METAPHYSICAL THEMES
IN THOMAS AQUINAS

STUDIES IN PHILOSOPHY
AND THE HISTORY OF PHILOSOPHY

Founding editor: John K. Ryan (1960–1978)
General editor: Jude P. Dougherty

Studies in Philosophy
and the History of Philosophy   Volume 10

Metaphysical Themes in Thomas Aquinas

by John F. Wippel

THE CATHOLIC UNIVERSITY OF AMERICA PRESS
Washington, D.C.

Library of Congress Cataloging in Publication Data
Wippel, John F.
  Metaphysical themes in Thomas Aquinas.

  (Studies in philosophy and the history of philosophy; v. 10)
  Includes index.
  1. Thomas, Aquinas, Saint, 1225?-1274 — Metaphysics — Addresses, essays,
lectures. 2. Metaphysics — History — Addresses, essays, lectures. I. Title.
II. Series. B21.S78 vol. 10 [B765.T54] 100s [110′.92′4] 83-7296
ISBN 0-8132-0578-6

Table of Contents

Acknowledgments

The previously published articles included in this volume are herewith listed together with the original publication information.

1. "Etienne Gilson and Christian Philosophy," in *Twentieth-Century Thinkers*, John K. Ryan, ed. (Staten Island, N.Y.: Alba House, 1965), pp. 59-87.

2. "Teaching Metaphysics: The Value of Aquinas for the Seminarian Today," in *Philosophy in Priestly Formation*, Ronald D. Lawler, ed. (Washington, D.C.: The Catholic University of America, 1978), pp. 101-29. Mimeographed reproduction.

3. "Thomas Aquinas and Avicenna on the Relationship between First Philosophy and the Other Theoretical Sciences: A Note on Thomas's *Commentary on Boethius's De Trinitate*, Q. 5, art. 1, ad 9," in *The Thomist* 37 (1973), pp. 133-54.

4. "The Title *First Philosophy* According to Thomas Aquinas and His Different Justifications for the Same," in *The Review of Metaphysics* 27 (1974), pp. 585-600.

5. "Metaphysics and *Separatio* According to Thomas Aquinas," in *The Review of Metaphysics* 31 (1978), pp. 431-70.

6. "Aquinas's Route to the Real Distinction: A Note on *De ente et essentia*, c. 4," in *The Thomist* 43 (1979), pp. 279-95.

7. "The Reality of Nonexisting Possibles According to Thomas Aquinas, Henry of Ghent, and Godfrey of Fontaines," in *The Review of Metaphysics* 34 (1981), pp. 729-58.

8. "Did Thomas Aquinas Defend the Possibility of an Eternally Created World? (The *De aeternitate mundi* Revisited)," in *Journal of the History of Philosophy* 19 (1981), pp. 21-37.

9. "Quidditative Knowledge of God According to Thomas Aquinas," in *Graceful Reason: Essays in Ancient and Medieval Philosophy Presented to Joseph Owens, CSSR, on the Occasion of His 75th Birthday,* Lloyd Gerson, ed. (Toronto: Pontifical Institute of Mediaeval Studies, 1983), pp. 273-99.

10. "Divine Knowledge, Divine Power and Human Freedom in Thomas Aquinas and Henry of Ghent," in *Divine Omniscience and Omnipotence in Medieval Philosophy,* Tamar Rudavsky, ed. (Dordrecht, Holland, and Boston, U.S.A.: D. Reidel Publishing Company, forthcoming): Proceedings of the

Conference on Divine Omniscience and Omnipotence in Medieval Jewish, Christian, and Islamic Philosophy, held at The Ohio State University, March 3 and 4, 1982, for which this paper was originally prepared.

Introduction

The studies included in the present volume treat of a number of different topics having to do with Thomas Aquinas's metaphysical thought. This variety in subject-matter is only to be expected, since these essays were originally written at different times and for different purposes. Nonetheless, enough of them deal with related issues to enable me to impose some order upon this collection. The first chapter combines into one two articles which appeared a number of years apart, but each of which deals with the same theme — the twentieth-century controversy concerning the appropriateness of describing Thomas's philosophical thought as "Christian philosophy." This discussion is important for anyone who would study Thomas's metaphysics; for it really centers around a question of methodology — the appropriate way to approach his writings in order to glean from them the elements of his metaphysical thought while taking into account the fact that they were written by one who was by profession a theologian. Chapters II and III treat of fairly fine points relating to Thomas's understanding of the nature of metaphysics (or first philosophy). Chapter II investigates his usage of Avicenna in explaining the interrelationship between first philosophy and other theoretical sciences. Chapter III examines his different reasons for naming this discipline "first philosophy." Chapter IV concentrates heavily on a technical operation named "separation" by Aquinas himself, and one which plays a critical role in his account of the way one reaches a metaphysical understanding of being, and hence of the subject of metaphysics. These three last-mentioned chapters, therefore, have this in common, that they are concerned with problems relating to the nature of metaphysics and the discovery of its subject.

In the subsequent chapters issues are considered which are more properly metaphysical in content rather than methodological or propaedeutic to metaphysics. Chapter V examines a well-known but frequently disputed text from one of Thomas's early works, ch. 4 of his *De ente et essentia,* and the argumentation offered there for real distinction between essence and existence in created beings. The second half of this chapter appears here for the first time. It contains my response to some difficulties and questions raised by Fr. Joseph Owens about the interpretation proposed in the first part of Chapter V. Chapter VI, without making any claim at being exhaustive, examines a number of other approaches used by Aquinas in reasoning to or defending real distinction between essence and existence in creatures. It, too, has been written especially for this volume.

Chapter VII is devoted to an examination of the ontological status of possibles in Aquinas, but also in two other later thirteenth-century thinkers — Henry of Ghent and Godfrey of Fontaines. In part this reflects my interest in these thinkers as well as in Thomas; but consideration of their views on this always intriguing topic will serve, it is hoped, both to illustrate the variety of solutions proposed for this problem by thirteenth-century thinkers and to cast Aquinas's own solution into sharper historical relief. Chapter VIII is not unrelated to Chapter VII, in that it concentrates on a particular version of the question of possibility — Thomas's views concerning the possibility of an eternally created universe. While it is generally conceded that Thomas denied that one can prove that the world began to be, the issue raised here is slightly different. Did Thomas also maintain that an eternally created world is possible? If so, this would mean that he defended an even stronger position and, within the doctrinal circumstances of his time, one that was more controversial.

Chapter IX is addressed to a difficult problem concerning Thomas's views about philosophical knowledge of God: In this life can we know what God is in any way? Chapter X concentrates on the issues of divine knowledge, divine power, and human freedom in Thomas and in Henry of Ghent.

In sum, therefore, the second part of Chapter V and all of Chapter VI appear here for the first time. Because Chapter I is based on two previous articles, a certain amount of editing has been required to unite these into one chapter. Apart from some editorial changes, some bibliographical updating, and some omissions in order to eliminate unnecessary repetition, the other chapters are substantially the same as their originally published versions.

At this point I would like to express my thanks to the various journal editors and publishers who have given permission for these articles to be reprinted in this volume. I would also like to acknowledge a debt of gratitude to Jude P. Dougherty, Dean of the School of Philosophy at Catholic University, for having encouraged me to bring these studies together in their present form. He originally suggested that I assemble a collection of previously published articles for inclusion in the Catholic University of America series Studies in Philosophy and the History of Philosophy. It soon became clear that many of my recent publications cluster around two different focal points — the metaphysical thought of Aquinas, and later thirteenth-century metaphysical thought. Included here are studies of the first type. Perhaps at some future date it will be possible for me to bring out another collection focusing on the post-Thomistic period. In any event, it is my hope that the present volume will be of some value to those who are currently interested in Aquinas's thought.

I would like to single out for special mention those many colleagues both here at Catholic University and from various other universities in North America and Europe who have taken the time and trouble to read one or more of these essays either before or after publication and who have been good enough to pass on their comments to me. Though they are too numerous for me to name each of them individually, their reactions, suggestions and criticisms are deeply appreciated. Of all of these no one else has read more of this material in its prepublication form than one of my colleagues here at Catholic University — Thomas Prufer. I am especially grateful to him for his many insightful comments over the years.

Finally, special thanks are due to Catholic University librarians Carolyn T. Lee, David J. Gilson, and Bruce Miller for their generous assistance in obtaining many scattered sources; to Mr. Frank Hunt for his careful copyreading of the manuscript; and to Dr. Thérèse-Anne Druart, Sister Patricia Flynn, and Elisabeth Lippens for their conscientious attention to many of the details involved in the final stages of preparing the text for publication.

Washington, D.C.
April, 1983

CHAPTER I

THOMAS AQUINAS AND THE PROBLEM OF CHRISTIAN PHILOSOPHY

During the revival of interest in the philosophical thought of Thomas Aquinas which marked the first six decades or so of the twentieth century, considerable attention was directed to his views concerning the proper relationship between faith and reason, and between philosophy and theology. Many participants in these investigations were not only interested in reaching a proper understanding of the historical Thomas's views concerning this relationship; they also wished to propose his solution as a working-model for twentieth-century thinkers who would be both believers and philosophers. In itself this is not surprising, since Thomas Aquinas stands out as one who had clarified the faith-reason relationship as perhaps no one else before his time.[1]

As historical research concerning Thomas and many of the other great schoolmen continued during the first half of our century, it became ever more evident that many of these thinkers, like Thomas himself, had spent their professional careers not as pure philosophers but as theologians. One of the towering figures in twentieth-century research concerning Thomas Aquinas in particular and medieval philosophy in general was, of course, Etienne Gilson.[2] His historical findings eventually led him to some highly

---

1. See, for instance, E. Gilson, *Reason and Revelation in the Middle Ages* (New York–London, 1950), Part III, "The Harmony of Reason and Revelation." Of the many texts from Aquinas which can be cited to illustrate this point, perhaps none makes it more effectively than the corpus of question 2, article 3 of his Commentary on the *De Trinitate* of Boethius. See *Expositio super librum Boethii De Trinitate,* B. Decker, ed. (Leiden, 1959), p. 94. Note in particular: "Et quamvis lumen naturale mentis humanae sit insufficiens ad manifestationem eorum quae manifestantur per fidem, tamen impossibile est quod ea, quae per fidem traduntur nobis divinitus, sint contraria his quae sunt per naturam nobis indita. Oporteret enim alterum esse falsum; et cum utrumque sit nobis a deo, deus nobis esset auctor falsitatis, quod est impossibile."
2. See M. McGrath, *Etienne Gilson: A Bibliography/Une Bibliographie* (Toronto, 1982).

original if controversial views concerning what he called "Christian Philosophy" and concerning Thomas Aquinas as a "Christian Philosopher." This chapter, therefore, will consist of two parts, one devoted to a presentation of Gilson's views about Christian philosophy in general and in Thomas Aquinas in particular; the other consisting of some reflections about Gilson's position and about the appropriate way in which Aquinas's metaphysics should be approached.

1: Etienne Gilson and Christian Philosophy

At first sight the very title "Christian Philosophy" appears to be self-destroying. If philosophy is to remain philosophy, if it is to be an investigation carried out under the light of natural reason, how can it be described as Christian? Insofar as it is philosophy it would seem to admit of no direct reference to faith or to theology.[3] Be that as it may, this was not the view of Etienne Gilson. Perhaps no other name has been linked more closely to a defense of the Christian character of patristic, medieval, and Thomistic philosophy. In order to understand more clearly how he gradually arrived at his notion of Christian philosophy and at his final views concerning the interrelationship between philosophy and theology, one may turn to his own works and in particular to his relatively late intellectual autobiography entitled *The Philosopher and Theology.*[4]

In the opening pages of this revealing study Gilson notes how deeply familiar with certain fundamental theological notions any well-instructed Catholic should be. Perhaps without realizing it, in learning his catechism and his creed, in his high school religion courses and thereafter, he has assimilated a set of beliefs which will serve him to his dying day. In the Apostles' Creed he finds answers to some of the most profound questions that have perplexed philosophers and theologians from time immemorial. If he does not know many things at this point in life, he believes a great deal as regards the origin and nature and destiny of man, and the existence and nature of God. More than that, and this is significant in Gilson's eyes, he has become familiar with some profound metaphysical notions without

---

3. See, for instance, M. Heidegger, *An Introduction to Metaphysics,* R. Manheim, tr. (Garden City, New York, 1961), p. 6. Note in particular: "A 'Christian philosophy' is a round square and a misunderstanding. There is, to be sure, a thinking and questioning elaboration of the world of Christian experience, i.e., of faith. That is theology." For the German see *Einführung in die Metaphysik* (Tübingen, 1958), p. 6.

4. Trans. by Cécile Gilson (New York, 1962). This English translation will be cited here.

having attempted in any way to separate them from his religious beliefs.[5] Witness the believer's surprise, comments Gilson, when he comes into contact with a set of purely philosophical propositions for the first time, many of them treating of notions which until now he had accepted on faith. Now some of these same truths may be presented to him as rationally demonstrable.[6]

Gilson's Discovery of Medieval Philosophy

Apparently Gilson himself underwent a similar experience when he first came into contact with pure philosophy presented as such. For some reason, as he readily acknowledges, his good marks notwithstanding, he seemed to understand very little of it. Failing to resolve this matter by his own reading, he then began to study philosophy formally at the University of Paris. In spite of diversity in outlook among his professors there, they were agreed on one point at least, and this a negative one. Each was convinced that he was a pure philosopher, free from any kind of religious influence in his philosophizing. One might be Protestant, Jewish, or Catholic, but this would never be reflected in one's teaching. And yet, Gilson notes that as a young Catholic student there he felt no particular embarrassment. If he had now entered into a different world, he was prepared. He expected no "revelation" concerning what he should hold as true. His religious faith had already decided that issue for him. Now he would test his own thought and investigate the foundations of that faith.[7]

At the same time, Gilson notes his surprise on coming into contact with certain Catholic theologians who seemed to be defending a kind of primacy of reason. They made great efforts never to believe in any truth which reason could establish. Apparently their motives were apologetic. In an age of scientism and rationalism they undoubtedly hoped to appeal to non-Catholic scholars by this emphasis on unaided reason. But if they were correct in asserting reason's rights when it comes to knowing truths such as God's existence, Gilson found it far more difficult to understand why they judged belief or continued belief in these same truths to be impossible. Granted that the first Vatican Council teaches that human reason can arrive at certain knowledge of God's existence, Gilson would not concede that the Council condemns belief in his existence or rejects such as impossible.[8]

---

5. See *The Philosopher and Theology,* pp. 10–15.
6. *Ibid.*, p. 15.
7. *Op. cit.,* pp. 21, 27, 34–36.
8. *Ibid.,* pp. 73–84. Also see "What Is Christian Philosophy?" in *A Gilson Reader,* A. Pegis, ed. (Garden City, N.Y., 1957), pp. 181–82, and 190, n. 4, where Gilson

He loves to hark back to a catechism of his youth with its statement: "I believe that there is a God because He Himself has revealed His existence to us." Only then does this 1885 edition add: "Yes, reason tells us there is a God because, if there were no God, heaven and earth would not exist." Gilson contrasts this catechism with a 1923 version which begins its discussion of the existence of God with a number of philosophical arguments, and only thereafter notes that God has revealed his existence. Finally, in seeming despair, he quotes a 1949 version: "I believe in God because nothing can make itself." After noting the questionable philosophy involved in this reply — the omission of an important step, the proof that something has been made or created — Gilson calls for a restoration of faith to its proper place.[9]

---

writes: "According to Thomas Aquinas, *everybody* is held *explicitly* and *always* to believe that God is and that he aims at the good of man." Gilson observes that there is no reason to think that Thomas is rejecting his other thesis that one cannot believe and know the same thing at the same time. In *Christianity and Philosophy*, R. MacDonald, tr. (New York, 1939), Gilson challenges the view which denies that the existence of God can ever be an object of faith. As Gilson sees it, God's existence must be accepted on faith by those who have not yet attained to demonstrative knowledge of it. See pp. 61–67. Then he goes on to suggest that it might be compatible with Thomistic teaching to say that in one sense the existence of God as known by us is not identical with the existence of God as believed by us. The Christian continues to say "Credo in Deum" even after he has become a philosopher. This will not be impossible in Thomism because one would then have faith and knowledge *de eodem* but not *secundum idem*. See pp. 70–71. In the *Elements of Christian Philosophy* (New York, 1960), pp. 25–27 and in his *Introduction à la philosophie chrétienne* (Paris, 1960), pp. 13–25, Gilson makes the same point. The philosopher should never forget that God has revealed his existence. Again, it is by an act of faith in the God of Moses that the theologian begins his research. To know that God exists will not dispense the Christian from believing in him whose existence is revealed by divine revelation. For the affirmation of God by faith is specifically distinct from the affirmation of God by philosophical reason. Belief in God is for the believer the first real grasp of that God who is the author of the economy of salvation and the first step on the path leading to man's ultimate supernatural end in the beatific vision. Granted that the existence of God can be demonstrated by natural reason, Gilson is not so sure that every man can be certain that his own reason is infallible in its effort to achieve such demonstrative knowledge. While pursuing the rational effort in its every detail, Gilson urges the believer to preserve his faith in that Word which reveals this truth to the simple as well as to the wise. See *Introduction,* p. 21. Gilson sees no contradiction between such a view and the proposition that it is impossible to believe and to know one and the same thing at the same time. See pp. 21–22. As he puts it in the *Elements*, p. 286, n. 15: " . . . while the God of faith is also the Prime Mover, the Prime Mover is not the God of faith."

9. "If I believe in the existence of God nothing untoward will happen on the day when some unbeliever will question the validity of my proofs. My religious life is not founded on the conclusions of any philosopher . . . . But if I have first been taught

But to return to Gilson, the youthful student of philosophy, it seems that his personal philosophical research gradually carried him to similar convictions concerning the mutual interrelations of philosophy and theology. At this point in his career he had as yet enjoyed no direct contact with scholastic philosophy or with the thought of Thomas Aquinas. At the same time, certain historical canons were accepted by practically everyone teaching philosophy at the University of Paris. One of these maintained that there are really only two philosophical periods in history, the ancient and the modern. The latter begins with Descartes and comes after the period of antiquity as though nothing had intervened. Between the decline of Greek philosophy and Descartes there was nothing but darkness, the darkness of the middle ages. At best one might admit that there had been a scholastic theology, based on revelation, and thus the very antithesis of philosophy.[10]

This rather negative attitude toward the medieval period notwithstanding, Professor Lévy-Bruhl suggested to Gilson as a research project the theme Descartes and Scholasticism. Gilson's 1913 thesis, *La liberté chez Descartes et la théologie*, was the result. Some of his conclusions were surprising. A number of philosophical positions were common to scholasticism and Descartes and apparently had passed from the former to the latter. At the same time, however, metaphysics as found in Descartes seemed to have undergone a decline. As Gilson sums it up: "On all these points the thought of Descartes, in comparison with the sources from which it derives, marks much less a gain than a loss." Yet this conclusion seems to violate the generally accepted law. If Descartes had borrowed metaphysical notions from the scholastics, how could it be that he came after the Greeks as though nothing philosophical had existed in between?[11]

The problem was to become more complicated. What had preceded Descartes seemed to have been theology. It appeared, therefore, that the theology of the scholastics had, at least in part, been transformed into the philosophy of Descartes. However, unless there had also been some philosophy in scholasticism, how could Descartes have borrowed metaphysical notions therefrom? This raised another problem. How was one to account for the presence of philosophy in medieval scholasticism? By appealing to

---

to hold that God exists on the strength of demonstrative reasoning, and only later to believe it, it is to be feared that the reverse will happen . . . . The man who thinks he knows that God exists and then realizes that he no longer knows it also realizes that he no longer believes it." *The Philosopher and Theology*, p. 72. See pp. 65–72 as well as *Christianity and Philosophy*, pp. 74–77.

10. *The Philosopher and Theology*, p. 87.
11. *Ibid.*, pp. 88–89. See *God and Philosophy* (New Haven, 1959), pp. xii–xv.

Aristotle, no doubt. And yet, the very notions which Descartes had retained from scholasticism seemed to be absent from Aristotle — the existence of one supreme being, creative cause of the universe, infinite and free, and a theory of man endowed with personal immortality. Not finding these notions in Aristotle, Gilson concluded that philosophy had changed considerably due to its contact with Christian theology. Consequently, he found himself forced to account for a twofold transition: from Greek philosophy to Christian theology, and from Christian theology to modern philosophy.[12]

With this background in mind Gilson then turned to a deeper study of Thomas Aquinas. Restricting himself in the main to Thomas's theological writings, his research resulted in the first edition of his *Le thomisme*. This was originally given as a course of lectures at the University of Lille in 1913–1914 and eventually published at Strasbourg in 1919. Gilson notes that it received sharp criticism, especially along three lines. Maurice De Wulf of Louvain pointed out certain weaknesses from the metaphysical side. Gilson grants the justice of this criticism. Secondly, Gilson had followed a theological order of exposition rather than a philosophical. This he would continue to do in his subsequent expositions of Thomas's philosophical thought. Thirdly, at least one Catholic theologian objected to his speaking of a "philosophy of Saint Thomas," apparently holding to the view promoted by De Wulf according to which all the scholastics maintained a common "scholastic synthesis" consisting fundamentally of the philosophy of Aristotle.[13]

Apparently stirred on by these rebukes, Gilson determined to test the last-mentioned point. Was the philosophy of St. Thomas to be identified with that of the other scholastics? He concentrated on Bonaventure and published *La philosophie de saint Bonaventure* in 1924.[14] His conclusion was that Bonaventure differed from Thomas on such fundamental notions as being, cause, intellect, and natural knowledge. Now he had discovered two medieval philosophies, or so he thought. For then the Dominican, Pierre Mandonnet, entered the discussion. Admitting that Gilson's presentation of Bonaventure's doctrine was sound enough, Mandonnet objected to the title. No doctrine wherein the distinction between faith and reason was so vague could rightfully be styled philosophy. The book should rather be called the "Theology of Saint Bonaventure."[15]

---

12. *The Philosopher and Theology*, pp. 89–90.

13. *Ibid.*, p. 91. The fifth edition of a considerably revised *Le thomisme* has appeared in English under the title *The Christian Philosophy of St. Thomas Aquinas*, L. K. Shook, tr. (New York, 1956). A sixth French edition appeared in 1965 (J. Vrin: Paris).

14. *The Philosopher and Theology*, pp. 91–92. *La philosophie de saint Bonaventure* has appeared in English as *The Philosophy of St. Bonaventure*, I. Trethowan and F. J. Sheed, trs. (New York, 1938).

15. *The Philosopher and Theology*, pp. 92–93.

Gilson now found himself in the middle. One critic apparently believed that Thomas Aquinas was the only thirteenth-century philosopher. Another denied that he had a distinctive philosophy of his own, suggesting rather that he shared in the common "scholastic synthesis." And then another Dominican, Gabriel Théry, struck the final blow. Granted that the doctrine of Bonaventure is a theology, so too is that of Aquinas. Both are theologians! Gilson had simply selected certain propositions from their writings and presented them as their philosophies. What he had dubbed their philosophies were really nothing but "truncated theologies."[16]

Reviewing matters, Gilson noted the following: (1) a series of propositions concerning God, man, and the universe, which could have been taught by the medieval theologians as well as by certain modern philosophers; (2) the fact that most of these were to be found explicitly stated in the theological writings of the great medieval thinkers; (3) the fact that in every comprehensive presentation of these same theses, the medievals had not followed the philosophical but the theological order (descending from God to creatures rather than ascending from creatures to God).[17] The problem then arose of finding an appropriate name which would be flexible enough to cover so complex a doctrinal situation.

Gilson's many years of subsequent research in medieval philosophy reinforced his conviction that a number of metaphysical conclusions are to be found there which cannot be simply identified with the philosophy of Aristotle, or with that of any other Greek thinker. As he sees it, only ignorance of the history of philosophy can lead one to proclaim the middle ages a long period of philosophical stagnation. In *The Spirit of Mediaeval Philosophy* he set forth a series of issues whose full philosophical development was due, in his eyes, to inspirations stemming from Christianity. Without denying the heavy debt of medieval philosophy to the Greeks, his purpose in this work was to emphasize the distinctively Christian elements, or more accurately phrased, those philosophical notions which appear there

---

16. *Ibid.,* p. 94.

17. *Ibid.,* p. 95. For Gilson's view that much of modern classical philosophy owes a far greater debt to Christian influences than is generally recognized see *The Spirit of Mediaeval Philosophy*, Gifford Lectures 1931-1932, A. H. C. Downes, tr. (London, 1936/repr. 1950), pp. 13-19. The notes of the French original (*L'Esprit de la philosophie médiévale* [Paris, 1932], 2 vols.) have been considerably shortened in the English version. For his criticisms of attempts to reconstruct a Thomistic philosophy by following the philosophical order, see *The Christian Philosophy of St. Thomas Aquinas*, p. 442, n. 33. To do so is to present a *"philosophia ad mentem sancti Thomae* as though it were a *philosophia ad mentem Cartesii"* (p. 443). Also see pp. 21-22. Gilson finds this distinction between the philosophical order and the theological order in the *Summa contra gentiles* II, ch. 4. See *Elements of Christian Philosophy*, p. 290, n. 42.

because of Judeo-Christian influences.[18] Gilson's position is that philosophy did receive new impulses and insights and, consequently, did attain to new heights precisely because it was exercised under Christian conditions. In this he is diametrically opposed to the position taken by Emile Bréhier in 1928 and again in 1931 and thereafter in the great debate concerning the possibility of a Christian philosophy.[19] Without spelling out in detail the particulars, a survey of the titles of some of the lectures in *The Spirit of Mediaeval Philosophy* will suffice to indicate areas where Gilson finds this positive Christian influence: "Being and Its Necessity," "Beings and Their Contingence," "Analogy, Causality and Finality," "The Glory of God," and "Christian Providence." It was only after he had completed the chapters which make up Vol. I of the French original of this monumental work, save for the first two, that the name "Christian Philosophy" occurred to him as best suited to describe the kind of philosophizing characteristic of the middle ages. With this in mind he devoted the first two chapters to this notion.[20] Gilson's research had now convinced him that there was a philosophy in the middle ages, to be sure, but a Christian philosophy.

Christian Philosophy

In attempting to understand precisely what Gilson means by Christian philosophy, one should never forget that for him it was originally a name which designated certain historically observable realities, namely, the philosophical doctrines which are to be found in the writings of the Fathers and the scholastic theologians. The historical premise on which the title rests is the existence in these thinkers of certain philosophical doctrines which are met in their works for the first time in this precise sense and form.[21]

18. *The Spirit of Mediaeval Philosophy*, p. 207. Also see the concluding pages of Gilson's *History of Christian Philosophy in the Middle Ages* (New York, 1955), pp. 540–45.

19. For brief surveys of this controversy see E. A. Sillem, "Notes on Recent Work: Christian Philosophy," *The Clergy Review* 46 (1961), pp. 151–58; and M. Nédoncelle, *Is There a Christian Philosophy?*, I. Trethowan, tr. (New York, 1960), pp. 85–99.

20. *Christianity and Philosophy*, pp. 93–94. On previous usage of the expression "Christian philosophy" see *L'Esprit de la philosophie médiévale*, pp. 413–40; *The Christian Philosophy of St. Thomas Aquinas*, p. 441, n. 19; "What Is Christian Philosophy?" in *A Gilson Reader*, pp. 178ff., 186, 190, n. 6; *The Philosopher and Theology*, pp. 175ff. Also see Sillem, "Notes on Recent Work," pp. 149–52; and Nédoncelle, *Is There a Christian Philosophy?*, p. 85. For a brief survey of philosophy in Christian times and of Christian philosophy as understood by Nédoncelle, cf. chs. 1–4 of the same.

21. Gilson (*The Christian Philosophy of St. Thomas Aquinas*, p. 441, n. 20) refers to his *Christianity and Philosophy* as follows: "The basic idea in this book is that the phrase 'Christian philosophy' expresses a theological notion of a reality observable in history." See also his "La possibilité philosophique de la philosophie chrétienne," *Revue des sciences religieuses* 32 (1958), p. 168.

One may ask why so many philosophers did in fact turn to Christianity to find a more satisfying solution for their philosophical difficulties. Gilson would refer one back to the very beginnings of Christianity. For a St. Paul, to be sure, Christianity is not simply another philosophy, but a religion which surpasses all that is normally known as philosophy. Christianity offers salvation by faith in Christ and is contrasted with the wisdom of the Greeks. If certain Pauline texts seem to reject Greek philosophy, their real intent, according to Gilson, is to "set aside the apparent wisdom of the Greeks which is really folly, so as to make way for the apparent folly of Christianity which is really wisdom." It is the salvation preached by Christ which is the true wisdom.[22]

Still, this seems to leave one with the problem of Christian philosophy. Faith may free one from the need for philosophy, but why, then, did some of the earliest writers of the patristic period gain philosophically by accepting Christianity? Gilson loves to cite Justin as a prime example. After his long search among the various Greek philosophies, Justin eventually came to the conclusion that Christianity itself is the only "sure and profitable philosophy." Referring to his conversion to Christianity, he notes that it was by becoming a Christian that he really became a philosopher. After seeking truth by reason alone and failing, Justin accepted the truth proposed by faith. Thereupon, his reason found satisfaction as well. For Justin, therefore, and others like him the happiest philosophical situation was no longer that of the pagan but that of the Christian.[23]

In the second chapter of *The Spirit of Mediaeval Philosophy,* Gilson detects a similar pattern in Augustine, Lactantius, Anselm, and Aquinas. For each of these thinkers Christianity was a way of salvation. In addition, faith offered a certitude not provided by reason alone. Yet, in each of these men reason had its role to play in Christian life, at least to the degree that they aspired to understand the content of revelation. And in every case, because reason existed under Christian conditions, Gilson finds its lot greatly improved.[24]

According to Gilson the "content of Christian philosophy is that body of rational truths discovered, explored or simply safeguarded, thanks to the help that reason receives from revelation."[25] Unless the formula, Christian philosophy, is to lose all its force, "it must be frankly admitted that nothing less than an intrinsic relation between revelation and reason will suffice to give it meaning."[26] This is not to say that Gilson's Christian philosopher

22. *The Spirit of Mediaeval Philosophy*, pp. 20–22.
23. *Ibid.,* pp. 23–30. For Justin see his *Dialogue with Trypho,* chs. 2–8.
24. *The Spirit of Mediaeval Philosophy,* pp. 29–34, 39–41.
25. *Ibid.,* p. 35. See "What Is Christian Philosophy?" *A Gilson Reader,* pp. 177–79.
26. *The Spirit of Mediaeval Philosophy,* p. 35.

will confuse philosophy with theology. Rather he seeks to determine whether, among those truths he holds on faith, there are not some which reason can also establish. In Gilson's own words:

> In so far as the believer bases his affirmations on the intimate conviction gained from faith he remains purely and simply a believer, he has not yet entered the gates of philosophy; but when amongst his beliefs he finds some that are capable of becoming objects of science then he becomes a philosopher, and if it is to the Christian faith that he owes this new philosophical insight, he becomes a Christian philosopher.[27]

Gilson goes on to tell us what he means by Christian philosophy.

> Thus I call Christian, *every philosophy which, although keeping the two orders formally distinct, nevertheless considers the Christian revelation as an indispensable auxiliary to reason.*[28]

Or again, as he describes it in his much later *Elements of Christian Philosophy,* "Christian philosophy is that way of philosophizing in which the Christian faith and the human intellect join forces in a common investigation of philosophical truth."[29]

Certain comments are in order if one will be fair to Gilson. First of all, he insists that the orders of philosophy and theology be kept formally distinct. In the formal order one is concerned with the essence of a thing. If it is of the essence of philosophy to operate in the light of natural reason, it is of the essence of theology to proceed under the light of revelation.[30] The two orders are formally distinct. Consequently, one will never find a simple abstract essence or quiddity to conform to the notion of Christian philosophy. What Gilson has in mind is a concrete historical reality, something to be described rather than defined, and something which includes

---

27. *Ibid.,* p. 36.

28. *Ibid.,* p. 37. See *Christianity and Philosophy,* pp. 100–101.

29. *Elements,* p. 5. Gilson insists that his view of Christian philosophy squares with that advocated by Leo XIII in the Encyclical *Aeterni Patris.* He is convinced that the Encyclical points to far more than a merely negative role for faith as regards human reason. As Gilson interprets it, a positive influence is called for by words such as the following: "Those, therefore, who to the study of philosophy unite obedience to the Christian faith, are philosophizing in the best possible way; for the splendor of the divine truths, received into the mind, helps the understanding, and not only detracts in no wise from its dignity, but adds greatly to its nobility, keenness, and stability." (Cited in Gilson's "What Is Christian Philosophy?" *A Gilson Reader,* p. 186.) Cf. *Christianity and Philosophy,* pp. 91–102, and *The Philosopher and Theology,* pp. 175–90.

30. *The Philosopher and Theology,* p. 192. Cf. *The Christian Philosophy of St. Thomas Aquinas,* pp. 20–23.

"all those philosophical systems which were in fact what they were only because a Christian religion existed and because they were ready to submit to its influence."[31] Gilson suggests that failure to make this distinction lies behind much of the controversy between philosophers and theologians concerning the notion of Christian philosophy.[32]

The distinction proposed here by Gilson seems to correspond with a distinction developed by Jacques Maritain in his doctrinal discussion of the problem. Maritain distinguishes between the nature (or essence) of philosophy, considered in itself and abstractly, and the state in which it exists in a given subject. In terms of its nature and as abstracted from its concrete conditions of existence, philosophy is a purely natural and rational discipline.[33] Considered in this way, philosophy is simply that—pure philosophy. It is not Christian. But Maritain contrasts this with philosophy considered according to its state, as found in the man who philosophizes. Here, because Christians also philosophize, one may speak of a Christian philosophy. From this perspective there will be a difference between the Christian and the non-Christian philosopher. The Christian believes that fallen nature is elevated and strengthened by grace. Furthermore, he finds that his faith reveals certain truths to him which unaided reason would in fact fail to discover. In Maritain's own words, the Christian

> . . . also believes that if reason is to attain without admixture of error the highest truths that are naturally within its ken it requires assistance, either from within in the form of inner strengthening or from without in the form of an offering of objective data.[34]

31. *The Spirit of Mediaeval Philosophy,* p. 37. See p. 36: "In this sense [considered according to its formal essence] it is clear that a philosophy cannot be Christian, nor, for that matter, Jewish or Mussulman, and that the idea of Christian philosophy has no more meaning than 'Christian physics' or 'Christian mathematics'."

32. *The Spirit of Mediaeval Philosophy,* p. 36; *The Philosopher and Theology,* pp. 192ff.

33. J. Maritain, *An Essay on Christian Philosophy,* E. H. Flannery, tr. (New York, 1955), p. 15. "Viewed as a formally constructed philosophy, Thomistic philosophy—I do not say Thomistic theology—is wholly rational: no reasoning issuing from faith finds its way into its inner fabric; it derives intrinsically from reason and rational criticism alone; and its soundness as a philosophy is based entirely on experimental or intellectual evidence and on logical proof."

34. *An Essay on Christian Philosophy,* p. 18. See pp. 15–18. See also Maritain, *Science and Wisdom,* B. Wall, tr. (London, 1940/repr. 1954), pp. 79–80, 90–93, 97. Here I am limiting myself to Maritain's treatment of speculative philosophy. For him speculative philosophy is Christian only by reason of its state, not by reason of its specifying object. Practical philosophy, on the other hand, will be Christian by reason of its state and by reason of its object. See *Science and Wisdom,* pp. 100, 127. For his general treatment of the Christian character of moral philosophy see the same, pp. 107–27 and Part II, as well as *An Essay on Christian Philosophy,* pp. 38ff.

For Maritain, therefore, Christian philosophy is not a simple essence but something complex, an essence plus the given state in which the Christian thinker finds himself. Because of its Christian state philosophy receives a certain guidance from the faith without thereby ceasing to be philosophy. Philosophy will always judge things in accord with its own principles and norms. This will apply even to the philosophical consideration of those naturally knowable truths which were not, in fact, clearly and accurately attained apart from some influence of Christian revelation.[35]

Maritain's distinction between philosophy considered according to its nature and philosophy considered in its concrete state of existence seems to correspond to Gilson's distinction between philosophy considered formally, or in the abstract, and philosophy taken as a concrete historical reality, found in philosophers. Gilson also grants that one will never find a simple abstract essence to correspond to Christian philosophy. What he intends to describe is rather a concrete way of philosophizing. It should not be forgotten, of course, that Gilson originally arrived at this notion by way of historical research, to resolve a historical problem. Nonetheless, he has referred to Maritain's study as the natural doctrinal complement to his historical investigations and has expressed his agreement with it.[36] If one

---

and 61-100. To return to his consideration of the Christian character of speculative philosophy, Maritain distinguishes between objective data which philosophy may receive from faith and from theology, and subjective aids and reinforcements. The objective data refer primarily to revealed truths of the natural order, i.e., those data which philosophical reasoning should be able to attain but which, in fact, the great pagan thinkers did not clearly grasp in their fullness. "Moreover, these *objective data* are also concerned with the repercussions of truths of the supernatural order on philosophical reflexion: and here the connexions and echoes really extend indefinitely." *Science and Wisdom,* p. 80. For more on these objective aids see *An Essay on Christian Philosophy,* pp. 18-24. By subjective reinforcements he refers to philosophical wisdom insofar as it is a habit of the intellect. As an intellectual habit, philosophical wisdom may be aided by higher habits such as faith, theological wisdom, and contemplative wisdom, provided of course that the philosopher is a Christian. Here Maritain speaks of a "dynamic continuity of *habitus*" which will reinforce philosophical activity subjectively by vivifying and purifying the philosophical *habitus*. See *An Essay . . . ,* pp. 24-29, and *Science and Wisdom,* pp. 80, 86-90. For a detailed exposition and critique of this aspect of Maritain's theory see A. Naud, *Le problème de la philosophie chrétienne: Eléments d'une solution thomiste* (Montreal, 1960), pp. 13-34. Naud emphasizes this notion of the subjective *confortations* so greatly that he may possibly minimize the importance of the objective contributions by faith and theology to philosophy according to Maritain's theory.

35. *An Essay on Christian Philosophy,* p. 29.

36. See *L'Esprit de la philosophie médiévale,* 2d ed. (Paris, 1948), pp. 439-40, n. 80. Though I am unaware of any detailed treatment by Gilson of Maritain's distinction

objects that, since philosophy is distinct from faith, the latter can have nothing to do with the former save in some purely extrinsic way, Gilson will no doubt agree that such is true in the formal order. But taken as a concretely observable reality, such will not be true of Christian philosophy. Here its Christian condition and mode of existence must be taken into account.

A second point should also be kept in mind in Gilson's description of Christian philosophy. An intrinsic relation between revelation and reason must be admitted. It is not enough to say that Christian philosophy will refer to faith and revelation as a negative norm, warning reason when it is in danger of contradicting revealed truth. According to Gilson faith will do this, of course, but more. Christian philosophy also will involve certain positive contributions which philosophy has received from its Christian state of existence.[37] First of all, this implies that philosophy has discovered certain naturally knowable truths only at the positive suggestion of revelation. Once such truths have been pointed out by faith, of course, the Christian philosopher is invited to investigate their rational foundations.[38]

In addition, Gilson sets down certain typical characteristics of the Christian philosopher and/or of Christian philosophy. Granted that the Christian philosopher has the right to investigate each and every philosophical problem, in fact he is selective. Questions concerning the existence and nature of God, and the origin and nature and destiny of man will be of paramount importance. A second characteristic of Christian philosophy has been its tendency to systematize. This is understandable, for in the Christian view of things there is a fixed frame of reference, man in his relationship to God. Finally, Christian philosophy has the necessary material at

---

between objective aids and subjective reinforcements (see n. 34) from which philosophy will benefit under Christian conditions, Gilson seems to empohasize the former without rejecting the latter in any way. In fact, in the present reference he tells us why. Granted that that which is most vital is the work of revelation and grace in the soul of the believing philosopher and granted that without this there would be no Christian philosophy, yet for the observer and in particular for the historian of philosophy the only means available to detect this inner action is to examine the outward evidence, that is, philosophy with revelation and philosophy without revelation. This is what Gilson has attempted to do, and this is why he has said that history alone can give meaning to the notion of Christian philosophy. He continues: "Je dirai donc que la philosophie chrétienne n'est une réalité objectivement observable que pour l'histoire, et que son existence n'est positivement démontrable que par l'histoire, mais que, son existence étant ainsi établie, sa notion peut être analysée en elle-même et qu'elle doit l'être comme vient de le faire M. J. Maritain. Je suis donc entièrement d'accord avec lui." Cf. *Le thomisme*, 6th ed., pp. 42–43.

37. *The Spirit of Mediaeval Philosophy*, pp. 35–41; "What Is Christian Philosophy?" p. 186.

38. *The Spirit of Mediaeval Philosophy*, pp. 40–41; *Elements of Christian Philosophy*, p. 25.

hand for its completion. To illustrate this point, Gilson appeals to Thomas Aquinas, *Summa contra gentiles* I, 4, where he notes that it was fitting for God to reveal certain truths which human reason can also attain. Otherwise, reasons Thomas, truths of this type (including certain truths necessary for salvation) would be grasped only by a few. The reasons offered by Aquinas for this confirm Gilson in his view that the Christian will be well advised to philosophize from within the faith. Without revelation the majority of men would never attain to such truths either because of a lack of native ability, or a lack of time for research, or a lack of interest in such matters. Even those who did finally succeed in reaching such truths would do so only with great effort and after a long period of time. Finally, according to Aquinas, the human intellect is so weakened in its present state that, unless it were reinforced by faith, that which might seem clearly demonstrated to some would remain doubtful to others. Error might be intermingled with the truths which the few had finally reached. If this is not an optimistic picture of the results to which unaided reason can attain in practice, Gilson insists that it is the view of Thomas Aquinas as regards such metaphysical truths.[39]

In sum, therefore, while admitting that a true philosophy considered formally in itself will stand or fall in virtue of its own rationality, Gilson would remind us that such a philosophy has not been constructed in fact without the help of revelation "acting as an indispensable moral support to reason." Both history itself and the words of Aquinas point to this conclusion. If one does find in history an influence exercised on the development of metaphysics by revelation, the reality of Christian philosophy is historically demonstrated. This, of course, is what Gilson claims to have done.[40]

Philosophy and Theology

One problem remains to be settled. If one follows Gilson in his historical development of the notion of Christian philosophy and agrees with him that, while distinct in the formal order, philosophy and religious faith are in

---

39. *The Spirit of Mediaeval Philosophy*, pp. 37–40. Also see "Thomas Aquinas and Our Colleagues," *A Gilson Reader*, p. 296, n. 7; "What Is Christian Philosophy?" *A Gilson Reader*, pp. 179–82; *Christianity and Philosophy*, pp. 60–61; *Elements of Christian Philosophy*, pp. 24–25.

40. See *The Spirit of Mediaeval Philosophy*, pp. 40–41. In addition to this work see Gilson's *History of Christian Philosophy in the Middle Ages*. As regards individual thinkers see also: *The Christian Philosophy of Saint Augustine*, L. E. M. Lynch, tr. (New York, 1960); *The Philosophy of Saint Bonaventure; The Christian Philosophy of St. Thomas Aquinas; Elements of Christian Philosophy; Introduction à la philosophie chrétienne; Jean Duns Scot: Introduction à ses positions fondamentales* (Paris, 1952).

fact found together in the believing philosopher, what remains of the distinction between philosophy and theology? In order to understand more fully the notion of philosophy, Gilson would direct our attention to it in its relationship with theology. He has insisted that the truly original philosophical contributions of Thomas Aquinas are to be found in his theological writings.[41] This squares, of course, with the Gilsonian view that the Christian who philosophizes does not find himself in the same state as the pagan. One must admit, therefore, some real connection between natural theology, on the one hand, and revealed theology on the other. Two reasons point to this conclusion. First of all, in the past the greatest masters of natural theology have also been professional theologians. Secondly, every historical attempt to separate philosophy from theology has, in Gilson's opinion, ended in disaster. To repeat, it is not enough to restrict the role of faith to a negative norm. Placed by God at the disposal of all, philosopher and non-philosopher, faith not only teaches those truths which one may not contradict. To the degree that some of the revealed truths admit of rational demonstration as well, as with the preambles of faith, the believing philosopher is invited to seek to demonstrate and to understand such truths insofar as this is possible.[42]

41. See *The Christian Philosophy of St. Thomas Aquinas,* p. 8: "The *Commentaries* of St. Thomas on Aristotle are very precious documents and their loss would have been deplorable. Nevertheless, if they had all perished, the two *Summae* would still preserve all that is most personal and most profound in his philosophical thought, whereas, if the theological works of St. Thomas had been lost, we should be deprived of his most important contribution to the common treasure of metaphysical knowledge." See p. 22: "There is a series of works in which St. Thomas used the philosophical method—the Commentaries on Aristotle and a small number of *Opuscula.* But each *opusculum* gives but a fragment of his thought, and the commentaries on Aristotle, bound to follow the meanderings of an obscure text, only let us suspect imperfectly what might have been the nature of a Summa of Thomistic philosophy organised by St. Thomas himself, with all the sparkling genius that went into the *Summa theologiae.*" Also see *Elements of Christian Philosophy,* p. 282, n. 6: "*Expositor* Thomas is not the author of the *Summa Theologiae;* he is the author of the commentaries on Aristotle, in which it is literally true to say that he seldom or never disagrees with the teaching of Aristotle. Now this is precisely the reason one cannot expound the philosophy of Saint Thomas out of his commentaries on Aristotle alone." Cf. *The Philosopher and Theology,* pp. 210–11: "In his commentaries on the writings of the Philosopher, Saint Thomas is not principally concerned with his own philosophy but with Aristotle's . . . . Saint Thomas is only a commentator in his writings on Aristotle. For his personal thinking one must look at the two *Summae* and similar writings, in which he shows himself an author in the proper sense of the word. Even in the astonishing tract, *On Being and Essence,* the level of theology is not far from the surface." Hence, if in this last quotation Gilson appears to take the *De ente* more seriously, apparently this is because he now regards it too as a theological work!

42. *Christianity and Philosophy,* pp. 77–79.

But in more recent writings, Gilson seems to go farther than this. He notes that in Thomas's time the theologian who used philosophy in his work was normally not described as a philosopher, but as a philosophizing theologian (*philosophans theologus*), or more simply, as a philosophizer (*philosophans*). The term "philosopher" was usually restricted to pagan thinkers. The thirteenth-century theologians do not seem, according to Gilson, to have considered explicitly the possibility of a person who would be at one and the same time a *philosophus* and a *sanctus*, that is, one sanctified by baptism.[43]

As regards Aquinas's relationship to Aristotle, Gilson judges it an over-simplification to say that Thomas simply "baptized" the Stagirite. In his commentaries on Aristotle, whenever Thomas finds him contradicting Christian teaching, he either admits as much or at the very least does not force conclusions upon him which he did not expressly defend. Thus Aquinas never uses the term *creatio* to describe the causality of the First Mover in his Commentary on the *Metaphysics*. Yet he did attempt to remove from Aristotle alleged contradictions to Christian truth which are not clearly there, but which interpretations such as those proposed by Averroes would imply. In Gilson's view, if one will speak of a Thomistic "baptism" of Aristotle, this took place in Thomas's theological writings.[44]

After having purified Aristotle, Thomas noted certain shortcomings in his thought. Here he found it necessary to complete the Stagirite. And yet, Aristotle was the philosopher *par excellence* and seemed to represent the best that unaided reason can achieve without the help of revelation. In his theologizing, however, Aquinas needed an adequate philosophy. To the extent that none was at hand he found it necessary to develop his own, which Gilson describes as a "reinterpretation of the fundamental notions of Aristotle's metaphysics in the light of Christian truth." Gilson cites the Thomistic notions of being, substance, and efficient cause as illustrations.[45]

---

43. See "Thomas Aquinas and Our Colleagues," pp. 288–89; *Elements of Christian Philosophy*, p. 12; *The Philosopher and Theology*, p. 194.

44. *Elements of Christian Philosophy*, p. 14.

45. *Ibid.*, p. 15. Granted that these same terms are also found in Aristotle, Gilson insists that in Aquinas they have taken on new meaning. In Gilson's eyes the only true gateway to a proper understanding of Thomistic metaphysics lies in a "certain metaphysical notion of being tied up with a certain notion of the Christian God." *Ibid.*, p. 6. To set forth this notion in some of its most important metaphysical ramifications is the avowed purpose of his *Elements of Christian Philosophy* as well as his *Introduction à la philosophie chrétienne*. Here again Gilson finds additional evidence pointing toward a positive influence of revelation and theology upon philosophy, this time because he regards it as highly plausible that the original inspiration for the Thomistic understanding of *esse* as act is to be traced back to the well-known biblical text: *Ego sum qui sum* (Exod. 3:14). Having been prompted by this text to conclude

This Thomistic development of the Aristotelian metaphysics was the work of a teacher of Christian truth and, Gilson insists, a teacher of Christian theology. In line with this theological mission, then, Aquinas found it necessary to develop a philosophy. But as Gilson interprets him, this philosophy is a part of Thomistic theology.

> This philosophy, which, according to Thomas himself, is part of his theology, appeals to no revealed knowledge; it is purely rational in both principles and method, and still, it is irreducible to the philosophy of Aristotle if only for the reason that the first principle of human knowledge, being, is not understood by Thomas and Aristotle in the same way.[46]

If one asks whether there is any philosophy in the works of Aquinas, Gilson will insist that there is. But he will remind us that it is always there in order to aid man in his knowledge of God. Thomas has worked out a philosophy with theological goals in mind. In connection with this Gilson cites with full approval Thomas's reply to the objection that the Christian monk should not busy himself studying letters. Thomas replies (*Summa theol.* II–IIae, q. 188, a. 5, ad 3) that monks should devote themselves to a study of the doctrine which is "according to godliness." They should interest themselves in the various branches of secular learning only insofar as such ministers to sacred doctrine. For Gilson this is a perfect expression of Thomas's attitude regarding philosophical speculation. Thomas never forgot that he himself was a religious. He would interest himself in philosophy to the extent that it could be of service to sacred science. Once more, suggests Gilson, Thomas will not be overly concerned about freeing his philosophy from all theological influences and goals.[47]

As has already been noted, Gilson's historical research had convinced him that there was such a thing as Christian philosophy. The fact that this philosophy had been worked out by theologians under the guidance of faith and for theological purposes continued to fascinate him, eventually leading him to his final view that Christian philosophy should in some way be

---

that God's essence is "to be" (*esse*), Thomas would then have easily moved to composition of essence and "to be" in all creatures by way of contrast with God. Once more Thomas would have followed the theological order rather than the philosophical. See *Elements*, pp. 124–35; *Introduction*, pp. 45–58. For difficulties involved in any purely philosophical approach to the essence-existence composition, also see *Introduction*, pp. 98–109. For a different view see my Ch. V below.

46. *Elements of Christian Philosophy*, p. 282, n. 6.

47. *Ibid.*, pp. 19–20 and 283, n. 11. Cf. *The Christian Philosophy of St. Thomas Aquinas*, pp. 6–7. In the first passage (*Elements*), Gilson is using the term "monk" broadly, as equivalent to "religious."

included in sacred theology. To account for this, he determined that the notion of theology would itself have to be broadened. According to a widely held view, conclusions deduced from naturally known premises are strictly philosophical. Gilson does not object. But many go on to conclude from this that philosophical reasoning has no function in theology. They would restrict theology to the task of deducing conclusions from premises, one at least of which is known by faith. Gilson finds such a view acceptable so far as it goes, but entirely too restrictive. If it is true that strictly theological conclusions do not enter into philosophical demonstrations, it does not follow that purely rational conclusions cannot contribute in some way to theological investigation. In fact, as Gilson sees the situation, it is of the essence of scholastic theology to employ philosophical reasoning. In his own words: "Because it draws on faith, it is a scholastic *theology*, but because of its distinctive use of philosophy, it is a *scholastic* theology."[48]

For Thomas theology or divine science is twofold. There is a theology in which divine things are considered not as the subject of the science, but rather as the principle or cause of the subject. This is metaphysics or natural theology and has as its subject *ens in quantum est ens.* It studies God (divine things) only as principle or cause of its subject, that is to say, of that which falls under its subject — being as being. There is another theology or divine science which considers divine things in their own right as its subject. This is the theology which is based on Sacred Scripture, and which we know as sacred theology. According to Aquinas this theology differs in genus from natural theology or metaphysics.[49]

Gilson is perfectly familiar with this Thomistic distinction, but sounds a note of warning. One should distinguish between the formal order, where such distinctions do apply, and the concrete order. In the formal order,

---

48. *The Philosopher and Theology,* p. 98. See "St. Thomas and Our Colleagues," *A Gilson Reader,* pp. 293–94. For Gilson, of course, this broader view of theology is that of Thomas himself. See *The Christian Philosophy of St. Thomas Aquinas,* pp. 9–10. To designate those philosophical elements "which have been integrated with a theological synthesis" Thomas used the term *revelabilia.* For discussion of the *revelabilia* see *ibid.,* pp. 9–15. For additional precisions, see *Le thomisme,* 6th ed., pp. 20–23.

49. *Expositio super librum Boethii De Trinitate,* B. Decker, ed., 2d ed. (Leiden, 1959), q. 5, a. 4, pp. 194–95. Note in particular: "Sic ergo theologia sive scientia divina est duplex. Una, in qua considerantur res divinae non tamquam subiectum scientiae, sed tamquam principia subiecti, et talis est theologia, quam philosophi prosequuntur, quae alio nomine metaphysica dicitur. Alia vero, quae ipsas res divinas considerat propter se ipsas ut subiectum scientiae, et haec est theologia, quae in sacra scriptura traditur" (p. 195:6–11). For the distinction in genus between sacred science and metaphysics also see ST I, q. 1, a. 1, ad 2.

sacred theology and metaphysics are generically distinct. But Gilson suggests that the concrete order is of greater concern to Thomas here.[50] It would seem to be in the concrete order that Gilson's "broadened" notion of theology finds its full application. In the concrete order sacred science notes certain possibilities for philosophical reasoning of which philosophy, left to its own devices, would remain unaware. The philosophy which the theologian applies in his theology remains philosophical in its nature, formally considered. But it is now employed in a higher task, the theological, and subjected to a higher light; and thereby it becomes a part of theology.[51]

One might object that theology itself is degraded insofar as it uses philosophical reasoning. Thomas faced such an objection in the *Summa theologiae*. If sacred science borrows from the lower sciences, it would seem to be inferior to them. Thomas replies that sacred teaching does not receive its principles from any lower science, but immediately from God by revelation. Therefore, it does not receive from the other sciences as from its superiors, but rather uses them as its inferiors and handmaids.[52]

On the other hand, one might protest that philosophy's condition is worsened by its theological state of service. Against this Gilson counters that to serve as the handmaid of theology is philosophy's highest honor. If some of the patristic writers had found that the most favorable situation for philosophy was not that of the pagan but that of the Christian, Gilson insists that in the same fashion philosophy as it exists within theology is in far better position than any kind of separated philosophy. However, it has also been objected that such a view turns philosophy into theology and thereby destroys one or the other or both. In his Commentary on the *De Trinitate* Thomas had faced a similar charge. He had been accused of mixing the water of philosophy with the wine of Scripture. He had replied that in a mixture both component natures are changed, resulting in some third substance. Here, however, there is no mixture. Philosophy passes under the authority of faith and thereby water is changed into wine. Gilson interprets this to mean that philosophy is changed into theology by being so used.[53]

---

50. *Elements of Christian Philosophy*, p. 27. See *Introduction à la philosophie chrétienne*, pp. 112ff. and 132.

51. *Elements*, p. 289, n. 36. Also see the text cited below and referenced in n. 54. Also cf. *The Philosopher and Theology*, pp. 100–101; "Thomas Aquinas and Our Colleagues," pp. 293–94.

52. ST I, q. 1, a. 5, ad 2. On this see *Elements of Christian Philosophy*, pp. 36–37.

53. *Expositio super librum Boethii De Trinitate*, q. 2, a. 3, ad 5 (p. 96). See *Elements*, pp. 289–90, n. 36; "Thomas Aquinas and Our Colleagues," p. 294; *The Philosopher and Theology*, p. 101.

Far from being harmful to philosophy, according to Gilson this transformation is rather a kind of "transfiguration" of it. He concludes from all of this:

> . . . the nature of the doctrine in the *Summa Theologiae* should be clear. Since its aim is to introduce its readers, especially beginners, to the teaching of theology, everything in it is theological. This does not mean that the *Summa* contains no philosophy; on the contrary, it is full of philosophy. Since the philosophy that is in the *Summa* is there in view of a theological end, and since it figures in it as integrated with that which is the proper work of the theologian, it finds itself included within the formal object of theology and becomes theological in its own right.[54]

As found in the theological writings of Thomas Aquinas, then (and this is where one must look to find his distinctive philosophy, according to Gilson), philosophy is there in view of a theological end. Consequently, it will be included within the formal object of theology and will thereby become theological. This seems to be Gilson's final conclusion. If in the concrete order the philosophy of Aquinas is not separated from his faith and his religious convictions and is thereby constituted a Christian philosophy, it now seems that insofar as this Christian philosophy was constructed by a theologian in theological writings and for theological goals, it has been changed into theology. It is perhaps this final point which has raised the greatest number of protests, even from among those who might defend some kind of Christian philosophy.

In line with the above, Gilson now broadens the notion of Christian philosophy itself. It will refer to any usage of philosophy made by the Christian in the service of theology and, in its most comprehensive meaning, "transcends the distinction of scholastic philosophy and scholastic theology." It is now taken to apply to the use the Christian makes of philosophy in either philosophy or theology insofar as he joins religious faith and philosophical reasoning.[55]

Practical Consequences

Some rather obvious practical consequences follow from Gilson's position, and he does not hesitate to draw them. If the Christian philosophy of Thomas Aquinas was at the same time a part of his theology insofar as it served as its instrument and was thereby changed into theology, what of the believing Christian who would philosophize today? He could, of course, attempt to philosophize without any reference to his religious belief. But such would not be the ideal for the Christian philosopher. Nor, according to Gilson, will it be

---

54. *Elements*, p. 42.
55. *The Philosopher and Theology*, p. 198.

enough for him to refer to his religious faith as a negative norm, warning him when his philosophical reasoning has gone astray. The modern Christian who wishes to philosophize, above all, the modern Thomist, should proceed in the way Thomas Aquinas did in his own day. If philosophy was changed into theology by being used as its instrument in the writings of Aquinas, it would seem to follow that the Christian who wants to philosophize today *ad mentem sancti Thomae* should first study theology. Then he will follow the order proposed by Thomas in his theological works, and will be in position to profit from the positive contributions which theology has to make to philosophy.[56]

Consistent as he is, Gilson does not stop short of such conclusions. In a lecture originally given at the Aquinas Foundation at Princeton University, March 7, 1953, he discusses this very issue. Basing himself on certain texts of Aquinas he concludes that, according to Thomas himself: (1) young people are not yet ready to study metaphysics; (2) "youth" ends at fifty; (3) the ancient philosophers used to wait until the later part of their lives to study metaphysics.[57] Gilson recalls that these points are verified by his own experience and by his unsuccessful attempts to understand the metaphysicians when he first attempted to do so as a youth of twenty.[58]

But what of Aquinas himself, one may ask, since he died at age forty-nine and had composed his *De ente et essentia* when he was perhaps only thirty-one? Gilson has a ready answer. Thomas did not regard himself as a philosopher but as a theologian. If he advised young people against studying metaphysics and natural theology and ethics, he did not say that they are not ready to study "revealed theology, including what of metaphysics and ethics it may contain."[59] As Thomas saw it, the pure philosopher, the one who would philosophize without the guidance of revelation, had best wait until late in life to take up the study of metaphysics. But as a Christian and a religious he had studied philosophy while still a youth in order to become a theologian. Thomas's advice as interpreted by Gilson would be this. If one wishes to become a metaphysician, he can hardly begin too late in life. If he wishes to become a theologian, he can hardly begin too soon. Aquinas had never regarded himself as a pure philosopher. Hence, if he had studied philosophy in his youth, he had done so in order to become a theologian.[60]

Gilson suggests that Thomas objects to the early study of metaphysics because of its extremely abstract character. Religion, on the other hand,

---

56. See *The Philosopher and Theology*, pp. 213–14.
57. "Thomas Aquinas and Our Colleagues," p. 286.
58. *Ibid.*, p. 287.
59. *Ibid.*, pp. 287–89. For the quotation see p. 289.
60. *Ibid.*, p.289.

can offer a concrete approach to certain notions presented abstractly by
metaphysics. If the notion of "pure act" elicits little response from a class of
undergraduates, a term such as "God" will fare much better. God is already
known to them by reason of their previous religious training. If we cannot
substitute the teaching of theology for metaphysics in Catholic liberal arts
colleges today, still, if we would introduce Christian students to Thomas's
metaphysics and ethics, the best short cut would be to teach them the relevant parts of his theology. At the very least we should create "around our
teaching of philosophy a like religious atmosphere."[61] And as regards the
training of future theologians, Gilson's position is unequivocal: "If you
want to teach your students both metaphysics and ethics, teach them
straight theology, provided only it be theology as Thomas Aquinas himself
understood it."[62] For if such a theology is really Thomistic, it will include
that Christian philosophy which serves as its instrument and handmaid.

2: Personal Reflections

In reacting to Gilson's views concerning Thomas Aquinas and Christian
philosophy, I shall first turn to a distinction proposed by Anton Pegis which
may serve to introduce some additional clarifications. Then I shall examine
critically two points which seem to be crucial to Gilson's historical interpretation of Aquinas concerning this issue, and which are of importance to
anyone interested in recovering Thomas's distinctive metaphysical thought.
With respect to these, alternative approaches will be proposed.

In one of his later writings, *The Middle Ages and Philosophy,* Pegis offers an
interesting precision. There he speaks of a certain ambivalence of medieval
philosophy. Considered as a philosophy, one finds that it was developed in
a religious atmosphere under the influence of a Christian *Weltanschauung.*
For this reason, one is not surprised to note that it bears the marks of its
Christian origins and is, in fact, a Christian philosophy. At the same time,
however, one finds that this same philosophy was used as an instrument of
theology and thereby involved in a task which carried it beyond the realm
of philosophy. Pegis and Gilson would agree, therefore, that in the case of
great medieval Schoolmen such as Thomas Aquinas, their philosophies
were developed by theologians in order to enable them to create and perfect
their theologies. Consequently, continues Pegis, when dealing with such a
philosophy one should distinguish between its "Christian character as a
philosophy and its theological state of service."[63]

---

61. *Ibid.,* pp. 290–92.
62. *Ibid.,* pp. 292–93.
63. A. Pegis, *The Middle Ages and Philosophy* (Chicago, 1963), p. 71.

Herein lies the ambivalence of medieval philosophy. On the one hand, maintains Pegis, it was a Christian philosophy: *philosophy,* because it was a work of human reason operating according to its proper light; *Christian,* because it was elaborated under the influence of revelation. On the other hand, it was not only a Christian philosophy, but was developed within a theology to serve as its instrument. As Christian this philosophy remained philosophical in substance, and for that reason deserves to be called Christian philosophy, not Christian theology. But as a theological instrument it was involved in a labor which was imposed on it neither as philosophy nor as Christian. Granted that it is one and the same Christian philosophy which was also used by theology, that which makes it Christian philosophy cannot be identified with that which makes it theological. As Pegis puts it, one must not confuse "what is Christian in the philosophy to be found in the *Summa* with what is *in addition* theological in the use St. Thomas made of it." If the Christian philosophy of Thomas Aquinas is not to be reduced to the philosophy of Aristotle, as Gilson has so effectively argued, at the same time it should not be "equated with the service to which he put philosophy in the interpretation of *sacra doctrina.*"[64]

In my opinion this is a helpful distinction, and it suggests another application. It is one thing to acknowledge that a given medieval thinker may have been influenced in some way by his faith in his philosophizing. In addition to the fact that he would have used his religious belief as a negative norm to warn him when he had reached philosophical conclusions opposed to his faith, it is more than likely that he also first accepted on faith certain positions which he might subsequently investigate philosophically. Gilson has, it seems to me, brought out this point very effectively. Issues such as the existence of one God, or life after death, or divine providence come to mind. Long before such a medieval Christian would have even heard of philosophy he would have accepted these as religious truths, based on faith. Once he began to study philosophy formally, or perhaps to develop his own, he might well investigate these same truths from the philosophical side. And he might do this, I would suggest, without having first become a theologian or without having incorporated them into his theology, for instance during his career as a student in arts or thereafter. In other words, one may readily admit that a typical Christian medieval thinker was influenced in his original acceptance of a given point by his prior religious belief in the same, or in what might be called the "moment of discovery." If one wishes to describe this procedure as "Christian philosophy" and to restrict this name to the order of discovery, I myself would have no great

---

64. *Ibid.,* pp. 69–81. For the quotations see pp. 77, 81.

difficulty with that usage of the name. Such a medieval thinker could never, of course, admit a revealed premise into his attempted philosophical demonstration of a given conclusion without thereby passing from philosophy to theology. The proper name for any such procedure would no longer be Christian philosophy but Christian theology. One should not, therefore, refer to philosophy as Christian in its "moment of proof."[65]

To make the same point another way, it is one thing to suggest that in a given case a medieval thinker may have moved from prior religious belief in a certain point to philosophical inquiry concerning the same. It is something else again to suggest that he must have moved from his theology to philosophical investigation of the same. In Gilson's later examinations of philosophy and theology in Aquinas, he seems to have ended by adopting the second of these proposals as well as the first. As will become clearer from my subsequent remarks, as regards the historical Thomas Aquinas's procedure in his philosophizing, I would accept only the first.

This brings me back to two other points in Gilson's historical interpretation and presentation of Aquinas's philosophy, especially his metaphysics, which in my opinion are open to criticism: (1) the kind of texts to which one should turn in seeking to discover Thomas's distinctive metaphysical views; (2) Gilson's insistence on presenting the philosophy of Aquinas according to the theological order.

As regards the first point, Gilson has insisted that Aquinas's most personal and most distinctive philosophical and metaphysical thought is to be found mainly if not exclusively in his theological writings. This view, of course, goes hand in hand with Gilson's conviction that Thomas was a theologian and not a philosopher, unless one means by this a Christian philosopher in the sense elaborated by Gilson. It also seems to follow from this that it will be foreign to the spirit of Aquinas to attempt to extract his

---

65. I do not wish to imply that Pegis himself is any way responsible for the point just made, or that he would have accepted it any more than Gilson himself would have. For some writers who apply this distinction between the "moment of discovery" and the "moment of proof" to the issue of Christian philosophy, see G. Klubertanz, "Metaphysics and Theistic Convictions," in *Teaching Thomism Today*, G. McLean, ed. (Washington, D.C., 1963), pp. 278–82; A. Naud, *Le problème de la philosophie chrétienne*, pp. 35–62; G. Grisez, "The 'Four Meanings' of Christian Philosophy," *The Journal of Religion* 42 (1962), pp. 113ff. On the other hand, F. Van Steenberghen has often distinguished between philosophy taken in the broad sense and in the strict sense, as well as between the status of the philosopher and philosophy. If there are Christian philosophers, there can be no Christian philosophies (taken in the strict sense). See his "Etienne Gilson, historien de la pensée médiévale," *Revue philosophique de Louvain* 77 (1979), pp. 496–507, with references to earlier treatments.

philosophical and especially his metaphysical thought from its original theological moorings.[66]

In considering possible sources upon which one might draw in attempting to discover Thomas's metaphysical thought, it may be helpful to propose a general classification of his works. One might divide them as follows: (1) philosophical commentaries including his commentaries on Aristotle and the *Liber de causis;* (2) commentaries on Sacred Scripture; (3) theological commentaries (as on the *De Trinitate* and the *De Hebdomadibus* of Boethius, on Pseudo-Denis's *The Divine Names,* or on the *Book of Sentences* — of these only two are commentaries in the strict sense, that is, on the *De Hebdomadibus* and on the *Divine Names;* the other two use the texts of Boethius and of Peter the Lombard as *occasiones,* as it were, for much fuller and highly personal expressions of Thomas's own views); (4) works of theological synthesis (see the two *Summae,* and the *Compendium of Theology*); (5) Disputed Questions and Quodlibetal Questions (delivered and/or prepared by Thomas as a Master of Theology); (6) theological opuscula; (7) philosophical opuscula (such as the *De ente, De principiis naturae, De unitate intellectus, De aeternitate mundi,* and perhaps *De substantiis separatis* [regarded by some rather as a theological opusculum in light of its final part]).[67]

As regards the sources one might utilize in developing Thomas's personal metaphysical thought, two of the above categories are obviously philosophical, that is, the commentaries on Aristotle and on the *Liber de causis,* and the philosophical opuscula. The others might be regarded as

66. See the references given above in n. 41. Here perhaps it will be appropriate for me to recall Professor Gilson's remarks during a public lecture delivered during my student days (in the 1950s) on the campus of The Catholic University of America and dealing with this very topic. After Gilson had contended that Thomas Aquinas was not a philosopher but a theologian, questions were raised by others about the commentaries on Aristotle and the philosophical opuscula. Gilson replied that the commentaries were exercises in the history of philosophy, not expressions of Thomas's personal thinking. There, too, Gilson minimized the philosophical importance of the philosophical opuscula.

67. For fundamentally the same classification see F. Van Steenberghen, *La philosophie au XIIIe siècle* (Louvain-Paris, 1966), pp. 310–14. I have included under the general class, theological opuscula, his listing of apologetical opuscula, theological opuscula, opuscula in defense of the Mendicants, and opuscula treating of spirituality. One might include the Commentary on the *Sentences* under works of theological synthesis. See Van Steenberghen, *op. cit.,* p. 311; J. Weisheipl, *Friar Thomas d'Aquino: His Life, Thought, and Work* (Garden City, New York, 1974), pp. 358–59. For a strong defense of the theological character of the *De substantiis separatis* as well as his insistence on including the term "Tractatus" in its title, see F. J. Lescoe, "*De substantiis separatis:* Title and Date," in *St. Thomas Aquinas 1274–1974: Commemorative Studies,* A. Maurer, ed. (Toronto, 1974), Vol. 1, pp. 54–55.

theological and are the kinds of writings one would expect from one who was a Master of Theology and a theologian by profession. This fact of itself, incidentally, seems to be sufficient to indicate why Thomas never took the time to write his own *Summa philosophiae*. By profession he was indeed a theologian. What is more surprising is the fact that he did devote so much time and energy to writing the philosophical opuscula and especially the philosophical commentaries.[68]

Given these two classes of philosophical writings, however, Gilson tends to downgrade their importance when it comes to discovering Thomas's personal metaphysical thought. In fact he has contended that the commentaries are not really expressions of the distinctive Thomistic philosophy at all, but exercises in the history of philosophy. What one finds in them is Thomas's understanding of the texts upon which he is commenting. As to the philosophical opuscula, to the extent that the later Gilson admitted that they are indeed philosophical, he tended to downgrade their importance as well. They are not all that significant as expressions of Thomas's personal and original philosophical thought.[69]

With respect to this I can only reply that the philosophical opuscula are surely philosophical works. Moreover, they are important sources for Thomas's personal philosophical views. Granted that the *De ente*, for instance, is an early work, one already finds therein many of the essential features of the mature Thomistic metaphysics. One need only think of the discussion of essence and *esse* in ch. 4 and the interesting argumentation for God's existence that appears there.[70] One finds more mature expressions of Aquinas's personal views in works such as the *De aeternitate mundi*,[71] or the *De unitate intellectus*,[72] or for that matter in the philosophical part of the *De substantiis separatis*.[73]

---

68. On this see the interesting view advanced by Weisheipl, *Friar Thomas d'Aquino*, pp. 281–85. Both Weisheipl and Van Steenberghen regard the Commentaries on Aristotle as important sources for one seeking Thomas's personal philosophical thought. See *La philosophie au XIIIe siècle*, pp. 310, 330, and n. 33, p. 330 (citing G. Verbeke to this same effect).

69. See my notes 41 and 66 above.

70. For more on this see Ch. V below.

71. For more on this and for references to other studies see my Ch. VIII below.

72. On this see F. Van Steenberghen, *Thomas Aquinas and Radical Aristotelianism* (Washington, D.C., 1980), pp. 49–67; *Maître Siger de Brabant* (Louvain-Paris, 1977), pp. 347–60.

73. See, for instance, the presentation and detailed refutation of Avicebron's universal hylemorphism which one finds in chs. 5 through 8, and especially the important statement of Thomas's views concerning essence and *esse* in creatures and his metaphysics of participation as found in ch. 8 (Lescoe edition, pp. 79–82).

As to the commentaries on Aristotle and the *De causis,* considerable care is required in utilizing these as sources for Thomas's original and personal thought. Some (Gilson in particular) hold that the Aristotelian commentaries are presentations of Thomas's understanding of Aristotle, and hence works in the history of philosophy. Others seem to go to the opposite extreme and assume that almost every statement made by Thomas in these commentaries is an expression of his personal view.[74]

My own view is, and here I shall concentrate on the Commentary on the *Metaphysics,* that one can neither discount it as a source for Thomas's personal thought nor automatically assume that every statement found therein expresses the same. Some passages admit of one interpretation, that is, they appear to be straightforward expressions of Aristotle's thought. Others seem to go beyond the thought of Aristotle. Moreover, with respect to the first type, one cannot automatically assume that when Thomas merely repeats and interprets Aristotle he is or is not also expressing a view that he himself holds. Some kind of control is needed, a control that is extrinsic to the body of the Commentary proper. In many instances one has such a control. One can often weigh points made in the Commentary against statements made elsewhere, for instance in the *Prooemium* to the Commentary itself or in other works where Thomas is obviously writing more independently.[75] If one finds Thomas saying the same thing in other treatises, then one can be reasonably certain that one is dealing with his personal thought even in the Commentary, always allowing for the possibility of development in his thinking, to be sure. But if one finds statements in Thomas's exposition of Aristotle which are difficult to reconcile with views expressed in more independent writings, one should proceed very cautiously before attributing the same to Thomas himself.[76]

---

74. For discussion of this see the references to Van Steenberghen and Weisheipl in note 68 above. In addition see the lengthy study devoted by J. Doig to the nature of Thomas's Commentary on the *Metaphysics: Aquinas on Metaphysics: A Historico-Doctrinal Study of the Commentary on the Metaphysics* (The Hague, 1972). Note the remarks and references given in Doig's "Introduction," pp. ix–xiv. For my review of Doig's book see *Speculum* 52 (1977), pp. 133–35.

75. For some illustrations of this see my discussion of the presuppositions for *separatio* according to Aquinas in Ch. IV below.

76. For recognition that non-Aristotelian elements have been introduced into Thomas's Commentaries on Aristotle at certain points, see J. Owens, "Aquinas as Aristotelian Commentator," in *St. Thomas Aquinas 1274–1974,* Vol. 1, pp. 213–38. However, Owens also seems strongly inclined to regard these as further instantiations of Thomas's overriding theological enterprise, wherein he "continues to change what was water in the other sciences into the wine of theology." See pp. 235–38. Owens does propose this view very cautiously in this context, it should be noted.

As to the other writings, those of a more theological nature, some distinctions are in order. It may be, as Fernand Van Steenberghen has suggested, that one finds there a philosophical discussion inserted as such into a theological work.[77] One might think of qq. 5 and 6 of the Commentary on the *De Trinitate* where Thomas treats of the division, respective subjects, distinctive knowing procedures, and levels of verification for the three theoretical sciences—physics, mathematics, and metaphysics. Or one might refer to the so-called Treatises on God and on Man in the *Summa theologiae*. To the extent that these are self-contained philosophical discussions, one can free them from their theological context and the biblical and patristic references found in their *videturs* and *sed contras* and use them as valuable sources for Thomas's thought.[78]

At other times one finds philosophy being used by Thomas as a rational instrument in his development of a strictly theological topic, for instance, in discussing questions related to the Trinity or the Incarnation. Here the philosophy in question has surely become theology, as Gilson would urge, and has lost its autonomy. Still, it may be helpful to study such texts in order to discover the philosophical choices that enabled Aquinas to develop his theological positions concerning the same. In short, it would seem that even such passages may be used as sources in recovering Thomas's metaphysical thought, although in this last instance one must proceed with great caution.[79]

77. *La philosophie au XIIIᵉ siècle*, p. 354.

78. For additional references to Thomas's discussions of these issues in the Commentary on the *De Trinitate*, see below in this same chapter, as well as Chapters II, III, and IV.

79. See Van Steenberghen, p. 354. For the sake of illustration, consider the following taken from Thomas's *Quaestiones disputatae de potentia Dei*, q. 3, a. 13, ad 4: "Ad quartum dicendum, quod illud quod habet esse ab alio, in se consideratum, est non ens, si ipsum sit aliud quam ipsum esse quod ab alio accipit; si autem sit ipsum esse quod ab alio accipit, sic non potest in se consideratum, esse non ens; non enim potest in esse considerari non ens, licet in eo quod est aliud quam esse, considerari possit. Quod enim est, potest aliquid habere permixtum; non autem ipsum esse, ut Boëtius dicit in libro *de Hebdomadibus*. Prima quidem conditio est creaturae, sed secunda est conditio Filii Dei." *Quaestiones disputatae*, Vol. 2, P. Bazzi et al., eds. (Rome-Turin, 1953), p. 79. The immediate context as well as the argumentation are surely theological, since Thomas is attempting to show that "aliquod ens ab alio possit esse aeternum." Here he has maintained that the Son, although naturally proceeding from the Father, is coeternal with the Father. His reply as quoted here tells one much about his metaphysical views, for instance, that if something is distinct from the *esse* that it receives from another, then viewed in itself it may be regarded as *non-ens*. This, he concludes, is true of a creature. This implies that the creature is distinct from (*aliud quam*) the *esse* that it receives, and also that the creature (in terms of its essence, presumably), can be described as nonbeing in some sense, that is, precisely because it is not identical with the *esse* that it receives.

In sum, therefore, it would seem that any and all of Thomas's writings, to the extent that they clearly employ metaphysical argumentation, may be regarded as legitimate sources for recovering his metaphysical thought.

But what, then, of the other point mentioned above, Gilson's contention that one should present Thomas's metaphysical thought according to the theological order in which one finds it in his theological writings? It would seem that Thomas himself has provided us with enough indications to suggest another approach. Even though he was never called upon to write a *Summa metaphysicae*, it is clear that he had worked out a metaphysics and a very thorough one. Moreover, it also seems that the development of this metaphysics was a necessary condition for him to create his own theology.[80] This, of course, is why so much of it appears in his theological writings. If one would reconstruct this metaphysics, therefore, and if Thomas has given us clear indications as to how he conceived this science in terms of its subject, the distinctive knowing processes required to arrive at that subject, and the relationship between its subject and God, one need only follow these indications. But Thomas has developed each of these points in considerable detail, especially in his Commentary on the *De Trinitate* of Boethius.[81]

According to Thomas's discussion in q. 5, a. 1 of that same Commentary, metaphysics is to be regarded as a theoretical science along with mathematics and natural philosophy. It differs from them in that it studies a

---

80. See Van Steenberghen, *La philosophie au XIIIe siècle,* pp. 350–51. Far from agreeing with Gilson that Thomas was a great philosopher because he was a great theologian, Van Steenberghen defends the exact opposite: "Thomas d'Aquin a été un théologien de génie parce qu'il a été un philosophe de génie." In order to show that, in Thomas's eyes, differences between theologians arise from their differences in philosophy, Van Steenberghen cites from *In II Sent.*, d. 14, q. 1, a. 2: "circa hanc quaestionem fuit philosophorum diversa positio . . . . Similiter etiam expositores Sacrae Scripturae in hoc diversificati sunt, secundum quod diversorum philosophorum sectatores fuerunt, a quibus in philosophicis eruditi sunt." See *Scriptum super libros Sententiarum,* P. Mandonnet, ed. (Paris, 1929), Vol. 2, p. 350. As will be evident to the reader, I am in agreement with Van Steenberghen on this point. The most I would concede to Gilson with respect to this is that, in the order of final causality, Thomas's desire to create an original theology may have inspired him, at least in part, to develop his original philosophy; but the development of his own philosophy, and especially of his own metaphysics, was a necessary condition for him to develop his theology. The philosophy must have been created first. The fact that it is already so well worked out in Thomas's first writings, such as the *De ente* or the Commentary on the *Sentences,* clearly testifies to this. This is not to deny that Thomas's philosophical (and theological) thought would mature considerably during the subsequent years of his career.

81. See in particular q. 5, a. 1; q. 5, a. 3; q. 5, a. 4; q. 6, a. 1; and q. 6, a. 2. For an excellent English translation along with a helpful Introduction see A. Maurer, *St. Thomas Aquinas, The Division and Methods of the Sciences,* 3d revised ed. (Toronto, 1963).

distinctive kind of object of theoretical knowledge (*speculabile*), the kind that does not depend on matter for its being (*esse*). This may be because the object of theoretical science is never found in matter (God and angels), or because it is found in matter in certain cases though not in others (illustrated by substance, quality, being, act and potency, the one and the many, etc.).[82] One might refer to the first type as the positively immaterial, in that such objects of theoretical science positively exclude matter. And one might refer to the latter kind as negatively or neutrally immaterial, in that they need not be found in matter, even though they can be.[83]

In q. 5, a. 3 Thomas observes that the intellect's first operation, the "understanding of indivisibles," is directed toward a thing's nature, whereas its second operation, that whereby it composes and divides, is directed toward a thing's *esse*. This text and others like it have been used to good effect by Gilson and others to show that, according to Aquinas, one cannot discover existence or being as existing by relying on the intellect's first operation. The intellect's second operation, often referred to as judgment, is required for this.[84]

Farther on in this same article Thomas discusses two kinds of abstraction when that term is taken strictly, the abstraction of the whole and the abstraction of the form. He connects the first with natural philosophy and the second with mathematics, presumably thereby implying that one must have recourse to these respectively to arrive at the subjects of physics and of mathematics. He then contrasts these with another way in which the mind distinguishes, this time by judging negatively, technically referred to here as "separation." This last-mentioned operation — separation — is then connected with metaphysics. Presumably Thomas means by this that through this second operation or negative judgment one explicitly frees the subject of metaphysics, being, from any necessary connection with matter and

---

82. *Ed. cit.* (Decker), pp. 164–65.

83. See Ch. IV below for fuller discussion of this distinction.

84. *Ed. cit.*, p. 182. Note in particular: "Secunda vero operatio respicit ipsum esse rei, quod quidem resultat ex congregatione principiorum rei in compositis vel ipsam simplicem naturam rei concomitatur, ut in substantiis simplicibus." Full credit must be given to Gilson for having stressed the crucial role played by judgment in one's discovery of being as existing or in one's discovery of existence. See in particular the all-important ch. VI of his *Being and Some Philosophers*, 2d ed. (Toronto, 1952). This theme has been developed by many and especially by J. Owens. See, for instance, his *An Interpretation of Existence* (Milwaukee, 1968), especially ch. II; "Aquinas on Knowing Existence," *The Review of Metaphysics* 29 (1976), pp. 670–90. At the same time, Owens's article indicates how greatly leading contemporary Thomistic scholars have differed in their explanations of Thomas's views concerning the discovery of existence.

motion. In short, one thereby judges that that by reason of which something is recognized as being need not be identified with that by reason of which it is recognized as a given kind of being. One thus arrives at a knowledge of being as such or of being as being, that is to say, at knowledge of the subject of metaphysics.[85]

And if one wonders how the kind of *speculabile* that need not be found in matter is to be correlated with the kind that cannot be found in matter, or in other words how being, the subject of metaphysics, is to be correlated with God, Thomas addresses himself to this in q. 5, a. 4. Both metaphysics and the theology grounded in Scripture treat of things separate from matter and motion. But there is this crucial distinction. Things separate from matter in the positive sense, that is, those which cannot be found in matter or divine things as Thomas here expresses it, constitute the subject of the theology grounded in Scripture. Things separate from matter and motion in the negative or neutral sense, which may or may not be found in matter, these are studied by metaphysics as its subject. In brief, as he has already remarked in this article, being as being is the subject of metaphysics; things separate from matter and motion in the positive sense — divine things — are studied by metaphysics only as principles of its subject.[86]

This same theme is developed in the *Prooemium* to Thomas's Commentary on the *Metaphysics*, and again therefore in a context where Thomas is writing freely and expressing his personal views rather than merely commenting. Once more he notes that the subject of metaphysics is not God or divine things, but being in general. Divine things, such as God and separate substances, are rather regarded as causes of being in general (*ens commune*). By this he must mean that these are causes of all that which falls under being in general. Far from assuming that one must begin with God and then move on to consider being in general and that which falls thereunder, that is, created being, Thomas here maintains that knowledge of the causes of a given science's subject-genus is rather the end or goal of that science's inquiry.[87]

---

85. *Ed. cit.,* pp. 183–86. For fuller discussion see my Ch. IV below.

86. *Ed. cit.,* pp. 194–95. See in particular: "Et ideo pertractantur in illa doctrina, in qua ponuntur ea quae sunt communia omnibus entibus, quae habet subiectum ens in quantum est ens . . . " (p. 194:24–26); "Theologia ergo philosophica determinat de separatis secundo modo sicut de subiectis, de separatis autem primo modo sicut de principiis subiecti" (p. 195:22–24).

87. Note in particular: "Unde oportet quod ad eamdem scientiam pertineat considerare substantias separatas, et ens commune, quod est genus, cuius sunt praedictae substantiae communes et universales causae. Ex quo apparet, quod quamvis ista scientia praedicta tria consideret [that is, first causes, being, separate substances], non tamen considerat quodlibet eorum ut subiectum, sed ipsum solum ens commune. Hoc enim est subiectum in scientia, cuius causas et passiones quaerimus,

Reference to these passages should be sufficient to show that in Thomas's mind there is no confusion between metaphysics, on the one hand, and the theology based on revelation, on the other. If metaphysics has as its subject being in general, theology has as its subject God and divine things. Far from presupposing or beginning with God, Thomas's metaphysics regards knowledge of the divine as the end or goal of the metaphysician's investigation. His metaphysics begins with the discovery of a metaphysical understanding of being as being. This itself is derived from one's knowledge of sensible entities and one's application thereto of the two kinds of judgment noted above. First there is a positive judgment of existence. This is directed towards a thing's *esse* and is required, I would suggest, even for one to get to a primitive or nonmetaphysical knowledge of being. Secondly there is a negative judgment (*separatio*), which is required for one to free one's primitive and original understanding of being from restriction to the material and changing. One may well debate Thomas's view concerning the presuppositions for this discovery of being as being or for *separatio*. But that is another matter.[88] For the present it is enough for us to note that there are ample indications in Thomas's writings concerning his views with respect to the nature, the subject-matter, and the method appropriate to metaphysics. It would seem, therefore, that if one wishes to recover the elements of this metaphysics from Thomas's various writings, one should present these elements according to the philosophical order outlined by Thomas himself, not according to the theological order proposed by Gilson.[89]

---

non autem ipsae causae alicuius generis quaesiti. Nam cognitio causarum alicuius generis, est finis ad quem consideratio scientiae pertingit." See *In duodecim libros Metaphysicorum Aristotelis expositio,* M.-R. Cathala and R. Spiazzi, eds. (Turin-Rome, 1950), p. 2.

88. See Ch. IV, Section II, for discussion of this.

89. For another text where Thomas clearly distinguishes these two orders, see *Summa contra gentiles* II, ch. 4, especially: "Exinde etiam est quod non eodem ordine utraque doctrina procedit. Nam in doctrina philosophiae, quae creaturas secundum se considerat et ex eis in Dei cognitionem perducit, prima est consideratio de creaturis et ultima de Deo. In doctrina vero fidei, quae creaturas non nisi in ordine ad Deum considerat, primo est consideratio Dei et postmodum creaturarum." See *Summa contra gentiles,* ed. Leonina manualis (Rome, 1934), p. 96. Presumably, therefore, if one wishes to present the metaphysics or the philosophy of Aquinas, one should do so according to the philosophical order as described by him rather than according to the theological order. For a considerably more critical reaction to Gilson's views concerning Christian philosophy, the reader may consult John M. Quinn, *The Thomism of Etienne Gilson: A Critical Study* (Villanova, 1971), ch. I ("Christian Philosophy and Philosophy"), pp. 1–16.

Finally, one may still wonder whether such an effort at reconstructing a metaphysics by drawing upon indications found in different types of writings, including many which are theological, will not result in a distortion of Thomas's true thought. Here another distinction seems to be in order. On the one hand, since Thomas himself has indicated his views concerning the nature, subject, and methodology appropriate to metaphysics, and since texts filled with metaphysics are scattered throughout his writings, one seems to be justified in being guided by and using the same in one's effort to recapture Thomas's personal metaphysical thought. In sum, if Thomas did develop a highly original and personal metaphysics and if such was a necessary condition for him to create his original theology, one does not do violence to his thought by following the philosophical and metaphysical order defined by Thomas himself in attempting to reconstruct that metaphysics. On the other hand, precisely because Thomas did not write a finished *Summa philosophiae* or even a *Summa metaphysicae*, considerable initiative and latitude are left to the individual contemporary scholar who attempts to discover and reassemble the various elements of that metaphysical thought. A sensitivity to the history of medieval thought in Thomas's own day is surely required, as well as some metaphysical skill on one's own part. Given the variety of individuals and the different backgrounds and approaches of those who turn themselves to this task in our time, variety and diversity of interpretation in these efforts at reconstruction are bound to result. Some efforts will undoubtedly be more successful than others, and failure will inevitably involve distortion to some degree. But this, in a sense, is what makes continued study of Aquinas so interesting and challenging a task, the kind of task required of all who would attempt to present metaphysics *ad mentem sancti Thomae.*

PART I

THE NATURE OF METAPHYSICS
AND ITS SUBJECT-MATTER

CHAPTER II

AQUINAS AND AVICENNA ON THE RELA-TIONSHIP BETWEEN FIRST PHILOSOPHY AND THE OTHER THEORETICAL SCIENCES
(*In De Trin., q. 5, a. 1, ad 9*)

In recent decades considerable progress has been made in investigating and identifying earlier philosophical sources for the thought of Thomas Aquinas. Among these sources Avicenna stands out as one whose work must be considered by anyone interested in the historical origins of Thomistic metaphysics. In addition to groundbreaking studies by Etienne Gilson illustrating the general influence of Arabic philosophy on Latin scholasticism,[1] a number of more recent efforts have been directed to particular examples of the Avicennian influence on Thomas himself. Some of these have investigated the Avicennian influence on particular doctrines while others have concentrated on Avicenna as a source for particular Thomistic works.[2]

---

1. "Pourquoi saint Thomas a critiqué saint Augustin," *Archives d'Histoire Doctrinale et Littéraire du Moyen Age* 1 (1926-1927), pp. 5-127; "Avicenne et le point de départ de Duns Scot," *ibid.* 2 (1927), pp. 89-149; "Les sources gréco-arabes de l'augustinisme avicennisant," *ibid.* 4 (1929), pp. 5-149.

2. See for instance, G. Smith, "Avicenna and the Possibles," *The New Scholasticism* 17 (1943), pp. 340-57; A. Lobato, *De influxu Avicennae in theoria cognitionis Sancti Thomae Aquinatis* (Granada, 1956); B. Zedler, "Saint Thomas and Avicenna in the 'De Potentia Dei,'" *Traditio* 6 (1948), pp. 105-59; "St. Thomas, Interpreter of Avicenna," *The Modern Schoolman* 33 (1955-1956), pp. 1-18; L. De Raeymaeker, "L'être selon Avicenne et selon s. Thomas d'Aquin," *Avicenna Commemoration Volume* (Calcutta, 1956), pp. 119-31; "La esencia avicenista y la esencia tomista," *Sapientia* 11 (1956), pp. 154-65. For a list of explicit citations of Avicenna by St. Thomas see C. Vansteenkiste, "Avicenna-Citaten bij S. Thomas," *Tijdschrift voor Philosophie* 15 (1953), pp. 457-507. For further bibliographical indications concerning Avicenna and his influence on Latin scholasticism see G. C. Anawati, *Essai de bibliographie avicennienne* (Cairo, 1950), section 4, "Les Travaux Sur Avicenne En Langues Autres

At the same time, qq. 5 and 6 of Thomas's Commentary on Boethius's *De Trinitate* contain his most extensive treatment of the division and nature of the speculative sciences and their respective methods. Renewed interest in these questions is indicated by the relatively recent appearance of two important editions of these questions,[3] by two English translations,[4] and by a series of articles treating of the Thomistic theory of abstraction and separation developed therein.[5] Finally, S. Neumann has devoted a monograph to the object and method of the theoretical sciences as found in these same questions.[6] However, although considerable attention has understandably

Que L'Arabe," and for a résumé of this bibliography in French his "La tradition manuscrite orientale de l'oeuvre d'Avicenne," *Revue thomiste* 51 (1951), pp. 407-40; also his "Chronique avicennienne 1951-1960," *Revue thomiste* 60 (1960), pp. 630-31; and "Bibliographie de la philosophie médiévale en terre d'Islam pour les années 1959-1969," *Bulletin de philosophie médiévale* 10-12 (1968-70), p. 361. Now also see his "Saint Thomas d'Aquin et la *Métaphysique* d'Avicenne," in *St. Thomas Aquinas 1274-1974: Commemorative Studies* (Toronto, 1974), Vol. 1, pp. 449-65 (with references to other studies); *La Métaphysique du Shifā' Livres I à V. Introduction, traduction et notes* (Paris, 1978), pp. 63-78 (with some additional references). Also see L. Gardet, "Saint Thomas et ses prédécesseurs arabes," in *St. Thomas Aquinas 1274-1974*, Vol. 1, especially pp. 435-38; A. Judy, "Avicenna's *Metaphysics* in the *Summa contra gentiles,*" *Angelicum* 52 (1975), pp. 340-84, 541-86; and vol. 53 (1976), pp. 185-226. Also see Gilson, "Avicenne en Occident au Moyen Age," *Archives d'Histoire Doctrinale et Littéraire du Moyen Age* 36 (1969), pp. 89-121.

3. *Thomas von Aquin, In librum Boethii De Trinitate, Quaestiones Quinta et Sexta,* P. Wyser, ed. (Fribourg-Louvain, 1948); *Sancti Thomae de Aquino Expositio super librum Boethii De Trinitate,* B. Decker, ed., 2d ed. (Leiden, 1959). In addition to being an edition of the entire Thomistic Commentary rather than merely of qq. 5 and 6, Decker's work has the added merit of having consulted other codices in addition to the autograph manuscript used by Wyser. See Decker, *op. cit.,* pp. 33ff.

4. *St. Thomas Aquinas, The Division and Methods of the Sciences: Questions V and VI of His Commentary on the De Trinitate of Boethius, Translated with Introduction and Notes,* A. Maurer, tr., 3d rev. ed. (Toronto, 1963); *The Trinity and The Unicity of the Intellect by St. Thomas Aquinas,* Sr. Rose Emmanuella Brennan, tr. (St. Louis, 1946), pp. 8-197 for a translation of all six questions of Thomas's Commentary on the *De Trinitate*. Maurer's translation is based on the autograph edition of Wyser, but in the third edition Decker's edition has also been used. See Maurer, pp. xxxix-xl. Although the Brennan translation is not restricted to qq. 5 and 6, it appeared before the Wyser and Decker editions and hence is not based on the better text now available.

5. For reference to many of these and for discussion of this issue see Ch. IV below.

6. S. Neumann, *Gegenstand und Methode der theoretischen Wissenschaften nach Thomas von Aquin aufgrund der Expositio super librum Boethii De Trinitate,* in Beiträge zur Geschichte der Philosophie und Theologie des Mittelalters 41:2 (Münster, 1965). Since the original appearance of my article in 1973, another book-length study of Thomas's Commentary has appeared: L. Elders, *Faith and Science: An Introduction to St. Thomas' Expositio in Boethii De Trinitate* (Rome, 1974). Moreover, H. Weidemann

been given to Aristotle and to Boethius as sources for Thomas in his writing of this commentary, Avicenna has received relatively little notice. Nonetheless, a comparison of q. 5 in particular with certain sections of the Latin Avicenna, above all with the opening book of the *Metaphysics* of his great encyclopedia of philosophy (*al-Shifā'*), suggests that the latter may also have to be numbered among the principal sources for this part of Thomas's commentary.[7] Rather than attempt to demonstrate this point in the present

---

has concentrated heavily on Thomas's Commentary in his *Metaphysik und Sprache: Eine sprachphilosophische Untersuchung zu Thomas von Aquin und Aristoteles* (Freiburg-Munich, 1975).

7. Thus Neumann, in the work cited in n. 6 above, devotes pp. 19–36 to Aristotle and pp. 36–57 to Boethius as background material for Thomas's Commentary. With rarest exceptions such as pp. 115 and 152, Avicenna is completely disregarded. Nonetheless, Vansteenkiste lists ten explicit citations of Avicenna by Thomas in this Commentary and four from questions 5 and 6 (q. 5, a. 1, ad 4; q. 5, a. 1, ad 9; q. 5, a. 4c; q. 6, a. 3c), *op. cit.*, pp. 458–60. In the footnotes of his edition Decker has indicated a number of further parallel passages between Avicenna and Aquinas in addition to the explicit citations. More recently, Elders has also noted a number of points in the Commentary where Thomas is influenced by Avicenna (*op. cit.*, Index), though he does not single out the passage which is of primary interest to me in the present chapter. Also, for some references to Avicenna and to my article see Weidemann, *op. cit.* The Avicenna known to Thomas and to which I shall here be referring is the Latin Avicenna, that is, the Latin translation of the *Metaphysics* of Avicenna's most important philosophical work, his *Kitāb al-Shifā'*. Although a major part of the original Arabic text was translated into Latin in the Middle Ages, this translation activity occurred in different stages. Moreover, certain sections were simply not translated at all. For an outline of the various parts of the *Shifā'* and a description of the various steps involved in the medieval Latin translation of the same, see M.-T. d'Alverny, "Avicenna Latinus I," *Archives d'Histoire Doctrinale et Littéraire du Moyen Age* 28 (1961), pp. 282–88. The most important step seems to have occurred at Toledo after the year 1150 and included an *Introduction, Isagoge,* ch. 7 of section 2 of the *Second Analytics, Physics* (in part), *De Anima,* and *Metaphysics.* Only a relatively small part of the *Logic* (about one-fourteenth) was translated into medieval Latin. See Anawati, "La tradition manuscrite orientale," p. 417. Both the Latin *Logic* and *Metaphysics* may be found in a 1508 edition: *Avicennae perhypatetici philosophi ac medicorum facile primi Opera in lucem redacta ac nuper quantum ars niti potuit per canonicos emendata* (Venice, 1508; repr. Frankfurt am Main, 1961), ff. 2–12 (*Logica*); ff. 70–109 (*Philosophia prima*). The *Metaphysics* is also available in a 1495 edition: *Metaphysica Avicennae sive eius Prima Philosophia* (Venice, 1495; repr. Louvain, 1961). More recently a critical edition of the Latin *Metaphysics* has appeared in two volumes: *Avicenna Latinus, Liber de Philosophia Prima sive Scientia Divina I–IV,* S. Van Riet, ed.; G. Verbeke, "Introduction doctrinale" (Louvain-Leiden, 1977); *V–X* (Louvain-Leiden, 1980). While forced to rely on the earlier noncritical editions and on an important manuscript contained in Godfrey of Fontaines' library and dating from ca. 1280 (Paris, Nat. Lat. 16.096) when originally writing the present article, here I shall follow the critical edition.

essay, however, I shall here limit myself to one issue and to one text wherein the Avicennian influence clearly appears and is, to some extent at least, explicitly acknowledged by Thomas. Analysis of this text in the light of parallel passages in Avicenna will not only enable me to study in some detail Thomas's usage of Avicenna but will also, it is to be hoped, cast some light on an apparent ambiguity in the Thomistic text itself.

Near the end of the corpus of q. 5, a. 1 of his Commentary on Boethius's *De Trinitate* Thomas indicates that three names may be applied to that branch of speculative knowledge which treats of things that do not depend upon matter for their being. It is known as theology or divine science because the foremost of those things studied in it is God. It is known as metaphysics or as "beyond physics" (*trans physicam*) because it is to be learned after physics. It is also known as first philosophy in that the other sciences receive their principles from it and come after it.[8] Avicenna also assigns this final function to first philosophy.[9].

---

8. Decker ed., p. 166. (All citations will be from this edition.) "De quibus omnibus est theologia, id est scientia divina, quia praecipuum in ea cognitorum est deus, quae alio nomine dicitur metaphysica, id est trans physicam, quia post physicam discenda occurrit nobis, quibus ex sensibilibus oportet in insensibilia devenire. Dicitur etiam philosophia prima, in quantum aliae omnes scientiae ab ea sua principia accipientes eam consequuntur." Cf. also q. 6, a. 1, of this same Commentary (*op. cit.,* p. 212). In the latter context, after having designated the method of reason as typical of natural science and the method of learning as characteristic of mathematics, Thomas assigns the method of intellectual consideration to divine science. Divine science gives principles to the other sciences inasmuch as intellectual consideration is the principle of rational consideration. Because of this divine science is also called first philosophy. He also notes in this same context that divine science is learned after physics and after the other sciences in that rational consideration terminates in intellectual consideration. For this reason it is described as metaphysics in that it is, as it were, *trans physicam,* since it comes after physics in the order of resolution. If in these passages Thomas names metaphysics first philosophy because it gives principles to the other sciences, in other contexts he assigns this same title to it because it treats of the highest being or of the first cause(s) of things. Cf. in particular his Commentary on Aristotle's *Metaphysics, Prooemium,* and elsewhere, where this reason for the title first philosophy or first science appears as a common theme. See J. Doig, "Science première et science universelle dans le 'Commentaire de la métaphysique' de saint Thomas d'Aquin," *Revue philosophique de Louvain* 63 (1965), pp. 43–46. For my attempt to resolve this apparent discrepancy in Thomas's reasons for naming metaphysics first philosophy, see Ch. III below.

9. In the opening chapter of Bk. I (*Tractatus Primus*) of his *Metaphysics,* after having first raised the question concerning the subject of this science, Avicenna notes that the reader is acquainted with the notion that it is the most certain philosophy, that it is first philosophy, and that it is the science which verifies the principles of the other sciences. See Van Riet ed., p. 3: "Et etiam iam audisti quod haec est philosophia certissima et philosophia prima, et quod ipsa facit acquirere verificationem principiorum

Given this view that metaphysics or first philosophy or divine science provides other sciences with their principles, an apparent difficulty arises. As Thomas puts it in the ninth objection of this same article, that science upon which others depend should be prior to them. But all other sciences depend upon divine science, since it pertains to the latter to establish their principles. Therefore divine science should be placed before and not after the other sciences.[10] Since Thomas explicitly refers to the text of Avicenna in replying to this objection, I shall present the texts from the two authors in parallel columns so as to facilitate comparison between them:

ceterarum scientiarum, et quod ipsa est sapientia certissime." While considering the divisions of this science in ch. 2 of this same Bk. I Avicenna writes that one part treats of the principles of the particular sciences. The principles of a less general science themselves are questions or problems to be investigated by a higher and more general science. Thus the principles of medicine are investigated by a higher science, natural philosophy, and the principles of measure are worked out in geometry. Consequently, it pertains to first philosophy to study the principles of the individual sciences and to establish their subjects. Their function will be to investigate that which follows from their subjects: "Contingit igitur ut in hac scientia monstrentur principia singularium scientiarum quae inquirunt dispositiones uniuscuiusque esse" (*op. cit.,* p. 15). Shortly thereafter he observes that this science is first philosophy because it is the science of the first cause of being. In addition to this he notes that that which is first from the standpoint of universality is being (*esse*) and unity. "Igitur quaestiones huius scientiae quaedam sunt causae esse, inquantum est esse causatum, et quaedam sunt accidentalia esse, et quaedam sunt principia scientiarum singularum. Et scientia horum quaeritur in hoc magisterio. Et haec est philosophia prima, quia ipsa est scientia de prima causa esse, et haec est prima causa, sed prima causa universitatis est esse et unitas" (pp. 15–16). In light of all of this, three reasons might be offered to justify describing this science as first philosophy: (1) because it gives principles and subjects to the particular sciences; (2) because it studies the First Cause of all being; (3) because it studies that which is most universal, being and unity. It is true, however, that Avicenna explicitly connects the name first philosophy with the second reason. Assumed here is the point that he has already established in this same chapter, namely, that metaphysics has as its subject being as being. For references see note 12 below. In his discussion of the usefulness of first philosophy in ch. 3 Avicenna again assigns a certain *utilitas* to it insofar as it contributes principles to the particular sciences and establishes knowledge as to what they are (*quid sint*) with respect to things that are common to the particular sciences even when they are not causal principles therein: "Utilitas igitur huius scientiae, cuius modum iam demonstravimus, est profectus certitudinis principiorum scientiarum particularium, et certitudo eorum quae sunt eis communia quid sint, quamvis illa non sint principia causalia" (p. 20).

10. *Op. cit.,* p. 163. "Praeterea, illa scientia, a qua aliae supponunt, debet esse prior eis. Sed omnes aliae scientiae supponunt a scientia divina, quia eius est probare principia aliarum scientiarum. Ergo debuit scientiam divinam aliis praeordinare."

Thomas, *op. cit.,* ad 9 (p. 172)

Ad nonum dicendum quod quamvis scientia divina sit prima omnium scientiarum naturaliter,[11] tamen quoad nos aliae scientiae sunt priores. Ut enim dicit Avicenna in principio suae Metaphysicae, ordo huius scientiae est, ut addiscatur post scientias naturales, in quibus sunt multa determinata, quibus ista scientia utitur, ut generatio, corruptio, motus et alia huiusmodi.

Avicenna, *Metaphysica* I, ch. 3
(Van Riet ed., pp. 20-21)

Ordo vero huius scientiae est ut discatur post scientias naturales et disciplinales. Sed post naturales, ideo quia multa de his quae conceduntur in ista sunt de illis quae iam probata sunt in naturali, sicut generatio et corruptio, et alteritas, et locus, et tempus, et quod omne quod movetur ab alio movetur, et quae sunt ea quae moventur ad primum motorem, et cetera.

According to Avicenna and Thomas, then, metaphysics should be learned after the natural sciences because various points are established in the latter which are presupposed by metaphysics. Thomas cites generation, corruption, motion, and things of this type, and to this Avicenna adds place, time, the axiom that whatever is moved is moved by another, knowledge of those things that are moved with respect to the first mover, etc. In each text the implication is that metaphysics is in some way dependent on the natural sciences for its awareness of such items. Receiving this data from the lower sciences, therefore, metaphysics will then be in a position to pursue its analyses from another point of view, that of being as being.[12]

Thomas continues to follow Avicenna in noting that metaphysics should also be studied after mathematics.

Thomas, *ibid.*

Similiter etiam post mathematicas. Indiget enim haec scientia ad cognitionem substantiarum separatarum cognoscere numerum et ordines orbium caelestium, quod non est possibile sine astrologia, ad quam tota mathematica praeexigitur.

Avicenna, p. 21

Post disciplinales vero, ideo quia intentio ultima in hac scientia est cognitio gubernationis Dei altissimi, et cognitio angelorum spiritualium et ordinum suorum, et cognitio ordinationis in compositione circulorum, ad quam scientiam impossibile est perveniri nisi

---

11. Here I have changed the punctuation of the Decker edition slightly by placing the comma after *naturaliter.* For the same interpretation see Maurer, *op. cit.,* p. 16, and n. 44.

12. On being as being as the subject of metaphysics in Aquinas see, for instance, the texts cited above in Ch. I, notes 86 and 87. For Avicenna see his *Metaphysics,* Bk. I, chs. 1 and 2. Note in particular: "Igitur ostensum est tibi ex his omnibus quod ens, inquantum est ens, est commune omnibus his et quod ipsum debet poni subiectum huius magisterii, et quia non eget inquiri an sit et quid sit . . . . Ideo primum subiectum huius scientiae est ens, inquantum est ens; et ea quae inquirit sunt consequentia ens, inquantum est ens, sine condicione" (pp. 12-13).

per cognitionem astrologiae; ad scientiam vero astrologiae nemo potest
pervenire nisi per scientiam arithme-
ticae et geometriae.

In shortened form Thomas again retains the essentials of the Avicennian text. According to each writer metaphysics should be studied after mathematics. As Thomas presents it, a knowledge of separate substances pertains to metaphysics. Such knowledge presupposes astronomy, which in turn requires mastery of mathematics. According to Avicenna the ultimate purpose of first philosophy is to arrive at a knowledge of God as supreme ruler as well as at knowledge of the angels and their orders and at knowledge of the heavenly spheres. In his text also one finds knowledge of astronomy laid down as an essential prerequisite for this together with the view that astronomy itself presupposes arithmetic and geometry. Needless to say, each author here assumes that angels or separate intelligences in some way move the heavenly bodies.[13] If such were the case, knowledge of the heavenly spheres and their movements would be regarded as essential for knowledge of the separate intelligences themselves. In brief, if metaphysical investigation should end in knowledge of God and the separate entities, and if an investigation of the heavenly spheres is required for such knowledge, then mathematics as presupposed by astronomy will also be presupposed by metaphysics.

Here it may be helpful to recall the opening lines of Thomas's reply to the ninth objection. There he distinguishes between the order of nature and the order of discovery (*naturaliter* and *quoad nos*). Metaphysics is prior to the other sciences in the order of nature. But as far as we are concerned it should be learned after physics and after mathematics, for it receives certain data from each of these sciences. Although Avicenna does not explicitly advert to this distinction in the immediate context under consideration here, it is presupposed by his discussion. In fact, some lines farther on, after a somewhat involved consideration of a possible objection to the view that metaphysics depends in some way on physics and mathematics, Avicenna refers to a similar distinction. There he notes that in the order of nature (*in ipsis rebus*) there is another way of proceeding. Rather than move from sense

---

13. On this view in Aristotle and Thomas see Maurer, *op. cit.*, p. 17, n. 46. For more on Thomas's views concerning the movers of the heavenly bodies see T. Litt, *Les corps célestes dans l'univers de saint Thomas d'Aquin* (Louvain-Paris, 1963), pp. 99–109; and J. Collins, *The Thomistic Philosophy of the Angels* (Washington, D.C., 1947), pp. 305–10. Also, for some interesting comments on this first part of Thomas's reply to objection 9 and for some reference to Avicenna, see G. Klubertanz, "St. Thomas on Learning Metaphysics," *Gregorianum* 35 (1954), pp. 10–13.

experience of an effect to knowledge of its cause, he mentions a deductive approach whereby one would arrive at a knowledge of a necessary being by application of self-evident universal propositions which would immediately lead to such knowledge. He then comments, however, that because of the weakness of our knowing powers we cannot follow this deductive route from principle to conclusion or from cause to effect except in certain restricted cases. Normally we must reason from effect to cause rather than from cause to effect. Because of this, therefore, although metaphysics is prior to the other sciences when it is viewed in itself, insofar as we are concerned it comes after the other sciences. The priority of physics and mathematics with respect to metaphysics applies to the order of learning or the order of discovery, not to the order of nature.[14] Once more we find Thomas in agreement with the thought of Avicenna.

Further comparison of the Thomistic and Avicennian texts reveals that the close parallelism continues.

Thomas, *ibid.*	Avicenna, *ibid.*
Aliae vero scientiae sunt ad bene esse ipsius, ut musica et morales vel aliae huiusmodi.	Musica vero et particulares disciplinalium et morales et civiles utiles sunt, non necessariae, ad hanc scientiam.

Again Thomas shortens the text of Avicenna. He simply notes that other sciences such as music and moral philosophy contribute to the perfection of metaphysics. The implication would seem to be that they are not necessary for one to arrive at metaphysics. Avicenna notes that music and the particular mathematical sciences as well as moral and political sciences are useful but not necessary for metaphysics. His text is more explicit than that of Thomas on this final point.

At this juncture an interesting objection is raised by Avicenna. Awareness of the same difficulty accounts for the corresponding Thomistic passage.

Thomas, *ibid.*	Avicenna, *ibid.*
Nec tamen oportet quod sit circulus, quia ipsa supponit ea, quae in aliis probantur, cum ipsa aliarum principia probet . . .	Potest autem aliquis opponere dicens quod, si principia scientiae naturalis et disciplinalium non probantur nisi in hac scientia et quaestiones utrarumque scientiarum probantur per principia earum, quaestiones vero earum fiunt

14. *Op. cit.*, pp. 23–24. Note in particular: "Sed nos propter infirmitatem nostrarum animarum non possumus incedere per ipsam viam demonstrativam, quae est progressus ex principiis ad sequentia et ex causa ad causatum, nisi in aliquibus ordinibus universitatis eorum quae sunt, sine discretione. Igitur ex merito huius scientiae in se est, ut ipsa sit altior omnibus scientiis; quantum vero ad nos posterioratur post omnes scientias" (p. 24).

principia huius, tunc haec argumen-
tatio est circularis et per ultimum eius
fit manifestatio sui ipsius.

Although it appears in shortened form in the Thomistic text, the objection
is fundamentally the same. If, as both writers have maintained, metaphysics presupposes both the natural sciences and mathematics in that it derives
certain points from them and if, at the same time, these sciences receive
their principles from metaphysics, how avoid the conclusion that circular
reasoning is involved? One seems to be asserting that certain conclusions of
the lower sciences are adopted by metaphysics for its own purposes and that
it uses them as principles to arrive at conclusions which will serve as principles in the same lower sciences. If the original conclusions of the lower
sciences follow from such principles given to them by metaphysics, it will
follow that these conclusions have now become their own principles of proof.

Thomas develops his first reply to this objection in the following lines:

. . . quia principia, quae accipit alia scientia, scilicet naturalis, a
prima philosophia, non probant ea quae idem philosophus primus
accipit a naturali, sed probantur per alia principia per se nota; et
similiter philosophus primus non probat principia, quae tradit
naturali, per principia quae ab eo accipit, sed per alia principia per
se nota. Et sic non est aliquis circulus in diffinitione.[15]

Because this text admits of two different interpretations I shall consider it
according to the following steps:

First Reading:

1. The principles which another science such as natural philosophy
receives from first philosophy:

a) are not used to prove those points which the first philosopher receives
from the natural philosopher;

b) rather they (the principles) are proved by means of other self-evident
principles, and apparently in first philosophy.

2. In like fashion, as regards the principles which the first philosopher
gives to a particular science, that is, natural philosophy:

a) they are not proved by means of principles derived from the natural
philosopher

b) but by means of other self-evident principles.

Conclusion: Therefore there is no vicious circle. This conclusion follows
from step 1 as well as from step 2. According to step 1-a there is no vicious
circle because the principles which the particular science receives from

15. *Op. cit.*, p. 172.

metaphysics are not used to prove those things which metaphysics derives from the particular science. According to step 2 there is no vicious circle because these same principles are not proved by means of principles derived from the particular science, but by means of other self-evident principles. Hence they will not be used to prove themselves, as might happen if they were established by means of conclusions of the particular science. In that case such conclusions might themselves derive from these same principles.

A certain difficulty follows from this reading, however, with respect to the role of step 1-b in the argumentation. In step 1-a our attention is directed to the function of principles given by metaphysics to a particular science, that is, natural philosophy. Such principles are not used to prove those things which first philosophy derives from the natural philosopher. But in step 1-b attention is shifted to the origin of these same principles. They are proved by means of other self-evident principles. The break in thought is rather surprising, and step 1-b hardly seems necessary in order to refute the argument about circular reasoning. Moreover, granted the presence of step 1-b, step 2-b seems to be repetitious. If according to step 2-a these same principles (which the first philosopher gives to the natural philosopher) are not proved by means of principles derived from natural philosophy, it is because they are derived from other self-evident principles (cf. step 2-b). But this has already been asserted in step 1-b. Again, step 1-a states that the principles given by first philosophy to a lower science are not used to prove the principles that first philosophy receives from that science. The question remains unanswered as to how the latter principles (those received by metaphysics from the lower science) are themselves established. However, it should be noted that in step 3 (see below) where a second argument appears, the demonstrations of natural philosophy will be grounded in sense experience.

To assume that *principia* is also the subject of *probantur* appears to be the more natural reading, at least at first sight. It is also the reading implied by A. Maurer in his translation of the same:

> For the *principles* that another science (such as natural philosophy) takes from first philosophy do not prove what the same first philosopher takes from the natural philosopher, but *they* are proved through other self-evident principles.[16] (Italics mine)

However, another reading is possible:

> For the principles that another science (such as natural philosophy) takes from first philosophy do not prove *those things* which

16. *Op. cit.*, p. 17.

> the same first philosopher takes from the natural philosopher, but *they* (the latter) are proved through other self-evident principles.

According to this reading the subject of *probantur* would not be the principles that another science receives from first philosophy but rather those things which the first philosopher receives from the natural philosopher. It is these that are proved through self-evident principles. Recalling our previous analysis of the text ("First Reading"), we find that this interpretation would lead to another reading.

Second Reading:

1. The principles which another science such as natural philosophy receives from first philosophy:

a) are not used to prove those things which the first philosopher receives from the natural philosopher.

b) Rather, the latter (those things which the first philosopher receives from the natural philosopher) are proved by means of other self-evident principles. Such proof, according to this reading, would take place in natural philosophy itself.

Step 2 would remain the same as in the First Reading.

Relative merits of the two readings:

According to the Second Reading, step 1-b now has a more logical function in the argumentation. It tells us precisely why the principles which another science receives from first philosophy are not to be used to prove the conclusions that first philosophy takes from the particular science. Such is true because the latter type of conclusion, that which first philosophy derives from a particular science such as natural philosophy, is proved by means of other self-evident premises within the particular science itself.[17] Then in step 2 attention is directed to the manner of proof for the principles of step 1-a. The principles that first philosophy gives to a particular science

---

17. Vernon Bourke translates the sentence at issue as follows: "In fact, the principles that another science, say, natural philosophy, takes from first philosophy do not prove the points which the first philosopher takes from the natural philosopher; rather, they are proved by means of different principles that are self-evident." See *The Pocket Aquinas* (New York: Washington Square Press, 1960; 6th printing, 1968), p. 152. While nicely capturing something of the ambiguity of the Latin text, this translation appears to support the Second Reading I am defending here. The same appears to be true of Klubertanz's rendering: " . . . the principles which another *scientia*, that is, natural *scientia*, received from first philosophy do not prove those things which the first philosopher accepts from the natural *scientia*, but they are proved by other principles which are known per se . . . " (*op. cit.*, p. 9).

are not only not to be used to prove those conclusions that first philosophy receives from natural philosophy. In addition they are not to be proved by means of principles derived from natural philosophy. They too are rather proved by means of other self-evident principles, and in metaphysics itself.

According to this Second Reading both steps enter into the refutation of alleged circularity, with each making a distinctive contribution. Step 1-b notes that those principles that first philosophy receives from natural philosophy themselves derive from self-evident principles and not from other premises in natural philosophy which themselves would be given to it by first philosophy. Steps 1-a, 2-a, and 2-b deal with those principles that first philosophy gives to a particular science such as natural philosophy. If such principles are not used to prove conclusions that metaphysics receives from natural philosophy (step 1-a), in like fashion they are not themselves proved by means of such conclusions (cf. step 2-a). Rather they too follow from other self-evident principles.

Moreover, this interpretation allows for a certain autonomy of the particular theoretical sciences. Granted that they do receive principles from metaphysics, in some way they can also discover their own starting points or first principles by grounding them in that which is self-evident. In the immediately following context Thomas develops this final point in what is really another argument or another reply to the objection about circular reasoning.

> Praeterea, effectus sensibiles, ex quibus procedunt demonstrationes naturales, sunt notiores quoad nos in principio, sed cum per eos pervenerimus ad cognitionem causarum primarum, ex eis apparebit nobis propter quid illorum effectuum, ex quibus probabantur demonstratione quia. Et sic et scientia naturalis aliquid tradit scientiae divinae, et tamen per eam sua principia notificantur.[18]

In this passage, which I shall describe as *step 3,* Thomas notes that the demonstrations of natural science depend on certain effects available to sense experience. These effects are more evident to us in the beginning, that is to say, they are prior with respect to us in the order of discovery. Presumably these sensible effects may also be described as "principles" in a broader sense, since they serve as starting points for demonstrations in natural philosophy. By means of them one comes to a knowledge of first causes. When this happens one will only have knowledge *quia* concerning these effects and concerning their causes. One will know *that* they exist but not *why.* However, Thomas suggests that when one has come to such

18. *Op. cit.*, pp. 172–73.

knowledge of their causes and has analyzed the knowledge of said causes in metaphysics, then one may be in position to reason back from the cause to the effect. That is to say, one will then have *propter quid* knowledge of the sensible effects, the starting points or principles of the natural science. In this way, concludes Thomas, natural philosophy may contribute something to divine science (knowledge concerning the existence of a cause or causes) and divine science may in turn contribute something to natural philosophy (knowledge of the reason for the effects in terms of the causes from which they follow, which effects themselves had served as starting points or as principles in natural philosophy).[19]

This argument (step 3) differs somewhat from that presented in steps 1 and 2. According to the earlier argumentation there is no vicious circle because different principles are involved. The principles that metaphysics gives to the particular science are not proved by means of principles derived from that science but by means of other self-evident principles. And according to our suggested reading, the principles that metaphysics receives from the particular sciences are not proved by means of principles given by metaphysics to that science but likewise by means of self-evident premises. In the present argument, however, it seems that one and the same "principle," a fact of sense experience, for instance, may be discovered by the particular science on the basis of experience and then reaffirmed by metaphysics in terms of *propter quid* knowledge of it as an effect following from its proper cause. According to this line of reasoning a vicious circle is avoided in that the "principle" of the particular science can be established in two different ways.

To return to the text of Avicenna, one finds a similar development there. However, since his reply is somewhat extended and more or less seems to repeat itself, I shall present it in three sections. In each section essentially the same reasoning reappears, although there is some development and the three steps involved in that reasoning are brought out most distinctly in Section C.

Section A:

> Dico igitur quod principium scientiae non est principium sic ut omnes quaestiones pendeant ex eo ad demonstrandum eas in actu vel in potentia, sed fortasse accipietur principium in demonstratione aliquarum. Possibile est etiam esse quaestiones in scientiis in quarum demonstrationibus non admittuntur ea

---

19. For more on this distinction between demonstrations *quia* and *propter quid* see Maurer, *op. cit.*, pp. 17–18, n. 47; W. Wallace, *The Role of Demonstration in Moral Theology* (Washington, D.C., 1962), pp. 17–22; John of St. Thomas, *Cursus Philosophicus Thomisticus*, Vol. 1, *Ars logica*, B. Reiser, ed. (Turin, 1930), II, 25, 4, pp. 785–91.

> quae posita sunt principia ullo modo, quia non admittuntur nisi propositiones quae non probantur ad hoc ut principium scientiae sit principium verissimum, per quod ad ultimum acquiratur certissima veritas, sicut est illa quae acquiritur ex causa. Si autem non acquirit causam, non dicetur principium scientiae sic sed aliter, quia fortasse dicetur principium, sicut sensus solet dici principium, eo modo quo sensus inquantum est sensus, non acquirit nisi esse tantum.[20]

According to this passage (1) in order for something to be regarded as a principle of a given science it is not necessary for all the conclusions of that science to follow from it. It may merely serve as a principle for demonstrating some of the conclusions of that science. (2) Again, certain points may be demonstrated in a particular science without using "principles" at all but merely by depending on undemonstrated premises, presumably because they are self-evident. (3) Finally, that alone is a "principle" of a science in the truest sense which leads to most certain knowledge as of a conclusion in terms of its cause. If it does not lead to such knowledge of the conclusion it should not be described as a principle of the science in this sense but from some other point of view, as for example, when one refers to sense knowledge as a "principle" insofar as the senses lead to a knowledge of *esse,* i.e., that something is.

Section B:

> Soluta est igitur quaestio, quoniam principium naturale potest esse manifestum per se, et potest esse ut manifestetur in philosophia prima per id per quod non fuerat probatum antea, sed per quod in illa probantur aliae quaestiones ita, quod est propositio in scientia altiori ad inferendum in conclusione illud principium, non in hoc assumatur principium ad concludendum illud, sed assumatur alia propositio. Possibile est etiam ut scientia naturalis et disciplinalis acquirant nobis demonstrationem de an est, et non acquirant nobis demonstrationem de quare est, sed haec scientia acquirit nobis demonstrationem de quare est, et praecipue in causis finalibus remotis.[21]

This section more or less repeats the reasoning of Section A, but with fuller development of certain points. (1) A principle of natural philosophy may be self-evident in itself. See Section A-2 above. (2) Such a principle may also be established in first philosophy by means whereby it was not previously proved, but by which (means) other conclusions are proved therein. Hence that which serves as a premise (*propositio*) in a higher science (first philosophy) to establish this principle (of natural philosophy) will not

20. *Op. cit.,* pp. 21–22.
21. *Op. cit.,* pp. 22–23.

be assumed in order to establish it. Some other premise will be assumed.[22]
(3) In Section A-3 Avicenna had remarked that only that which leads to certain knowledge of a conclusion in terms of its cause is a principle of a science in the strict sense. Here he observes that natural science and mathematics may simply result in a demonstration that something is (*an est*) rather than in a demonstration as to why it is (*quare est*). But first philosophy may lead to knowledge as to why it is, particularly in terms of remote final causes.

Section C:

> Manifestum est igitur quod de quaestionibus scientiae naturalis id quod est principium huius scientiae aliquo modo, (1) vel non manifestabitur ex principiis quae manifestantur in hac scientia, sed ex principiis quae sunt per se nota, (2) vel manifestabitur ex principiis quae sunt quaestiones in hac scientia, sed non convertuntur ut fiant principia illarum earumdem quaestionum sed aliarum, (3) vel illa principia erunt principia aliquorum huius scientiae quae significarunt illud esse de quo quaeritur manifestari in hac scientia quare est. Constat igitur quod, cum ita sit, non erit praedicta probatio circularis ullo modo, ita ut ipsa sit probatio in qua aliquid idem accipiatur in probatione sui ipsius.[23]

As regards a principle derived from a lower science such as natural philosophy and employed by metaphysics, the three steps of the above reasoning are now proposed by Avicenna as three possibilities. (1) It may be that the principle in question is not derived from premises which are established in metaphysics but rather from self-evident principles. Cf. Sections A-2 and B-1 above. (2) It may be that such a principle is derived from premises which are *quaestiones* to be established in metaphysics. So long as these *quaestiones* are not used as principles to establish themselves but to establish other conclusions, there will be no vicious circle.[24] See Section A-1 above. (3) It may happen that such a principle of a lower science will be used by metaphysics to establish the factual existence of that whose reason for existing is to be determined by metaphysics on other grounds. Cf. Avicenna's distinction above

---

22. This is a difficult passage even in the Latin critical edition. Thus in lines 3–4 ("sed per quod in illa") the *quod* might be taken to refer to the principle of natural philosophy or to the metaphysical premise which is used to establish that natural principle in metaphysics. I have here taken it in the latter sense. In the Van Riet edition, the following literal translation is offered from the Arabic for the section running from "non in hoc" to "illud": "(ce qui est prémisse dans la science supérieure) ne sera pas pris en considération . . . en tant qu'il produit ce principe: (au contraire celui-ci aura une autre prémisse)." For a slightly different rendering of the Arabic, see Anawati, *La Métaphysique du Shifā'* . . . , p. 99.

23. *Op. cit.*, p. 23.

24. Perhaps this is the point the difficult text in Section B-2 is attempting to make. See note 22.

between demonstrations *an est* and *quare est* and between causal and non-causal knowledge of a conclusion in Sections A-3 and B-3. Avicenna concludes by observing that in each of these situations circular reasoning will be avoided.

In addition to serving as a key for more clearly singling out the steps in the reasoning of Sections A and B, this passage is also helpful as a frame of reference for comparing the Avicennian text with that of Thomas. The parallel between the Avicennian passages and the Thomistic text is not perfect. Aquinas has greatly abbreviated Avicenna's rather extended presentation. Moreover, Thomas focuses his discussion on those principles which a lower science receives from first philosophy. The Avicennian passages concentrate on the principles which first philosophy receives from the lower science. By concentrating on the latter type of principle in reading the Thomistic text, however, one finds the essentials of the Avicennian reasoning.

Before making this comparison, it may be helpful to recall these steps once more. According to Avicenna, then: (1) A principle of a lower science such as natural philosophy (which is also used by metaphysics) may be self-evident in itself. Insofar as it does not lead to knowledge of conclusions in terms of their causes it is not a principle of that science in the strict sense but according to broader usage (cf. A-2, B-1, C-1). (2) Such principles may be used by metaphysics to arrive at certain conclusions therein. Such principles may also be established in metaphysics itself, but never in such a way that the metaphysical premise used to establish a principle is itself derived from that same principle (cf. A-1, B-2, C-2). (3) Such a principle of a lower science may only serve to establish the fact that something is (demonstration *an est*), its reason for existing being determined in metaphysics by knowledge of it in terms of its cause (demonstration *quare*). Cf. A-3, B-3, C-3.

As suggested above, one finds these three basic points in Thomas's text and more completely so according to the Second Reading which I have proposed. As regards the principles which first philosophy receives from natural philosophy Thomas holds: (1) They are not proved by means of the principles that first philosophy has given to natural philosophy. According to the First Reading of the Thomistic passage the discussion as to the origin of such principles ends with this observation, the remainder of steps 1 and 2 concentrating rather on the origin of those principles which first philosophy gives to a lower science. According to the Second Reading proposed above, however, Thomas goes on to note that such principles (taken by first philosophy from a lower science) are proved by means of other self-evident principles. The parallel with step 1 of Avicenna's reasoning as outlined above is more perfectly maintained by this Second Reading. (2) If Thomas again seems more interested in the principles which first philosophy gives to other sciences, he also writes that they are not themselves proved by means of principles derived by metaphysics from other sciences but by means of other self-evident principles. While apparently concentrating on those particular principles that metaphysics borrows from lower sciences, Avicenna also writes that they too may be established in metaphysics (cf. step 2 above). But like Aquinas he warns that the grounds for establishing such a principle in metaphysics must not themselves derive from that same principle. Here Thomas seems to have generalized Avicenna's reasoning so as to apply it to any principle of a lower science that metaphysics can establish. Avicenna's texts seem to be concerned more directly with principles taken from a lower science by first philosophy for its own purposes, which principles first philosophy may also be in position to demonstrate according to its proper method. Fundamentally the same argumentation is present in both authors, however. (3) Aquinas notes that the demonstrations of natural science proceed from sensibly observable effects. By reasoning from them one may conclude to the existence of their causes. At this point, however, one would only know that these effects are. One would not yet know the reason for their existence, the *why*. By examining their causes in first philosophy, one might then be in position to reason back from cause to effect, thus establishing the reason for their existence. This reasoning reproduces that found in step 3 of Avicenna's text, but again in shortened form. Avicenna has indicated that the demonstration *quare* provided by metaphysics should give knowledge of the effect in terms of its cause, above all in terms of its final cause. While Thomas speaks of a knowledge of first causes as providing *propter quid* knowledge of the effect, he does not here single out any one cause for special emphasis.

In conclusion, then, the preceding analysis suggests two points with respect to Thomas's reply to this ninth objection in his Commentary on Boethius's *De Trinitate*. First, his dependence on Avicenna is far greater here than the brief reference in his text might indicate.[25] He appears to be heavily dependent on Avicenna both for the objection concerning possible circular reasoning and in formulating the various steps of his reply to that objection. Second, as to interpreting the difficult passage cited above in Thomas's text, added evidence appears for the Second Reading as I have proposed it in light of his general dependency on Avicenna in this context. This dependency of itself does not suffice to prove that Thomas reasoned in the way suggested here. Nevertheless, if I am correct in finding the Second Reading more likely on the grounds of internal consistency, then the similarity between the reasoning implied by that Reading and the general argumentation found in the Avicennian text serves as a supporting argument for my view.

25. See p. 42 of my text above.

CHAPTER III

"FIRST PHILOSOPHY"
ACCORDING TO THOMAS AQUINAS

In q. 5, a. 1 of his Commentary on the *De Trinitate* of Boethius, Thomas Aquinas divides the theoretical sciences on the basis of the different degrees to which objects of theoretical knowledge (*speculabilia*) may be viewed as separated from or joined to matter and motion. He appeals to this criterion in this context to show that the division of speculative science into three parts is fitting.[1] Thus there are certain objects of theoretical knowledge that depend on matter for their very being (*secundum esse*). The proof lies in the fact that they cannot exist except in matter. But these may be subdivided into two classes. Some depend on matter both for their being and for being understood, that is, those whose definition includes sensible matter. Consequently, they cannot be understood without sensible matter and fall under the consideration of physics or natural science. Others, however, even though dependent on matter for their being, do not depend on it for being understood, since sensible matter is not included in their definition. These are the things studied by mathematics.[2]

In addition to the above Aquinas notes that there are other objects of theoretical knowledge that do not depend on matter for their being, since they can exist apart from matter. Some of these are never found in matter, such as God or an angel. Others, such as substance, quality, being, potency, act, the one and the many, etc., exist in matter in certain cases although not in others. The fact that such objects exist without matter in certain instances

---

1. *Ed. cit.*, p. 165. Q. 5, a. 1 is directed to this question: "Utrum sit conveniens divisio qua dividitur speculativa in has tres partes: naturalem, mathematicam et divinam" (p. 161).

2. *Op. cit.*, p. 165. Note in particular: " . . . quaedam dependent a materia secundum esse et intellectum, sicut illa, in quorum diffinitione ponitur materia sensibilis . . . . Quaedam vero sunt, quae quamvis dependeant a materia secundum esse, non tamen secundum intellectum, quia in eorum diffinitionibus non ponitur materia sensibilis, sicut linea et numerus . . . ."

suffices to establish Thomas's point here, that they do not depend on matter in order to exist. Such objects, therefore, those that do not depend on matter for their being, will be treated by a third theoretical science, sometimes known as theology or divine science, sometimes as metaphysics, and sometimes as first philosophy.

Thomas comments that this science is entitled theology or divine science because the primary object studied therein is God. He indicates that it is known as metaphysics or as *trans physicam* because it is to be learned by us after physics. In support of this apparent pedagogical reason he appeals to a fundamental tenet of his theory of knowledge, according to which one must proceed from a knowledge of sensibles to knowledge of things that are not sensible. He then notes that it is called first philosophy because all the other sciences, deriving their principles from it, come after it.[3]

My primary concern in this chapter is with this third title, first philosophy, and the reasons given here and elsewhere by Thomas in this same work and in his Commentary on the *Metaphysics* for so naming this science. Were one to restrict oneself to this passage, the matter would appear to be quite simple. Insofar as other sciences receive their principles from this science, they may be said to come after it. When it is compared with the other sciences, then, it will be called first philosophy because of their dependence upon it. It is interesting to note that in replying to the ninth objection of this same article, Thomas indicates that metaphysics presupposes conclusions proved in the other sciences and also proves the principles of the other sciences. In that immediate context, where metaphysics is viewed as supplying principles for the other sciences, he again refers to it as first philosophy and to its practitioner as the first philosopher.[4]

---

3. For this and the preceding paragraph, see pp. 165–66. With respect to the three names Thomas writes: "De quibus omnibus est theologia, id est scientia divina, quia praecipuum in ea cognitorum est deus, quae alio nomine dicitur metaphysica, id est trans physicam, quia post physicam discenda occurrit nobis, quibus ex sensibilibus oportet in insensibilia devenire. Dicitur etiam philosophia prima, in quantum aliae omnes scientiae ab ea sua principia accipientes eam consequuntur" (p. 166).

4. *Op. cit.*, p. 172. For discussion of this see Ch. II above. For an indication of various ways in which other sciences depend on metaphysics according to Aquinas see A. Moreno, "The Nature of Metaphysics," *The Thomist* 30 (1966), pp. 132–34. In brief, the particular sciences borrow from metaphysics those concepts that are common to all the sciences such as cause, effect, similitude, substance, accident, relation, essence, existence, etc. They also borrow from it general principles of knowledge such as those of noncontradiction, identity, etc. It pertains to metaphysics to establish the existence and define the natures of the subjects of the particular disciplines, rejecting those that are in opposition to its own. It should direct other sciences to its own end.

In the *Prooemium* to his Commentary on the *Metaphysics* of Aristotle Thomas again lists the same three titles for this science, theology, metaphysics, and first philosophy. There he has already reasoned that when a number of things are directed to a single goal, one must be director or ruler, and the others directed or ruled. But all the sciences and arts are ordered to one end, the perfection of man, which is happiness. Therefore, one of these sciences should direct or rule the others, and this will deserve the title wisdom. In seeking to determine which science this is, Thomas suggests that it will be the one that is most intellectual. The most intellectual science is that which treats of those things that are most intelligible.[5]

Things may be described as most intelligible from different perspectives, first of all in terms of the order of knowing (*ex ordine intelligendi*). Viewed from this standpoint that science which considers the first causes of things appears to be ruler of the other sciences in fullest measure. This is so because those things from which the intellect derives certitude are most intelligible. Since such are the causes, a knowledge of the causes appears to be most intellectual.

Again, things may be described as intelligible on the basis of a comparison between sense and intellect. While sense knowledge is directed toward particulars, intellectual knowledge has to do with universals. Given this, that science is most intellectual which treats of the most universal principles, that is, being and those things that follow upon it such as the one and the many, potency and act. Since things of this kind should not remain entirely undetermined and since they should not be treated by any one of the particular sciences, they should rather be examined in one universal science. Being most intellectual, such a science will rule the others.[6]

Finally, something may be described as most intelligible from the standpoint of intellectual knowledge itself. Since a thing has intellective power to the extent that it is free from matter and since intellect and intelligible object must be proportioned to one another, things that are most separate from matter are most intelligible. But those things are most separate or removed from matter which not only abstract (1) from designated matter (*materia signata*) but also (2) from sensible matter altogether, and (3) this not only in the order of thought or definition (*secundum rationem*) but also in the order of being (*secundum esse*). As Thomas had already indicated in q. 5, a. 1

---

5. *In duodecim libros Metaphysicorum Aristotelis expositio*, M.-R. Cathala and R. Spiazzi, eds. (Turin-Rome, 1950), pp. 1–2. Note in particular: " . . . ita scientia debet esse naturaliter aliarum regulatrix, quae maxime intellectualis est. Haec autem est, quae circa maxime intelligibilia versatur" (p. 1).

6. *Ibid.*

of his Commentary on the *De Trinitate* and as he again observes here, the first type is studied by natural philosophy, the second is represented by mathematicals, and the third by God and intelligences. Therefore, the science that treats of this last-named type of intelligible seems to be most intellectual and chief or mistress of the other sciences.[7]

One might wonder whether or not these different kinds of intelligibles will be investigated by one and the same science. Thomas hastens to make the point that such is indeed the case. The above-mentioned separate substances are universal and primary causes of being (cf. the first and third instances of intelligible objects). Moreover, it belongs to one and the same science to investigate the causes proper to a given genus and to investigate that genus itself. Therefore it will belong to one and the same science to investigate both the separate substances and *ens commune*, for the latter is the "genus" of which the separate substances are the common and universal causes. In other words, while this science considers the three aforementioned classes of intelligible objects, it studies only one of them, *ens commune*, as its subject. As Thomas indicates, the subject of a science is that whose causes and properties one investigates rather than the causes themselves of the genus under investigation. Knowledge of the causes of a given genus is rather the end or goal toward which the consideration of the science is directed.[8].

At this point Thomas returns to a distinction among those things that do not depend on matter either for their being or their intelligibility, a distinction we have already seen him making while commenting on the *De Trinitate*, q. 5, a. 1. As he phrases it here, not only things that are never found in matter such as God and intelligences are said to be separated from matter *secundum esse et rationem*, but also those that may be found without matter, such as *ens commune*.[9]

---

7. *Ibid.* For his discussion of this in his Commentary on the *De Trinitate* see *op. cit.*, pp. 165–66.

8. *Prooemium*, pp. 1–2. Note in particular the text quoted above in my Ch. I, n. 87. On this also see q. 5, a. 4 of his Commentary on the *De Trinitate* of Boethius, pp. 190–200. For general discussion of these points see: A. Zimmermann, *Ontologie oder Metaphysik? Die Diskussion über den Gegenstand der Metaphysik im 13. und 14. Jahrhundert* (Leiden-Köln, 1965), pp. 159–80; L. Oeing-Hanhoff, *Ens et Unum Convertuntur: Stellung und Gehalt des Grundsatzes in der Philosophie des. Hl. Thomas von Aquin* (Münster Westf., 1953), pp. 7–20; S. Neumann, *Gegenstand und Methode der theoretischen Wissenschaften nach Thomas von Aquin aufgrund der Expositio super librum Boethii De Trinitate* (Münster Westf., 1965), pp. 113–19; also, J. Doig, "Science première et science universelle dans le 'Commentaire de la métaphysique' de saint Thomas d'Aquin," *Revue philosophique de Louvain* 63 (1965), pp. 41–96; *Aquinas on Metaphysics: A Historico-Doctrinal Study of the Commentary on the Metaphysics* (The Hague, 1972), pp. 55–94; J. Counahan, "The Quest for Metaphysics," *The Thomist* 33 (1969), pp. 519–72.

9. *Prooemium*, p. 2; *In Boeth. De Trinitate*, p. 165.

Then, in the concluding lines of the *Prooemium,* Thomas cites the same three titles for this science that we have already found in his Commentary on the *De Trinitate.* It is to be called divine science or theology insofar as it studies separate substances. It is known as metaphysics insofar as it considers being and that which follows upon it. Here Thomas notes that these transphysicals are discovered by the process of analysis (*in via resolutionis*) just as the more universal is discovered after the less universal. It is described as first philosophy insofar as it considers the first causes of things.[10]

Comparison of the reasons offered here in the *Prooemium* for these three titles with those presented in the Commentary on the *De Trinitate* reveals one striking difference. There, as will be recalled, this science was described as first philosophy insofar as the other sciences receive their principles from it and come after it. In the *Prooemium* it receives this title because it considers the first causes of things, which first causes Thomas has now identified with the separate substances, that is, God and the intelligences. Moreover, there are other instances in his Commentary on the *Metaphysics* where this second reason is offered to justify entitling this science first philosophy.[11]

My purpose in the present study, therefore, is this, to attempt to determine more precisely why Thomas sometimes refers to metaphysics as first philosophy because it gives principles to the other sciences, and why he sometimes applies this same name to it because it investigates the first causes. The fact that he does so has been noted by other writers. Why he does so has not, to my knowledge, been satisfactorily determined.[12] It

---

10. "Dicitur enim scientia divina sive *theologia,* inquantum praedictas substantias considerat. *Metaphysica,* inquantum considerat ens et ea quae consequuntur ipsum. Haec enim transphysica inveniuntur in via resolutionis, sicut magis communia post minus communia. Dicitur autem *prima philosophia,* inquantum primas rerum causas considerat. Sic igitur patet quid sit subiectum huius scientiae, et qualiter se habeat ad alias scientias, et quo nomine nominetur" (p. 2).

11. For other references see Doig, "Science première et science universelle," p. 43 and n. 4. See in particular *In VI Metaph.,* lect. 1, n. 1170: "Sed, si est aliqua substantia immobilis, ista erit prior substantia naturali; et per consequens philosophia considerans huiusmodi substantiam, erit philosophia prima."

12. See Oeing-Hanhoff, *op. cit.,* p. 17. In commenting on our two passages he writes that this name, first philosophy, "charakterisiert die Metaphysik nicht nur, insofern sie nach den ersten Ursachen der Dinge fragt, sondern bezeichnet sie auch als die Wissenschaft, die, keine andere voraussetzend, sich selbst begründen muss." However, it should be noted that in the reference from the Commentary on the *De Trinitate* (cited in n. 3 above) Thomas does not explicitly state that this science is to be called first philosophy because, in presupposing no other, it must ground itself. Granted that this may be a legitimate deduction from Thomas's observation that it is called first philosophy because the other sciences, receiving their principles from it, come after it, it is for this latter reason that it is entitled first philosophy according to

appears, however, that an important clue is given in this same context where Thomas notes that it is called metaphysics insofar as it studies being and those things that follow upon being. He observes that such things which transcend the physical are discovered by the process of analysis just as more universal things are discovered after less universal ones. His reference to analysis at least raises the question as to what process he might be following when he names this science first philosophy because it studies the first causes of things. In any event, one would seem to be well advised at this point to turn to his description of and contrast between analysis and synthesis in q. 6, a. 1, of that same Commentary on the *De Trinitate* of Boethius.

In the third major part of q. 6, a. 1, Thomas is attempting to show that one should proceed according to the method of intellect (*versari intellectualiter*) in divine science.[13] In support of this contention he recalls that one may attribute the method of reason (*rationabiliter procedere*) to natural philosophy because this method is most closely followed there.[14] So, too, he will now maintain that the method of intellect is to be attributed to divine science because it is in this science that this method is most closely followed. After a brief discussion of the difference between reason and intellect,[15] Thomas comments that rational consideration terminates in intellectual consideration according to the process of analysis, but that intellectual consideration

---

Thomas in this context. Moreover, Oeing-Hanhoff leaves unanswered our primary question in the present study: Why does Thomas sometimes say that it is called first philosophy insofar as it studies first causes, and why does he sometimes say that it is so named because it gives principles to the other sciences and therefore comes after them? Takatura Ando, in his *Metaphysics: A Critical Survey of Its Meaning* (The Hague, 1963), discusses the passages from the Commentary on the *De Trinitate* and the *Prooemium*. Thus on p. 30 he notes that it is called first philosophy "because it deals with the principles which synthetically explain everything that is involved in the special science." But after commenting on the *Prooemium* as well, he does not cite the three reasons offered there by Thomas for the three names, nor does he advert to the different reason offered there for naming it first philosophy. Also, see J. Lotz, "Ontologie und Metaphysik," *Scholastik* 18 (1943), p. 8 and n. 44. While noting the two reasons offered by Thomas to account for the title first philosophy, Lotz does not attempt to resolve our problem. So too Doig, in his *Aquinas on Metaphysics* . . . . Compare p. 69 with pp. 57, 82–83, 86, 91, 173, and 188.

13. *Op. cit.*, pp. 210–13.

14. For this see the first part of this same q. 6, a. 1, pp. 205–7. Note in particular Thomas's concluding remark in the corpus of that part: "Attribuitur ergo rationabiliter procedere scientiae naturali, non quia ei soli conveniat, sed quia ei praecipue competit" (p. 207).

15. *Op. cit.*, p. 211. For fuller discussion of the relationship and distinction between *intellectus* and *ratio* in Thomas see J. Peghaire, *Intellectus et Ratio selon S. Thomas d'Aquin* (Paris-Ottawa, 1936).

is the principle or starting point (*principium*) of rational consideration according to the process of synthesis or discovery (*secundum viam compositionis vel inventionis*). As he also indicates here, in the process of analysis reason gathers one simple truth from many things. In the process of synthesis, on the other hand, the intellect grasps a multitude of things in one.[16]

Two points have been introduced in this context that are of importance for our purposes: first, the distinction between the process of analysis and that of synthesis; second, the observation that intellectual consideration may be regarded as the terminus of rational consideration according to the process of analysis, while it may be regarded as the beginning or starting point of rational consideration according to the process of synthesis. Since Thomas is attempting to establish the point that the method of intellect is to be attributed to divine science, he then comments that the kind of consideration which is the terminus of all human reasoning is intellectual to the maximum degree. According to the process of analysis, all rational consideration in all the sciences terminates in the consideration of divine science.[17]

In support of this Thomas now introduces a further distinction. As he has already indicated above,[18] reason sometimes moves from knowledge of one

16. "Sic ergo patet quod rationalis consideratio ad intellectualem terminatur secundum viam resolutionis, in quantum ratio ex multis colligit unam et simplicem veritatem. Et rursum intellectualis consideratio est principium rationalis secundum viam compositionis vel inventionis, in quantum intellectus in uno multitudinem comprehendit" (*op. cit.*, p. 211). If Thomas here associates *ratio* with analysis and *intellectus* with synthesis, this follows from an analogy which he has just drawn between multitude and unity, on the one hand, and analysis and synthesis, on the other. Thus: "Differt autem ratio ab intellectu, sicut multitudo ab unitate . . . . Est enim rationis proprium circa multa diffundi et ex eis unam simplicem cognitionem colligere . . . . Intellectus autem e converso per prius unam et simplicem veritatem considerat et in illa totius multitudinis cognitionem capit . . . " (*ibid.*). In brief, then, reason, which gathers one simple truth by starting from a many, is characteristic of the process of analysis (resolution); whereas intellect, which first contemplates one truth and in that truth grasps a many, is more characteristic of the process of synthesis (composition). For a general discussion of the distinction between analysis and synthesis in Thomas see L. M. Régis, "Analyse et synthèse dans l'oeuvre de saint Thomas," in *Studia Mediaevalia in honorem admodum reverendi patris Raymundi Josephi Martin* (Bruges, 1948), pp. 303–30; also, S. Edmund Dolan, "Resolution and Composition in Speculative and Practical Discourse," *Laval théologique et philosophique* 6 (1950), pp. 9–62; Doig, *Aquinas on Metaphysics*, pp. 64–76.

17. *Op. cit.*, pp. 211–12. "Illa ergo consideratio, quae est terminus totius humanae ratiocinationis, maxime est intellectualis consideratio. Tota autem consideratio rationis resolventis in omnibus scientiis ad considerationem divinae scientiae terminatur."

18. Q. 6, a. 1, first part (pp. 206–7): "Secundo, quia cum rationis sit de uno in aliud discurrere, hoc maxime in scientia naturali observatur, ubi ex cognitione unius rei in cognitionem alterius devenitur, sicut ex cognitione effectus in cognitionem causae. Et non solum proceditur ab uno in aliud secundum rationem, quod non est

thing to knowledge of another in the order of reality (*secundum rem*), as when there is demonstration through extrinsic causes or effects. Reason may thus advance either according to the process of synthesis, by moving from cause to effect, or according to the process of analysis, by moving from effect to cause. This application of synthesis and analysis to cause and effect reasoning can be made because causes are simpler, more unchangeable, and more constant than their effects, and because, as has been observed above, in the process of analysis one gathers one simple truth from a many.[19] Hence in this case by the process of analysis one arrives at knowledge of that which is simpler (the cause) by moving from knowledge of that which is less simple (the effect). Consequently, the ultimate term of the process of analysis when one reasons *secundum rem* or in terms of extrinsic causes is a knowledge of supremely simple causes, that is, the separate substances.[20]

At other times, however, reason moves from one thing to another in the order of reason (*secundum rationem*), as when one proceeds in terms of intrinsic causes. This too can occur either according to the process of synthesis or according to the process of analysis. In the first case one advances from the most universal forms to the more particular. In the second case one proceeds in reverse order, that is, from the more particular to the most universal. This is so, suggests Thomas, because what is more universal is simpler and, as has already been noted, in its process of analysis reason gathers one simple truth from a many, here the most universal from the more particular.[21] But, continues Thomas, the most universal things are those which are common to all beings. Therefore, the ultimate terminus of analysis in this movement of reason in terms of intrinsic causes (*secundum rationem*) is a consideration of being and that which pertains to being as such.[22]

---

aliud secundum rem, sicut si ab animali procedatur ad hominem. In scientiis enim mathematicis proceditur per ea tantum, quae sunt de essentia rei, cum demonstrent solum per causam formalem . . . . Sed in scientia naturali, in qua fit demonstratio per causas extrinsecas, probatur aliquid de una re per aliam rem omnino extrinsecam."

19. *Op. cit.*, p. 212. "Ratio enim, ut prius dictum est, procedit quandoque de uno in aliud secundum rem, ut quando est demonstratio per causas vel effectus extrinsecos: componendo quidem, cum proceditur a causis ad effectus; quasi resolvendo, cum proceditur ab effectibus ad causas, eo quod causae sunt effectibus simpliciores et magis immobiliter et uniformiter permanentes."

20. *Ibid.* "Ultimus ergo terminus resolutionis in hac via est, cum pervenitur ad causas supremas maxime simplices, quae sunt substantiae separatae."

21. *Ibid.* "Quandoque vero procedit de uno in aliud secundum rationem, ut quando est processus secundum causas intrinsecas: componendo quidem, quando a formis maxime universalibus in magis particularia proceditur; resolvendo autem quando e converso, eo quod universalius est simplicius."

22. *Ibid.* "Et ideo terminus resolutionis in hac via ultimus est consideratio entis et eorum quae sunt entis in quantum huiusmodi."

In sum, therefore, Thomas has now shown that the ultimate term of the process of analysis when one reasons in terms of extrinsic causes (*secundum rem*) is a knowledge of separate substances. Its ultimate term when one proceeds according to intrinsic causes (*secundum rationem*) is a knowledge of being and the properties that follow from being as such. But as he has already shown above in q. 5, a. 1 and q. 5, a. 4, these two, being and separate substances, are the things of which divine science treats.[23] Moreover, since he has already indicated in the present context that that consideration is intellectual to the maximum degree which is the terminus of all human reasoning, one is not surprised to find him concluding that the consideration of divine science is supremely intellectual.[24]

At this point in the discussion Thomas again briefly considers the different names assigned to divine science. The name divine science itself is not at issue here, since this is the title used by Boethius in the text upon which Thomas is commenting, and primarily by Thomas himself until this point in q. 6, a. 1.[25] Because intellectual consideration is the principle or starting point of rational consideration, Thomas now comments that divine science gives principles to all the other sciences. For this reason it is called *first philosophy*. But because intellectual consideration may also be regarded as the terminus of rational consideration, this science is learned after physics and the other sciences. For this reason it is called *metaphysics*, beyond physics, as it were, because it comes after physics according to the process of analysis.[26]

With respect to the title first philosophy, therefore, it will be recalled that Thomas holds that intellectual consideration is the principle of rational consideration according to the process of synthesis. If he now styles this science first philosophy because it gives principles to the other sciences, this is because intellectual consideration is the principle of rational consideration.

23. *Op. cit.*, pp. 165–66, 195.
24. *Op. cit.*, p. 212.
25. Note that q. 6, a. 1 is directed to the following question: "Utrum oporteat versari in naturalibus rationabiliter, in mathematicis disciplinabiliter, in divinis intellectualiter" (*op. cit.*, p. 201). As noted previously, in the third part of this question Thomas attempts to show that one should proceed according to the method of intellect in divine science (*op. cit.*, pp. 210ff.). For the text of Boethius see his *De Trinitate*, 2 (*Boethius: The Theological Tractates with an English Translation*, H. F. Stewart and E. K. Rand, trs. [Cambridge, Mass., 1968]), p. 8: " . . . in naturalibus igitur rationabiliter, in mathematicis disciplinaliter, in divinis intellectualiter versari oportebit . . . ."
26. *Op. cit.*, p. 212. "Et exinde etiam est quod ipsa largitur principia omnibus aliis scientiis, in quantum intellectualis consideratio est principium rationalis, propter quod dicitur prima philosophia; et nihilominus ipsa addiscitur post physicam et ceteras scientias, in quantum consideratio intellectualis est terminus rationalis, propter quod dicitur metaphysica quasi trans physicam, quia post physicam resolvendo occurrit."

But according to what we have now seen, this in turn is true only according to the process of synthesis, not according to the process of analysis. Consequently, when Thomas names this science first philosophy because it gives principles to the other sciences, I conclude that he is then regarding its consideration as the principle or starting point of the other sciences, to be sure, but that when he so correlates this science and others he is considering the movement from one to the other according to the process of synthesis.

Moreover, in the preceding context he has distinguished between the advance of reason in the order of intrinsic causes (*secundum rationem*) and its advance according to extrinsic causes (*secundum rem*). He has noted that the processes of synthesis and analysis may be applied to either of these. The ultimate terminus of analysis in the movement of reason according to intrinsic causes was identified with being and the properties that belong to being as such. Consequently, it would seem to follow that when Thomas entitles this science first philosophy because it gives principles to the other sciences, he is then viewing the movement from this science to the others according to the process of synthesis rather than according to the process of analysis, as has already been suggested, and in the order of intrinsic causes (*secundum rationem*) rather than in the order of extrinsic causes (*secundum rem*). In other words, he is viewing it as the science of being as being and suggesting that it gives principles to the other sciences insofar as more particular concepts and more particular principles follow from the most general concepts (being, etc.) and most general principles. As he indicates in other contexts, just as it pertains to this science to study being as being, so too does it pertain to it to examine and defend the principles that follow immediately from being as being.[27] Granted that this is a fuller explanation of his reasoning for so entitling this science than one finds explicitly stated in the text itself, it seems to be a logical deduction from distinctions he has made there, and also appears to be consistent with the view expressed in q. 5, a. 1. There, it will be recalled, this science is named first philosophy because the other sciences, receiving their principles from it, come after it.[28]

As we have seen above, in the *Prooemium* to his Commentary on the *Metaphysics* Thomas offers a different reason for describing this science as first

---

27. On this see the remarks and texts found in Moreno's study, "The Nature of Metaphysics," cited in n. 4 above. Also see J. Counahan, *op. cit.*, pp. 531–33; Oeing-Hanhoff, *op. cit.*, p. 18. Note the following from Thomas's *Summa contra gentiles* III, ch. 25: "Hoc autem modo se habet philosophia prima ad alias scientias speculativas, nam ab ipsa omnes aliae dependent, utpote ab ipsa accipientes sua principia, et directionem contra negantes principia: ipsaque prima philosophia tota ordinatur ad Dei cognitionem sicut ad ultimum finem, unde et scientia divina nominatur." Ed. Leonina Manualis (Rome, 1934), pp. 252–53.

28. For the text see note 3 above.

philosophy. There he writes that it is so named because it considers the first causes of things. In that context it is clear that the latter are to be understood as extrinsic causes.[29] Hence, if one may apply the distinction between the movement of reason in terms of intrinsic causes (*secundum rationem*) and in terms of extrinsic causes (*secundum rem*) of q. 6, a. 1 of his Commentary on the *De Trinitate* to the present context, the *Prooemium,* it is reasoning in terms of extrinsic causes (*secundum rem*) that Thomas now has in mind. Moreover, if one wonders whether the process of analysis or that of synthesis is at issue here, it appears to be the former rather than the latter. As Thomas has already stated in q. 6, a. 1, the ultimate term of the process of analysis when one reasons in terms of extrinsic causes is attained when one arrives at a knowledge of supremely simple causes, that is to say, the separate substances.[30] Consequently, when metaphysics is described as first philosophy because it gives principles to the other sciences, it is being viewed in terms of intrinsic causes (*secundum rationem*) and according to the process of synthesis with respect to these sciences. Such is the standpoint of q. 5, a. 1 and q. 6, a. 1 of the Commentary on the *De Trinitate.* But when it is so named because it studies the first causes, it is being viewed in terms of extrinsic causes (*secundum rem*) and apparently according to the process of analysis with respect to these causes, since according to this perspective one reasons from a knowledge of effects to a knowledge of separate substances as their causes. Such is the standpoint implied by Thomas's explanation of the reasons for this title in the *Prooemium* to the Commentary on the *Metaphysics*.

Two further possibilities present themselves at this juncture. Why not view this science in terms of extrinsic causes (*secundum rem*), but according to the process of synthesis? Or why not view it in terms of intrinsic causes (*secundum rationem*), but according to the process of analysis? According to the first suggestion one would then move in this science from a knowledge of God and separate substances to a knowledge of effects that follow from the same. While such might indeed obtain in a universe wherein man enjoys some kind of direct insight into the divine essence and wherein there is no freedom on the part of God to create or not to create, neither of these conditions would be conceded by Thomas Aquinas. Hence there would have been little point in his viewing metaphysics in terms of extrinsic causes according to the process of synthesis.

As to the second suggestion, considering metaphysics in terms of intrinsic causes (*secundum rationem*) and according to the process of analysis with respect to its relationship to the other sciences, Thomas does concede this possibility, but suggests that it should be called metaphysics (rather than

29. For the text see note 10 above.
30. See note 20 above.

first philosophy) when it is so viewed. Thus in q. 6, a. 1 he notes that it is learned after physics and the other sciences because intellectual consideration is the terminus of rational consideration. As he has explained in this same context, when one advances according to intrinsic causes (*secundum rationem*) by the process of analysis, one proceeds from the more particular to the more universal. Since that which is most universal is common to all beings, the ultimate term of analysis *secundum rationem* is being and that which pertains to being as such. To return again to his discussion of the title, metaphysics, he then comments that it is for this reason that this science is called metaphysics or *trans physicam*, because it comes after physics according to the way of resolution (analysis).[31]

This simply reinforces the view expressed in q. 5, a. 1, according to which it is called metaphysics or *trans physicam* because it is to be learned by us after physics. There he has noted that we must move from a knowledge of sensible things to a knowledge of things that are not sensible.[32] In that immediate context he does not explicitly indicate whether these not-sensible things include the two classes of things that do not depend on matter for their being and to be defined, that is, those that are never found in matter such as God and the angels, and those that are sometimes found in matter and sometimes not, such as substance, quality, being, etc. He simply notes that this science treats of them all and that it is known as theology, as metaphysics, and as first philosophy. Perhaps, then, in q. 6, a. 1, one might extend his reason for naming it metaphysics to both classes, and suggest that it is so named or comes after physics in the order of resolution (analysis) both as applied in terms of intrinsic causes (*secundum rationem*), hence to being and its properties, and in terms of extrinsic causes (*secundum rem*), hence to God and separate entities. However, in light of the discussion of the title metaphysics in the *Prooemium,* I am more inclined to restrict his reason for so entitling it in q. 5, a. 1 and q. 6, a. 1 to the first of these. Thus in the *Prooemium* he notes that it is called metaphysics insofar as it considers being and those things that follow upon being. For these transphysicals are discovered by way of analysis (*in via resolutionis*) just as the more general is discovered after the less general.[33] Here it is clear that he is appealing to the process of analysis and to the movement of reason according to intrinsic causes (*secundum rationem*) alone when it comes to justifying the name metaphysics. It would seem more likely, then, that such was also his intention in the two discussions in the Commentary on the *De Trinitate.*

31. See note 26 above.
32. See note 3 above.
33. See note 10 above.

In conclusion, therefore, when Thomas styles this science metaphysics whether in the Commentary on the *De Trinitate* or in the *Prooemium* to his Commentary on the *Metaphysics,* it is because it comes after physics in the order of analysis. This is so because it studies being and its properties and because these are discovered after one has investigated sensible things, at least to some extent, and because one is dealing with a movement of reason according to intrinsic causes (*secundum rationem*) rather than according to extrinsic causes (*secundum rem*). When he names it first philosophy because it gives principles to other sciences, this is because he is viewing the movement of reason from it to other sciences in terms of intrinsic causes (*secundum rationem*) once again, to be sure, but according to the process of synthesis rather than the process of analysis. When he names it first philosophy because it studies the first causes of things he is now viewing the movement of the mind according to extrinsic causes (*secundum rem*), and according to the process of analysis or the way of resolution rather than according to the process of synthesis.

CHAPTER IV

METAPHYSICS AND *SEPARATIO* IN THOMAS AQUINAS

Considerable attention has been paid in recent years to the intellectual processes involved in one's explicit discovery of being, especially of being as real or existing, according to Thomas Aquinas. Inspired in large measure by the work of E. Gilson and also of J. Maritain, many recent commentators on Thomas have stressed the role of the mind's second operation, often referred to as judgment, when it comes to one's discovery of being as existing. Judgment, it is argued, is required if one is not to have an incomplete notion of being, a notion of being that would be reducible to the level of an essence or quiddity. Only judgment can assure one that one's notion of being embraces being as existing, an *est* as well as an *id quod*, an "is" as well as a "that which."[1]

Some attention has also been devoted to a particular kind of judgment or a particular form of the intellect's second operation, sometimes named *separatio* by Thomas. Important editions of qq. 5 and 6 of Thomas's Commentary on the *De Trinitate* of Boethius in 1948 and 1955 and the groundbreaking study by L. B. Geiger in 1947[2] have set the stage for further emphasis on this distinctive type of intellectual operation when it comes to one's discovery of

1. On this see, for instance, E. Gilson, *Being and Some Philosophers*, 2d ed. (Toronto, 1952), ch. 6 ("Knowledge and Existence"), pp. 190-215; *The Christian Philosophy of St. Thomas Aquinas* (New York, 1956), pp. 40-45; J. Maritain, *Existence and the Existent* (New York, 1948), pp. 22-35; J. Owens, *An Elementary Christian Metaphysics* (Milwaukee, 1963), pp. 45-56, 248-58; *An Interpretation of Existence* (Milwaukee, 1968), ch. 2 ("Grasp of Existence"), pp. 14-43; "Judgment and Truth in Aquinas," *Mediaeval Studies* 32 (1970), pp. 138-58.
2. As will be seen below, questions 5 and 6 of this Commentary are the most important sources for any study of *separatio* in Aquinas. Here as in the previous chapters citations will be taken from the Decker edition. For Geiger's article see "Abstraction et séparation d'après s. Thomas *In de Trinitate*, q. 5, a. 3," *Revue des sciences philosophiques et théologiques* 31 (1947), pp. 3-40; also his *La participation dans la philosophie de S. Thomas d'Aquin*, 2d ed. (Paris, 1953), pp. 318-21.

being, or better, of that notion of being that can serve as subject of a science of being as being rather than a science of being as material or as quantified. While this new development has remained largely unnoticed in certain regions of Thomistic scholarship for a number of years, it has been pursued in depth by other writers.[3] At the same time, investigation of the same nicely dovetails with the renewed emphasis on existence and on judgment as the process required to discover being as existing referred to above. For as will be seen below, at least one passage in Thomas's Commentary (q. 5, a. 3) reinforces the contention that one must pass beyond simple apprehension to the mind's second operation or to judgment if one is to grasp being explicitly as existing. This particular point, however, is not my primary concern here.

In this chapter I wish to concentrate on questions relating to *separatio* as such insofar as it is involved in one's discovery of being as being, that is to say, of being as presupposed for a science of being as being, a metaphysics. For the sake of simplicity I shall consider this issue in three steps: (1) a historical review of the textual evidence pointing to a distinctive teaching with respect to *separatio* in Thomas; (2) an effort (also historical) to determine what is presupposed by Aquinas for the judgment known as *separatio* to function, that is to say, the kind of knowledge presupposed for one's discovery of being as being; (3) a more theoretical discussion of the possibility of *separatio* without prior awareness that immaterial and/or divine being exists.

I

Questions 5 and 6 of Thomas's Commentary on the *De Trinitate* of Boethius are our richest source of information with respect to his views concerning the proper division of and relationship between the theoretical sciences. This has already been implied by remarks made in Chapters I, II, and III above. Thomas's Commentary originates from his first Parisian teaching period and can be dated between 1255 and 1259 (1258–1259, according to

---

3. For some of these see R. Schmidt, "L'emploi de la séparation en métaphysique," *Revue philosophique de Louvain* 58 (1960), pp. 376–93. See pp. 373–75 for earlier treatments of the same. Among these earlier treatments, Schmidt rightly stresses the importance of that by L.-M. Régis, "Un livre: *La philosophie de la nature*. Quelques 'Apories'," *Etudes et Recherches* 1 (1936), pp. 127–56. See in particular pp. 134–38. Also, L. Sweeney, *A Metaphysics of Authentic Existentialism* (Englewood Cliffs, N.J., 1965), pp. 307–29. See pp. 307–8, nn. 13, 15, 16 for other literature on the topic. Also, J. Owens, "Metaphysical Separation in Aquinas," *Mediaeval Studies* 34 (1972), pp. 287–306. See p. 302, n. 39 for references to other studies. Also see S. Neumann, *Gegenstand und Methode der theoretischen Wissenschaften*, pp. 72–97, 145–51; L. Elders, *Faith and Science*, pp. 105–11. H. Weidemann, *Metaphysik und Sprache*, pp. 27–32, 43–47, 75–78.

Weisheipl).[4] In any event, therefore, it is a relatively early work in Thomas's career. To refer to it as a "commentary" is somewhat misleading, for it is far more than that. A few lines taken from the *De Trinitate* serve as the occasion for Thomas's deeply personal reflection on the points at issue, and in qq. 5 and 6, for his development of his own views on the nature and divisions of the theoretical sciences. Even the Latin title found in various early catalogues of his works, *Expositio in librum Boethii de Trinitate*, only partly indicates the true nature of this writing.[5]

As we have already seen, in q. 5, a. 1 the issue is raised as to whether speculative science is appropriately divided into three parts—natural philosophy, mathematics, and what Thomas there, following the text of Boethius, calls "divine science."[6] His answer, of course, is in the affirmative; but the criterion proposed to justify this division is of immediate interest, since it is based upon the degree to which an object of theoretical science, a *speculabile*, depends on or is free from matter and motion. As Thomas phrases it, separation from matter and motion or connection with the same pertains to an object of theoretical science considered precisely as such. Therefore, theoretical sciences are differentiated according to the degree of freedom from matter and motion of their respective objects (*speculabilia*).[7]

Thomas then goes on to apply this criterion. Some objects of speculation depend on matter for their very being (*secundum esse*) since they can exist only in matter. Among these he introduces a subdivision. Some depend on matter not only for their being, but also in order to be understood. By these he has in mind those objects of theoretical knowledge whose definition includes sensible matter. Sensible matter, matter insofar as it is subject to sensible qualities, is necessarily involved in one's understanding of such an object of theoretical science. Thus flesh and bones are included in one's understanding of man. Physics or natural science treats of such objects, according to Thomas.[8]

---

4. See Wyser, *Thomas von Aquin, In librum Boethii De Trinitate*, pp. 17–18, for the 1255–1259 dating. For Weisheipl see his *Friar Thomas d'Aquino*, pp. 381 and 136–37.

5. On this see Wyser, pp. 3–4.

6. Decker ed., p. 161.

7. *Op. cit.*, p. 165. Note in particular: "Sic ergo speculabili, quod est obiectum scientiae speculativae, per se competit separatio a materia et motu vel applicatio ad ea. Et ideo secundum ordinem remotionis a materia et motu scientiae speculativae distinguuntur" (ll. 12–15).

8. *Op. cit.*, p. 165:16–21. On Thomas's understanding of common sensible matter see L.-M. Régis, "Un livre: *La philosophie de la nature*," p. 146, and other references given there. Thus in one passage from his Commentary on the *Metaphysics* Thomas defines it as follows: "Sensibilis [materia] quidem est, quae concernit qualitates sensibiles, calidum et frigidum, rarum et densum, et alia huiusmodi, cum qua quidem materia concreta sunt naturalia, sed ab ea abstrahunt mathematica" (*In VIII Met.*, lect. 5, n. 1760).

Other objects of theoretical science (*speculabilia*) while also depending on matter for their being, do not depend on sensible matter in order to be understood or defined, continues Aquinas. Such is true of lines and numbers, in short, of the kinds of things studied by mathematics. Common sensible matter, that is, matter insofar as it can be grasped by the senses, is not included in the definition of mathematicals. Yet, according to Thomas, such mathematicals can never in fact exist apart from matter, not even apart from sensible matter.[9]

In contrast with objects of theoretical knowledge that depend on matter and motion, Thomas now refers to another kind. Some objects of theoretical knowledge do not even depend upon matter for their being (*esse*). These are of two types, those that are never found in matter (God and angels), and those that are found in matter in certain cases but not in others (substance, quality, being [*ens*], potency, act, the one and the many, and things of this kind).[10] Thomas goes on to observe that the science that treats of all of these is called "theology" or "divine science," also "metaphysics," and also "first philosophy." Without pausing here to examine again his three reasons for these three different titles, let it suffice for me to stress one point. These are three different names for one and the same science, that science whose subject is being as being or being in general.[11]

One important point has been made with respect to our topic. According to Thomas there are two classes or types of *speculabilia* that do not depend on matter either to be or to be defined. God (and angels) constitute the first class. A whole host of what one might dub "metaphysicals" are listed as representative of the second, including, be it noted, substance and being. If, as Thomas holds elsewhere and as will be seen below, the subject of a science is that whose causes and properties one investigates in that science, and if as he also holds, *ens commune* or *ens inquantum ens* is the subject of metaphysics, a problem immediately arises. Must one presuppose the existence of the two kinds of *speculabilia* that do not depend on matter in the order of being if one is to begin metaphysics? In other words, will knowledge of the second type of "immaterial," the "neutrally immaterial," if one may so phrase it, be

9. Decker ed., p. 165:21–24.

10. *Ibid.*, p. 165:24–28. "Quaedam vero speculabilia sunt, quae non dependent a materia secundum esse, quia sine materia esse possunt, sive numquam sint in materia, sicut deus et angelus, sive in quibusdam sint in materia et quibusdam non, ut substantia, qualitas, ens, potentia, actus, unum et multa et huiusmodi."

11. On Thomas's reasons for entitling this science "first philosophy" see Ch. III above. On being as being or being in general as the subject of this science see, for instance, in this same Commentary on the *De Trinitate*, q. 5, a. 1, ad 6 (p. 171:16–26); q. 5, a. 4 (pp. 194–95); the *Prooemium* to his Commentary on the *Metaphysics*, and further discussion below in the present chapter.

sufficient to begin metaphysics? Will knowledge of this kind of immaterial even be possible without presupposing the reality of the immaterial in the first or stronger and positive sense? In short, must one already know that positively immaterial being (God or angelic being) exists in order to discover being as such or being as being?

Before leaving q. 5, a. 1, one more point should be noted. The sixth objection protests that a whole should not be divided from its parts. But divine science seems to be a whole with respect to physics and mathematics. The subjects of physics and mathematics (changeable substance and quantity, respectively) are parts of being, the subject of divine science. Therefore, divine science should not be contradistinguished from natural science and mathematics.[12]

Thomas begins his reply by conceding that the subjects of physics and mathematics, changeable being and quantified being, are parts of being, and that being (*ens*) itself is the subject of metaphysics. Still, he counters, it does not follow that these other sciences are parts of metaphysics. For each particular science treats of one part of being in a special way (*secundum specialem modum considerandi*), distinct from the way in which metaphysics considers being. Therefore, the subject of the particular science is really not a part of the subject of metaphysics. For it is not a part of being from that standpoint under which being itself is the subject of metaphysics.[13] In brief, then, metaphysics has as its subject being in general rather than being as restricted to the changeable or the quantitative. Moreover, it studies being as being rather than as changing or as quantified.

Thomas's reply is of interest for our immediate purposes because he is here treating of the second class of things that may be said to be separate from matter and motion, the neutrally immaterial, represented in this instance by being. He is suggesting that even changing being or quantified being can be studied by our science insofar as it is being, that is, from the standpoint of being.[14] At the same time, of course, this reply again gives rise to the question: Must one presuppose the existence of immaterial being in the positive sense (God and/or angels) in order to study being as being rather than merely as changing or as quantified? Before attempting to

12. *Op. cit.*, p. 162:18-24.

13. *Op. cit.*, p. 171:16-24.

14. This point is important for it shows that even in the discussion of q. 5, a. 1 wherein Thomas has directed the reader's attention to the different kinds of *speculabilia* corresponding to the different theoretical sciences, he does not reduce the subject of a science to the sum total of things considered therein. The subject also includes the formal perspective of that science, its distinctive *modus considerandi*. Thomas's reply to the seventh objection reinforces this same point (p. 171:27-30). For more on his understanding of the subject of a science see Zimmermann, *Ontologie oder Metaphysik?*, pp. 160-65.

discern Thomas's answer to this question, I shall first turn to q. 5, a. 3 of this same Commentary on Boethius's *De Trinitate*.

In this article Thomas raises the question: Does mathematics treat, without matter and motion, of what exists in matter?[15] He already has suggested in q. 5, a. 1 that mathematics does treat of such things. But in preparing to develop this position here he introduces some important precisions with respect to the intellectual processes involved in arriving at the distinctive subjects of each of the theoretical sciences. It is within this same general context that he presents key texts touching on *separatio*.

Thomas begins by observing that one must understand how the intellect in this operation is able to abstract (*abstrahere possit*) if one is to throw light on this question. Taking his cue from Aristotle's *De anima* he notes that according to the Philosopher the operation of the intellect is twofold. There is one operation whereby it knows what something is, called the understanding of indivisibles (*intelligentia indivisibilium*). There is another whereby it composes and divides, that is to say, by forming affirmative and negative propositions.[16] Thomas then comments that these two intellectual operations correspond to two factors found in things. The first operation is directed toward a thing's nature, according to which it enjoys a certain rank, whether it be a complete thing or even an incomplete thing such as a part or an accident. The second operation has to do with a thing's *esse*, which results from the union of its principles in the case of composites, or accompanies the simple nature itself, as in the case of simple substances.[17] Needless to say, this text, together with its parallels, strongly supports those who insist that for Thomas one must have recourse to judgment, not merely to simple apprehension, if one is to grasp being as existing or as real, or if one is to grasp existence as such.[18]

15. "Utrum mathematica consideratio sit sine motu et materia de his quae sunt in materia" (*op. cit.*, p. 179).

16. *Op. cit.*, pp. 181:17–182:5. For Aristotle see *De anima* III, ch. 6 (430a26–28).

17. "Et hae quidem duae operationes duobus, quae sunt in rebus, respondent. Prima quidem operatio respicit ipsam naturam rei, secundum quam res intellecta aliquem gradum in entibus obtinet, sive sit res completa, ut totum aliquod, sive res incompleta, ut pars vel accidens. Secunda vero operatio respicit ipsum esse rei, quod quidem resultat ex congregatione principiorum rei in compositis vel ipsam simplicem naturam rei concomitatur, ut in substantiis simplicibus." (*Op. cit.*, p. 182:5–12.)

18. See the authors cited in n. 1 of this chapter. For a helpful survey of recent Thomistic discussions of judgment see A. McNicholl, "On Judging," *The Thomist* 38 (1974), pp. 789–825; also see his "On Judging Existence," *ibid.* 43 (1979), pp. 507–80. This should be supplemented by recent studies by J. Owens cited above in n. 1 as well as by his "Aquinas on Knowing Existence," *The Review of Metaphysics* 29 (1976), pp. 670–90. For a rather critical evaluation of the Gilson position on this point see J. M. Quinn, *The Thomism of Etienne Gilson*, pp. 53–91. Quinn's evaluation of Gilson has

So far, then, Thomas has been discussing two intellectual operations, often known as simple apprehension and judgment. While the first is directed towards a thing's nature or essence, the second has to do with its *esse*. Thomas had initiated this discussion by suggesting that one must investigate the various ways in which the intellect can *abstract*. Now, after this brief general reference to simple apprehension and judgment, he again turns to that issue. Since the truth of the intellect results from its conformity to reality, in its second operation (judgment) it cannot truly abstract (*abstrahere*) that which is in fact united in reality.[19] This is so because when one abstracts according to this second operation one indicates that there is a corresponding separation (*separatio*) in reality. Thomas illustrates this with the case of a white man. If I say that he is not white, I assert that there is a separation in reality. If the man is indeed white, my judgment is erroneous.[20]

Thomas contrasts the second operation of the intellect with the first on this score. According to the mind's first operation, he continues, one can indeed abstract things which are not separated in reality. This is true in certain cases although not in others. In brief, such is possible when and only when the intelligibility of that which is abstracted does not depend on the other thing with which it is united in reality.[21] In judgment, however, one can never truthfully abstract that which is united in reality.

At this point Thomas introduces a new element into his theory of abstraction and separation:

---

been disputed and defended. See A. Maurer, review of *The Thomism of Etienne Gilson: A Critical Study, The Thomist* 37 (1973), pp. 389–91; L. Kennedy, review of Quinn's book, *The New Scholasticism* 49 (1975), pp. 369–73; John Beach, "A Rejoinder to Armand A. Maurer's Review of *The Thomism of Etienne Gilson: A Critical Study* by John M. Quinn," *The Thomist* 38 (1974), pp. 187–91; and Beach, "Another Look at the Thomism of Etienne Gilson," *The New Scholasticism* 50 (1976), pp. 522–28. For parallel texts in Thomas see *In I Sent.*, d. 19, q. 5, a. 1, ad 7 (Mandonnet ed., Vol. 1, p. 489): " . . . prima operatio respicit quidditatem rei; secunda respicit esse ipsius." Also, *In I Sent.*, d. 38, q. 1, a. 3, sol. (p. 903): "Cum in re duo sint, quidditas rei, et esse eius, his duobus respondet duplex operatio intellectus. Una quae dicitur a philosophis formatio, qua apprehendit quidditates rerum, quae etiam a Philosopho, in III *De anima*, dicitur indivisibilium intelligentia. Alia autem comprehendit esse rei, componendo affirmationem, quia etiam esse rei ex materia et forma compositae, a qua cognitionem accipit, consistit in quadam compositione formae ad materiam, vel accidentis ad subjectum."

19. "Et quia veritas intellectus est ex hoc quod conformatur rei, patet quod secundum hanc secundam operationem intellectus non potest vere abstrahere quod secundum rem coniunctum est, quia in abstrahendo significaretur esse separatio secundum ipsum esse rei . . . . " (Decker ed., p. 182:12–15).

20. *Ibid.*, p. 182:16–18.

21. *Op. cit.*, pp. 182–83.

Accordingly, through its various operations the intellect distinguishes one thing from another in different ways. Through the operation by which it composes and divides, it distinguishes one thing from another by understanding that the one does not exist in the other. Through the operation, however, by which it understands what a thing is, it distinguishes one thing from another by knowing what one is without knowing anything of the other, either that it is united to it or separated from it. So this distinction is not properly called *separation* [*separatio*], but only the first. It is correctly called *abstraction*, but only when the things, one of which is known without the other, are one in reality. (Italics mine)[22]

Here, then, within the general context of the different ways in which the intellect can "distinguish" one thing from another, Thomas has differentiated between one kind of operation referred to as *separatio,* and another referred to as abstraction. Abstraction has now taken on a narrower meaning, being restricted to the intellect's first operation. *Separatio* refers to the intellect's second operation or judgment, and since it is a distinguishing or dividing operation, is often described by commentators on Thomas as a "negative judgment."

Thomas goes on in this same article to distinguish two further subdivisions of abstraction taken in this strict and narrow sense, corresponding to two modes of union. To union of part and whole there corresponds the abstraction of the whole, the abstraction of the universal from the particular. To union of form (the accidental form of quantity) and its appropriate matter there corresponds abstraction of the form. Though Thomas's development of these two types of abstraction is rather detailed, here it will be enough for us to note that he then correlates *separatio* and the two types of abstraction taken strictly with his threefold division of theoretical science.

We conclude that there are three kinds of distinction in the operation of the intellect. There is one through the operation of the intellect joining and dividing which is properly called separation; and this belongs to divine science or metaphysics.

---

22. See A. Maurer, *The Division and Methods of the Sciences*, p. 30. For direct translations, I shall follow Maurer. For the Latin see the Decker ed., p. 183:23–31: "Sic ergo intellectus distinguit unum ab altero aliter et aliter secundum diversas operationes; quia secundum operationem, qua componit et dividit, distinguit unum ab alio per hoc quod intelligit unum alii non inesse. In operatione vero qua intelligit, quid est unumquodque, distinguit unum ab alio, dum intelligit, quid est hoc, nihil intelligendo de alio, neque quod sit cum eo, neque quod sit ab eo separatum. Unde ista distinctio non proprie habet nomen separationis, sed prima tantum. Haec autem distinctio recte dicitur abstractio, sed tunc tantum quando ea, quorum unum sine altero intelligitur, sunt simul secundum rem."

There is another through the operation by which the quiddities of things are conceived which is the abstraction of form from sensible matter; and this belongs to mathematics.

And there is a third through the same operation which is the abstraction of a universal from a particular; and this belongs to physics and to all the sciences in general, because science disregards accidental features and treats of necessary matters.[23]

In short, therefore, a particular kind of judgment, a negative judgment or *separatio,* is here associated with the third degree of theoretical science, that is to say, with metaphysics.

In an effort to reconstruct Thomas's teaching on the discovery of *esse, separatio,* and the subject of metaphysics, it will be helpful to recall the following points.

First of all, by way of contrast with the mind's first operation, simple apprehension, its second operation or judgment is said to be directed towards a thing's *esse.* Given this, there is strong reason to suggest that an existential judgment or a judgment of existence has some role to play in one's discovery of being as existing according to Thomas.[24]

Secondly, if one or a series of individual judgments of existence is (are) directed to objects that have originally been grasped by the senses, the subject of every such judgment will be concrete, material, and changing, that is, the kind of thing that can be grasped by the senses. If one stops at this point in formulating his notion of being, he will hardly have arrived at an understanding of being as being rather than as changing and material.

---

23. Maurer trans., pp. 33–34. For the Latin see the Decker ed., p. 186:13–21. "Sic ergo in operatione intellectus triplex distinctio invenitur. Una secundum operationem intellectus componentis et dividentis, quae separatio dicitur proprie; et haec competit scientiae divinae sive metaphysicae. Alia secundum operationem, qua formantur quiditates rerum, quae est abstractio formae a materia sensibili; et haec competit mathematicae. Tertia secundum eandem operationem [quae est abstractio] universalis a particulari; et haec competit etiam physicae et est communis omnibus scientiis, quia in scientia praetermittitur quod per accidens est et accipitur quod per se est."

24. See n. 18 above and the references indicated therein as well as in n. 1. I phrase my statement in these terms because, as I read Aquinas, for him one's understanding or notion of being is complex, involving both a quidditative aspect (an *id quod*) and an existential aspect (*esse*). Hence, according to his theory of knowledge an adequate understanding of being as real or as existing presupposes sense experience, the intellect's first operation (whereby the quidditative aspect is grasped), and a judgment of existence, whereby existence itself is grasped. J. Owens seems to have taken my statement as referring only to existence rather than to being as existing. Hence the need for this clarification. See his "Stages and Distinction in *De Ente:* A Rejoinder," *The Thomist* 45 (1981), p. 110, n. 14.

Hence he will not yet be in a position to develop a science of being as being or being as such. He may have arrived at what might be termed a primitive notion of being, that is, of being as restricted to the material and changing.[25]

Thirdly, in order to overcome this restricted notion of being, appeal may be made to a negative judgment, or to Thomas's *separatio*. This seems to be why he asserts that *separatio* is characteristic of metaphysics, the science of being as being, while the subject-matters of the other theoretical sciences can be attained by some process of abstraction taken strictly, or simple apprehension.[26]

As to identifying more precisely the role of *separatio,* our task would be considerably easier had Thomas devoted an article or question to its function as such. Lacking this, however, we may take our clues from a number of explicit references to *separatio* in q. 5, a. 3. As has been noted, it is a judging operation whereby one distinguishes one thing from another by understanding that the one is not found in the other.[27] In short, it is a negative judgment. Thomas also states that in the case of things that can exist separately, separation obtains rather than abstraction.[28] Hence, when he speaks most precisely, he carefully distinguishes it from abstraction. Again, he notes that substance, the intelligible matter of quantity, can exist without quantity. Therefore, the consideration of substance without quantity belongs to the order of separation rather than to that of abstraction.[29] It will be recalled that according to Thomas's treatment in q. 5, a. 1, substance and being were cited as instances of that which is found in matter in certain cases but not in others, that is to say, of that which is negatively or neutrally immaterial rather than positively immaterial.[30] Therefore, one may conclude that the consideration of being as such rather than as material or

25. For some other contemporary interpreters of Thomas who also distinguish between this "primitive" notion of being and a truly metaphysical notion, see H. Renard, "What is St. Thomas' Approach to Metaphysics?" *The New Scholasticism* 30 (1956), p. 73; A. M. Krapiec, "Analysis formationis conceptus entis existentialiter considerati," *Divus Thomas* (Piac.) 59 (1956), pp. 341–44; G. W. Klubertanz, *Introduction to the Philosophy of Being*, 2d ed. (New York, 1963), pp. 45–52; R. W. Schmidt, "L'emploi de la séparation en métaphysique," *Revue philosophique de Louvain* 58 (1960), pp. 377–80.

26. For helpful remarks on *separatio*'s role in detaching being from limited determinations see J.-D. Robert, "La métaphysique, science distincte de toute autre discipline philosophique, selon saint Thomas d'Aquin," *Divus Thomas* (Piac.) 50 (1947), pp. 216–17.

27. See q. 5, a. 3 as cited in n. 22 above.

28. Decker ed., pp. 185:31–186:1. "In his autem quae secundum esse possunt esse divisa, magis habet locum separatio quam abstractio."

29. *Ibid.*, p. 186:10–12. "Substantia autem, quae est materia intelligibilis quantitatis, potest esse sine quantitate; unde considerare substantiam sine quantitate magis pertinet ad genus separationis quam abstractionis."

30. See p. 72 of our text above.

quantified pertains to *separatio* rather than to abstraction. Finally, we have seen that *separatio* belongs to metaphysics or to divine science. If one bears in mind that for Thomas metaphysics has as its subject being as being and that it treats of the kind of things that do not depend on matter either for their existence or to be defined, it follows that for him *separatio* is the intellectual process whereby one attains to that particular kind of subject-matter.

To express Thomas's understanding of *separatio* in other terms, it is the process through which the mind explicitly acknowledges and asserts that that by reason of which something is recognized as being need not be identified with that by which it is recognized as material being, or changing being, or being of a given kind. One may describe it as a negative judgment in that it denies that that by reason of which something is described as being is to be identified with that by reason of which it is being of a given kind, for instance, material and changing being, or quantified being, or, for that matter, spiritual being. One may describe it as *separatio* because by reason of this judgment one distinguishes or separates that intelligibility in virtue of which something is described as being from all lesser and more restrictive intelligibilities that indicate its kind of being. As a result of *separatio*, therefore, one asserts that in order for something to be or to be real, it need not be material or changing or quantified. Thus one asserts the negative immateriality, the neutral character, of being.

If one concedes that metaphysics is indeed the science of being as being and that its subject is being in general rather than this or that particular kind of being,[31] then one can understand why Thomas links *separatio* with metaphysics and contrasts it with the abstractions characteristic of the other theoretical sciences. This is why his distinction between abstraction in the strict sense and *separatio* in q. 5, a. 3 is so important when it comes to grounding metaphysics or to one's discovery of a metaphysical understanding of being. It is by appealing to this negative judgment that one frees

---

31. For some other texts wherein Thomas distinguishes the metaphysician's perspective, see *In III Sent.*, d. 27, q. 2, a. 4, sol. 2: " . . . sicut philosophia prima est specialis scientia, quamvis consideret ens secundum quod est omnibus commune, quia specialem rationem entis considerat secundum quod non dependet a materia et motu" (*Scriptum super Sententiis*, Vol. 3 [Paris, 1933], pp. 886–87). *In IV Met.*, lect. 1, n. 530: "Dicit autem 'secundum quod est ens', quia scientiae aliae, quae sunt de entibus particularibus, considerant quidem de ente, cum omnia subiecta scientiarum sint entia, non tamen considerant ens secundum quod ens, sed secundum quod est huiusmodi ens, scilicet vel numerus, vel linea, vel ignis, aut aliquid huiusmodi." *In VI Met.*, lect. 1, n. 1147: "De quolibet enim ente inquantum est ens, proprium est metaphysici considerare." It pertains to metaphysics to treat of being in general therefore, or without restriction, precisely insofar as it is being rather than insofar as it is being of a given kind.

one's understanding of being from the restrictions involved in a merely primitive notion of being. As to Thomas's assertion of this distinction between abstraction in the strict sense and *separatio*, it is interesting to note that he himself settled on it only after some false starts. Examination of the transcription of his autograph of this discussion shows that in an earlier version he used the language: "Patet quod triplex est abstractio. . . . "[32] In the final version he clearly distinguishes between *separatio* and abstraction and reserves the name *separatio* for the intellect's second operation. It is this that he regards as proper to metaphysics.

In order to highlight the importance of *separatio* for Aquinas, suppose, for the sake of illustration, that one were to reject this distinction and reduce the formation of the notion of being to a more refined kind of abstraction. Thus one might first abstract from the individuating differences between material and changing things, thereby ending with a general or universal concept that still included reference to sensible matter, e.g., man, horse, animal. One would then be on the level of physics or philosophy of nature. One might then abstract from common sensible matter as well, retaining only common intelligible matter or being insofar as it is quantified. One would now have reached the subject of mathematics. Finally, one might then abstract from common intelligible matter as well, thereby arriving at the notion of being as being.

The difficulty with such a procedure is that being then becomes another abstracted notion. As such it can hardly serve as subject (of a science) that is so universal and so transcendental that it not only applies to that which is insofar as it is, but even to the individual differences between things. If one abstracts from individual differences, from sensible matter, and from quantity in arriving at one's notion of being, how can one apply such an abstracted notion to these same individual differences, to sensible matter, and to quantity? Perhaps by adding something to the notion of being that does not fall under the same. But that could only be nonbeing. Such an abstract notion of being might be univocal, it would seem, but not truly analogical and not sufficiently transcendental to serve as subject of a science of being as being.[33] Hence Thomas's earlier suggestion that the mind's second

32. For Decker's transcription of the same see p. 233:20–23: "Patet ergo quod triplex est abstractio, qua intellectus abstrahit. Prima quidem secundum operationem secundam intellectus, qua componit et dividit. Et sic intellectum abstrahere nihil est aliud hoc non esse in hoc." See p. 232. On the different redactions see Geiger, "Abstraction et séparation," pp. 15–20.

33. In his Commentary on *Metaphysics* I, Thomas attributes such reasoning to Parmenides: "Quicquid est praeter ens, est non ens: et quicquid est non ens, est nihil: ergo quicquid est praeter ens est nihil. Sed ens est unum. Ergo quicquid est praeter unum, est nihil. In quo patet quod considerabat ipsam rationem essendi

operation is ordered to a thing's *esse*. Reliance solely on the mind's first operation has been rejected by him as insufficient to grasp being as real, or as existing. Were one to move by simple abstraction from the primitive notion of being attained through judgment to a metaphysical notion of being, one would, presumably, abstract from existence as well as from individual differences, from common sensible matter, and from quantity. But all of these should be included under the resulting metaphysical notion of being.[34] Hence Thomas's second appeal to judgment, this time, to the negative judgment, *separatio*. As he himself has shown, in certain cases of abstraction one can mentally distinguish things that are not distinguished in reality. Not so in judgment, however. By appealing to a negative judgment, to *separatio,* therefore, one asserts that that by reason of which something is recognized as being is not to be identified with that by reason of which it is material or quantified or of a restricted kind. In short, one asserts that being, in order to be such, need not be material, or changing, or quantified, etc. Therefore one asserts the legitimacy of investigating being as being rather than as changing or as quantified.

The terminological differentiation between "abstraction" and "separation" is, perhaps, not so important. But the difference between that which is signified by the term "abstraction," the intellect's first operation, and that which is signified by "separation," the intellect's second or judging operation, is indeed crucial. If, therefore, at later points in his career Thomas does not always rigorously preserve this distinction in terminology between

---

quae videtur esse una, quia non potest intelligi quod ad rationem entis aliquid superveniat per quod diversificetur: quia illud quod supervenit enti, oportet esse extraneum ab ente. Quod autem est huiusmodi, est nihil. Unde non videtur quod possit diversificare ens. Sicut etiam videmus quod differentiae advenientes generi diversificant ipsum, quae tamen sunt praeter substantiam eius" (lect. 9, n. 138). Thomas comments: "Sed in hoc decipiebantur, quia utebantur ente quasi una ratione et una natura sicut est natura alicuius generis; hoc enim est impossibile. Ens enim non est genus, sed multipliciter dicitur de diversis" (n. 139). Were one to regard being simply as the most abstract of all notions, one might well encounter a problem similar to that of Parmenides. One would hardly have safeguarded its analogical character. See the remarks by Robert, "La métaphysique, science distincte," pp. 213–15, esp. 214, n. 29. As Robert observes, the differences which contract being are still included within being, though in a confused way. But specific and individual differences are only potentially present in non-transcendental concepts. Robert refers the reader to the *De veritate*, q. 1, a. 1.

34. Geiger's comment bears quotation: "Mais dire cela, c'est dire équivalemment que l'être ne peut être abstrait à proprement parler ni de la matière ni des réalités immatérielles, puisque tout cela est de l'être. Finalement c'est donc le caractère transcendental, et avec lui le caractère analogique propre aux données transcendentales qui exige le jugement de séparation . . . . " ("Abstraction et séparation," p. 28).

abstraction and *separatio* but uses abstraction more generally so as to apply to both ways of distinguishing, this does not imply any change in doctrine. For in these later texts he still distinguishes clearly between one operation (simple apprehension) and the other (judgment), and still connects the latter with metaphysics.[35]

II

If the above has been an accurate interpretation of Thomas's mind with respect to *separatio,* a second historical problem remains to be examined. According to Aquinas, what does *separatio* presuppose? For one to judge that being, in order to be such, need not be material or changing, must one already know that positively immaterial being exists? Must one presuppose the existence of some entity such as the First Mover of the *Physics* or a spiritual soul? The majority of contemporary scholars who have studied Thomas's views on *separatio* have concluded that such is his view. According to many, Thomas grounds *separatio,* and therefore the very possibility of metaphysics, on the demonstration of the First Mover of the *Physics* (or according to some, on the demonstration of the existence of a spiritual soul). If immaterial being does in fact exist, it can exist. Therefore, one may conclude that in order for something to be realized as being, it need not be material. As one writer phrases it: "Is the existence of immaterial beings an absolute necessity for

---

35. Thus in *Summa theologiae* I, q. 85, a. 1, ad 1, he writes: "Ad primum ergo dicendum quod abstrahere contingit dupliciter. Uno modo, per modum compositionis et divisionis; sicut cum intelligimus aliquid non esse in alio, vel esse separatum ab eo. Alio modo, per modum simplicis et absolutae considerationis: sicut cum intelligimus unum, nihil considerando de alio. Abstrahere igitur per intellectum ea quae secundum rem non sunt abstracta, secundum primum modum abstrahendi, non est absque falsitate. Sed secundo modo abstrahere per intellectum quae non sunt abstracta secundum rem, non habet falsitatem." After discussing the abstraction of the universal from the particular in the same context, and again in his reply to the second objection, Thomas also considers the kind of abstraction appropriate to mathematics, that of quantity from sensible qualities (common sensible matter). He concludes his reply to the second objection by observing: "Quaedam vero sunt quae possunt abstrahi etiam a materia intelligibili communi, sicut ens, unum, potentia et actus, et alia huiusmodi, quae etiam esse possunt absque omni materia, ut patet in substantiis immaterialibus. Et quia Plato non consideravit quod dictum est de duplici modo abstractionis [see our quotation above from his reply to objection 1], omnia quae diximus abstrahi per intellectum, posuit abstracta esse secundum rem." Although he does not here name this kind of "abstraction" *separatio* there can be no doubt that he is referring to the intellect's judging operation (*per modum compositionis et divisionis*). Hence his doctrine has not changed.

metaphysics? If by metaphysics we mean a science specifically different from physics, then, their existence is absolutely necessary."[36]

One of the most interesting defenses of the view that *separatio* must be grounded on prior knowledge of the existence of immaterial being is found in Geiger's article. After strongly asserting that this judgment presupposes awareness that immaterial beings actually exist, and after singling out two texts from Thomas's Commentary on the *Metaphysics,* Geiger briefly suggests that the concept of being itself enjoys a certain mode of being. Because its mode of being is immaterial, there is at least one immaterial being given with the concept of being initially drawn from the material world. He suggests that this is the procedure used by Thomas to demonstrate the existence of the purely immaterial activity of our intellect and, thereby, the immateriality of the power of the intellect itself and of the human soul.[37]

Consideration of the texts he cites leads one back to the historical issue: Does Thomas himself ground *separatio* and the very possibility of metaphysics on prior awareness that immaterial being exists? A first text is taken from his Commentary on the *Metaphysics,* Bk. I, lect. 12, n. 181. Here Thomas reports with approval Aristotle's criticism of the position of the ancient philosophers of nature. Thomas notes that they were mistaken

36. See A. Moreno, "The Nature of Metaphysics," *The Thomist* 30 (1966), p. 113. Although he does not emphasize the role of *separatio*, Vincent Smith is a fine illustration of those who ground the possibility of metaphysics on the demonstration of an immaterial and First Mover at the conclusion of physics. See his "The Prime Mover: Physical and Metaphysical Considerations," *Proceedings of the American Catholic Philosophical Association* 28 (1954), pp. 78–94; *The General Science of Nature* (Milwaukee, 1958), p. 382: "A science called metaphysics now becomes possible . . . . we do not discover that there is such a subject [being as being] without our proof that there is an immaterial and immobile world and without proof that mobile being, hitherto taken by reason as the only reality, is not truly so . . . . . While the science of nature and metaphysics remain distinct disciplines, metaphysics presupposes the science of nature as a material condition."

37. Geiger, "Abstraction et séparation," pp. 24–25. Note his comment on p. 24: "Pour que l'intelligence puisse le prononcer en toute vérité scientifique, faut-il donc qu'elle sache qu'il existe des êtres immatériels avant de commencer la métaphysique? Sans aucun doute. Et S. Thomas le dit explicitement dans deux textes au moins . . . " He then cites two texts from Thomas's Commentary on the *Metaphysics,* for which see below. For his argument from the immateriality of the concept of being, see the following: "Alors que l'objet des concepts portant sur les essences est limité à cette essence, et donc au contenu du concept—le concept de cheval n'est pas un cheval, mais signifie le cheval—le concept de l'être signifie l'être et est lui-même de l'être, parce que l'être est transcendant à toute catégorie. Le concept est lui-même un certain mode de l'être, et puisqu'il est immatériel, c'est un certain être immatériel qui est donné avec le concept de l'être tiré du monde matériel" (p. 25).

in positing nothing but corporeal principles. Against them he observes that there are not only corporeal but also certain incorporeal things, as is evident from the *De anima*.[38] This text is interesting for our purposes, it would seem, because in denying that only physical or corporeal realities exist, Aquinas does refer in passing to the *De anima,* and presumably to what he regards as a demonstration of the incorporeal therein. But this text of itself does not show that the possibility of metaphysics in general or of *separatio* in particular must be grounded on such a presupposition. Hence I find little support in it for Geiger's contention.

Geiger's second text is also taken from Thomas's Commentary on the *Metaphysics,* this time from Bk. IV, lect. 5, n. 593. There Thomas again finds Aristotle criticizing the ancient philosophers of nature, this time for having concerned themselves with examining the first principles of demonstration. This is understandable in light of the ancients' view that only corporeal and mobile substance exists. Thomas observes that because of this the philosophers of nature were thought to treat of the whole of nature, and therefore of being as being as well as of the first principles that are considered together with being. This view is false, Thomas counters, because there is still another science that is superior to natural philosophy. Nature, or natural being, is only one given class (*genus*) within the totality of being. But not all being is of this type. (Here one appears to have an instance of *separatio*, the judgment that not all being is physical or material.) In support of this judgment, Thomas then appeals to the existence of an immobile being as established in Bk. VIII of the *Physics*. He comments that this immobile being is superior to and nobler than mobile being, which the physicist considers. And then, in a passage which expands considerably upon the text of Aristotle, he writes: "And because the consideration of *ens commune* pertains to that science to which it also belongs to consider the first being, therefore the consideration of *ens commune* also belongs to a science different from natural philosophy." Hence it will pertain to that science to study such principles.[39]

38. "Quia in rebus non solum sunt corporea, sed etiam quaedam incorporea, ut patet ex libro *de Anima*. Sed ipsi non posuerunt principia nisi corporea . . . " (*ed. cit.*).

39. See n. 593 of Thomas's Commentary. Note in particular: "Hoc autem falsum est; quia adhuc est quaedam scientia superior naturali: ipsa enim natura, idest res naturalis habens in se principium motus, in se ipsa est unum aliquod genus entis universalis. Non enim omne ens est huiusmodi; cum probatum sit in octavo *Physicorum* esse aliquod ens immobile. Hoc autem ens immobile superius est et nobilius ente mobili, de quo considerat naturalis. Et quia ad illam scientiam pertinet consideratio entis communis, ad quam pertinet consideratio entis primi, ideo ad aliam scientiam quam ad naturalem pertinet consideratio entis communis." Although it cannot be assumed that the Latin text of the *Metaphysics* printed with Thomas's Commentary is

Geiger concludes from this text and the previous one that the negative judgment which grounds the immateriality of the object of metaphysics draws its objective value from the demonstration of immaterial beings effected in the philosophy of nature: the First Mover of *Physics* VIII, and the human soul with its agent and possible intellect as established in the *De anima*. For Geiger this is only to be expected, since Thomas also affirms on other occasions that metaphysics should be taught after physics.[40]

As regards the text from Thomas's Commentary on *Metaphysics* IV, one might contend that he here justifies *separatio* by appealing to the fact that immobile being exists, something that he takes *Physics* VIII to have established. Moreover, he justifies the existence of the science of *ens commune* by asserting that it belongs to one and the same science to study the first being and to study *ens commune*. Hence he seems to justify *separatio,* the science of the first being, and the science of *ens commune,* by appealing to the existence of the Immobile and First Mover demonstrated in the *Physics.*

However, this passage of itself does not appear to be conclusive proof that in Thomas's eyes one must ground metaphysics and *separatio* on the conclusions of the *Physics.* The situation is dialectical. Thomas is commenting on Aristotle's criticism of the earlier natural philosophers and their restriction of reality to the material. Against this it would only be natural for him to cite a counterfact, the existence of immaterial being as established at the end of the *Physics.* Given this, it is not surprising to find him also arguing that the science that studies this first and immaterial being, because it also studies being in general, is distinct from and higher than physics. Hence, granted that in this particular case he reasons from the fact that immaterial being exists to the distinctive character of the science of that first entity and the science of *ens commune,* it need not follow that he could only proceed in this manner. It was only natural for him to do so here, because of the context, that is, the refutation of the early naturalists, and because of his ultimate purpose in the immediate context, to show that the study of first principles does not belong to them but to the science that studies being

---

always identical with the version on which he commented, I will cite it and then the corresponding Greek text in order to facilitate comparison between Aristotle's statement and Thomas's expanded affirmation of identification of the science of the first being and the science of *ens commune:* "Sed quoniam est adhuc physico aliquis superior, unum enim aliquod genus est natura entis, ipsius universalis et circa substantiam primam theorizantis, et de his erit perscrutatio" (n. 323, p. 163); ἐπεὶ δ' ἔστιν ἔτι τοῦ φυσικοῦ τις ἀνωτέρω (ἓν γάρ τι γένος τοῦ ὄντος ἡ φύσις), τοῦ καθόλου καὶ τοῦ περὶ τὴν πρώτην οὐσίαν θεωρητικοῦ καὶ ἡ περὶ τούτων ἂν εἴη σκέψις (1005a33–1005b1).

40. Geiger, "Abstraction et séparation," p. 25. See below for consideration of such passages wherein Thomas recommends studying metaphysics after physics.

in general. Finally, Thomas is here interpreting the text of Aristotle. If in more independent texts one should find him suggesting a different procedure, then greater weight should be given to those texts when it comes to a determination of Thomas's personal thought on the matter in question. This final suggestion will be developed below.

Perhaps the most forceful text pointing toward the dependence of metaphysics and presumably, therefore, of *separatio* upon the conclusions of natural philosophy is to be found in Thomas's commentary on the final lines of ch. 1 of Bk. VI of Aristotle's *Metaphysics* (and in his commentary on the parallel passage in book XI).[41] Here Thomas follows Aristotle's text very closely and raises the question to which Aristotle himself explicitly adverts. One might well wonder whether first philosophy is universal in that it studies being in general, or whether its consideration is rather directed to a particular genus and a particular nature (separate and immobile reality).[42] The question, of course, arises naturally from earlier developments in Bk. IV, chs. 1 and 2, and Bk. VI, ch. 1 of Aristotle's *Metaphysics*. Aristotle's own resolution of this same difficulty has caused considerable perplexity for his commentators, as is well known.[43]

In commenting on the solution offered by Aristotle in Bk. VI, Thomas repeats his text with slightest modification. If there is no other substance apart from those that exist according to nature and of which physics treats, then physics will be the first science. But if there is some immobile substance, this will be prior to natural substance. Therefore, the philosophy which considers this kind of substance will be first philosophy. And because it is first it will therefore be universal. It will belong to it to study being as

---

41. See nn. 1169–1170, commenting on Aristotle's *Metaphysics* VI, ch. 1 (1026a23–32); and nn. 2266–67, commenting on *Metaphysics* XI, ch. 7 (1064b6–14).

42. See n. 1169: "Tertio movetur quaedam quaestio circa praedeterminata: et primo movet eam, dicens, quod aliquis potest dubitare, utrum prima philosophia sit universalis quasi considerans ens universaliter, aut eius consideratio sit circa aliquod genus determinatum et naturam unam." For the parallel from his Commentary on Bk. XI, see n. 2266: " . . . et dicit: Dubitabile est, utrum istam scientiam, quae est circa entia separabilia, oporteat poni universalem scientiam entis, inquantum est ens, aut non . . . "

43. See, for instance, the solutions proposed by J. Owens, *The Doctrine of Being in the Aristotelian Metaphysics,* 3d ed. (Toronto, 1978); P. Merlan, *From Platonism to Neoplatonism,* 2d ed. (The Hague, 1960), ch. 7; A. Mansion, "L'objet de la science philosophique suprême d'après Aristote, *Métaphysique* E I," *Mélanges de philosophie grecque offerts à Mgr A. Diès* (Paris, 1956), pp. 151–68; "Philosophie première, philosophie seconde et métaphysique chez Aristote," *Revue philosophique de Louvain* 56 (1958), pp. 165–221; P. Aubenque, *Le problème de l'être chez Aristote: Essai sur la problématique Aristotélicienne* (Paris, 1962); E. König, "Aristoteles' erste Philosophie als universale Wissenschaft von den ARXAI," *Archiv für Geschichte der Philosophie* 52 (1970), pp. 225–46.

being, both what it is, and the attributes which pertain to being as being.[44] And then, in a significant addition to Aristotle's text, Thomas concludes: for the science of the first being and the science of being in general are one and the same, as has been maintained in the beginning of Bk. IV.[45] Thomas's commentary on the passage in Bk. XI parallels the above very closely. But there he offers a justification for the concluding statement which he had added to his commentary on Bk. VI. To prove that the science that studies the first being(s) is the same as the universal science, he observes that the first beings are the principles of the others.[46]

One might, therefore, well argue from Thomas's commentary on the passage from *Metaphysics* VI (and the parallel text from *Metaphysics* XI) that metaphysics (and *separatio* as required to discover being as being) presupposes prior awareness that immaterial and immobile being exists. Negatively expressed, Thomas has written that if there is no substance beyond the physical, physics will be the first science. Positively phrased, he states that if there is some immobile substance, the philosophy that studies this kind of substance will be first, and because it is first, it will also be universal and the science of being as being. Moreover, if one wonders how Aristotle himself justifies the transition from first philosophy to the universal science in this passage (see *Metaphysics* VI 1026a30ff.), Thomas has asserted the identity of the two in commenting on *Metaphysics* VI. In commenting on *Metaphysics* XI, he has supplied an added reason: the first being(s) are the principles of

44. N. 1170. Thomas's final sentence reads: "Et quia est prima, ideo erit universalis, et erit eius speculari de ente inquantum est ens, et de eo quod quid est, et de his quae sunt entis inquantum est ens: eadem enim est scientia primi entis et entis communis, ut in principio quarti habitum est." Compare with the Latin version printed in the Marietti text: "Et quia prima et de ente inquantum est ens, eius utique est speculari, et quod quid est, et quae insunt inquantum ens" (p. 294, n. 542). For the Greek see 1026a29–32: εἰ δ' ἔστι τις οὐσία ἀκίνητος, αὕτη προτέρα καὶ φιλοσοφία πρώτη, καὶ καθόλου οὕτως ὅτι πρώτη· καὶ περὶ τοῦ ὄντος ᾗ ὄν, ταύτης ἂν εἴη θεωρῆσαι, καὶ τί ἐστι καὶ τὰ ὑπάρχοντα ᾗ ὄν. Also see Thomas, *In III Met.*: "Sicut si non essent aliae substantiae priores substantiis mobilibus corporalibus, scientia naturalis esset philosophia prima, ut dicitur infra in sexto" (n. 398). As Thomas himself indicates in this paragraph, this statement is to be read in the light of Aristotle's procedure in *Metaphysics* VI and XI.

45. *Ibid.* For the text see n. 44 above.

46. N. 2267. "Sed de naturali manifestum est; quia si naturales substantiae, quae sunt substantiae sensibiles et mobiles, sunt primae inter entia, oportet quod naturalis scientia sit prima inter scientias; quia secundum ordinem subiectorum, est ordo scientiarum, ut iam dictum est. — Si autem est alia natura et substantia praeter substantias naturales, quae sit separabilis et immobilis, necesse est alteram scientiam ipsius esse, quae sit prior naturali. Et ex eo quod est prima, oportet quod sit universalis. Eadem enim est scientia quae est de primis entibus, et quae est universalis. *Nam prima entia sunt principia aliorum*" (italics mine).

the others. The implication seems to be: in studying the first principle, one studies all else. In sum, therefore, if all being is physical, if there is no immaterial and immobile being in the positive sense, it seems that one could not reason that being, in order to be, need not be material. In short, one would not be justified in distinguishing being as such from being as material and changeable by means of *separatio*. Therefore, one would be unable to arrive at a science of being as being rather than a science of being as changing.[47] It should also be noted that prior knowledge of immaterial, separate, and immobile beings appears to be required. In other words, prior knowledge of the existence of a spiritual human soul is not implied by these texts from Thomas's Commentary. Hence they offer little support for the view that one might ground *separatio* on this conclusion rather than on the existence of an immaterial and immobile being, viz., the First and Unmoved Mover.

In attempting to evaluate the importance of this text and its parallel, two points should be recalled. (1) Thomas is here writing as a commentator on Aristotle and is following his text with greatest care. In fact, he presents this as Aristotle's answer to Aristotle's question. Can one automatically assume that this reflects Thomas's own opinion, unless further evidence can also be offered from other texts where Thomas is clearly expressing his personal views? One's hesitation in replying in the affirmative will, of course, increase if one finds Thomas suggesting a different procedure in such texts.[48] (2) The concluding sentence, as has already been noted above, has been added by Aquinas and appeals to the identity of the science that studies the first being and the science that studies being in general, as established in the beginning of Bk. IV. For the sake of convenience, these two points will now be considered in reverse order.

47. For such an interpretation of these passages see Moreno, "The Nature of Metaphysics," pp. 113–15; T. O'Brien, *Metaphysics and the Existence of God* (Washington, D.C., 1960), p. 160 (citing *In VI Met.*, n. 1170); J. Doig, *Aquinas on Metaphysics*, p. 243, n. 1; p. 303, n. 1; J. Weisheipl, "The Relationship of Medieval Natural Philosophy to Modern Science: The Contribution of Thomas Aquinas to Its Understanding," *Manuscripta* 20 (1976), pp. 194–96.

48. On the difficult point of determining whether Thomas in this Commentary is simply exposing Aristotle's thought as he understands it, or whether he is using the Commentary as an *occasio* to express his personal metaphysical views, or whether he proceeds in one way at times and in the other at other times, see J. Doig, *Aquinas on Metaphysics: A Historico-Doctrinal Study of the Commentary on the Metaphysics.* For my review of the same see *Speculum* 52 (1977), pp. 133–35. For an examination of Thomas's role as commentator on Aristotle in general, but with special emphasis on the Commentary on the *Metaphysics*, see J. Owens, "Aquinas as Aristotelian Commentator," *St. Thomas Aquinas 1274–1974: Commemorative Studies,* 2 vols. (Toronto, 1974), Vol. 1, pp. 213–38.

As regards the second point, Thomas makes an interesting remark in commenting on the opening chapter of *Metaphysics* IV. He observes that the Philosopher (Aristotle) is there attempting to show that the science under examination has *ens* for its subject. He notes that every principle is a per se principle and cause with respect to some nature. But in this science we seek after the first principles and ultimate causes of things, he continues, repeating Aristotle's text, and refers to Bk. I of the *Metaphysics* for support for the same.[49] Therefore, these first principles and ultimate causes must also be per se principles and causes of some nature. But that "nature" can only be *ens*. Following Aristotle, he writes that those philosophers who investigated the elements of things insofar as they are beings were seeking principles of this type (*prima et altissima*). Therefore, continues Thomas, in this science we must investigate the principles of being as being. And in an addition to Aristotle's text he concludes: "Therefore being [*ens*] is the subject of this science, because every science seeks after the proper causes of its subject."[50]

In sum, therefore, Thomas here is surely stating his personal view, a view which he attributes to Aristotle as well, that is, that *ens* or being is the subject of this science. One can be certain that this is his personal opinion because of statements in other texts as well.[51] But if it is his view that being is the subject of metaphysics, and secondly that it is the business of a science to investigate the principles and causes of its subject, and finally that God (the First Unmoved Mover) is such a principle, it would seem strange for him to suggest that one must prove the existence of the First Unmoved Mover (or God) in physics before discovering the subject of this science (metaphysics).[52]

---

49. See chs. 1 and 2 and Thomas's commentary on the same.

50. *In IV Met.*, n. 533. See in particular: " . . . ergo ens est subiectum huius scientiae, quia quaelibet scientia est quaerens causas proprias sui subiecti."

51. See, for instance, the references given in n. 11 above.

52. Note the concluding sentence of Thomas's Commentary on the *Physics:* "Et sic terminat Philosophus considerationem communem de rebus naturalibus, in primo principio totius naturae, qui est super omnia Deus benedictus in saecula. Amen." P. M. Maggiòlo, ed. (Turin-Rome, 1954), n. 1172. For a general discussion of the contested point as to whether in Thomas's view the First Mover of *Physics* VIII is, in fact, God, see A. Pegis, "St. Thomas and the Coherence of the Aristotelian Theology," *Mediaeval Studies* 35 (1973), pp. 67–117. For reference to some who would deny this see p. 68 and n. 3. See especially J. Paulus, "La théorie du Premier Moteur chez Aristote," *Revue de philosophie*, n.s. 4 (1933), pp. 259–94 and 394–424; J. Owens, "Aquinas and the Proof from the 'Physics,'" *Mediaeval Studies* 28 (1966), pp. 119–50. Pegis himself strongly defends this identity. See, for instance, pp. 97ff. Whether or not Thomas has in fact reasoned to the existence of God in his Commentary on the *Physics,* and if so whether he has or has not introduced some surreptitious metaphysical reasoning into the argumentation lies beyond the scope of the present study. I must content myself with the observation that in his final sentence

Yet such seems to be implied by his Commentary on *Metaphysics* VI, ch. 1
and in the parallel passage in *Metaphysics* XI, as we have seen above. And
such seems to be implied by the more traditional insistence that, according
to Aquinas, one must move from a demonstration of the First Mover in
physics to the discovery of being as being or to *separatio* as required for
metaphysics. It would rather seem that Thomas should have one begin by
discovering being as such or being in general (as achieved by a judgment of
existence and by separation according to my interpretation), and then, as
part of the business of metaphysics, reason to the existence of the cause or
principle of *ens commune,* that is to say, God. If it is difficult to reconcile this
procedure with the statements found in his Commentary on *Metaphysics* VI
and XI, it may be that in those texts he does not present his personal view,
but his understanding of Aristotle's text. And it may be that on this particular point, the two do not coincide. This brings us back to the first point
singled out above: In implying that prior knowledge of immaterial and immobile being is needed if one is to begin metaphysics while commenting on
Metaphysics VI and XI, was Thomas merely presenting Aristotle's position,
or was he also expressing his personal view?

For further clarification of this one is well advised to turn to the *Prooemium*
to Thomas's Commentary on the *Metaphysics.* Here, in any event, he is
surely writing in his own name. As we have already seen in some detail in
Chapter III above, here he lists the same three titles for this science which
one finds in his Commentary on the *De Trinitate* of Boethius—theology,
metaphysics, and first philosophy.[53]

Here he has already reasoned that one of the sciences should direct or
rule the others, and that it will therefore deserve to be entitled "wisdom." In
an effort to determine which science this is, he writes that it will be the one
that is most intellectual. But the most intellectual science is that which
treats of that which is most intelligible. As will be recalled from our discussion above in Chapter III, Thomas notes that things may be described as
most intelligible from different perspectives, three of which he singles out

---

therein he does assert that Aristotle's first principle of the whole of nature, in which
the *Physics* terminates, is God. And I would like to stress the point that the difficult
passages from Thomas's Commentary on *Metaphysics* VI and XI seem to require
prior knowledge of immaterial, separate, and immobile being in order to justify
metaphysics. Neither prior knowledge of the human soul nor of a sphere-soul that
moves itself without being absolutely unmoved and separate would appear to suffice, if one insists that these passages reflect Thomas's personal view.

53. For the texts from the *Prooemium* and from the Commentary on the *De
Trinitate* see above, Ch. III, nn. 10 and 3 respectively.

here. First of all, considered from the standpoint of the order of under-standing (*ex ordine intelligendi*), those things from which the intellect derives certitude are more intelligible than others. Since such are the causes, the science that considers the first causes appears to be most intellectual and best qualified to direct the others.

Secondly, things may be regarded as most intelligible from the stand-point of the relationship between sense and intellect. From this standpoint that science is most intellectual which treats of the most universal prin-ciples, that is, of being and that which follows upon it such as the one and the many, potency and act.

Thirdly, something may be viewed as most intelligible insofar as it is most separate from matter. But those things are most separate or removed from matter which abstract from sensible matter altogether, not only in the order of thought but also in the order of being. As examples Thomas cites God and the intelligences. Hence from this standpoint the science that treats of God and the intelligences is the most intellectual and thus chief or mistress of the others.[54]

Thomas then raises the obvious question. One might wonder whether or not these different kinds of intelligibles are to be investigated by one and the same science. His solution bears repeating again here. Thomas first observes that the above-mentioned separate substances (see class three) are universal and primary causes of being (see class one). Moreover, he con-tinues, it pertains to one and the same science to investigate the causes proper to a given genus and to investigate that genus itself. Thus the natural philosopher considers the principles of natural body. Therefore, it belongs to one and the same science to investigate both the separate substances and *ens commune* (see class two). This is so because *ens commune* is the "genus" of which the separate substances are common and universal causes.[55]

In other words, Thomas has distinguished three classes of intelligible ob-jects and has endeavored to show that while all three of these are studied by the science in question, only one of them, *ens commune*, is its subject. As Thomas also indicates, the subject of a science is that whose causes and

54. For all of this see the *Prooemium*, p. 1.
55. "Haec autem triplex consideratio, non diversis, sed uni scientiae attribui debet. Nam praedictae substantiae separatae sunt universales et primae causae essendi. Eiusdem autem scientiae est considerare causas proprias alicuius generis et genus ipsum: sicut naturalis considerat principia corporis naturalis. Unde oportet quod ad eamdem scientiam pertineat considerare substantias separatas, et ens com-mune, quod est genus, cuius sunt praedictae substantiae communes et universales causae" (*Prooemium*, pp. 1–2).

properties one investigates rather than those causes themselves. Knowledge of the causes is the end or goal toward which the science's investigation is directed.[56]

Here, then, one has reinforcement for the view being proposed in this chapter, the suggestion that one begins the science of metaphysics with its subject, the notion of being in general already achieved by *separatio*, and then, as part of the business of metaphysics, one seeks for the cause or causes of that same genus, that is to say, God and separate substances. Rather than presuppose the existence of immaterial being in the positive sense (God and separate entities), such knowledge is here held out as the end or goal towards which the metaphysician's investigation strives.

Finally, Thomas makes it clear here that not only immaterial being in the positive sense is at issue. Not only are those things said to be separate from matter *secundum esse et rationem* which are never found in matter, such as God and intellectual substances, but also those which can be without matter, such as *ens commune*.[57] As he had noted in q. 5, a. 4 of his Commentary on the *De Trinitate* of Boethius:

> . . . something can exist separate from matter and motion in two distinct ways: First, because by its nature the thing that is called separate in no way can exist in matter and motion, as God and the angels are said to be separate from matter and motion. Second, because by its nature it does not exist in matter and motion; but it can exist without them, though we sometimes find it with them.[58]

56. "Ex quo apparet, quod quamvis ista scientia praedicta tria consideret, non tamen considerat quodlibet eorum ut subiectum, sed ipsum solum ens commune. Hoc enim est subiectum in scientia, cuius causas et passiones quaerimus, non autem ipsae causae alicuius generis quaesiti. Nam cognitio causarum alicuius generis, est finis ad quem consideratio scientiae pertingit" (*Prooemium*, p. 2). For the same view with respect to the relationship between a science, its subject-genus, and its principles, see the Commentary on the *De Trinitate*, q. 5, a. 4, c. (pp. 192–95). There, too, Thomas notes that "divine things" are studied by the philosophers only insofar as they are the principles of all things. Hence they are treated in that discipline which studies that which is common to all beings and which has as its subject "ens in quantum est ens" (p. 194:23–26).

57. "Quamvis autem subiectum huius scientiae sit ens commune, dicitur tamen tota de his quae sunt separata a materia secundum esse et rationem. Quia secundum esse et rationem separari dicuntur, non solum illa quae nunquam in materia esse possunt, sicut Deus et intellectuales substantiae, sed etiam illa quae possunt sine materia esse, sicut ens commune. Hoc tamen non contingeret, si a materia secundum esse dependerent" (*Prooemium*, p. 2).

58. Maurer trans., p. 45. For the Latin see the Decker ed., p. 195:12–18: " . . . secundum quod dupliciter potest esse aliquid a materia et motu separatum secundum

It is clear that it is this second type of immateriality, negative or neutral immateriality, that applies to *ens commune*, the subject of metaphysics. As Thomas also comments in that same article from his Commentary on the *De Trinitate*:

> . . . We say that being and substance are separate from matter and motion not because it is of their nature to be without them . . . but because it is not of their nature to be in matter and motion, although sometimes they are in matter and motion . . . [59]

As we have indicated above, it is this kind of immateriality that is achieved by *separatio*. And in light of Thomas's discussion both in the body of q. 5, a. 4 of this same Commentary and in the *Prooemium* to his Commentary on the *Metaphysics*, it does not seem that discovery of the same presupposes prior awareness that immaterial being in the positive or stronger sense actually exists.

In the *Prooemium* Thomas had appealed to the position of the natural philosopher in order to show that one and the same science may investigate the causes of its subject genus and that genus itself.[60] As regards Thomas's own attitude with respect to the science that has *ens commune* as its subject, one might develop the parallel he has suggested there as follows. As natural philosophy is to its subject and the causes of its subject, so is metaphysics to its subject and the causes of its subject. But natural philosophy does not presuppose the existence of the cause of its subject, but reasons to the same. Therefore metaphysics does not presuppose the existence of the cause(s) of its subject (God and/or separate entity), but reasons to the same. If, as at times appears to be the case, Thomas has identified the First Mover of *Physics* VIII with God, then he could hardly make prior knowledge of the existence of this First Mover a

---

esse. Uno modo sic, quod de ratione ipsius rei, quae separata dicitur, sit quod nullo modo in materia et motu esse possit, sicut deus et angeli dicuntur a materia et motu separati. Alio modo sic, quod non sit de ratione eius quod sit in materia et motu, sed possit esse sine materia et motu, quamvis quandoque inveniatur in materia et motu." As Thomas goes on to observe in the immediate context, it is in this second way that being (*ens*), substance, and potency and act are separate.

59. Q. 5, a. 4, ad 5 (Maurer trans., pp. 48–49). For the Latin see the Decker ed., p. 199:4–9: "Ad quintum dicendum quod ens et substantia dicuntur separata a materia et motu non per hoc quod de ratione ipsorum sit esse sine materia et motu, sicut de ratione asini est sine ratione esse, sed per hoc quod de ratione eorum non est esse in materia et motu, quamvis quandoque sint in materia et motu, sicut animal abstrahit a ratione, quamvis aliquod animal sit rationale." This text and the one cited in the previous note bring out quite well what I have styled the negative or neutral immateriality of the notion of being.

60. See the text cited in n. 55 above.

necessary presupposition for beginning metaphysics.[61] To do so would be to have the metaphysician presuppose prior knowledge of the existence of the cause of the subject of his science. But knowledge of this cause has been proposed as the end or goal of the metaphysician's investigation.

On the other hand, one might meet the above contention by suggesting that Thomas has distinguished between the First Mover of the *Physics* (an immanent and self-moving principle of change) and the First Principle of the *Metaphysics* (an absolutely immobile and separate cause of being, or God).[62] Then one might argue that according to Thomas prior knowledge of this First Mover as established in physics is required if one is to discover being as being. Still, this suggestion will not do. If one insists that according to Thomas one must reason from the fact that immaterial, immobile, and separate being exists (as implied by the Commentary on *Metaphysics* VI and XI) in order to justify *separatio,* appeal to an immanent self-moving mover will not suffice.[63] If one must reason from the fact that immaterial, immobile,

---

61. See n. 52 above for the concluding sentence of Thomas's Commentary on the *Physics* and for the studies by Pegis as well as those by Owens and Paulus.

62. As noted by Owens and Pegis, *Summa contra gentiles* I, 13 is particularly difficult to interpret on this point. One paragraph might well be taken to imply that Thomas here distinguishes between the primary immobile mover as a sphere soul established by Aristotle in *Physics* VIII and the God who is proven in *Metaphysics* XII: "Sed quia Deus non est pars alicuius moventis seipsum, ulterius Aristoteles, in sua *Metaphysica,* investigat ex hoc motore qui est pars moventis seipsum, alium motorem separatum omnino, qui est Deus" (see in his discussion of the "secunda via," the par. "sed quia"; ed. Leonina manualis [Rome, 1934], p. 14). For Owens's discussion of this see his "Aquinas and the Proof from the 'Physics,'" pp. 132–37. Note in particular his concluding comment with respect to the treatment in SCG I, 13: "Here in the same chapter the interpretations of the argument as leading in the *Physics* to a sphere soul and to God occur side by side, without any feeling of embarrassment being shown by the writer" (p. 137). For a different interpretation of the same see Pegis, "St. Thomas and the Coherence of the Aristotelian Theology," pp. 78–86, 108–12. As already noted above (see n. 52), Pegis maintains that for Thomas, in proving the existence of the prime mover in the *Physics* Aristotle was proving the existence of God. Owens, on the other hand, finds no definite indication that Thomas himself thought that a demonstration on the level of natural philosophy can prove God's existence (p. 149). For his view that the "first way" of ST I, q. 2, a. 3 is metaphysical rather than pertaining to the philosophy of nature see his "The Conclusion of the Prima Via," *The Modern Schoolman* 30 (January 1953), pp. 109–21.

63. Thomas's texts from his Commentary on *Metaphysics* VI and XI do imply that if there were no immaterial, immutable, and separate entity, physics would be first philosophy (see nn. 1163, 1164, 1169, 1170, 2266, 2267). Hence, if this does indeed reflect Thomas's personal view rather than his interpretation of Aristotle, knowledge of an immanent and self-moving principle of change, that is, a sphere soul, will be no more adequate than knowledge of the human soul.

and separate being exists to the possibility of considering being as being rather than as material, changeable, and immanent, appeal to such an immanent mover will be of little avail.

Before concluding this historical investigation, it is incumbent upon me to consider one final point. There can be little doubt that Thomas frequently enough recommends that one move from a study of physics to metaphysics when he discusses the order of learning. This fact might be raised against the interpretation just proposed and in support of the claim that for Aquinas both *separatio* and the very possibility of metaphysics presuppose the conclusions of physics. Although limitations of space will not permit detailed consideration of each of these passages, some general remarks are in order. In the interests of simplification, one might divide these texts into two general categories: (1) those based on the incapacity of the learner, when too young, to learn metaphysics; (2) those treating of the relationship between metaphysics and other intellectual disciplines, especially physics (natural philosophy).[64]

One of the finest illustrations of the first is to be found in Thomas's Commentary on Bk. VI of Aristotle's *Ethics*. Aristotle's query as to why a boy may become a mathematician but not a wise man or a philosopher of nature serves as the occasion for Thomas's reflections.[65] Thomas takes the term "wise man" to refer to a metaphysician. He begins by expanding on Aristotle's reply. Mathematicals are grasped by abstraction from sensible things of which even a boy (*puer*) has awareness. But natural principles are not simply abstracted from sensible things but are acquired by experience, for which considerable time is required. As regards wisdom, continues Thomas, Aristotle observes that young men (*iuvenes*)[66] do not attain metaphysical truths with their minds even though they may verbally utter them. In support of this Thomas also comments that mathematical definitions (*rationes*) pertain to things that can be imagined, whereas those of wisdom (metaphysics) are purely intelligible. If young men (*iuvenes*) can grasp that which is imaginable, they find it difficult to attain that which exceeds this level.[67]

64. On this see G. Klubertanz, "St. Thomas on Learning Metaphysics," *Gregorianum* 35 (1954), pp. 3–17. Also see his "The Teaching of Thomistic Metaphysics," *Gregorianum* 35 (1954), pp. 187–205.

65. For Aristotle see *Ethics* VI, ch. 8 (1142a16ff.).

66. On the meanings to be assigned to the terms *puer* and *iuvenis* in Thomas's usage see Klubertanz, "St. Thomas on Learning Metaphysics," pp. 5–8.

67. *In VI Ethic.*, lect. 7 (Spiazzi ed. [Turin: Marietti, 1964], nn. 1209–10). Note in particular: "Iuvenes autem de facili capere possunt ea quae sub imaginatione cadunt. Sed ad illa quae excedunt sensum et imaginationem non attingunt mente, quia

With this background in mind, then, Thomas proposes the following order for learning. Boys (*pueri*) should first be instructed in logic, and then in mathematics. They should then study natural things (natural philosophy presumably). For while natural things do not transcend the level of sense and imagination, knowledge of them does require experience. Then only should they be introduced to moral science, and last of all, to wisdom and the study of divine things which transcend the imagination and require a powerful intellect.[68] One finds a similar progression of disciplines reported by Thomas in his Commentary on the *Liber de causis*.[69] But in both of these texts the concern appears to be pedagogical, that is to say, with the gradually developing capacities of the learning subject. There is no indication that one should study metaphysics after natural philosophy because the former depends upon the latter for knowledge of its starting point. Hence texts

---

nondum habent intellectum exercitatum ad tales considerationes, tum propter parvitatem temporis, tum propter plurimas mutationes naturae."

68. *Ibid.,* n. 1211. "Erit ergo congruus ordo addiscendi ut primo quidem pueri logicalibus instruantur, quia logica docet modum totius philosophiae. Secundo autem instruendi sunt in mathematicis quae nec experientia indigent, nec imaginationem transcendunt. Tertio autem in naturalibus; quae etsi non excedunt sensum et imaginationem, requirunt tamen experientiam. Quarto in moralibus quae requirunt experientiam et animum a passionibus liberum, ut in primo habitum est. Quinto autem in sapientialibus et divinis quae transcendunt imaginationem et requirunt validum intellectum." That this text does reflect Thomas's own view and not merely his interpretation of Aristotle's thought is indicated both by the fact that it is an addition to the text being commented on and by comparison with Thomas's correlation of sense, imagination, and intellect with physics, mathematics, and divine science in terms of their respective levels of termination in his Commentary on the *De Trinitate,* q. 6, a. 2, *passim.*

69. Here Thomas presents the same learning order as that which the philosophers themselves had followed: "Et inde est quod philosophorum intentio ad hoc principaliter erat ut, per omnia quae in rebus considerabant, ad cognitionem primarum causarum pervenirent. Unde scientiam de primis causis ultimo ordinabant, cuius considerationi ultimum tempus suae vitae deputarent: primo quidem incipientes a logica quae modum scientiarum tradit, secundo procedentes ad mathematicam cuius etiam pueri possunt esse capaces, tertio ad naturalem philosophiam quae propter experientiam tempore indiget, quarto autem ad moralem philosophiam cuius iuvenis esse conveniens auditor non potest, ultimo autem scientiae divinae insistebant quae considerat primas entium causas." *Sancti Thomae de Aquino super Librum de causis expositio,* H. D. Saffrey, ed. (Fribourg-Louvain, 1954), p. 2. For an interesting discussion as to how Thomas would apply the order recommended by the text cited in n. 68 above to medieval pre-theological students, see Klubertanz, "St. Thomas on Learning Metaphysics," pp. 14–16. Klubertanz (p. 5, n. 3) lists some other texts on the difficulty of learning metaphysics or which assign it to last place. Of these see *In Isaiam,* ch. 3; SCG I, ch.4; *In I Met.,* lect. 2, n. 46.

such as these surely do not point to an essential or intrinsic dependency of metaphysics upon the conclusions of physics, and especially not with respect to discovery of the subject of metaphysics, being as being as attained by *separatio*.

Other texts treat of the relationship that obtains between metaphysics, on the one hand, and other disciplines, especially natural philosophy, on the other. One of the fullest is to be found in q. 5, a. 1 of Thomas's Commentary on the *De Trinitate* of Boethius, hence in that same work wherein he was to develop and present his views on *separatio*. There, in replying to the ninth objection, he writes:

> Although divine science is by nature the first of all the sciences, with respect to us the other sciences come before it. For, as Avicenna says, the position of this science is that it be learned after the natural sciences, which explain many things used by metaphysics, such as generation, corruption, motion, and the like. It should also be learned after mathematics, because to know the separate substances metaphysics has to know the number and dispositions of the heavenly spheres, and this is impossible without astronomy, which presupposes the whole of mathematics. Other sciences, such as music, ethics, and the like, contribute to its fullness of perfection.[70]

Reference has already been made above in Chapter II to this passage and the immediately following lines in order to illustrate Thomas's usage of Avicenna therein.[71] Even so, I find no reason to deny that this text does represent Thomas's personal view. According to this text, therefore, divine science (metaphysics) is to be learned after the other sciences, though it is by nature first of all the sciences. Following Avicenna's lead, Thomas notes that it is to be learned after the natural sciences in which various things are determined which this science (first philosophy) uses. Avicenna had listed the following illustrations: generation, corruption, alteration, place and time, the axiom that whatever is moved is moved by another, and an indication of those things which are moved with respect to the first mover.[72] As already noted in Chapter II, Thomas has abbreviated Avicenna's list and omitted therefrom explicit mention of alteration, place and time, the axiom of motion, and the first mover. After citing generation and corruption he simply mentions motion and other things of this kind. For our

70. Maurer trans., pp. 16–17. For the Latin see Decker ed., p. 172:3–12; cited in my Ch. II above, pp. 42, 44.

71. See Ch. II, pp. 42–49.

72. For Avicenna see his *Metaphysics* (*Philosophia prima*), Bk. I, ch. 3 (Van Riet ed., pp. 20–21), cited above in Ch. II, p. 42.

immediate purposes it is important to note that Thomas does not say that metaphysics derives knowledge of its subject-matter and/or justifies *separatio* by relying on the philosophy of nature.[73]

Thomas has also indicated that metaphysics should be studied after mathematics. A knowledge of astronomy and hence of mathematics is required to enable one to arrive at knowledge of the number and of the order of the separate substances and therefore of the heavenly spheres. Again there is no indication that metaphysics depends on mathematics for knowledge of its starting point, being as being, or in order to justify *separatio*. Thomas's remarks about music, ethics, and the like obviously do not point to formal or intrinsic dependence of metaphysics upon these disciplines.

Then, in continuing dependency upon Avicenna, Thomas refutes the charge of circularity that might seem to follow from admitting that metaphysics both proves the principles of the other sciences and yet borrows some points from them. In his discussion of this he concentrates on the relationship between metaphysics and natural science. Reference has already been made in Chapter II to Thomas's reply. No vicious circle is involved because the principles which natural science receives from first philosophy are not used to prove those points which the first philosopher takes from the natural philosopher. Without repeating here the detailed analysis of this passage already offered in Chapter II, it will be enough for us to note one point.[74] There is no indication in this text that first philosophy derives its starting point or its subject from natural philosophy, or that *separatio* depends upon natural philosophy's proof of a First Mover. Indeed, if such were implied by this text, one might well wonder whether or not the charge of a vicious circle had been evaded. One would have to show that the argument for the First Mover in physics did not itself employ principles derived from and proven in metaphysics and therefore dependent on prior knowledge of being in general or of the subject of metaphysics.

In what appears to be another refutation of the charge of circularity, Thomas then introduces some further precisions:

> Moreover, the sensible effects on which the demonstrations of
> natural science are based are more evident to us in the beginning.
> But when we come to know the first causes through them, these

73. See Ch. II above, pp. 42–43. Given all of this, Klubertanz's remark is pertinent: "This text is as interesting for what it does not say as for what it says . . . . St. Thomas does *not* say that metaphysics receives its object from the philosophy of nature" ("St. Thomas on Learning Metaphysics," p. 10).

74. Decker ed., p. 172:13–20. For discussion of two different ways in which this passage might be interpreted and for fuller justification of the reading followed here see Ch. II above, pp. 45–48.

causes will reveal to us the reason for the effects, from which they were proved by a demonstration *quia*. In this way natural science also contributes something to divine science, and nevertheless it is divine science that explains its principles. That is why Boethius places divine science last, because it is the last relative to us.[75]

Here Thomas reasons that the demonstrations of natural science are based on sensible effects, and that such effects are more evident to us in the beginning. He suggests that one can reason to knowledge of the "first causes" by means of these effects and that, having done so, knowledge of such causes will reveal the reason for the effects. Thus natural science contributes something to divine science, and at the same time the former's principles are explained by the latter.

One might wonder what it is that natural science contributes to divine science, merely some knowledge of the sensible effects on which its (divine science's) demonstrations are based, or also the discovery of the first cause by means of these effects.[76] It seems that the text could be interpreted either

---

75. *Ibid.*, pp. 172:21–173:4. "Praetera, effectus sensibiles, ex quibus procedunt demonstrationes naturales, sunt notiores quoad nos in principio, sed cum per eos pervenerimus ad cognitionem causarum primarum, ex eis apparebit nobis propter quid illorum effectuum, ex quibus probabantur demonstratione quia. Et sic et scientia naturalis aliquid tradit scientiae divinae, et tamen per eam sua principia notificantur. Et inde est quod Boethius ultimo ponit scientiam divinam, quia est ultima quoad nos." Maurer trans., pp. 17–18.

76. As Owens has pointed out, the text states that it is through these sensible effects that one reaches knowledge of the first causes. "The text does not say that the first causes are reached by the demonstrations of natural philosophy." See his "Aquinas and the Proof from the 'Physics,'" p. 131. According to Owens: "In Aristotle, the separate substances are reached in metaphysics, in a process of reasoning that takes its starting point from the demonstrations of the eternity of the cosmic motion in natural philosophy." In this Peripatetic setting, natural philosophy would be of necessary help to metaphysics. But Thomas here uses the "neutral phrasing of 'first causes' instead of 'separate substances', " and hence can view the argumentation from sensible effects both as leading to first causes and as permitting natural philosophy to contribute something to metaphysics (pp. 131–32). Owens's interpretation, if correct, would square nicely with the view that we have found elsewhere in Aquinas, that it is the business of metaphysics by metaphysical reasoning to establish the existence of the cause(s) or principle(s) of its subject. Still, one might take this text as implying that one may reason from sensible effects to a knowledge of first causes in natural philosophy itself. For this reading see Ch. II above, p. 49. Viewed in itself, the text appears to be open to either interpretation. If one assumes that by "first causes" in this discussion Thomas has in mind God, then of course the issue touched on above reappears, that is, whether the First Mover established in natural philosophy is to be identified, in Thomas's eyes, with the Unmoved Mover of the *Metaphysics* (God). Without attempting to resolve that issue, however, it seems to me that neither interpretation of this passage forces one to conclude that Thomas would require a physical demonstration of the First Mover in order for one to begin metaphysics.

way. If natural science only contributes knowledge of those sensible effects which are then used by the metaphysician in his reasoning to the existence of first causes, there would be no evidence in this passage for thinking that Thomas would ground the starting point of metaphysics on natural philosophy's demonstration of the First Mover. But if the demonstration *quia* or discovery of first causes is itself assigned to natural philosophy by this text, some doubt might remain. Still, even if one interprets it in this way, there is no indication here that metaphysics depends on natural philosophy's demonstration of a First Mover in order to *begin* its own investigations and, therefore, in order to establish its starting point, being as being. Hence, according to neither reading should this text be so construed. At most it might imply that in addition to receiving some help from natural philosophy with respect to the items Thomas had earlier mentioned, metaphysics might benefit from the latter when it comes to *scientia quia* with respect to knowledge of the existence of (the) first cause(s). If one interprets it in the first way indicated above, not even this implication will follow from this passage. In sum, therefore, Thomas's reply to the ninth objection does not imply that metaphysics must receive its subject-matter from natural philosophy or that the demonstration of the First Mover by the latter is a necessary condition for the metaphysician to discover being as being or for *separatio*.[77]

77. Klubertanz distinguishes between the part of metaphysics that deals with being and its immediate principles, and that part which treats of God. "With the possible exception of one point (that there are distinct kinds of change), the philosophy of nature is not a necessary presupposition" for the first part. But some conclusions of the philosophy of nature are "necessarily presupposed" for the second part. He cites the points listed by Avicenna and suggests that they are necessary for establishing certain "negative attributes of spiritual substances, such as the immutability, immensity, and eternity of God" (p. 13). For knowledge of separate substances he also suggests that Thomas would presuppose knowledge of the human intellect and cites *In I De anima,* lect. 1 (A. Pirotta, ed. [Turin: Marietti, 1959], n. 7): "Quia si ad Philosophiam primam attendamus, non possumus devenire in cognitionem divinarum et altissimarum causarum, nisi per ea quae ex virtute intellectus possibilis acquirimus. Si enim natura intellectus possibilis esset nobis ignota, non possemus scire ordinem substantiarum separatarum, sicut dicit Commentator super *undecimo Metaphysicae.*" While acknowledging that there are Aristotelian physical arguments in support of the axiom of motion and with respect to the things immediately moved by the First Mover (see Avicenna's list of physics' contributions to metaphysics), there are also metaphysical arguments for the same. It is to the metaphysical argumentation that Thomas turns, continues Klubertanz, except when he is "expounding the *Physics*"(p. 13). The fact that Thomas did not list these particular items in his abbreviation of Avicenna makes me wonder whether he would indeed agree that metaphysics must borrow them from physics. But I am in fullest agreement with Klubertanz's contention that Thomas does not base his metaphysics on the philosophy of nature (p. 17). To determine Thomas's mind on this point is, of course, a major purpose of the present inquiry.

It is true that in discussing the reasons for entitling this science "metaphysics" Thomas writes that it comes "to us after physics among subjects to be learned; for we have to proceed from sensible things to those that are non-sensible" (Commentary on the *De Trinitate* of Boethius, q. 5, a. 1).[78] In q. 6, a. 1 of this same work he observes that this science is learned after physics and the other sciences because intellectual consideration is the terminus of rational consideration. Hence it is called "metaphysics" or *trans physicam* because it comes after physics according to the process of analysis (*resolutio*).[79] This reference to analysis or resolution reappears in the *Prooemium* to his Commentary on the *Metaphysics*. Here he writes that this science is called "metaphysics" because it considers being and its properties; for these transphysicals are discovered by the process of resolution just as the more universal is discovered after the less universal.[80]

But it should also be recalled that in q. 5, a. 1 of the Commentary on the *De Trinitate* he refers to it as "first philosophy" insofar as the other sciences, deriving their principles from it, follow after it.[81] Again in q. 6, a. 1 of this same work, he names it first philosophy for this same reason and, insofar as according to the process of composition or synthesis, intellectual consideration (which he has there associated especially with this science) is the "principle" of rational consideration (which he has associated with natural philosophy).[82] These discussions obviously involve the difficult issue to which Thomas addressed himself in replying to the ninth objection of q. 5, a. 1 of the Commentary on the *De Trinitate,* that is, the different ways in which metaphysics can derive certain points from the other sciences and still contribute principles to the same. The distinction between resolution (analysis) and composition (synthesis) is also of importance with respect to that issue. But these passages do not state or imply that metaphysics must receive knowledge of the existence of the First or Unmoved Mover from physics so as to be able to discover its own subject, being as being, by means of *separatio*.[83]

78. Maurer trans., pp. 8–9. See the Decker ed., p. 166:2–4: "quae alio nomine dicitur metaphysica, id est trans physicam, quia post physicam discenda occurrit nobis, quibus ex sensibilibus oportet in insensibilia devenire."

79. Decker ed., p. 212:22–25.

80. "Haec enim transphysica inveniuntur in via resolutionis, sicut magis communia post minus communia" (p. 2).

81. Decker ed., p. 166:4–6.

82. *Ibid.,* p. 212:20–22.

83. For discussion of the different reasons offered by Thomas for entitling this science "first philosophy" in the Commentary on the *De Trinitate,* on the one hand, and in the Commentary on the *Metaphysics,* on the other, and his use of the distinction between resolution and composition with respect to the same, see Ch. III above, *passim*.

In sum, therefore, in Thomas's mind there were strong pedagogical indications suggesting that metaphysics be studied after physics. As regards
the order of learning, one should move from the easier to the more difficult,
from the more concrete to the more abstract, from the more particular to
the more universal. Moreover, certain points developed by physics might
be of value to particular areas of metaphysical investigation. Nonetheless,
with the exception of the difficult texts drawn from his Commentary on
Metaphysics VI and XI and analyzed above, I have not found Thomas
stating or implying that one must presuppose the existence of positively immaterial being in order to begin metaphysics. On the contrary, such a suggestion is countered by his own view that it is the business of metaphysics to
reason to the existence of the principles of its subject. Far from presupposing the existence of an Unmoved Mover or of God as given to it by physics,
his personal view rather is that it is the task and goal of metaphysics to establish the same. Hence one may conclude that it is historically defensible
to suggest that for Aquinas the possibility of metaphysics and, therefore,
the possibility of *separatio* need not rest on a prior demonstration of a First
Mover or Unmoved Mover in physics. Those texts just referred to from his
Commentary on *Metaphysics* VI and XI that point to the opposite should,
therefore, in my opinion, be viewed as his interpretation of Aristotle's text
but not as his personal view.

III

If the above is a historically defensible interpretation of Thomas's personal thought on *separatio* and the subject of metaphysics, another and more
speculative issue remains. Within the framework of his metaphysical perspective is it possible for one to make a grounded judgment of separation,
to distinguish that by reason of which something is described as being from
that by reason of which it is described as being of a given kind, without
presupposing prior awareness that positively immaterial being exists in fact?

In considering this issue, certain points should be recalled. First of all,
one is interested in arriving at an understanding of being as being that
might serve as subject of a science of being as being rather than at an understanding of being that is restricted to the material and changeable. Secondly,
according to Thomas himself, it is quite possible for one to study material
being in metaphysics, not insofar as it is subject to change, but insofar as it
is being.[84] Thirdly, when giving what one may regard as illustrations of

---

84. See *In VI Met.*, n. 1165: "Advertendum est autem, quod licet ad considerationem primae philosophiae pertineant ea quae sunt separata secundum esse et

separatio, Thomas at times implies that things discovered thereby are without matter and motion. At other times he writes that they can be without matter and motion.[85] It is my contention that awareness of the latter (the negatively immaterial) is sufficient for him to arrive at a metaphysical understanding of being, which will serve as subject of the science in question. Finally, recourse to prior knowledge of the existence of a spiritual human soul, or even of a besouled first mover of the universe will not of itself be sufficient to prove that being, in order to be such, need not be material and *changing.* In short, if one can only justify separation by moving from prior awareness that the kind of being pointed to by this judgment does in fact exist, appeal to spiritual but changing being will not, of itself, prove that being, in order to be such, need not be changing.

Given these considerations, then, I would invite the reader to reflect upon the distinctive intelligibilities implied by two different kinds of questions that may be raised. One question searches for that by reason of which something may be recognized as being or as real. Another searches for that by reason of which something is recognized as a given kind of being. If one is justified in distinguishing these two questions and therefore these two intelligibilities from one another, one should then be in position to make this judgment: that by reason of which something is recognized as being need not be identified with or restricted to that by reason of which it is recognized as being of a given kind. (In fact, to deny this would be to deny that there can be different kinds of being, a conclusion that runs counter to our experience of different kinds of being, for instance, nonliving beings, living beings, canine beings, human beings, etc.) But to be recognized as material and changing is to be recognized as enjoying a given kind of being. Therefore, being, in order to be recognized as such, need not be recognized as material and changing. Here, then, one has formulated a negative judgment or *separatio,* and one should now be in position to study being simply as being rather than as nonliving or living or canine or human or as material and changing. The fact that one can, according to Thomas, study any kind of being, including material being, in metaphysics suggests that this procedure is not at odds with his understanding of the conditions required to ground the science in question.

---

rationem a materia et motu, non tamen solum ea; sed etiam de sensibilibus, inquantum sunt entia, Philosophus perscrutatur. Nisi forte dicamus, ut Avicenna dicit, quod huiusmodi communia de quibus haec scientia perscrutatur, dicuntur separata secundum esse, non quia semper sint sine materia; sed quia non de necessitate habent esse in materia, sicut mathematica."

85. See the texts from q. 5, a. 3 of the Commentary on the *De Trinitate* cited above in nn. 22, 28, and 29; and from q. 5, a. 4 of the same work, as cited in nn. 58 and 59.

In light of this negative judgment, therefore, it would seem that in order for being to be realized as such, it need not be realized as material and changing. At the least *separatio* will have indicated that, insofar as one can determine, there is nothing within the intelligible content of being as such to imply that it must be material. This, of course, will not be enough to prove that any positively immaterial being does in fact exist. But if in the subsequent course of one's metaphysical investigations one concludes to the existence of an immaterial and unchanging being, one will then be justified in predicating being of it, albeit analogically. According to Aquinas, however, one should not even then conclude that such an unchanging (and divine) being falls under *ens commune* — the proper subject of metaphysics. Such a being can be studied by metaphysics only indirectly, as the principle or cause of that which does fall under its subject-matter — *ens commune*.[86] And this understanding of being as being — initially achieved by *separatio* — need not itself presuppose previous knowledge of the existence of the human soul or of the First Mover of the *Physics* and/or of God.[87]

86. This point is clearly implied by the reasoning of q. 5, a. 4 of Thomas's Commentary on the *De Trinitate,* and by the *Prooemium* to his Commentary on the *Metaphysics.* Cf. in his Commentary on the *Divine Names:* " . . . omnia existentia continentur sub ipso esse communi, non autem Deus, sed magis esse commune continetur sub eius virtute." *In Librum Beati Dionysii De divinis nominibus expositio,* C. Pera, ed. (Turin-Rome, 1950), n. 660. See the immediately surrounding context for further discussion of God and *esse commune.* Also see ST I-IIae, q. 66, a. 5, ad 4. There, while defending the view that wisdom is a greater virtue than *intellectus,* Thomas writes: "Cognoscere autem rationem entis et non entis, et totius et partis, et aliorum quae consequuntur ad ens, ex quibus sicut ex terminis constituuntur principia indemonstrabilia, pertinet ad sapientiam: quia ens commune est proprius effectus causae altissimae, scilicet Dei." If *ens commune* is a proper effect of God, the highest cause, then God cannot be included under *ens commune.* For more on this see Zimmermann, *Ontologie oder Metaphysik?,* pp. 173–80. Also see Zimmermann's discussion of the relationship between created separate substances and the subject of metaphysics in that same context.

87. Most if not all of the authors cited above who find Aquinas grounding the very possibility of metaphysics and of *separatio* on prior knowledge that positively immaterial being exists would, of course, differ with my position. On the other hand, Klubertanz appears to go to the opposite extreme: "Hence, it is illusory to attempt to base a knowledge of being as being on the demonstrated existence of immaterial things. Either 'is' is freed from its sensible and changing context (prior to the proof of the existence of immaterial being, and thus is meaningful when we conclude to the existence of such being) or 'is' remains as we first find it immersed in sensibility and change. In the latter case, 'is' means 'is sensible, material and changeable', and to assert that 'An *immaterial, immobile* thing is *sensible, material and changeable'* is a contradiction" (*Introduction to the Philosophy of Being,* p. 52, n. 28). In my opinion it may be possible for one to reason from knowledge of the existence of positively immaterial and immobile being to the discovery of being as being (against Klubertanz), but this is not the only way of discovering being as being (in agreement with Klubertanz here and against the more traditional view).

PART II

THE METAPHYSICS OF CREATED
AND UNCREATED BEING

CHAPTER V

ESSENCE AND EXISTENCE IN THE *DE ENTE,* CH. 4

This brief chapter from one of Aquinas's earliest works has occasioned much disagreement on the part of commentators not only with respect to the validity of the argumentation found therein, but also with respect to Thomas's purpose in penning the same. Thus it is often contended that in this chapter he offers an argument based on one's understanding of essence (*intellectus essentiae* argument) in support of real distinction or real composition of essence and existence in creatures.[1] Not only is the validity of this argumentation contested by many, but some maintain that it was not even intended by its author to establish such real distinction or composition.[2] In a subsequent phase of what appears, at least at first sight, to be continued argumentation for this same distinction and composition, reference is made to the impossibility of there being more than one being in which essence and existence are identical. Surprisingly, the importance of this part of Thomas's argumentation is passed over lightly or even ignored by many commentators.

Immediately thereafter Thomas offers what seems to be a philosophical argument for God's existence. One might wonder whether or not this argument

---

1. For discussion of this argument see C. Fabro, *La nozione metafisica di partecipazione,* 2d ed. (Turin, 1950), pp. 218-19; U. Degl'Innocenti, "La distinzione reale nel 'De ente et essentia' di S. Tommaso," *Doctor Communis* 10 (1957), pp. 165-73; L. Sweeney, "Existence/Essence in Thomas Aquinas's Early Writings," *Proceedings of the American Catholic Philosophical Association* 37 (1963), pp. 105-9 (Sweeney lists passages from other early works where the *intellectus essentiae* approach is also found); J. Bobik, *Aquinas on Being and Essence* (Notre Dame, Ind., 1965), pp. 162-70; J. Owens, "Quiddity and Real Distinction in St. Thomas Aquinas," *Mediaeval Studies* 27 (1965), pp. 1-22 (see n. 2 of Owens's study for further references); A. Maurer, *St. Thomas Aquinas, On Being and Essence* (Toronto, 1968), pp. 21ff.

2. See Maurer, *op. cit.,* pp. 22-23; Owens, *op. cit.,* pp. 12-14. As Owens also indicates in note 2, A. Forest denies that this argument leads to real distinction of essence and existence. See his *La structure métaphysique du concret selon saint Thomas d'Aquin,* 2d ed. (Paris, 1956), pp. 148-49.

of itself presupposes real distinction and/or composition of essence and existence as its point of departure. It could hardly do so, of course, for those who deny that it was Thomas's intention to establish such distinction and/or composition in the preceding sentences. According to one interpretation it is only after having established God's existence by means of this argument that Thomas is in a position to conclude to real distinction of essence and existence in creatures.[3] According to another view, what appears to be an argument for God's existence is really not intended by Thomas to serve as such after all.[4] Given these varied interpretations of one and the same text, therefore, further clarification seems to be desirable with respect to Thomas's intent in writing this chapter. Hopefully, the following remarks will contribute in some way to this.

For the sake of context, it will be recalled that Thomas begins this chapter by announcing as his purpose an examination of essence as it is found in separate substances, that is, in the soul, in intelligences, and in the First Cause.[5] While all acknowledge the simplicity of the First Cause, he continues, some endeavor to introduce composition of form and matter into intelligences and into the soul. He suggests that Avicebron (Ibn Gabirol) is responsible for this theory in his *Fons vitae*. Thomas then observes that this view, that separate substances are composed of matter and form, is generally rejected by the philosophers. Thomas apparently agrees with them in holding that the strongest argument against admission of such composition in separate substances rests upon the fact that they are equipped with the ability to understand. After developing this point in some detail he concludes that there is no matter-form composition in the soul or in intelligences. But there is, he immediately adds, composition of form and existence (*esse*). In fact, he cites the *Liber de causis* in his support.[6]

---

3. See Owens, pp. 15–19. Note his remark on p. 19: "The foregoing considerations make clear that the real distinction between essence and existence cannot be known prior to the demonstration of the existence of God."

4. E. Gilson, "La preuve du 'De ente et essentia,'" *Acta III Congressus Thomistici Internationalis: Doctor Communis* 3 (Turin, 1950), pp. 257–60; "Trois leçons sur le problème de l'existence de Dieu," *Divinitas* 5 (1961), pp. 26–28.

5. "Nunc restat videre per quem modum sit essentia in substantiis separatis, scilicet in anima et in intelligentia et in causa prima." *Le 'De ente et essentia" de s. Thomas d'Aquin*, ed. M. D. Roland-Gosselin, repr. (Paris, 1948), pp. 29:32–30:1. Citations will be from this edition but as checked against the Leonine edition. For which see *Sancti Thomae de Aquino opera omnia*, Vol. 43, p. 375. Nonsubstantive differences will not be noted.

6. Roland-Gosselin ed., pp. 30:1–32:6/Leonine ed., pp. 375:3–376:40. For Thomas's reference to the *De causis* see: "Sed est ibi composicio forme et esse; unde in

Thomas then argues for the plausibility of this view, that intelligences are composed of form (essence) and existence, by noting that it is form that gives existence to matter, not vice versa. Therefore, while it is impossible for one to find matter without some form, it is not impossible for there to be some form without matter. In a separated substance, therefore, the essence or quiddity will be identical with the form itself, while in a composite substance the essence includes both form and matter.[7]

After isolating two further differences that will obtain between the essences of simple substances and those of composites, Thomas suggests that while simple substances are forms alone without matter, their simplicity is not so great as to free them from all potentiality and thus render them pure act.[8] The importance of this text should be emphasized because in it Thomas indicates his purpose in introducing the subsequent argumentation, that is, to show that substances whose essences are not composed of matter and form are not so simple as to be identical with Pure Act. It seems, therefore, that he is going to have to establish the presence of some kind of mixture of act and potency, some kind of composition in such entities, if he is to maintain his thesis. Since he then immediately introduces what appears to be argumentation for distinction ("otherness") of essence and existence, the distinction and composition for which he is about to argue must be sufficient, in his eyes, to eliminate total simplicity from such entities. In short, if the nonsimplicity he is about to defend in such entities is not purely logical or conceptual but obtains in some way in the order of reality, it would seem that the distinction and composition of essence and existence that he proposes therein should also be more than logical or conceptual. Merely logical or conceptual composition of such entities will hardly be sufficient for him to support his claim, that such entities are not in fact pure actualities. It would seem, then, that it was his intention in the subsequent argumentation to establish some kind of real distinction and composition of essence and existence in separate substances. Acknowledgment of this point does not, however, necessarily show that the first argument or

---

commento none propositionis libri *De causis* dicitur quod intelligentia est habens formam et esse; et accipitur ibi forma pro ipsa quiditate vel natura simplici" (Roland-Gosselin, p. 32:2–6/Leonine, p. 376:36–40). For the text from the *De causis* see the edition by A. Pattin, published by the *Tijdschrift voor Filosofie,* p. 69: "Et intelligentia est habens *yliathim* quoniam est esse et forma . . . . "

7. Roland-Gosselin ed., pp. 32:7–33:18/Leonine, p. 376:41–65.

8. "Huiusmodi autem substantie, quamvis sint forme tantum sine materia, non tamen in eis est omnimoda simplicitas naturae ut sint actus purus, set habent permixtionem potencie, et hoc sic patet" (p. 34:4–7/Leonine, p. 376:90–93).

the first phase of his argumentation results or was even intended to result in such real composition and distinction.[9]

Here, then, Thomas introduces the first phase of that argumentation, the well-known *intellectus essentiae* approach. Whatever is not included in the notion of an essence or quiddity comes to it from without and enters into composition with it. But every essence or quiddity can be understood without anything being understood with respect to its existence (*esse*). Therefore, existence is distinct from essence unless, he adds, there is something whose quiddity is its existence.[10] Here it seems that the first phase of the argumentation ends.

In support of the major, the contention that whatever is not included in the notion of an essence or quiddity comes to it from without and enters into composition with it, Thomas observes that no essence can be understood without those things which are parts of the essence.[11] And in support of the minor, that an essence or quiddity can be understood without its existence also being understood, Thomas appeals to two examples. One can understand what a man is, or what a phoenix is, without knowing whether it exists in reality.[12]

9. Fabro distinguishes three arguments in the text that follows and suggests that the first (the *intellectus essentiae* argument) is logical in nature, while the other two are metaphysical. As he divides the text the second argument is based on the impossibility of there being more than one *ipsum esse subsistens,* while the third reasons from the fact that the *esse* of the creature is extrinsically caused and ends by applying the Aristotelian act-potency couplet to the relationship between essence and *esse.* See his *La nozione metafisica* . . . , pp. 218–20. Also see his "Un itinéraire de saint Thomas: l'établissement de la distinction réelle entre essence et existence," *Revue de philosophie* 39 (1939), pp. 285–310. One might regard these as three arguments or perhaps more accurately as three phases of one continuous argumentation.

10. "Quicquid enim non est de intellectu essentie vel quiditatis hoc est adveniens extra et faciens compositionem cum essentia . . . . Omnis autem essentia vel quiditas potest intelligi sine hoc quod aliquid intelligatur de esse suo . . . . Ergo patet quod esse est aliud ab essentia vel quiditate. Nisi forte sit aliqua res cuius quiditas sit ipsum suum esse" (*op. cit.,* p. 34:7–16/Leonine ed., p. 376:94–104).

11. " . . . quia nulla essentia sine hiis que sunt partes essentie intelligi potest" (p. 34:9–10/Leonine ed., p. 376:96–97).

12. " . . . possum enim intelligere quid est homo vel fenix et tamen ignorare an esse habeat in rerum natura" (p. 34:12–14/Leonine ed., p. 376:100–101). For interesting discussions of the proper translation of *ignorare* in the text just cited see R. Masiello, "A Note on Essence and Existence," *The New Scholasticism* 45 (1971), pp. 491–94 and J. Owens, "'Ignorare' and Existence," *The New Scholasticism* 46 (1972), pp. 210–19. Masiello contends that the text cited in n. 12 above should be rendered: "I can know what a man is or a phoenix, and yet I can ignore (i.e., leave out of consideration) whether they have existence in the nature of things" (p. 491). Owens argues in part from parallel passages in Thomas's Commentary on the *Sentences* and concludes that the more common meaning of *ignorare* should be retained for this passage: "I can know what a man is or a phoenix, and yet not know whether he has

It would seem that the term "understand" is being taken here to signify fairly comprehensive knowledge, the kind that is sufficient for one to grasp a thing's essence and, therefore, its essential parts. One might wonder whether Thomas would in other contexts concede such knowledge to us either with respect to the essences of separate substances or with respect to those of sensible substances. He has here just stated, it will be recalled, that every (*omnis*) essence or quiddity can be understood without its existence also being understood. In other contexts dating more or less from this same period in his career, Thomas greatly restricts man's capacity to arrive at knowledge of the essences of immaterial substances.[13] Perhaps this is why he here turns to sensible substances, one fictitious (phoenix) and one real (man), in offering evidence for his minor. But even in the case of sensible substances Thomas is reluctant to admit that one can arrive at knowledge of them that penetrates to their specific differences. Hence, one might still wonder whether, in his view, merely generic knowledge of such a corporeal

---

being in reality" (p. 214). He finds this translation more consistent with the logic of the paragraph (pp. 215-16). As to possible sources for Thomas's argumentation here, Avicenna's general influence on the *De ente* and on this chapter has been highlighted by others (see, for instance, Roland-Gosselin, *op. cit.*, p. 187; A. Forest, *op. cit.*, pp. 148ff.; F. Van Steenberghen, "Le problème de l'existence de Dieu dans le 'De ente et essentia' de saint Thomas d'Aquin," *Mélanges Joseph De Ghellinck, S. J.* [Gembloux, 1951], pp. 837-47). William of Auvergne's influence as a source for Thomas in writing this particular chapter and even this particular argument has also been stressed. See Roland-Gosselin, p. 187; Van Steenberghen, *op. cit.*, p. 840; and Maurer, *op. cit.*, pp. 23-24. For another likely source wherein both man and phoenix appear as examples, see the following from Algazel: "Similiter, cum intelligis, quid est homo, non est necesse te intelligere eum esse vel esse album. Nec tamen potes eum intelligere, nisi intelligas quod est animal; quamvis non satisfaciat tuo intellectui hoc exemplum, eo quod tu es homo et omnes alii qui nunc sunt. Pone ergo aliud exemplum—sicut de phoenice vel de aliquo alio extraneo—et ibi manifestabitur tibi, quia esse accidentale est omnibus quae sunt. Animal vero essentiale est homini, similiter color nigredini et numerus quaternario." "*Logica Algazelis,* Introduction and Critical Text," ed. by C. Lohr in *Traditio* 21 (1965), p. 247:26-33. For another citation of the phoenix example, see Thomas, *In II Sent.*, d. 3, q. 1, a. 1, ed. Mandonnet (Paris, 1929), Vol. 2, p. 87: "Quaedam enim natura est de cujus intellectu non est suum esse, quod patet ex hoc quod intelligi potest esse cum hoc quod ignoretur an sit, sicut phaenicem, vel eclipsim, vel aliquid hujusmodi."

13. See, for instance, his *Expositio super librum Boethii De Trinitate*, q. 6, a. 3, especially pp. 221:7-10 and 222:21-223:5, and dating, according to J. Weisheipl, from 1258-1259. He dates the *De ente* before 1256. See his *Friar Thomas d'Aquino*, pp. 381 and 136-37; pp. 386 and 79. Not only does Thomas here deny that one can arrive at direct insight into the essence of God or of other separate substances, he also eliminates the possibility of one's attaining to some positive but obscure knowledge of their essences by knowing them in terms of their genus and accidents.

essence is sufficient to show that one can understand its essence without also being aware of its existence. Owens has connected Thomas's procedure in the present argument with his earlier discussion in the same *De ente* of the possibility that one may consider an essence or nature absolutely or in itself, without taking into account either its existence in an individual thing or its existence in the mind. In light of this Owens concludes that "merely generic knowledge of a thing as a body, therefore, amply suffices to show that the quidditative content of anything corporeal does not include existence."[14]

To return to Thomas's argument, then, let it be granted that one can have such generic knowledge of a corporeal essence without being aware that it exists. Thomas has argued that whatever is not included in one's understanding of an essence or quiddity comes to it from without and enters into composition with it. He now concludes that existence is other than essence or quiddity.[15] If this "otherness" or distinction of essence and existence is indeed real in Thomas's eyes, it would seem that he could

---

14. For Owens see his "Quiddity and Real Distinction . . . ," pp. 3–4, 6–7; and p. 7 for the citation in our text. For Thomas see the *De ente,* ch. 3, pp. 23–29, and especially pp. 24:1–26:10. Note the following: "Ergo patet quod natura hominis absolute considerata abstrahit a quolibet esse, ita tamen quod non fiat precisio alicuius eorum" (p. 26:8–10/Leonine ed., p. 374:68–70). For another interesting treatment of three ways in which nature (or essence) may be considered see Thomas's Quodlibet 8, q. 1, a. 1. There Thomas explicitly acknowledges his debt to Avicenna for this distinction: "Dicendum, quod, secundum Avicennam in sua *Metaphysica,* triplex est alicuius naturae consideratio. Una, prout consideratur secundum esse quod habet in singularibus; sicut natura lapidis in hoc lapide et in illo lapide. Alia vero est consideratio alicuius naturae secundum esse suum intelligibile; sicut natura lapidis consideratur prout est in intellectu. Tertia vero est consideratio naturae absoluta, prout abstrahit ab utroque esse; secundum quam considerationem consideratur natura lapidis, vel cuiuscumque alterius, quantum ad ea tantum quae per se competunt tali naturae." *Quaestiones quodlibetales,* ed. R. Spiazzi (Marietti: Rome-Turin, 1956), p. 158. This work also dates from Thomas's first Parisian period, that is, Christmas, 1257. See Weisheipl, *op. cit.,* p. 367. One might wonder whether this Avicennian view of the three ways in which nature may be considered continued to be so central to the later Thomas, but that issue cannot be pursued here. For more on the Avicennian background see Owens, "Common Nature: A Point of Comparison between Thomistic and Scotistic Metaphysics," *Mediaeval Studies* 19 (1957), pp. 1–4. For two very different ways in which this Avicennian doctrine was interpreted and applied by Henry of Ghent and Godfrey of Fontaines, see my *The Metaphysical Thought of Godfrey of Fontaines: A Study in Late Thirteenth-Century Philosophy* (Washington, D.C., 1981), pp. 72–74, 76–77. On the difficulty of arriving at knowledge of essential differences in sensible entities (and in spiritual substances), see *De ente,* ch. 5, p. 40:3–13/Leonine ed., p. 379:72–84. For Roland-Gosselin's listing of other texts where Thomas acknowledges this same difficulty with respect to knowledge of sensible substances see *loc. cit.,* n. 2.

15. See the text cited above in n. 10.

immediately conclude that existence comes to essence from without and enters into composition with it. Interestingly enough, however, he will appeal to the point that existence comes from without only when introducing what I shall regard as the third phase of his argumentation, that is, the (apparent) proof for God's existence.[16] And only after completing that proof will he conclude to the act-potency structure or composition of essence and existence in such caused beings, and hence of the intelligences.[17] Here, however, he limits himself to the conclusion that essence and existence are other or distinct in such entities.

Moreover, if one were to extract Thomas's argumentation from the following context, one might wonder whether it has in fact established real otherness or real distinction of essence and existence in such entities. One might counter that it shows only that it is different for one to recognize something as possible (to know what it is) and to recognize it as actual (to know that it exists). Granted that this entails two different intellectual operations, often referred to as simple apprehension and judgment, does it establish the reality of two really and ontologically distinct principles in such a being, an essence principle on the one hand, and an existence principle (*esse*) on the other, which latter would be required to account for the fact that the entity in question does exist and therefore can be so recognized? One might rather contend that it only establishes logical or conceptual distinction, the distinction between that which is grasped by one's concept of what something is, and one's judgment of it as actually existing.[18] But perhaps the difficulty lies in assuming that Thomas ever intended this argument to stand alone. Perhaps this is why he immediately conjoins to it a second argument or, as I prefer to regard it, a second phase in his argumentation.

To return to his text once more, then, Thomas has concluded that essence is not to be identified with existence unless, perhaps, there is some

16. *Op. cit.,* p. 35:3–11/Leonine ed., p. 377:127–37.
17. *Op. cit.,* pp. 35:19–36:3/Leonine ed., p. 377:147–66.
18. For this see Maurer, *op. cit.,* pp. 22–23; Owens, "Quiddity and Real Distinction . . . ," pp. 10–14. See in particular his remark on p. 12: "Just in itself, consequently, the inspection of the thing's quidditative content shows only a conceptual distinction between the thing and its being." There Owens also stresses the point that this argument from inspection of a thing's quiddity is "but a stage in a larger demonstration. It is the initial step toward proving the existence of the first efficient cause, subsistent being" (p. 17). While agreeing with him in the main on both of these points, my interpretation will suggest that the *intellectus essentiae* argument is but the initial step in a larger demonstration that leads to real otherness and distinction of essence and existence (phase two) and then only to the existence of the first efficient cause (phase three). Owens rather makes the argument for God's existence a necessary step for concluding to real distinction or otherness of essence and existence (see the text cited in my note 3 above, and see below).

entity whose quiddity is its very existence (*esse*). He immediately attempts to show that there can be at most one such being, whose quiddity is its existence (*esse*). So far he has not assumed that such a being does, in fact, exist. His contention is rather that if there is such a being, it must be unique. In every other being, therefore, essence and existence are not to be identified.[19] Presumably, this conclusion will obtain, in Thomas's view, whether or not this one possible and unique exception does exist. It should also be noted that Thomas does not restrict this contention to corporeal entities or to separate entities, but applies it to every being with this one possible exception.

In order to show that there can, at most, be one being in which essence and existence are identical, Thomas now suggests that there are three different ways in which something can be multiplied: (1) by the addition of some difference, as a generic nature is multiplied in species; (2) or by reason of the fact that the same kind of form is received in different instances of matter, as when a specific nature is multiplied in different individuals; (3) or else in that one thing exists in separation but another instance of the same is received in something else. If, for example, there were a separated heat, it would thereby be distinguished from non-separate or received instances of heat.[20]

But if it be maintained that there is a thing which is *esse* or existence alone so that existence itself is subsistent, continues Thomas, then no difference can be added to it. For then it would no longer be existence alone but existence plus some form that would differentiate one subsisting *esse* from another.[21]

Much less, continues Thomas, will it do for one to have recourse to the second alternative, that is, to multiply subsisting existences by suggesting that different instances of the same are received in different parts of matter. In that eventuality, counters Thomas, one's hypothetical subsisting existences would not be existence alone, but material existence.[22] Presumably, the second alternative is rejected because it would imply that the allegedly pure and subsistent existences would not be pure existence, but instead existence plus individuating instances of matter. Again Thomas finds the proposal self-refuting.

Rather than return explicitly to the third alternative, according to which one subsisting existence exists apart or in separation from all else, and other

---

19. *Op. cit.,* p. 34:15–32/Leonine ed., pp. 376:103–377:123. Note in particular: "Nisi forte sit aliqua res cuius quiditas sit ipsum suum esse. Et haec res non potest esse nisi una et prima . . . " (15–16). " . . . Unde oportet quod in qualibet alia re preter eam aliud sit esse suum et aliud quiditas vel natura seu forma sua" (30–32).

20. *Op. cit.,* p. 34:16–24/Leonine, pp. 376:104–377:113.

21. *Op. cit.,* p. 34:24–27/Leonine, p. 377:113–17.

22. *Op. cit.,* p. 34:27–29/Leonine, p. 377:117–19.

instances of existence are received in something else, Thomas immediately reasserts his conclusion as established. There can only be one thing which is its very existence (*esse*).[23] The implication is that the third alternative really concedes his point. Then there would only be one separate and subsisting existence. In all others, existence would be received by something else. But this is to acknowledge that any such being would consist of existence and that which receives it.

Having eliminated, at least to his own satisfaction, the possibility of there being more than one entity in which essence and existence are identical or whose essence is its existence, Thomas then draws the conclusion: Wherefore, it necessarily follows that in every other entity apart from this unique possible exception, existence and quiddity (or nature or form) must differ (literally: "must be other"). Whence it also follows that in the intelligences essence (form) and existence differ.[24]

Certain comments are in order as regards this phase of Thomas's argumentation. First of all, his conclusion does not appear to be hypothetical. It is true that he has not yet attempted to show that God, that unique entity whose essence is his existence, does in fact exist. But this does not imply that his immediate conclusion with respect to other entities is hypothetical.[25] His reasoning is rather that there can at most be one being whose essence is its existence or in which essence and existence are identical. In all other entities essence and existence differ whether or not that unique possible exception to the rule does in fact exist. If he has successfully shown that it is impossible for there to be more than one being in which essence and existence are identical, then he can conclude to factual otherness of essence and existence in all other entities. It is true that in other

23. *Op. cit.,* p. 34:29–30: "Unde relinquitur quod talis res que sit suum esse non potest esse nisi una." (Leonine ed., p. 377:119–21.) For similar developments of the ways in which multiplicity or plurality may be accounted for see *In I Sent.,* d. 8, q. 4, a. 1, ad 2; *Comp. theol.,* ch. 15. In the latter text, as Fabro remarks, the process is both simplified and rendered metaphysically more rigorous: "Duplex est modus quo aliqua forma potest multiplicari: unus per differentias, sicut forma generalis, ut color in diversas species coloris; alius per subiectum, sicut albedo." *Opuscula theologica,* Vol. 1 (Marietti, 1954), p. 17. For Fabro see *La nozione metafisica,* p. 220.

24. *Op. cit.,* pp. 34:30–35:2/Leonine, p. 377:114–26. See the final sentence of the text cited in n. 19 above. It is immediately followed by Thomas's application of his conclusion to the intelligences: "Unde oportet quod in intelligenciis sit esse preter formam, et ideo dictum est quod intelligencia est forma et esse."

25. Here my reading differs from that proposed by L. Sweeney, "Existence/Essence in Thomas Aquinas's Early Writings," pp. 116–17. At this point in the text Sweeney finds Thomas concluding to "at least a hypothetical otherness and composition of form/*esse* in intelligences" and to factual otherness and composition only after the proof for God's existence (p. 117).

contexts he first offers a demonstration of the existence of God or accepts this as given and then, by way of contrast, moves on to factual otherness of essence and existence in all else.[26] But that is not his procedure here. He rather reasons here from the impossibility of there being more than one being in which essence and existence are identical to their factual otherness in all other entities.

Secondly, the argument and its conclusion are not restricted to separate intelligences. On the contrary, Thomas first concludes to otherness of essence and existence in all else, with the one possible exception. Then only does he make the more particular application to separate intelligences.[27]

Thirdly, in Thomas's eyes the validity of this phase of his argumentation does not presuppose his subsequent proof for God's existence. If one may distinguish between otherness or diversity or distinction of essence and existence, on the one hand, and composition of the same as of potency and act, on the other, it is the former that he has attempted to establish in this step. It is only after introducing his proof for God's existence that he will conclude to potency-act composition of essence and existence in the intelligences.[28]

---

26. See for instance, his procedure in the *Summa contra gentiles*. In Bk. I, ch. 13, he offers a series of arguments for God's existence. In ch. 22 he concludes that in God essence and existence (*esse*) are identical. In Bk. II, ch. 52, he offers a series of arguments to show that in created intellectual substances there is some composition because in them *esse* and *quod est* (existence and essence) are not identical ("Invenitur enim in eis aliqua compositio ex eo quod non est idem in eis esse et quod est"). The first argument presented is interesting for our purposes. If *esse* is not present in some subject, there will be no way in which it can be united with something that is different from itself (*praeter esse*). But *esse*, insofar as it is *esse*, cannot be diversified. It can only be diversified by something that is other than *esse*. Thus the *esse* of a stone is distinct from (*aliud ab*) the *esse* of a man (presumably because the essence of the stone is different from its existence and different from the essence of the man). Therefore, continues Thomas, that which is subsistent *esse* can only be one. But, observes Thomas, he has already shown that God is his own subsisting *esse* (Bk. I, ch. 22). Therefore, nothing apart from God can be its own *esse*. Therefore, in every substance apart from God, (its) substance (essence) and its *esse* (*existence*) are other (or distinct). Granted that this argument takes God's existence and the fact that he is his own *esse* as given, if valid in itself it should hold whether or not one has already established these two points. Given the structure of the *Contra gentiles*, it is only natural for Thomas here to appeal to his earlier treatment of each of these points. But if its structure had been otherwise, as in ch. 4 of the *De ente*, the same conclusion should still follow, it would seem, because it is based on the impossibility of there being more than one being whose essence is its *esse* or existence.

27. *De ente*, pp. 34:30–35:2/Leonine, p. 377:119–26.

28. *Op. cit.*, p. 35:19–25/Leonine, p. 377:147–54. Central to his reasoning there is the notion that that which receives something from something else is in potency to that which it receives, while that which is received in it is in act. Having by then established to his own satisfaction both the fact that that whose essence differs from its existence

In sum, if, as appears to be the case, Thomas is here contending that in all beings with one possible exception essence and existence are really not identical, then it seems unlikely that he would agree with the claim that one must first have demonstrated God's existence in order to demonstrate the real distinction between essence and existence.[29] If it is impossible for there to be more than one being whose essence is its *esse*, then it follows that in all other beings essence and existence are not identical. And this follows whether or not that single exception has already been assumed or proven to exist, or whether it is simply regarded as a possibility.

To return once more to Thomas's text in the *De ente,* only now does he address himself to the question of God's actual existence. Everything that belongs to something is either caused by the principles of its nature (as man's ability to laugh), or comes to it from without from some extrinsic principle (as light's presence in air is due to the sun). Although Thomas does not explicitly refer to it here, a third possibility should be mentioned. That which belongs to a thing might be identical with that thing itself. But, continues the text, existence itself cannot be caused (efficiently) by the form or quiddity of a thing, for then something would produce itself. So much for the first possibility. Therefore, it is necessary for every such thing whose existence (*esse*) is other than its nature to derive that existence from another. So much for the third possibility to which reference was made above. Thomas has eliminated it by concentrating on entities in which essence (nature) and existence differ.[30] And such nonidentity, he has just maintained, is true of every being, including intelligences, with only one possible exception. He continues: because that which exists through another must be traced back to that which exists of itself as to its first cause, there

receives its existence from something else and the existence of God, Thomas is in position to conclude that the quiddity or form which is the intelligence is in potency with respect to the existence it receives from God, while that existence is received after the manner of an act. Hence the presence of act and potency in intelligences, though not of matter and form when taken strictly.

29. See Owens, "Quiddity and Real Distinction in St. Thomas," p. 19, as cited in my note 3 above.

30. According to the reading being proposed here, Thomas has already established such distinction between essence and existence in the second phase of his argumentation. Admission of such nonidentity strengthens his contention that the existence of such a being derives from something else or that it is efficiently caused: "Ergo oportet quod omnis talis res cuius esse est aliud quam natura sua habeat esse ab alio" (*op. cit.,* p. 35:10–11/Leonine, p. 377:135–37). It appears to me that he takes this nonidentity of essence and existence to be real, granted that in the *De ente* he will not apply the terminology "real distinction" to essence and existence here or in his application of them as potency and act to the intelligences.

must be something which serves as cause of existence for all (other) entities by reason of the fact that it is existence alone. Otherwise, observes Thomas, one would regress to infinity in a series of caused causes.[31]

At this point in his argumentation, therefore, he has concluded to the factual existence of that single possible being to which he had previously referred, that being whose essence is its *esse*. According to the interpretation presented above, this does not indicate that only now does Thomas believe that he has established the factual otherness of essence and existence in all other things. He has rather used the very factual otherness and distinction of essence and existence as his point of departure for the present step in his argument which is, or so it seems to this writer, an argument for God's existence and a highly interesting and metaphysical one at that. For it is based on a metaphysical conclusion which, according to the interpretation presented above, he has established in phase two of his argumentation, that is, real otherness or real distinction of essence and existence in all beings with this single exception.

Certain difficulties might be raised against this interpretation of Thomas's procedure. First of all, one might wonder why he found it necessary or even helpful to include this argument for God's existence in the immediate context, if it is not a necessary step in his effort to establish real otherness of essence and existence in creatures and in intelligences. Secondly, one might wonder whether Thomas either intended to or succeeded in establishing real otherness or real distinction of essence and existence in the second phase of his argumentation, especially so since we ourselves have, along with others, acknowledged certain reservations about his intention to do so in the first phase (the *intellectus essentiae* argument).

As regards the first difficulty, one obvious reply is to suggest that Thomas included the argumentation for God's existence for the sake of completeness, in order to show that the single possible exception to universal otherness of essence and existence is more than a possibility, an actuality. But the following lines of his text present another reason for his introduction of this argumentation here. He now returns to the structure of those intelligences with which so much of his earlier discussion was concerned. It is therefore clear, he remarks, that an intelligence is a form and *esse* and that it receives its existence from that first being which is existence alone, and which is God. While the first point had been established before his introduction of the proof for God's existence, the second point follows from that same proof.

---

31. *Op. cit.,* p. 35:3–16/Leonine, p. 377:127–43. As should be clear from the above, it is our view that this is intended by Thomas to be an argument for God's existence. For another opinion see the references to Gilson in n. 4 above.

"There must be something which is the cause of existence for all things by reason of the fact that it is existence alone."[32] Because the intelligence receives its existence from another, it is in potency with respect to that existence, and that same existence which it receives is its act. Therefore, the quiddity or form or essence which is the intelligence is in potency with respect to the existence it receives from God. Thus, reasons Thomas, one does find potency and act in intelligences, but not matter and form (unless the latter terms be applied equivocally).[33]

In sum, therefore, Thomas has found it helpful to introduce the argumentation for God's existence in order to establish the point that existence is related to essence in separate intelligences as act to potency. Therefore, even though he had rejected matter-form composition in the same, he has retained act-potency composition therein. And it was to establish this very point that he had initiated the general discussion including the first and second phases of his argumentation for otherness of essence and existence and the proof for God's existence.[34]

As regards the second difficulty, it would seem that if, in other contexts, after having established God's existence in fact or taken it as a given, Thomas can reason by way of contrast from the impossibility of there being more than one entity in which essence and existence are identical to real otherness or real distinction of the same in every other being, then the same conclusion should follow from his procedure in the present text.[35] And this

---

32. *Op. cit.,* p. 35:16–19. For the text just cited see p. 35:13–14: " . . . oportet quod sit aliqua res que sit causa essendi omnibus rebus ex eo quod ipsa est esse tantum . . . ." For the Leonine ed. see p. 377:139–46.

33. *Op. cit.,* p. 35:19–25/Leonine, p. 377:147–54.

34. *Op. cit.,* p. 34:4–7/Leonine, p. 376:90–93.

35. See, for instance, his procedure in SCG II, ch. 52, as indicated in n. 26 above. According to the second argument offered there it is impossible for there to be more than one *esse separatum per se subsistens.* Therefore, nothing else apart from this being (God) can be its own *esse.* In his *Tractatus de substantiis separatis* he once again endeavors to show that if spiritual substances lack matter, they must still be distinguished from God. Some potency is found in them insofar as they are not *esse* itself but rather participate in it. There can only be one self-subsistent being which is *esse* itself, just as any form could only be one if it should be considered as separate. Therefore, it is impossible apart from this one exception for there to be anything which is existence (*esse*) alone. "Est igitur in quocumque praeter primum et ipsum esse tanquam actus et substantia rei habens esse tamquam potentia receptiva huius actus qui est esse" (ed. by F. Lescoe [West Hartford, Conn., 1963], p. 79). While Thomas does not explicitly state that essence and existence are "really" distinct in creatures in either of these texts, the distinction and hence the composition for which he is arguing is surely intended to be extramental, not merely something that results from different ways in which one and the same ontological principle may be viewed.

conclusion should follow whether or not such a single and unique exception does in fact exist. Since in these other contexts he has already had occasion to offer argumentation for God's existence or else to take this as granted, he naturally assumes it as a given in reasoning to real otherness of essence and existence in all else. But in the *De ente* he has not yet introduced his argumentation for God's existence. Hence, or so it seems to this writer, he need not and does not presuppose the existence of God in order to conclude to real otherness of essence and existence in other entities. The impossibility of there being more than one being in which essence and existence are identical is sufficient ground for him to conclude to their real (*add.* to original version) and factual otherness in all else.

A Reply to Fr. Owens

In a recent issue of *The Thomist*, Fr. Joseph Owens has examined my interpretation of ch. 4 of the *De ente* at some length. As one might expect, he disagrees with my contention that Thomas does not presuppose prior knowledge or proof of God's existence in order to conclude to real distinction of essence and existence in creatures.[36] Without repeating in detail all points in Fr. Owens's article, it may be of interest here for me to concentrate on four "presuppositions" which he finds in my text, and which he regards as essential to my interpretation.

According to Owens my first latent presupposition is this — that mention of the real or conceptual character of the distinction between essence and existence "should have had some importance" in Thomas's procedure.[37] A second implicit tenet is said to be metaphysical in character. Owens asks whether, before having demonstrated that God exists, we can know *what* existence is in sufficient fashion to determine its real implications. Apparently he takes my interpretation as assuming that such is the case. As a third implicit tenet Owens suggests that my interpretation implies that from "the content of a concept of existence one can reason immediately or almost immediately to its conditions in reality." He even suggests that "shades of the ontological argument at once arise, even though here the existence, aside from the distinction, is known as real from the start." As a fourth implicit tenet, Owens suggests that my discussion assumes that "the designation 'real'

For some interesting reflections on Thomas's failure to identify explicitly as real the kind of distinction for which he was ultimately arguing in the *De ente* see Owens, *op. cit.*, pp. 19–22.

36. "Stages and Distinction in *De ente*: A Rejoinder," *The Thomist* 45 (1981), pp. 99–123.

37. *Ibid.*, p. 99.

adequately expresses the way things are distinguished from their being" within the perspective of Thomas's metaphysics.[38]

In addressing himself more fully to the first "implicit tenet" in my argumentation, Owens offers some interesting historical observations about the fact that in Aquinas's writings there is no set formulation to express the relationship and distinction between essence and existence, or as Owens prefers to phrase it, between a thing's nature and its being. He and I are in agreement that the issue in question has to do with the relationship between an individual thing's nature or essence, on the one hand, and its existence or being, on the other.[39]

Owens also argues from a parallel passage in the Commentary on the *Sentences* where, he writes, Thomas distinguishes between being and quiddity "in the way the rational aspect is distinguished from the animal aspect in man." Such a distinction arises from two different concepts and is, for Aquinas, only conceptual. Hence Owens, after noting that this text parallels the reasoning found in the opening lines of the *De ente* argumentation, comments that this should suffice to identify the distinction between essence and existence argued for there (in what I have called phase one of that argumentation) as conceptual. As Owens observes, on this point he and I are also in accord. Aquinas does not establish real distinction between essence and existence in this phase of his argumentation, and apparently did not intend to do so there.[40]

38. *Ibid.*, pp. 99–101.

39. See pp. 101–3. As Owens observes, various expressions such as distinction, difference, diversity, composition, other than, over and above (*praeter*), incidental to (*accidit*), shared by, received by, are used by Thomas to express the relationship between existence (*esse*) and essence in creatures (p. 101). For concrete illustrations he refers to Sweeney's study ("Existence/Essence in Thomas Aquinas's Early Writings," *passim*). Perhaps I should comment in passing that I am somewhat uneasy about referring to the distinction in question as that which obtains between a thing and its being, as Owens often does and not without justification (see pp. 102, 119, n. 28), rather than as that between a thing's nature or essence and its existence (*esse*). My reason for this reluctance is that such usage might confuse some readers. On occasion *res* ("a thing") is used by Aquinas to designate one of the transcendentals and therefore that which is really identical with that which is signified by *ens*. While the name *res* is derived from the essence of a given entity and the name *ens* is taken from its *actus essendi* (see *De ver.*, q. 1, a. 1), both *ens* and *res* may be used by Thomas to designate the concrete existing entity. This, of course, includes both that individual thing's essence or nature, on the one hand, and its *esse* or existence, on the other. Hence the issue concerning the real distinction for Aquinas centers on the appropriate relationship between these two, the essence principle and the *esse* principle within a given concrete entity. See *In IV Met.*, ed. cit., p. 155, nn. 553, 558.

40. See p. 103. For the text from *In I Sent.*, see the following note.

Here, however, perhaps I should comment in passing that in the text from Thomas's Commentary on I *Sentences*, his purpose is to show that *esse* may be said to be "accidental" to a creature's quiddity in the sense that it is not included in one's understanding of that quiddity, just as rational may be said to be "accidental" to animal because the former is not included in one's understanding of the latter. While Owens is correct in noting that such reasoning leads to nothing more than conceptual distinction between essence and existence, this text should not be interpreted to imply that for Thomas the two distinctions — that between a thing's essence and existence and that between the rational and the animal aspect in man — are on a par. Owens himself recognizes this. As he comments, from such an initial conceptual distinction between a thing and its being (or between its essence and existence as I shall often phrase it), Thomas's argumentation in the *De ente* moves on in the direction of a real distinction between them. As Owens puts it: "The one point at issue is the exact stage where the real distinction is reached."[41]

In the case of the relationship and distinction between essence and *esse*, Owens specifies, whether Thomas refers to this distinction as real or describes it as conceptual, "the one implies the other for real things." Hence Owens regards it as neither "negligence nor anomaly" on Thomas's part

---

41. In this same context (p. 103) Owens singles out in passing four texts where Thomas does use the terminology "real" or its equivalent in order to identify the diversity or difference or composition or otherness of a thing and its *esse: In I Sent.*, d. 13, q. 1, a. 3, sol. (*ed. cit.*, Vol. 1, p. 307); *In I Sent.*, d. 19, q. 2, a. 2 (Vol. 1, p. 471); *De ver.*, q. 27, a. 1, ad 8; *In Boeth. De Hebdomadibus*, lect. 2 (Calcaterra ed., n. 32). For the passage from the Commentary on I *Sentences* just mentioned in my text see *In I Sent.*, d. 8, exp. primae partis textus (Vol. 1, p. 209). There Thomas is commenting on this text: "Esse non est accidens Deo." He notes that one might say the same of any creature, since nothing is more essential to a thing than its own *esse*. To this Thomas responds: " . . . quod accidens dicitur hic quod non est de intellectu alicuius, sicut rationale dicitur animali accidere; et ita cuilibet quidditati creatae accidit esse, quia non est de intellectu ipsius quidditatis; potest enim intelligi humanitas, et tamen dubitari, utrum homo habeat esse." Thomas's point in this reply is to show that *esse* may be said to be "accidental" to a creature's quiddity in the sense that it is not included in one's understanding of it; this is not to imply that *esse* is to be regarded as a predicamental accident. For another interesting text where Thomas also refers to a thing's *esse* as "accidental" in the sense indicated above see Quodlibet 2, q. 2, a. 1 (Spiazzi ed., p. 24). Note in particular: "Unde, cum omne quod est praeter essentiam rei, dicatur accidens; esse quod pertinet ad quaestionem *an est*, est accidens." This is why he can also without inconsistency deny that *esse* is an accident (predicamental accident), as in *In IV Met.*, n. 558; or in Quodlibet 12, q. 5, a. 1 (p. 227): "Et sic dico quod esse substantiale rei non est accidens, sed actualitas cuiuslibet formae existentis . . . . Et quod Hilarius dicit, dico quod accidens dicitur large omne quod non est pars essentiae; et sic est esse in rebus creatis, quia in solo Deo esse est eius essentia."

not to specify in given contexts whether the distinction at issue is real or conceptual. Owens does acknowledge, nonetheless, that this point continues to have interest for us today, in light of controversies concerning the essence-existence relationship in creatures which arose within two years after the death of Aquinas.[42]

So much, then, for the first implicit "tenet" in my interpretation of the argumentation in the *De ente*. Granted that Thomas did not explicitly identify as real the distinction he was there defending between essence and existence in creatures, and granted that it was not necessary there for him to do so, the issue quickly became important in later thirteenth-century thought. Moreover, one might add, the issue continues to be of both philosophical and historical importance for us today. Not only is it legitimate for us to ask whether or not, in Thomas's view, the distinction between a thing's essence and its *esse* is merely conceptual or whether it obtains in reality; it is also legitimate for us to ask, if this distinction is indeed real in Thomas's eyes, as both Owens and I maintain, what evidence does Thomas offer for that conclusion in ch. 4 of the *De ente*?

In discussing the second "implicit tenet" in my reading of the argumentation in the *De ente*, Owens first asks rhetorically whether if existence is to be known as really distinct from the nature it actuates, it will not "first have to be recognized as having in itself the status of a real nature." In other words, will not one first have to demonstrate that God exists in order to draw out the metaphysical implications that follow for existence to be realized in creatures and hence to show that existence must be really distinct from any creaturely essence? Owens obviously believes that this is the case but, in my opinion, offers neither convincing textual nor convincing philosophical evidence for his position. Rather, without any real proof, he concludes that only "after existence has been known to be a real nature" will it become apparent that essence and existence are not merely conceptually distinct in creatures.[43]

Owens goes on to argue that because existence as a real nature (as realized in God—self-subsistent *esse*) is infinite and unique, where found in other things it must be "really over and above their natures."[44] And to know

---

42. Owens, *op. cit.*, pp. 104–8. For my own investigation of some of these later thirteenth-century controversies concerning the essence-existence relationship in creatures see my *The Metaphysical Thought of Godfrey of Fontaines*, ch. II (pp. 39–99); "The Relationship between Essence and Existence in Late-Thirteenth-Century Thought: Giles of Rome, Henry of Ghent, Godfrey of Fontaines, and James of Viterbo," in *Philosophies of Existence: Ancient and Medieval* (New York, N.Y., 1982), ch. 9 (pp. 131–64); and "Essence and Existence," in *The Cambridge History of Later Medieval Philosophy* (Cambridge, 1982), ch. 19, pp. 385–410.

43. *Op. cit.*, pp. 108–9.

44. *Ibid.*, p. 109.

that existence is a nature is to have proved that God exists. This, concludes Owens immediately, "should indicate emphatically that a real distinction between a thing and its being cannot be shown until after completion of the demonstration that God exists." Only then, maintains Owens, is one in "position to see that existence cannot coalesce in reality with any finite being."[45]

This is an interesting claim on Owens's part but, as I have suggested, one that remains unproven either philosophically or textually. As regards the philosophical evidence offered in this section of Owens's article, it is one thing to admit that one may reason from prior knowledge of God's existence to the conclusion that in all other beings essence and *esse* must differ and really differ. This is indeed a path followed by Aquinas on a number of other occasions, as I have already pointed out in nn. 26 and 35 of this chapter. But such is no indication that this is the only way in which Aquinas either could have reasoned or in fact did reason. The philosophical evidence offered by Owens may perhaps convince those who have accepted the Gilsonian views concerning Christian philosophy and who believe that in presenting Thomas's metaphysics one must follow the theological order rather than the philosophical. Since I have already expressed my disagreement with that position in Chapter I, there will be no need for me to reexamine that issue here.

Secondly, Owens's interpretation does not do full justice, in my opinion, to the text of the *De ente* itself, above all not to the argumentation presented by Thomas in its second phase. There Thomas does argue that there can at most be one being whose essence is identical with its *esse*. And then, without assuming that that being actually exists, he goes on to conclude that in every other being essence and *esse* are not identical. If the argumentation which Owens presents as the only way to establish the real distinction between essence and existence in creatures is indeed valid, then, I would maintain, the argumentation offered by Aquinas in phase two of the *De ente* is also valid. And since both Owens and I agree that Thomas's argument to prove the existence of God appears only in phase three, I submit again that in phase two Thomas has proven, or believes that he has proven, that in all other beings essence and *esse* are really not identical, which is to say that they are distinct.[46]

45. *Ibid.*, p. 110.

46. For references to the appropriate texts see above nn. 19–24. For fuller development of my claim that phase three of the argumentation in the *De ente* offers no more compelling evidence for real distinction between essence and *esse* than does phase two, see the closing paragraphs of this chapter. What phase three does contribute to Thomas's views concerning the essence-*esse* relationship in creatures is not, in my opinion, additional proof that they are really distinct but rather explicit

But this brings us to the third latent presupposition, according to Owens, in my interpretation. Here Owens finds me reasoning (or having Thomas reason) from the content of a concept (existence) to its real distinction from the subject in which it inheres. As already noted, he even sees certain "shades of the ontological argument" implied by my interpretation, even though, as he recognizes, the existence with which one begins the reasoning process is recognized as real, that is, as the existence of a really existing (nondivine) entity, from the outset.

> Even though the reasoning has been carried to the point where it has shown that the distinction [between essence and existence] does not hold in God, there is as yet no ground for projecting it as real. It would be reasoning from the presence of a distinction in the mind to a corresponding distinction in reality. In that perspective the reasoning would seem to have an ontological cast.[47]

In replying to this, two different situations should be distinguished: one, wherein one reasons from the content of a positive concept to its realization in actuality, as for instance, from one's understanding of God as that than which no greater can be thought to his real and extramental existence; another, where one reasons from the impossibility of something (based on the incompatibility or contradictory character of the notes it would involve) to its nonexistence in reality—for instance, from the incompatibility of combining squareness with circle to the conclusion that such cannot and therefore does not obtain in reality. Thomas would certainly reject the first kind of reasoning, as is clear from his criticism of the Anselmian argument

---

evidence to show that in addition to this they are also (really) composed as potency and act. Here there will be no need for me to delay over the section in his article where Owens endeavors to show that while the later Gilson no longer counted the argumentation for God's existence found in the *De ente* as a proof of God's existence in the technical sense, he did not thereby reject its cogency (pp. 110-17). As Owens comments, both he himself and I do recognize it as intended by Thomas to prove that God exists. I would only note in passing that others seem to have read the later Gilson as I have done (see n. 4 above), such as A. Maurer, *St. Thomas Aquinas, On Being and Essence*, 2d revised ed. (Toronto, 1968), p. 20, n. 33, and pp. 25-26; J. Knasas, "Making Sense of the *Tertia Via*," *The New Scholasticism* 44 (1980), pp. 497-99; and perhaps F. Van Steenberghen, *Le problème de l'existence de Dieu dans les écrits de S. Thomas d'Aquin* (Louvain-la-Neuve, 1980), pp. 47-48, n. 29. Van Steenberghen regards the argumentation in the *De ente* as an unsuccessful attempted proof for God's existence—unsuccessful because it is based on an unsuccessful attempt to demonstrate real distinction and composition of essence and *esse* in finite beings (see pp. 37-43). As regards his criticism of the argumentation for the essence-existence distinction, Van Steenberghen concentrates only on phase one of Thomas's argumentation, not on phase two.

47. *Op. cit.*, pp. 117-20. For the quotation see p. 120.

for God's existence.[48] On the other hand, Thomas just as clearly recognizes the validity of the second kind of reasoning and employs it. This will be illustrated more fully in my discussion of his views concerning that which is impossible in the absolute sense (see Chapter VII below). If one can show beyond the shadow of a doubt that something is intrinsically contradictory, then, according to Aquinas, not even God could bring it into being. This is so, not because of any deficiency on the part of God's power, but because the thing in question simply cannot be done — it is absolutely impossible in itself.[49]

One may now apply this distinction to the case at hand. According to my reading of the *De ente*, there is no question of Thomas's reasoning from one's conception of essence and existence as distinct to the conclusion that they are really distinct. In other words, contrary to Owens's suggestion, the first type of reasoning which I have distinguished in the previous paragraph does not apply here.

On the other hand, according to my interpretation, Thomas does reason in the second way just distinguished. If his claim that in all beings with only one possible exception essence and *esse* are not identical is validly established, this can only be because Thomas has already demonstrated to his own satisfaction that it is not possible for there to be more than one entity in which essence and *esse* are identical. If one grants the validity of this reasoning, it will follow that if more than one being does in fact exist in the extramental world, in every such being with one possible exception essence and *esse* are not identical. And this will follow whether or not one has already demonstrated the existence of that one hypothetical being in which essence and *esse* are identical.

To restate my point in other terms, Thomas does not here reason from possibility (of real distinction between essence and existence in all other

48. For Thomas's rejection of the Anselmian argumentation see *In I Sent.*, d. 3, q. 1, a. 2, ad 4; *In Boeth. De Trinitate*, q. 1, a. 3, ad 6; *De ver.*, q. 10, a. 12, ad 2; and especially SCG I, chs. 10 and 11; ST I, q. 2, a. 1, ad 2. For discussion see M. Cosgrove, "Thomas Aquinas on Anselm's Argument," *The Review of Metaphysics* 27 (1974), pp. 513–30; Van Steenberghen, *Le problème de l'existence de Dieu*, pp. 21–23, 72–82, 100–101, 105–8, 157–59.

49. See for instance, *De pot.*, q. 3, a. 14 (*ed. cit.*, p. 80): "E contrario vero impossibile, quando sibi invicem repugnant; ut simul esse affirmationem et negationem impossibile dicitur, non quia sit impossibile alicui agenti vel patienti, sed quia est secundum se impossibile, utpote sibi ipsi repugnans." Also see the remark in his *De aeternitate mundi:* "Secundo modo dicitur propter repugnantiam intellectuum aliquid non posse fieri, sicut quod non potest fieri ut affirmatio et negatio sint simul vera; quamvis Deus hoc possit facere, ut quidam dicunt. Quidam vero dicunt quod nec Deus hoc posset facere, quia hoc nihil est. Tamen manifestum est quod non potest facere ut hoc fiat, quia potentia qua ponitur esse destruit se ipsam" (in *Opuscula omnia*, J. Perrier, ed. [Paris, 1949], Vol. 1, n. 2). For the Leonine ed. see Vol. 43, pp. 85:42–86:49.

beings) to actuality (assertion of such real distinction in such beings). On the contrary, he reasons from impossibility in the conceptual order (of there being more than one entity in which essence and *esse* are identical) to impossibility in actuality (of there actually being more than one entity in which essence and *esse* are identical). So much, then, for the third suggested "latent" tenet in my interpretation of phase two of the argumentation in the *De ente*. The procedure suggested by my interpretation is diametrically opposed to that involved in the ontological argument.[50]

As regards the fourth suggested "latent assumption" in my interpretation, Owens is troubled by my seeming treatment of "real otherness" and "factual otherness" as synonymous.[51] In the interest of clarification, I should specify that by "factual" otherness of essence and *esse* in beings other than God I simply wish to suggest that Aquinas, at the end of phase two of his argumentation, has concluded to a nonidentity or distinction of essence and *esse* in such beings which is not merely hypothetical. Moreover, this distinction obtains in reality independently of the mind's consideration. Given this, I have also referred to this kind of distinction as "real." The more critical point of division between Owens's reading and my own, of course, concerns whether or not in this second phase of his argumentation Thomas believes that he has already established such a "factual" and "real" distinction in such entities.

Before concluding this discussion, it may be helpful for me to return to the last-mentioned issue. Owens is willing to admit that at the end of stage three, after having offered his argument for God's existence, Thomas does conclude to a distinction between essence and *esse* in other beings which is not merely conceptual and which can therefore be referred to as "real."[52] This is granted even though Thomas himself does not use this terminology in that context. Hence the absence of reference by Aquinas to this distinction as "real" applies both to the conclusions of stages two and three of his argumentation. Given this, the presence or absence of such language will not help in deciding the issue between Owens and myself.

On the other hand, in a number of other contexts Aquinas does reason from prior knowledge of God's existence to otherness or distinction of essence

---

50. To make this point still another way, one might say that the two procedures are as opposed as affirmation and negation or even as being and nonbeing. According to the Anselmian procedure, one reasons from possibility (of a being than which nothing greater can be thought) to its actuality. According to Thomas's procedure in phase two of the *De ente* argumentation, one reasons from the impossibility of that which is self-contradictory to the conclusion that it cannot and therefore does not exist.

51. *Op. cit.*, pp. 120–22.

52. *Ibid.*, pp. 104, 110, 123.

and *esse* in creatures; but even in those contexts rarely if ever is the resulting distinction explicitly described as "real." In other words, Thomas uses fundamentally the same terminology to describe the distinction between essence and *esse* which he has already employed in phase two of the *De ente* argumentation.[53] To carry this one step farther, if Thomas's reasoning in these other contexts is valid and successfully shows that there can only be one being in which essence and *esse* are identical, then his conclusion will follow whether or not that single exception to the rule exists. In every other being essence and *esse* will not be identical but will differ. In these parallel passages the reasoning is essentially the same as in phase two of the *De ente*. Because it is not possible for there to be more than one being in which essence and *esse* are identical, in every other being essence and *esse* are not identical. Because in these other contexts Thomas has already either proven or taken as granted God's existence, it is only natural for him to assume this as a given. But since in the *De ente* he has not yet established God's existence, here he argues that given the existence of more than one being and given the impossibility of there being more than one being in which essence and *esse* are identical, in every other being essence and *esse* are not identical. To repeat my point, if the reasoning he has employed in other contexts such as those just mentioned is valid, it will also be valid as it appears in phase two of the *De ente*. And such reasoning need not rest on prior knowledge of God's existence.[54]

53. See, for instance, SCG II, ch. 52 ("Quod in substantiis intellectualibus creatis differt esse et quod est"), and the way this conclusion is expressed in the text of the chapter: "Invenitur enim in eis aliqua compositio ex eo quod non est idem in eis esse et quod est" (end of 1st par.); " . . . esse aliud ipsam substantiam et esse eius" (end of 1st arg.); "nihil aliud praeter ipsum est suum esse" (end of 2d arg.). Also see in his *Tractatus de substantiis separatis*, ch. 8, n. 42: "Impossibile est igitur quod praeter ipsum sit aliquid subsistens quod sit esse tantum . . . . Est igitur in quocumque praeter primum et ipsum esse tanquam actus et substantia rei habens esse tamquam potentia receptiva hujus actus qui est esse" (Lescoe ed., p. 79/Leonine ed., Vol. 40, p. D 55:181–87). One may compare these formulations with those found in the *De ente*: "Ergo patet quod esse est aliud ab essentia vel quiditate" (end of phase one/ p. 34:14–15/Leonine ed., p. 376:102–3); "Unde oportet quod in qualibet alia re preter eam aliud sit esse suum et aliud quiditas vel natura seu forma sua. Unde oportet quod in intelligenciis sit esse preter formam . . ." (end of phase two/pp. 34:30–35:1/Leonine, p. 377:121–25). "Ergo oportet quod omnis talis res cuius esse est aliud quam natura sua habeat esse ab alio" (as starting point for the proof for God's existence/p. 35:10–11/Leonine, p. 377:135–37). As in the *De ente* it seems clear enough that Thomas must have real distinction of essence and *esse* in mind in these other passages; for in these contexts as in the *De ente* he must ultimately show how his rejection of matter-form composition of created intelligences does not entail that they are as simple as is God and therefore that they can be distinguished from God.

54. See, for instance, the series of arguments offered in SCG II, ch. 52, to show that if created intellectual substances lack matter-form composition, they are still

One might, of course, cast doubt on the reasoning employed by Thomas in phase two of his argumentation in the *De ente*, or at least upon the validity of my claim that according to Aquinas one can show by such reasoning that in all beings, with one possible exception, essence and *esse* are really not identical and are therefore distinct. As will be recalled from the first part of this chapter, Thomas there reasons that there can only be one being whose quiddity is its very *esse*. This follows, he argues, because things can be multiplied in only three ways: (1) by the addition of some difference, as when the nature of a genus is multiplied in its species; (2) by reason of the fact that a form which retains its specific identity is received in different instances of matter; (3) or by reason of the fact that one instance of the perfection is separate (*absolutum*) and other instances of that perfection are received in something else.[55] Owens comments that in the first two cases the relevant distinctions obtain between generic nature and specific nature, on the one hand, and between specific nature and an individual, on the other. "These," he writes, "are clearly conceptual distinctions."[56]

As regards the first of these and Owens's comment, it would seem to be more faithful to Thomas's text to refer to the distinction which will obtain between a difference, on the one hand (such as rational), and a generic concept (such as animal), on the other. Even so, Owens can rightly maintain that for Aquinas the distinction between my understanding of man as rational and as animal is only conceptual. However, when one returns to

---

composed in some way because in them *esse* and *quod est* are not the same. For the first argument there see my n. 26 above. Here it will be enough to stress the point that Thomas there reasons that that which is *esse subsistens* can only be one ("Illud ergo quod est esse subsistens, non potest esse nisi unum tantum"). In other words, it is impossible for there to be more than one being which is *esse subsistens*. Therefore, given the fact that God has been shown to be *esse subsistens* in Bk. I, ch. 22, Thomas now concludes that nothing other than God can be its *esse*. Apart from the appeal to his earlier demonstration of God's existence (implicit appeal) and to God's identity with his *esse* (explicit appeal), the logic here is the same as in stage two of the *De ente* argument. If valid, the argument should also hold here even without appeal to prior knowledge of God's existence; for it too rests upon the impossibility of there being more than one *esse subsistens*. As noted above (n. 35), the second argument offered in ch. 52 is based upon the impossibility of there being more than one *esse separatum per se subsistens*. The third shows that there cannot be two completely infinite *esse*s. Hence, given the infinity of *esse subsistens* (based on the fact that it is not limited by any subject), the same conclusion is drawn: there can only be one *esse subsistens*. In each of these cases the conclusion is enough for Thomas to maintain that there is some composition in such beings (created intellectual substances) because in them *esse* and *quod est* are not identical. For similar reasoning in his *Tractatus de substantiis separatis* see n. 35.

55. See n. 20 above and my text which corresponds to it.
56. *Op. cit.*, pp. 117–18.

Thomas's elimination of this as a viable way of accounting for multiplication of beings which would be identical with their respective *esses*, one finds a different kind of argument. If there is a being which is pure *esse* so as to be *esse subsistens*, it will not admit of the addition of any difference; for then it would not be pure *esse* (*esse tantum*), but *esse* plus some form. In short, Thomas is here assuming that in order for a being which is pure *esse* to be multiplied in the first proposed way, an additional form would have to be added to it. It would no longer be pure *esse* but *esse* plus the added form, and therefore, we may conclude, really composed of its *esse* and that distinct form. In other words, while the distinction between a genus and a difference is only conceptual, the ontological condition required to allow for any such multiplication of *esse* is real: real distinction of *esse* and form in any such being. Perhaps this is why on other occasions Thomas argues that membership in a genus or species requires distinction of essence and *esse* on the part of beings so multiplied.[57]

Thomas also rejects the possibility of multiplying subsisting *esse* in the second way, where like a form *esse* would be received in different instances of matter. But, counters Thomas, if one were to attempt to multiply pure and subsisting *esse* in this way, one would no longer have subsisting *esse* but *esse materiale*. Though one might suggest that the distinction between a specific nature and the individual in which it is realized is only conceptual, as Owens has pointed out, within Thomas's metaphysics even this distinction presupposes a more fundamental and real distinction—that between matter and form. Moreover, Thomas has argued, in the present case one would no longer have pure and subsisting *esse* but material *esse*.[58] This would be contrary to the hypothesis according to which one might multiply pure and subsisting *esse* in this way. One would now have united *esse* and matter in every such being, just as one might unite form and matter in different individuals of the same species. If the latter kind of distinction is real rather than conceptual, so would the former be, one might reason.

---

57. See *Compendium theologiae*, ch. 14, 2d arg. "Plura individua sub una specie contenta differunt secundum esse, et tamen conveniunt in una essentia. Ubicumque igitur sunt plura individua sub specie una, oportet quod aliud sit esse, et aliud essentia speciei." See *Opuscula theologica*, Vol. 1, R. Verardo, ed. (Rome-Turin, 1954), p. 17/Leonine ed., Vol. 42, p. 87:12–16. The reasoning in this text parallels that frequently found in what I shall describe in Ch. VI below as Thomas's "genus" argument for the real distinction. In the final analysis, of course, Thomas could not admit that *esse* is multiplied in the way a genus is, that is, by the addition of some difference. Since it is not a genus, *esse* can only be multiplied by being received in this or that subject. See SCG II, ch. 52, 2d arg., cited below in my Ch. VI, n. 29. For the point that being (*ens*) is not a genus also see *In I Met.*, lect. 9 (*ed. cit.*, n. 139).

58. The text reads: "et multo minus recipiet additionem materie quia iam esset esse non subsistens set materiale" (p. 34:27–29/Leonine ed., p. 377:117–19).

One might attempt to multiply instances of pure and subsisting *esse* in the third way, by suggesting that in one case *esse* is pure and unreceived, and that in every other case it is received in something else. It is evidently in this third way that Aquinas thinks *esse* is in fact multiplied.[59] Owens notes the example offered here by Aquinas — heat which would exist in separate and unreceived fashion, on the one hand, and heat as received, on the other. From this Owens concludes that Thomas is here concerned not with the distinction between participated heat and its subject, but only with that between separate heat and participated heat.[60] However, Thomas has suggested that according to this hypothesis, in only one being will *esse* be separate. In all other beings *esse* will be received just as heat is received in a body or subject. Hence one may infer that, according to Aquinas, in every other being *esse* will be received by some subject. And if there is real distinction between heat and the subject which receives it, the implication is that there will be real distinction between *esse* and the subject which receives it. This is a point which Aquinas spells out on other occasions.[61] If in the present context he leaves this final point unsaid, this is because here he has now shown to his own

---

59. "Unde relinquitur quod talis res que sit suum esse non potest esse nisi una" (p. 34:29–30/Leonine, p. 377:120–21).

60. *Op. cit.*, p. 118.

61. Frequently enough, Thomas makes this point within the perspective of the metaphysics of participation. See for instance *In I Sent.*, d. 48, q. 1, a. 1. There Thomas distinguishes two ways in which things may be similar: (1) by participating in a single form, as when two white men share in whiteness; (2) when one, by participating in a form, imitates that which another has *essentialiter*. It is only in the latter way that a creature can be like God. Such similitude implies composition in the participant, and simplicity in the unparticipated source: "Sicut si corpus album diceretur simile albedini separatae, vel corpus mixtum igneitate ipsi igni. Et talis similitudo quae ponit compositionem in uno et simplicitatem in alio, potest esse creaturae ad Deum participantis bonitatem vel sapientiam, vel aliquid hujusmodi, quorum unumquodque in Deo est essentia ejus" (*ed. cit.*, Vol. 1, p. 1080). Also see the important text on participation (to be discussed more fully below in the following chapter) from Quodlibet 2, q. 2, a. 1: "Quandocumque autem aliquid praedicatur de altero per participationem, oportet ibi aliquid esse praeter id quod participatur. Et ideo in qualibet creatura est aliud ipsa creatura quae habet esse, et ipsum esse eius" (*ed. cit.*, p. 24). Also see *De spiritualibus creaturis*, a. 1, especially: "Unde dicimus, quod Deus est ipsum suum esse. Hoc autem non potest dici de aliquo alio; sicut enim impossibile est intelligere quod sint plures albedines separatae; sed si esset albedo separata ab omni subiecto et recipiente, esset una tantum; ita impossibile est quod sit ipsum esse subsistens nisi unum tantum. Omne igitur quod est post primum ens, cum non sit suum esse, habet esse in aliquo receptum, per quod ipsum esse contrahitur; et sic in quolibet creato aliud est natura rei quae participat esse, aliud ipsum esse participatum" (M. Calcaterra and T. Centi, eds., in *Quaestiones disputatae*, Vol. 2 [Rome, 1953], pp. 370–71). The similarity between the reasoning employed here and that of the texts analyzed above in n. 54 will be evident to the reader.

satisfaction that in only one being can essence and *esse* be identified. In every other thing "aliud sit esse suum et aliud quiditas vel natura seu forma sua."[62]

In stage three of his argumentation Thomas will go on to correlate essence and *esse* as potency and act. But in the course of doing this he first reasons that what receives something from another is in potency with respect to it, and what is received in it is its act. In other words, he reasons from the fact that *esse* is received by essence to the conclusion that they are composed as act and potency. This, of course, comes after his proof for God's existence. But it is not so much the fact of God's existence which enables him to say that essence and *esse* are correlated as that which receives and that which is received. It is even more so the fact that in any such being essence (or nature) and *esse* differ. This, of course, was the conclusion established at the end of phase two of his argumentation.[63]

In sum, therefore, to return to a point already mentioned in passing above, while explicit application of act-potency composition to the essence-*esse* couplet occurs only in phase three of Thomas's argumentation, presupposed for this is the distinction between that which receives and that which is received. If the act-potency composition of essence and existence is real for Aquinas, as both Owens and I agree, then the distinction between that which receives and that which is received must also be real. But no more proof is offered to make this point in phase three of the argumentation than in phase two. Hence here one has additional confirmation for my claim that it is in phase two that Thomas believes he has established real otherness or real distinction between essence and *esse* in all beings with only one possible exception. This is not for me to suggest that this is the only way in which Aquinas argues for real distinction between essence and existence in created entities. Other ways are found in other texts; but more will be said about this in the following chapter.

62. *Op. cit.*, p. 34:31–32/Leonine ed., p. 377:122–23.
63. *Ibid.*, p. 35:3–23/Leonine ed., p. 377:127–49.

CHAPTER VI

ESSENCE AND EXISTENCE IN OTHER WRITINGS

As is well known, texts dealing with the relationship between essence and existence (*esse*) are scattered throughout Thomas Aquinas's writings. A number of these seem to offer some kind of argumentation for real distinction and/or real composition of essence and existence in created beings. Here no attempt will be made to gather all of these texts together. Rather, by drawing on a limited sampling of these, I shall illustrate a number of distinctive ways in which Aquinas seems to reason to this distinction. In the course of doing this, another issue already discussed within the confines of the *De ente* (see Ch. V above) will be kept in mind. In these other approaches to establishing real distinction and/or real composition of essence and *esse* in creatures, does Thomas always presuppose prior knowledge of God's existence?

Various attempts have been made by contemporary scholars to classify Thomas's different approaches to this problem.[1] While acknowledging my debt to these, my own examination of Thomas's texts leads me to propose the following different ways in which Thomas argues for real distinction of essence and *esse* in beings other than God: (1) the *intellectus essentiae* argument, already examined in Chapter V as it appears in the *De ente;* (2) what Leo Sweeney has dubbed the "genus" argument; (3) various forms of what we might call "God-to-creatures" argumentation; (4) arguments based on participation (many of which also clearly move from God to creatures); (5) argumentation based on the finite or limited character of individual entities.

Here I shall not delay longer over the first class — *intellectus essentiae* argumentation, since at least as it appears in what I have called phase one

---

1. See in particular, C. Fabro, *La nozione metafisica di partecipazione*, 2d ed. (Turin, 1950), pp. 212-44; J. de Finance, *Etre et agir dans la philosophie de Saint Thomas*, 2d ed. (Rome, 1960), pp. 94-111; L. Sweeney, "Existence/Essence in Thomas Aquinas's Early Writings," *Proceedings of the American Catholic Philosophical Association* 37 (1963), especially pp. 105-31. My own classification will be very close to that proposed by Sweeney.

of the argumentation in the *De ente*, it seems to be inconclusive.[2] Moreover, one may well doubt that, at least in that context, Thomas himself regarded it as sufficient to conclude to real distinction of essence and *esse* in created beings. I shall turn immediately, therefore, to an examination of each of the other suggested approaches.

1: The "Genus" Argument

In his study of Thomas's argumentation for the real distinction in his early works, Sweeney has singled out six different passages where this reasoning appears. In only two of these texts do we have what might pass for a genuine argument for the real distinction. (Two others are content to appeal to Avicenna's authority to make the point that whatever is present in a genus has a quiddity which differs from its *esse*. According to another, that which has an *esse* which is other than its quiddity must fall into a genus, again on the authority of Avicenna.) Of these two the first is taken from *In I Sent.*, d. 8, q. 4, a. 2, and the second from *De veritate*, q. 27, a. 1, ad 8.[3]

In the first text Thomas is attempting to show that God does not fall within the genus substance. The third argument in support of this position is referred to by Thomas as *subtilior* and is said to be taken from Avicenna. It runs as follows. Whatever is present in a genus has a quiddity which differs from its *esse*, as is true of a man. In proof Thomas argues that actual existence (*esse in actu*) is not due to humanity insofar as it is humanity. Thus humanity can be understood without there being knowledge whether some man exists. (Here, of course, the *intellectus essentiae* argument has been inserted.) And the

2. Sweeney finds other examples of the *intellectus essentiae* argumentation in *In I Sent.*, d. 8, expositio primae partis textus (*ed. cit.*, Vol. 1, p. 209); *ibid.*, q. 4, a. 2 (p. 222), where it appears as part of the "genus argument"; *In II Sent.*, d. 1, q. 1, a. 1 (Vol. 2, p. 12), where interestingly enough it enters into one of three arguments offered by Thomas to establish the fact that there is only one first principle; though there it does not seem to rest necessarily on prior knowledge of God's existence, one may well doubt that it leads to or is even intended to lead to real distinction of essence and *esse;* also in *In II Sent.*, d. 3, q. 1, a. 1 (p. 87); *De ver.*, q. 10, a. 12 (*ed. cit.*, p. 220), where the reasoning runs in reverse fashion, that is, from the essence-*esse* distinction to the conclusion that *esse* is not perfectly included in one's understanding of the intelligible content (*ratio*) of any creature. On this point, of course, that the *intellectus essentiae* argumentation in the *De ente* does not of itself establish more than conceptual distinction between essence and existence, Owens and I are in accord. In addition to references already given in Ch. V above see the remarks in his *Aquinas on Being and Thing* (Niagara University Press, 1981), pp. 8–9.

3. See Sweeney, *op. cit.*, p. 109. The four additional texts cited by Sweeney include *In I Sent.*, d. 19, q. 4, a. 2, sol. (Vol. 1, p. 483); *In II Sent.*, d. 3, q. 1, a. 1, ad 1 (Vol. 2, p. 88); *ibid.*, a. 5 (pp. 99–100); *ibid.*, a. 6 (pp. 102–3).

reason for this, adds Thomas, is this. The common characteristic which is predicated of things which are present in a genus predicates quidditatively (*praedicat quidditatem*), since genus and species are predicated of quiddity. But existence (*esse*) is not due to a quiddity except insofar as it is realized in this or that individual. Therefore the quiddity of a genus or species is not communicated to all members of that class in terms of a single *esse*, but only in terms of the common intelligible content (*ratio*). From this Thomas concludes that the *esse* of any such being (which belongs to a genus) is not identical with its quiddity.[4]

Before attempting to analyze the reasoning involved in the above argumentation, it may be helpful to consider the second and slightly later version found in the *De veritate*. Here Thomas is considering the question whether grace (*gratia gratum faciens*) is something positively created in the human soul. In defending the affirmative position, as he does, Thomas must meet the eighth objection. According to this objection, only things composed are present in a genus. But grace, being a simple form, is not composed. Therefore it is not present in any genus. But since everything created is in a genus, grace is not something created.[5]

Granted the theological context for this objection, Thomas's reply is highly philosophical. He agrees with the objection's claim that whatever is present in the genus of substance is composed, and by a *real composition,* it should be noted. But real composition is not required for something to fall into one of the accidental predicaments (also generic); a composition of reason — that of genus and difference — will suffice. So much for his reply to the theological objection. Our concern here, however, is with his claim that whatever is present in the genus of substance must be composed and really composed. How does he prove this? Whatever is present in the predicament of substance subsists in its own *esse*, he argues. Hence its *esse* must be other than itself (its essence). One may immediately ask why. Thomas replies that if

4. "Tertia ratio subtilior est Avicennae, tract. V. *Metaph.*, cap. iv, et tract. IX, cap. 1. Omne quod est in genere, habet quidditatem differentem ab esse, sicut homo; humanitati enim ex hoc quod est humanitas, non debetur esse in actu; potest enim cogitari humanitas et tamen ignorari an aliquis homo sit. Et ratio hujus est, quia commune, quod praedicatur de his quae sunt in genere, praedicat quidditatem, cum genus et species praedicentur in eo quod quid est. Illi autem quidditati non debetur esse nisi per hoc quod suscepta est in hoc vel in illo. Et ideo quidditas generis vel speciei non communicatur secundum unum esse omnibus, sed solum secundum unam rationem communem. Unde constat quod esse suum non est quidditas sua." *Ed. cit.*, Vol. 1, p. 222.

5. "Et primo quaeritur utrum gratia sit aliquid creatum positive in anima" (Spiazzi ed., pp. 511-13/Leonine ed., Vol. 22.3, pp. 789-92). For objection 8 see p. 511/ Leonine, p. 790:51-55.

this were not the case, if the *esse* of any such being were not distinct from its quiddity, it could not in fact differ in terms of its *esse* from other things with which it agrees in quidditative content. But this is required of all things which are included directly in a predicament — that they agree in quidditative content. Therefore, concludes Thomas, whatever is directly included in the predicament of substance is composed at least of *esse* and *quod est* (of existence and of that which it is, or essence).[6]

This argument, especially as it appears in the text from the *De veritate*, is interesting for a number of reasons. First of all, it explicitly distinguishes between a purely logical or conceptual kind of composition which obtains between genus and difference and a real composition which holds between *esse* and quiddity in the case of things directly included in the predicament of substance. Secondly, it does not seem to rest in any explicit or implicit manner upon prior knowledge of God's existence, even though in terms of the general context Thomas can assume the existence of God as a given within the *De veritate*. Thirdly, it also appeals, as its main presupposition — one which plays an equally central role in the text from *In I Sent.* — to the claim that insofar as things fall within a genus they must agree in intelligible content or in quidditative content with all other members of that genus. At the same time every such thing must differ from other members of that same class in terms of its individual *esse* (according to *In I Sent.*) or its substantial *esse* (as the *De veritate* passage specifies). Since the substantial *esse* of individual members of such a class is not shared in common with other members of that same class, and since their quidditative content in some way is, Thomas concludes to otherness of essence and *esse* in all such beings. Finally, it is interesting to note that both versions of the argument first

---

6. For his general reply to objection 8 see p. 513/Leonine, p. 792:221-31. For the argument of concern to us here, note the following: "Ad octavum dicendum, quod omne quod est in genere substantiae, est compositum *reali compositione;* eo quod id quod est in praedicamento substantiae est in suo esse subsistens, et oportet quod esse suum sit aliud quam ipsum, alias non posset differre secundum esse ab illis cum quibus convenit in ratione suae quidditatis; quod requiritur in omnibus quae sunt directe in praedicamento: et ideo omne quod est directe in praedicamento substantiae, compositum est saltem ex esse et quod est" (ital. mine). For the contrast between the real composition that must apply to what is directly present in the predicament substance and the logical composition entailed by presence in other predicaments, note the following: "Et ideo, ad hoc quod aliquis sit in praedicamento aliquo accidentis, non requiritur quod sit compositum compositione reali, sed solummodo compositione rationis ex genere et differentia: et talis compositio in gratia invenitur" (*ibid.*). The absence of any role for the *intellectus essentiae* argument within the genus argument as it is presented in the *De veritate*, taken together with its absence from later versions of the genus argument to be mentioned below, suggests that it plays no essential role in the version cited in n. 4 above from *In I Sent.*

conclude to otherness (or distinction) of essence and *esse* in members of a genus, i.e., of substance. While the version in the *De veritate* ultimately wishes to conclude to real composition of these, it does so only after first establishing otherness or distinction between them.

For confirmation of this way of interpreting the argumentation, one may turn to a much later and rather succinct version, in the *Summa theologiae* I, q. 3, a. 5. There again (as in the argument from *In I Sent.*), Thomas is attempting to show that God does not fall under any genus. His third argument to make this point runs as follows. All things present in a given genus share in the quiddity or essence of that genus. This, says Thomas, follows because genus is predicated of them in terms of their quiddity (*in eo quod quid est*). But such things differ in terms of their *esse*. In support Thomas comments that the *esse* of a man is not the same as the *esse* of a horse; nor is the *esse* of this man the same as the *esse* of that man. Therefore, it follows that in things which are present in a genus, their *esse* and their *quod quid est* — their essence as Thomas specifies — differ.[7] Essentially the same kind of argumentation appears in the slightly earlier *Summa contra gentiles* I, ch. 25, again where Thomas is trying to show that God is not included under any genus; also in *De potentia*, q. 7, a. 3, where Thomas is making the same point. In simplified fashion it is used in the *Compendium theologiae* to prove that God himself is not a species which would be predicated of various individuals.[8]

In sum, therefore, this argument appears both in Thomas's earlier and in his later writings. In his earliest usages of it he often explicitly ascribes it to Avicenna.[9] The argument seems to combine logical and metaphysical considerations, ultimately accounting for membership in a genus (or species)

---

7. "Tertio, quia omnia quae sunt in genere uno, communicant in quidditate vel essentia generis, quod praedicatur de eis *in eo quod quid est*. Differunt autem secundum esse: non enim idem est esse hominis et equi, nec huius hominis et illius hominis. Et sic oportet quod quaecumque sunt in genere, differant in eis esse et *quod quid est*, idest essentia" (P. Caramello ed., published by Marietti [Turin-Rome], 1950), p. 18.

8. Of the respective versions of this argument considered here the earliest is that found in *In I Sent.* (ca. 1252). This is followed by *De veritate*, q. 27 (1258–1259), *Summa contra gentiles* I (1258–1259), *De potentia*, q. 7 (1265–66), ST I (1266), and the *Compendium theologiae* (1269 or thereafter). For these datings see Weisheipl, *Friar Thomas d'Aquino*, "A Brief Catalogue of Authentic Works," pp. 355ff. On the other hand, the *De ente* seems to date from ca. 1252–1256. Sweeney follows Roland-Gosselin in placing it between *In I Sent.*, d. 25, and before *In II Sent.* (*op. cit.*, pp. 99–100, n. 7). The validity of the genus argument seems to be assumed by Thomas in the *De ente*, ch. 5 (p. 37:16–21/Leonine ed., p. 378:9–14).

9. See Sweeney's comment on the difficulty of finding this argument explicitly presented as such in Avicenna, Thomas's frequent references to Avicenna (in his earlier presentations of it) notwithstanding (*op. cit.*, p. 110, n. 21).

by postulating something metaphysical—real distinction and composition of essence and *esse* in all such beings. It does not seem to presuppose prior knowledge of God's existence, as is especially clear from its presentation in the *De veritate* and from the structure of the argument itself. At the same time it was referred to by Thomas himself as *subtilior*. It was obviously not accepted by Thomas's contemporaries and by those who came after him who rejected his views on the essence-*esse* distinction and relationship.[10] And it still causes some uneasiness on the part of followers of Aquinas today.

For instance, one may ask, does it not move in some way without justification from the order of logic and conceptual distinction to the order of reality and real distinction? In the final analysis it rests upon the fact that the members of the same genus (or species) have something in common (which falls on the side of quiddity) and something unique and distinct (their *esse*). Need this point to anything more than composition within the essences of such beings, for instance, of matter and form?[11]

As Sweeney has commented, this reply would be true enough for authors who do not share Thomas's metaphysical perspective. For Aquinas, however, this reasoning does not merely lead to composition within the essence of such beings, but to a composition that holds within them viewed as existents, hence a composition of essence and *esse*. Still, why not take *esse* in this case simply as referring to such beings as individuals, and essence as referring to that which they have in common with one another? Or why not suggest that essence as used here merely points to nature (essence as common and specific) and *esse* to the supposit (essence as realized in this individual)? Against this, as Sweeney notes, de Finance has countered that Thomas does not restrict this kind of reasoning to material entities, but also applies it to angelic beings. Since for Thomas there is no matter-form composition in such beings and no multiplicity of individuals within species, the composition and distinction argued for must be more fundamental than this. Hence, as Thomas has indeed written, it must apply to essence and *esse*—meaning thereby this individual thing's essence, on the one hand, and its *esse* (existence), on the other.[12]

10. For instance, for an extended effort to show how, though not composed either of matter and form or of essence and existence, there is sufficient potentiality and actuality in angels for them to be included in some kind of genus—a logical genus rather than a real or natural one—see Godfrey of Fontaines, Quodlibet 7, q. 7 (M. De Wulf and J. Hoffmans, eds., in *Les Philosophes Belges*, Vol. 3, pp. 349–63). For discussion see my *The Metaphysical Thought of Godfrey of Fontaines*, pp. 92–97.

11. See Sweeney, pp. 110–12 for discussion of the validity of this argument.

12. For de Finance, see his *Etre et agir*, pp. 95–96. In defending this argument against such charges, de Finance suggests that one should understand quiddity as pointing to a generic nature itself. Multiplicity of individuals within the same species

For my part, it seems evident enough to me that Thomas intends to establish real distinction and composition between essence and *esse* in all members of genera (or species) by this argumentation. The statement in the version found in the *De veritate* could hardly be clearer on this score. Moreover, as I have already noted above, the argument does not presuppose prior knowledge of God's existence either in terms of its inner logic or in terms of Thomas's intent in developing it. This, of course, is not enough to decide the other issue — the validity of the argument considered on its own merits. Here philosophical evaluations of its probative value will undoubtedly continue to vary, and not without good reason, in my opinion. The argument does seem to need some kind of metaphysical strengthening in order to escape from criticisms such as those just mentioned.

2: *God-to-Creatures Argumentation*

Reference has already been made to this kind of argumentation in Chapter V above.[13] Without agreeing with Owens that phase two of the argumentation in the *De ente* presupposes prior knowledge that God actually exists, even my interpretation of the argument uses the notion that there can at most be one being whose essence is its *esse* in order to conclude to real otherness of essence and *esse* in all else. In many other contexts Thomas takes the existence of God as a given and then reasons from this to the conclusion that in all else essence and *esse* are not identical, or are distinct. Here I shall concentrate on some representative texts where this last-mentioned procedure appears. With reference to these texts a further distinction seems

---

could be adequately accounted for, he reasons, by appeal to matter-form composition. This will not suffice, he continues, to account for plurality within a genus, since the categories (hence substance) surpass the limits of corporeal being. Hence to account for the fact that such beings can still be grasped by our concepts as having something in common, on the one hand, and something unique, on the other, a more radical composition is required, that of essence and *esse*. If the argumentation starts from quiddity taken universally and as generic, it concludes to a distinction within the concretely existing being between its individual essence and its individual *esse*. While not entirely satisfied with de Finance's defense of the argument, Sweeney also defends it. It seems to me, however, that in doing so he imports a central feature of what I shall regard as another approach to the real distinction, the limited character of being as realized in every finite being, and the need to account metaphysically for this — the limitation of *esse* (which, as we shall see below, is not self-limiting for an Aquinas). See *op. cit.*, p. 112, n. 23, 2d par. In effect, my final comment in the following paragraph may not really be at odds with Sweeney's defense of this argument.

13. Apart from the issue concerning the proper interpretation of *De ente*, ch. 4, see the texts cited in Ch. V, nn. 35, 54, and 61.

to be in order. At times Thomas simply reasons from the fact that only in God (*esse subsistens*) are essence and *esse* identified. Hence, by way of contrast, he concludes to distinction and/or composition of essence and *esse* in creatures. On the other hand, as Fabro points out,[14] at times Thomas reasons from the caused character of creatures to the distinction within them of essence and *esse*. In some of the following passages both lines of reasoning will appear.

Sweeney has presented a number of texts from Thomas's earlier writings where such argumentation appears.[15] For instance, in *In I Sent.,* d. 8, q. 5, a. 1, Thomas is attempting to determine whether or not any creature is simple.[16] Before answering this question Thomas comments that whatever comes forth from God and differs in essence from him must fall short of his simplicity. But, cautions Thomas, it does not follow that everything which falls short of the divine simplicity is itself composed. In explaining this Thomas notes that creatures are of two kinds. One kind enjoys complete being (*esse*) in itself, such as a man or anything of this type. Any such creature falls short of the divine simplicity by being composed. But, adds Thomas, there is another kind of creature which does not exist of itself but only in something else. As examples he cites prime matter, any form, or a universal. Such creatures can only exist within a particular subsistent entity. Hence they do not fall short of the divine simplicity by being composed.[17]

To return to the first kind of creature, a substance, if you will, one may wonder why Thomas insists that such creatures fall short of the divine simplicity by being composed. In proof he reasons that in God alone is his *esse* his quiddity. Hence in every creature, whether corporeal or spiritual, there must be both quiddity or nature, on the one hand, and the creature's *esse*, on the other, which it receives from God. Thomas adds that God's essence is his *esse*. Hence, concludes Thomas, in every such creature (creaturely substance) there is composition of *esse* (or *quo est*) and *quod est* (or essence).[18]

14. *Op. cit.*, pp. 214–15.

15. *Op. cit.*, pp. 112–20. He also lists argumentation from ch. 4 of the *De ente.* Since this has already been discussed above in Ch. V, I shall not include it here.

16. *Ed. cit.*, Vol. 1, pp. 226–27.

17. *Ibid.* After having strongly defended the need to admit the second kind of creature, Thomas concludes that such will fall short of the divine simplicity either because it is divisible in potency or *per accidens* (as with prime matter, form, and a universal), or because it can enter into composition with something else (*componibile alteri*). While Thomas's thinking concerning this point merits further study, it will be necessary for me to reserve fuller consideration of it for another occasion.

18. " . . . et talis creatura ita deficit a simplicitate divina quod incidit in compositionem. Cum enim in solo Deo esse suum sit sua quidditas, oportet quod in qualibet creatura, vel in corporali vel in spirituali, inveniatur quidditas vel natura sua, et

In attempting to unpack the reasoning implied by this argument, one may ask how Thomas justifies his claim that in every creaturely substance there must be both essence and *esse* (existence) and that it must be composed of these. Two possibilities come to mind, though they are not mutually exclusive. First of all, Thomas is here concerned with protecting the uniqueness of the divine simplicity. Given his conviction that in God essence and existence are identical and his unwillingness to admit matter-form composition in created spiritual entities (see his following article in the same question), this may be enough for him to conclude to the need for essence-*esse* distinction and composition in things other than God. The implication would be that since creaturely substances must fall short of the divine simplicity and since some of them are not composed of matter and form, they must be composed of essence and *esse*. Another possible interpretation would be that because a creature receives its *esse* from God, it must be composed of its essence and of the *esse* it receives from its cause. In other words, implied in this reasoning would also be an argument based on the efficiently caused character of creatures. According to this suggestion, the God-to-creatures argument would here be combined with one based on the efficiently caused character of creatures.[19]

Finally, one may ask, how does Thomas know that God is his very *esse*? This conclusion would follow for Thomas from both lines of reasoning just suggested. Thomas has already argued for the complete and total simplicity of God in q. 4, a. 1 of this same distinction. Moreover, two of the arguments found in the *sed contra* of that article (and therefore defending divine simplicity) are based on the fact that God as first principle gives being to all else. This being so, God cannot be composed of anything else (including essence and existence), for then his being would depend upon the components.[20] In short, distinction or composition of essence and existence in God would be incompatible both with his perfect simplicity and with his uncaused character as the first cause.

In turning to the next text (*In I Sent.*, d. 8, q. 5, a. 2), one finds Thomas discussing the question of the soul's simplicity. After rejecting matter-form composition of the soul, he argues that it is composed in another way. If there is a quiddity which is not composed of matter and form, that quiddity

---

esse suum, quod est sibi acquisitum a Deo, cuius essentia est suum esse; et ita componitur ex esse, vel quo est, et quod est" (*ibid.*).

19. As the text quoted in the previous note indicates, Thomas does refer to the fact that the *esse* of any creature is given to it by God. Whether Thomas regards this as a premise or conclusion in the argument is difficult to determine.

20. *Ed. cit.*, pp. 218–19, args. 1 and 2 in the *sed contra*.

will either be identical with its *esse* or it will not be. If it is its very *esse*, reasons Thomas, it will be the essence of God himself (whose essence is his very *esse*) and it will be completely simple. If it is not its *esse*, it must have an *esse* given to it by something else, as is true of every created quiddity. Thomas then goes on to reason from this that the quiddity will therefore be potential (*possibilis*) with respect to the *esse* which it receives from its cause. Hence there will be composition of potency and act, i.e., of essence and *esse*. [21]

The most important step in this reasoning for my immediate purpose is the claim that if a given quiddity is identical with its *esse*, it will be God and will be perfectly simple. If this is granted, one can then conclude by way of contrast that anything which is not God cannot be identified with its *esse*. [22] Unfortunately, however, Thomas does not really prove this point in the present text; therefore it is really not a complete proof or argument for the real distinction. Perhaps the implicit presupposition is that anything whose essence is identical with its *esse* must be uncaused. On the other hand, Thomas has stated that any such being wherein quiddity and *esse* are identical is completely simple. Perhaps this is why he assumes that if something is not God and therefore not perfectly simple, it cannot be identified with its *esse*. Once more, however, this needs to be spelled out more clearly.

For another interesting version of the God-to-creatures argument one may turn to *In II Sent.*, d. 3, q. 1, a. 1. Here Thomas is rejecting matter-form composition in angels. Nevertheless, he continues, there is some kind of composition in them. He notes that there are two kinds of natures: one type in which *esse* is not included in one's understanding of that nature (which, Thomas comments, is evident because such a nature can be understood without one's knowing whether or not it exists — as with a phoenix or an eclipse, etc.); another kind which includes *esse* in its intelligible content and in which its *esse* is its very nature. *Esse* of this kind is not received from something else, since that which a thing has by reason of its quiddity it has of itself. But, continues Thomas, everything other than God receives its *esse* from something else. Therefore, only in God is *esse* identical with quiddity or nature. In all other things *esse* is other than the nature which receives *esse*. The argument goes on to conclude that in angelic beings there is composition of *esse* and *quod est* (quiddity), or of *quo est* and *quod est* and then relates these as act and potency. [23]

While the *intellectus essentiae* argument makes a brief appearance here, its function is not directly to prove that essence and *esse* in such beings are

---

21. *Ed. cit.*, pp. 229–30.

22. "Si illa quidditas sit esse suum, sic erit essentia ipsius Dei, quae est suum esse, et erit omnino simplex" (p. 229).

23. *Ed. cit.*, Vol. 2, pp. 85–89. See in particular pp. 87–88.

distinct. Its purpose rather seems to be to show that there is a kind of being in which *esse* is not included in one's understanding of that thing's nature. This is contrasted with another kind of nature which is its very *esse* and whose existence is here simply conceded. Given this, Thomas then argues that such a being is uncaused. By way of contrast with this one uncaused being, Thomas concludes that in everything else *esse* is acquired from something else. In other words, every such being is caused. Therefore, concludes Thomas's argument, in God alone is *esse* identical with quiddity. In everything else *esse* is distinct from the nature which receives it.

If one wonders how Thomas establishes distinction of essence and *esse* here, his argument seems to rest heavily on the caused character of the *esse* of every such being. Because such a being receives its *esse* from something else, or because it is caused, it (or its quiddity) is not identical with its *esse*. The argument moves from God to creatures, but does so by emphasizing the uncaused character of God and the caused character of every other entity. Given this, it then moves on to distinction or otherness of essence and *esse* in all else. Even though the argument is especially concerned with establishing the nonsimplicity of angels, it seems to apply to everything apart from God ("in omnibus autem aliis esse est praeter quidditatem, cui esse acquiritur"). While reminding one in some respects of the complex argumentation in the *De ente*, it differs from that reasoning in many respects. Moreover, it seems less polished and less persuasive than that argumentation.

A much briefer version of this kind of argument appears in another early work, Quodlibet 9, q. 4, a. 1.[24] There again Thomas is rejecting matter-form composition in angels. After having completed his refutation of any such composition in such entities, he comments that because the substance of an angel is not its *esse*, we find in the angel both its substance or quiddity, on the one hand, and its *esse*, on the other (whereby it subsists). Hence one may say that an angel is composed of *quo est* and *quod est,* or of *esse* and *quod est.* Thomas then correlates these as act and potency in angelic beings. For our immediate purposes the most interesting step is his claim that the substance of an angel is not its *esse*. In proof he merely states that identity of substance and *esse* is true of God alone, to whom *esse* is due and not derived from another.[25] Here again, therefore, he contrasts creatures with God. In

---

24. Spiazzi ed., pp. 184–85.

25. "Sed quia substantia angeli non est suum esse (hoc enim soli Deo competit, cui esse debetur ex seipso, et non ab alio); invenimus in angelo et substantiam sive quidditatem eius, quae subsistit, et esse eius, quo subsistit, quo scilicet actu essendi dicitur esse, sicut actu currendi dicimur currere" (p. 185). The latter part of this citation with its reference to *esse* as the *actus essendi* leaves little doubt that Thomas is here speaking of *esse* in the sense of existence as an intrinsic principle by reason of which such a substance exists.

support he argues that God's *esse* is due him of his very nature and not derived from another. In all other things, by way of contrast, Thomas maintains that essence and *esse* are not identical. There seem to be two presuppositions at work here. First, God's essence is his *esse* because he is the uncaused cause. Secondly, because this is true of God alone, everything else derives its *esse* from another (this is implied rather than explicitly stated). From this Thomas concludes that in an angel quiddity and *esse* differ, apparently because anything which receives its *esse* from something else (or is caused) differs from its *esse*. Though all of this could be spelled out more fully for the reader, here again the movement from God to creatures is closely joined to an argument based on the uncaused character of God, and the caused character of all else.

Interesting and perhaps clearer versions of this kind of argumentation also appear in Thomas's later writings. Here representative texts will be considered from SCG II, ch. 52 (ca. 1262); the Disputed Question *De spiritualibus creaturis* (1267–1268); the Commentary on *Physics* VIII (1269–1270); and the *Treatise on Separate Substances* (1271–1273).

As already noted above,[26] in Bk. II, ch. 52 of the *Summa contra gentiles*, Thomas is attempting to show that if created intellectual substances lack matter-form composition, they are still composed of essence (*quod est*) and existence (*esse*). As we have already seen, one argument in support of this claim is based on the impossibility of there being any being other than God which is its very *esse*.[27] A second argument is based on the impossibility of there being more than one *esse subsistens*. Since Thomas has already proved in Bk. I, ch. 22 that God is *esse subsistens*, nothing else can be its very existence (*esse*). Both of these are clearly examples of God-to-creatures argumentation, therefore.[28]

In setting the stage for his conclusion in the second argument, Thomas begins by noting that any nature, if it is understood as being separate, can only be one, granted that there may be many individuals which share in that nature. In illustration he cites the case of the nature of animal. If such a nature could subsist in itself and in separation, it would not possess that which is proper to man or to ox, for instance; otherwise it would not be

---

26. See Ch. V, n. 26.

27. Note in particular: "Illud ergo quod est esse subsistens, non potest esse nisi unum tantum. Ostensum est [lib. I, cap. 22] autem quod Deus est suum esse subsistens. Nihil igitur aliud praeter ipsum potest esse suum esse. Oportet igitur in omni substantia quae est praeter ipsum, esse aliud ipsam substantiam et esse eius" (*ed. cit.*, p. 145).

28. The reader will of course recall that already in Bk. I, ch. 13, Thomas had offered a series of arguments to prove that God exists.

animal alone, but man or ox. Once specific differences are removed, therefore, the nature of the genus remains undivided. Consequently, continues Thomas, if *esse* itself were to exist in such separate and subsisting fashion like our hypothetical subsisting genus, it too could only be one. And since *esse* in fact is not divided by differences, as is a genus, but rather by reason of its being realized in this or that particular being, it is even more evident that there can only be one self-existing *esse*. Given the fact that God is his *esse*, this can be true of nothing else.[29]

As I have already suggested above, in both of these God-to-creatures arguments Thomas assumes that he has already proven God's existence in Bk. I. Nonetheless, if the inner logic of each of these arguments is sound, then in each case the argument should hold even without presupposing God's existence. Each argument rests on the impossibility of there being more than one self-subsisting being. In all other beings, by way of contrast, essence and existence (*esse*) are not to be identified.[30]

The third argument in this same ch. 52 runs as follows. It is impossible for there to be two completely infinite beings. Completely infinite being embraces the total perfection of being. Hence, if such infinity were present in any two beings, there would be no way of distinguishing one from the other. But *esse subsistens* must be infinite because it is not limited (*terminatur*) by any receiving subject. Therefore it is impossible for there to be any other *esse subsistens* apart from the first being.[31] Presumably the reader is expected to draw the conclusion that by way of contrast, essence and existence (*esse*) must differ in every other being. This argument also assumes the existence of a self-subsistent being as already proven. On the other hand, it seems to me that it need not do so any more than the first two just considered. If it is impossible for there to be more than one infinite being, and if two or more beings do exist, one may infer that all of these with one possible exception are finite. Hence, if finite they cannot be self-subsisting being or *esse subsistens*. Therefore, in them essence and existence are not identical.

---

29. Note the following: "Sic igitur, si hoc ipsum quod est esse sit commune sicut genus, esse separatum per se subsistens non potest esse nisi unum. Si vero non dividatur differentiis, sicut genus, sed per hoc quod est huius vel illius esse, ut veritas habet; magis est manifestum quod non potest esse per se existens nisi unum. Relinquitur igitur quod, cum Deus sit esse subsistens, nihil aliud praeter ipsum est suum esse" (*ibid.*).

30. See Ch. V above, n. 54, and the corresponding text.

31. "Adhuc. Impossibile est quod sit duplex esse omnino infinitum: esse enim quod omnino est infinitum, omnem perfectionem essendi comprehendit; et sic, si duobus talis adesset infinitas, non inveniretur quo unum ab altero differret. Esse autem subsistens oportet esse infinitum: quia non terminatur aliquo recipiente. Impossibile est igitur esse aliquod esse subsistens praeter primum" (*ibid.*).

A fourth argument reaches this same conclusion by invoking reasoning based on causality, and by contrasting the uncaused cause with everything else. If there is some self-subsisting being, it must be uncaused. Therefore, no caused being is its very existence (*esse*). Though not spelled out for us in detail, the assumption seems to be that any caused being must differ from its existence (*esse*).[32] The latter part of this argumentation does not really have to presuppose God's existence, even though this is understandably again taken as a given here. That the movement from being caused to distinction of essence and existence in any such being does not itself presuppose God's existence is confirmed by the fifth argument. The substance of any given thing belongs to it of itself and not by reason of something else. But the existence of any created entity is given to it by something else; otherwise it would not be caused. Therefore the existence (*esse*) of any created substance is not identical with its essence (*substantia*).[33]

This fifth argument does not directly reason from God to creatures, therefore, though it is based on the caused (and even the created) character of particular beings. If one can show that such beings are caused in this radical sense, that is, that they receive their existence from something else, the argument immediately concludes that in them essence and existence are not identical. As a theoretical issue, of course, one may wonder whether it is possible to prove that finite beings are truly dependent on something else for their very existence without having already shown that in them essence and existence are not identical. Since many of Aquinas's arguments for God's existence (his five ways, for instance) do not begin with this presupposition and do, in his opinion, conclude to the existence of a God whom he can eventually show to be a creator, he evidently thinks that such a procedure is possible.

In q. 1, a. 1 of his *De spiritualibus creaturis* Thomas is again rejecting matter-form composition of spiritual substances. He then notes that there are still two (principles) in created spiritual substances, one of which is related to the other as potency to act. In proof of this he first argues that God, the first being, is unlimited act. Given this, he concludes that God's *esse* is not received in a distinct nature; for then it would be limited to that nature. Hence we say that God is his very *esse*. This, Thomas comments, cannot be said of anything else. Just as it would be impossible for there to

---

32. "Item. Si sit aliquod esse per se subsistens, nihil competit ei nisi quod est entis inquantum est ens . . . . Esse autem ab alio causatum non competit enti inquantum est ens: alias omne ens esset ab alio causatum . . . . Illud igitur esse quod est subsistens, oportet quod sit non causatum. Nullum igitur ens causatum est suum esse" (*ibid.*).

33. "Amplius. Substantia uniuscuiusque est ei per se et non per aliud . . . . Sed cuilibet rei creatae suum esse est ei per aliud: alias non esset causatum. Nullius igitur substantiae creatae suum esse est sua substantia" (*ibid.*).

be more than one separate whiteness, if whiteness could exist apart from every subject and recipient, so is it impossible for there to be more than one *esse subsistens*. Every other being, therefore, since it is not its existence, has an existence which is received in something else which limits that existence.[34]

Thomas goes on in this text to apply the language of participation to the essence-existence structure. In every creature the nature which participates in *esse* is one thing and its participated *esse* is something else. Therefore, he concludes, participated *esse* is related to the nature which participates in it as act to potency.[35]

This argument for distinction between essence and existence again reasons from the identity of the same in God, and the impossibility of there being more than one such being, to distinction and eventually to potency-act composition of essence and existence (*esse*) in every other. It clearly takes God's existence as given, although once more, as regards the explicit reasoning leading to real distinction between essence and existence, it would not have to do so. Once again the argument rests on the impossibility of there being more than one *esse subsistens*.

The next text, from Thomas's Commentary on *Physics* VIII, appears within the context of a discussion of the presence or absence of matter-form composition in heavenly bodies. Here I shall bypass that issue which proved to be so troublesome for Thomas and his contemporaries.[36] After arguing for matter-form composition (of some kind) in heavenly bodies, Thomas comments that even if it were conceded that such bodies lack this composition, it would still be necessary to hold that potency is present in them in some way. Every simple and subsisting substance is either identical with its existence (*esse*) or else it participates in existence. But there can only be one simple substance which is its very existence (*ipsum esse subsistens*), just as, if there were a subsisting whiteness, it could only be one. Therefore, concludes Thomas, every other substance which comes after the first simple substance participates in *esse*. But every participant is composed of that which participates and of that in which it participates. And that which participates is in potency to that in which it participates. Consequently, every

---

34. *Ed. cit.* (Calcaterra-Centi ed.), pp. 370–71. The central part of this argument is quoted in Ch. V above, n. 61.

35. " . . . et sic in quolibet creato aliud est natura rei quae participat esse, et aliud ipsum esse participatum. Et cum quaelibet res participet per assimilationem primum actum in quantum habet esse, necesse est quod esse participatum in unoquoque comparetur ad naturam participantem ipsum, sicut actus ad potentiam" (p. 371).

36. On this in Aquinas see especially T. Litt, *Les corps célestes dans l'univers de saint Thomas d'Aquin* (Louvain-Paris, 1963), ch. III, pp. 54–90. For the very different solution to this problem proposed by Godfrey of Fontaines see my *The Metaphysical Thought of Godfrey of Fontaines*, pp. 285–91.

substance apart from the first substance, no matter how simple it may be, is in potency with respect to existence (*potentia essendi*).[37]

Though this is also a God-to-creatures kind of argument, it leads to distinction and composition of essence and existence by introducing the theme of participation. The impossibility of there being more than one substance which is identical with its existence continues to play a central role in the reasoning.

Reference has already been made in Chapter V to the next text, taken from Thomas's *Treatise on Separate Substances*.[38] The context is familiar—refutation of matter-form composition in such entities. It will not follow, counters Aquinas, that if created spiritual substances lack matter, they cannot be distinguished from God. Granting that there is no matter in them, a certain potency remains insofar as they are not *esse* but merely participate in it. In proof, reasons Thomas, there can be only one self-subsistent being which is its very *esse*. Again he draws an analogy with other forms. If any such form is considered simply in itself, it is only one. And just as it is one in the order of thought when it is so viewed, it would be one in the order of reality if it could exist as such. Thomas suggests that the same applies to a genus in relationship to its species—if it could exist apart from its species it too could only be one. Finally, he says, we come to *esse* itself which is most general. Given this, he concludes that self-subsisting *esse* can only be one. And then, by contrasting all other beings with self-subsisting *esse*, he concludes that aside from God there can be no other subsisting entity which is pure *esse*. But since everything which exists has *esse*, in all such beings one must admit the presence both of existence (*esse*), viewed as act, and the substance (or essence) of that which has existence and is a potency with respect to its corresponding act (existence), which it receives.[39]

---

37. See *In VIII Physc.*, lect. 21, n. 1153 (Maggiòlo ed., p. 615). Note in particular: "Sed dato quod corpus caeleste non sit compositum ex materia et forma, adhuc oportet in ipso ponere aliquo modo potentiam essendi. Necesse est enim quod omnis substantia simplex subsistens, vel ipsa sit suum esse, vel participet esse. Substantia autem simplex quae est ipsum esse subsistens, non potest esse nisi una, sicut nec albedo, si esset subsistens, posset esse nisi una. Omnis ergo substantia quae est post primam substantiam simplicem, participat esse. Omne autem participans componitur ex participante et participato, et participans est in potentia ad participatum. In omni ergo substantia quantumcumque simplici, post primam substantiam simplicem, est potentia essendi."

38. See Ch. V, nn. 35, 54 (and the corresponding text).

39. See Lescoe ed., n. 42/Leonine ed., Vol. 40, p. D 55. Note in particular: "Ipsum igitur esse secundum se subsistens est unum tantum. Impossibile est igitur quod praeter ipsum sit aliquid subsistens quod sit esse tantum. Omne autem quod est esse habet. Est igitur in quocumque praeter primum et ipsum esse tamquam actus et substantia rei habens esse tamquam potentia receptiva huius actus qui est esse."

This text bears close similarities with others taken from Thomas's later writings and examined above. Once again it argues for the uniqueness of that being in which essence and existence are identical, and then, by contrasting this with all else, concludes that in everything else there is both existence, viewed as act, and substance (or essence) which as a corresponding potency receives existence. In support of the first point — the uniqueness of the being in which essence and existence are identical — it develops a line of thought already familiar to us from other texts such as SCG II, ch. 52 (2d arg.), *De spiritualibus creaturis,* and *In Physics VIII* (where it is mentioned in passing). The central thrust of that reasoning seems to be this: if any more restricted form (more restricted than *esse*) is considered in itself, it is one and undivided. If any such form could subsist in itself apart from everything else, it would then be one in the order of being. *Esse* itself is more general than anything else. Therefore, since *esse* does subsist in one case it too must be unique. Here one would do well to bear in mind an important distinction mentioned by Thomas in SCG II, ch. 52 (arg. 2). In fact *esse* is not divided by differences, as is a genus, but by being received in this or that subject. Nor, according to Aquinas, can one identify God (*esse subsistens*) with being in general.[40]

Like other versions of God-to-creatures argumentation considered above, the one found in the *Treatise on Separate Substances* then moves from the impossibility of there being more than one being which is its *esse* to the nonidentity (and in this case to act-potency composition) of essence and existence in all else. As I have already pointed out on a number of occasions, it seems to me that if this step in Thomas's reasoning is valid, it would hold even if one did not already know or assume that God exists; for it is based on the impossibility of there being more than one entity in which essence and existence are identical. As with some other texts dating from Thomas's later period, this one is set within the metaphysics of participation. But this observation brings us to another way in which Thomas approaches or argues for the real distinction — one based on participation.

---

40. See Ch. I above, nn. 86 and 87, where Thomas states that being as being or being in general (*ens commune*) is the subject of metaphysics. As we have seen in that same context, for him God is not the subject of metaphysics but is studied by it only insofar as he is a principle or cause of that which is included under *ens commune*. For explicit refusal to identify God with *esse commune* see Thomas's Commentary on the *Divine Names* (*In Librum B. Dionysii De divinis nominibus expositio,* C. Pera, ed. [Turin-Rome, 1950], p. 245, n. 660). See, for instance: " . . . alia existentia dependent ab esse communi, non autem Deus, sed magis esse commune dependet a Deo . . . . Secundo, quantum ad hoc quod omnia existentia continentur sub ipso esse communi, non autem Deus, sed magis esse commune continetur sub eius virtute . . . ."

3: Arguments Based on Participation

At various points in his career Thomas argued from the participated character of particular beings to the essence-existence distinction and/or composition within them. This type of argumentation seems to be relatively rare in Thomas's earlier writings, but appears more frequently in later works.[41] At the same time, in many cases it is closely joined with what we have called God-to-creatures argumentation, as is clear from some passages examined in the previous section. It would be premature, however, to assume that in using argumentation based on participation Thomas always proceeds from God, the unparticipated source, to participation and then to distinction of essence and existence in everything else. It is also interesting to observe that at times Thomas seems to reason from the participated character of particular beings to essence-existence distinction within them; at other times he reverses his procedure, by moving from essence-existence distinction to participation. In one interesting text, Quodlibet 2, q. 2, a. 1, both procedures seem to appear.[42]

Here I shall begin with two texts taken from Thomas's early writings, his Commentary on the *De Hebdomadibus* of Boethius, and *De veritate,* q. 21, a. 5. Since these two texts seem to date from roughly the same period, ca. 1256–1259, we shall first turn to the more fully developed presentation, that found in the Commentary on the *De Hebdomadibus,* lect. 2. As regards the remote context, Thomas is here commenting on the oft-quoted Boethian axiom: *diversum est esse et id quod est.*[43] In beginning his discussion

---

41. See Fabro, *La nozione metafisica di partecipazione,* p. 217. Also see the fine collection of texts based on participation running from pp. 222–43.

42. This text, dating from Christmas, 1269, gives an excellent overview of some of Thomas's thinking on participation. For the particular passages I have in mind, see: "Secundum ergo hoc dicendum est, quod ens praedicatur de solo Deo essentialiter, eo quod esse divinum est esse subsistens et absolutum; de qualibet autem creatura praedicatur per participationem; nulla enim creatura est suum esse, sed est habens esse" (Spiazzi ed., p. 24). Here he seems to reason from the essential presence of being in God to the participated character of being in every creature. But then, in seeming support of this point, he notes that no creature is its *esse,* but merely *has* esse. There he seems to reason from distinction in a creature of essence and *esse* to participation ("habens esse"). Shortly thereafter, however, he writes: "Quandocumque autem aliquid praedicatur de altero per participationem, oportet ibi aliquid esse praeter id quod participatur. Et ideo in qualibet creatura est aliud ipsa creatura quae habet esse, et ipsum esse eius . . . . ." Here he reasons from participation to otherness or distinction of *esse* (existence) and essence.

43. For this see *S. Thomae Aquinatis Opuscula theologica,* Vol. 2 (Turin-Rome, 1954), *In librum Boetii De Hebdomadibus expositio,* M. Calcaterra, ed., pp. 396ff. For discussion see Fabro, *La nozione,* pp. 24–32; *Partecipazione e causalità* (Turin, 1960), pp. 204–13; *Participation et causalité selon s. Thomas d'Aquin* (Louvain-Paris, 1961),

of this Thomas observes that the diversity mentioned by Boethius does not at this point refer to things (*res*) but rather to intelligibilities or intentions (*rationes seu intentiones*). In other words, Boethius is not here speaking of real distinction between *esse* and *id quod est*.[44] In this same context Thomas distinguishes between *id quod est* and *esse* as between a concrete subject, or being, on the one hand, and that which is signified abstractly, on the other. The concrete subject is identified as the subject of being. Hence one can say that a being (*ens*) is insofar as it participates in the act of being, or existence (*actus essendi*). See nn. 22–23. Farther on Thomas uses another Boethian axiom as the occasion to present one of his most interesting descriptions of participation (n. 24). Since this text has been exploited to good advantage by others, there will be no need to delay over it here.[45]

Still farther on, Thomas considers two more Boethian axioms. According to one of these, in every composite entity its *esse* and that which it is are not one and the same. According to the other, in every simple entity its *esse* and that which it is are identical. Thomas first takes up the question of composites (n. 32). He remarks here that just as *esse* and *id quod est* differ in intention or conception in the case of simple beings, in the case of composites they differ really (*differunt realiter*).[46] His argument in support of this is interesting. He recalls that according to his earlier remarks in this Commentary, *esse* does not participate in anything. Nor does *esse* admit of anything extraneous which might be mixed with it. Therefore, he continues, *esse* itself is not composed. Given this, he quickly concludes that a composite thing (*res*) is not its existence (*esse*).[47]

---

pp. 268–80; G. Schrimpf, *Die Axiomenschrift des Boethius (De Hebdomadibus) als philosophisches Lehrbuch des Mittelalters* (Leiden, 1966), pp. 119–34; Sweeney, *op. cit.*, pp. 120–23.

44. "Dicit ergo primo, quod diversum est esse, et id quod est. Quae quidem diversitas non est hic referenda ad res, de quibus adhuc non loquitur, sed ad ipsas rationes seu intentiones" (p. 296, n. 22).

45. Note the following from par. n. 23: " . . . et ideo sicut possumus dicere de eo quod currit, sive de currente, quod currat, inquantum subiicitur cursui et participat ipsum; ita possumus dicere quod ens, sive id quod est, sit, inquantum participat actum essendi." For discussion of the text on participation (n. 24), see Fabro, *La nozione*, pp. 27–28; Sweeney, *loc. cit.*, pp. 120–21; W. N. Clarke, "The Meaning of Participation in St. Thomas Aquinas," *Proceedings of the American Catholic Philosophical Association* 26 (1952), pp. 147–57.

46. "Est ergo primo considerandum, quod sicut esse et quod est differunt in simplicibus secundum intentiones, ita in compositis differunt realiter. . . ." (p. 398).

47. " . . . dictum est enim supra, quod ipsum esse neque participat aliquid, ut eius ratio constituatur ex multis; neque habet aliquid extraneum admixtum, ut sit in eo compositio accidentis; et ideo ipsum esse non est compositum. Res ergo composita non est suum esse . . . ." (n. 32, p. 398).

Essential to Thomas's argument is the claim that *esse* is not composed. Earlier in this Commentary (n. 24) he had noted that *esse* does not participate in anything in the way matter participates in a form, or a subject participates in an accidental form, or a particular participates in that which is universal. As he had there specified, *esse* itself is indeed participated in by other things. Thus it is the concrete subject which participates in it (existence or the *actus essendi* as he there describes it). Because he had there contrasted existence (*esse*) and *id quod est* as that which is signified abstractly, on the one hand, and the concrete subject, on the other, he had also argued that while the concrete subject can admit of the addition of something extraneous such as an accidental form, such is not true of existence (*esse*). It was for these reasons that he had there concluded that existence (*esse*) itself is not composed.[48] To return to his argument for real distinction of essence and existence, it rests upon this conclusion. If existence is simple and therefore not composed, it cannot be identified with any composite essence. Therefore Thomas can conclude, as we have seen, that in every composite entity (composed of matter and form, presumably) existence (*esse*) and essence (*id quod est*) differ and, for Thomas though not for Boethius, differ really.[49]

One might wonder, however, whether this kind of argument can lead to real distinction of essence and existence in entities whose essence itself is not composed, for instance in souls or in angels. In this case the argument just used seems to break down. Granted that the existence of such beings is not composed, neither is their essence.

Thomas's recognition of this difficulty may account for the next step in his Commentary. With Boethius he agrees that in simple entities existence and essence are really identical (n. 33). If essence and existence were really distinct in such entities, the beings in question would not be simple but composite. At this juncture Thomas introduces a precision. Something may be simple in one sense without being entirely simple. Hence if one discovers certain forms which are not present in matter, each of these may be regarded as simple insofar as it lacks matter. But since every such form does determine *esse*, no such form is *esse* itself but rather merely has *esse*. What Thomas has in mind is that any such form, being more restricted in extension than *esse* itself, must determine or specify *esse* to some degree if it is to "have" *esse*.[50]

---

48. Note in particular: " . . . unde ipsum quidem participatur in aliis, non autem participat aliquid aliud. Sed id quod est, sive ens, quamvis sit communissimum, tamen concretive dicitur; et ideo participat ipsum esse, non per modum quo magis commune participatur a minus communi, sed participat ipsum esse per modum quo concretum participat abstractum" (n. 24, p. 397).

49. See n. 32, p. 398.

50. See n. 34, p. 398. Note especially: " . . . quia tamen quaelibet forma est determinativa ipsius esse, nulla earum est ipsum esse, sed est habens esse."

Here Thomas introduces a rather surprising example. Suppose that Plato was correct and that certain Platonic forms or ideas do subsist, a form of horse, for instance, and a form of man, any such form would not be *esse commune* but would only participate in it. The same will hold, continues Thomas, if with Aristotle we admit that there are other separate substances of even higher rank than Plato's forms. Each of these, insofar as it is a given entity and distinguished from others, will participate in *esse*. Therefore no such form will be perfectly simple. Given all of this, Thomas concludes that there will be only one truly simple being. This being does not merely participate in *esse*. It is subsisting *esse*. And such a being, continues Thomas, can only be one. For if *esse* (taken as the *actus essendi* or existence) can admit of nothing extraneous which might be mixed with it, it is equally impossible for that subject which is existence itself to be multiplied by anything which might diversify it.[51]

What is one to say of this lengthy and complicated argumentation? First of all, it has the merit of distinguishing clearly between a merely conceptual distinction and a real distinction between essence and existence. If it begins by finding only the former in the Boethian text, it ends by defending the latter. Secondly, it involves two different ways of reasoning to such real distinction. In the case of matter-form composites, Thomas recalls the Boethian position that *esse* is not composite or composed. This being so, it cannot be identified with the essence of any composite being. As regards nondivine entities whose essences are not composed, however, another kind of argumentation has been introduced. Any such being enjoys only a given kind of being when compared with the perfection of *esse* simply viewed in itself. Given this, any particular immaterial entity only has being or participates in being (*esse*). Hence it cannot be identical with its *esse*. In other words, in this second approach Thomas reasons from the participated character of any such being to real distinction of it (its essence) from the *esse* (existence) in which it participates. This approach suggests that there may be a less complicated way of reasoning from the participated character of any being (whether composed of matter and form or not) to real distinction of essence and existence in that being. And as it appears here, this argument does not seem to rest on or presuppose prior knowledge of the existence of God. On

---

51. See p. 398, nn. 34–35. Note in particular: " . . . unaquaeque illarum, inquantum distinguitur ab alia, quaedam specialis forma est participans ipsum esse; et sic nulla earum erit vere simplex" (n. 34). Also: "Hoc autem non potest esse nisi unum; quia si ipsum esse nihil aliud habet admixtum praeter id quod est esse, ut dictum est, impossibile est id quod est ipsum esse, multiplicari per aliquid diversificans" (n. 35).

the contrary, it moves from distinction of essence and existence in other beings to identity of the same in God.[52]

As our second text from Thomas's earlier writings we shall turn to *De veritate*, q. 21, a. 5. There Thomas is seeking to determine whether any created good is good of its essence. In bringing out certain differences between divine goodness and the goodness of creatures, Thomas mentions this along with others. In a creature one does not discover its essential goodness merely by attending to its nature viewed in itself (*secundum considerationem naturae absolutam*), but by considering it (the creature) in terms of its *esse*. This is so because humanity does not possess the intelligibility of goodness except insofar as it exists (*habet esse*). But, continues Thomas, the divine essence is its *esse*. The nature or essence of any created thing, however, is not its *esse* (existence), but rather participates in *esse* from something else. Hence, concludes Thomas, because God is his subsisting existence, pure existence (*esse*) is realized in him. But in creatures existence (*esse*) is received and participated.[53]

Though cited both by Sweeney and Fabro,[54] this text is not so much an argument for the real distinction as a simple statement that while the divine essence is identical with its existence, such is not true of any creature. In what might perhaps be taken as an argument for this claim, Thomas immediately adds that creatures participate in *esse* from something else. Hence in this text he seems to connect closely or perhaps even to identify participation with being efficiently caused. Perhaps the argument is intended to

---

52. Central to this second argument seems to be the view that any particular being can be considered as participating in being (*esse*) when it is compared with the fullness of being simply viewed in itself, that is, with *esse commune*. One might wonder whether the kind of participation discovered by such a comparison is more than logical or conceptual, that is, one involving concepts. Thomas seems to think that it is, apparently because here he believes that if we examine any particular being we find that it enjoys only a particular kind and degree of being. Hence it cannot be identified with being as such, or with existence. On the other hand, on other occasions he will establish the participated character of created being by beginning with a given being, the divine, and by reasoning by way of contrast to the participated character of everything else. See the texts cited above in n. 42. This suggests that for Aquinas one may speak of participation by particular beings in being, meaning thereby the divine being (as when an effect participates in its cause, for instance), or meaning thereby having without exhausting the fullness of being (participating without exhausting *esse commune*). When Thomas establishes the participated character of particular beings in the first way, he does, of course, presuppose the existence of God.

53. *Ed. cit.*, p. 385/Leonine ed., Vol. 22.3, p. 606. Note in particular: "Ipsa autem natura vel essentia divina est eius esse; natura autem vel essentia cuiuslibet rei creatae non est suum esse, sed esse participans ab alio."

54. Sweeney, pp. 125–26; Fabro, *La nozione*, p. 224.

move from the contrast between God, in whom essence and existence are identical, to the participated character of created existence, and from this to distinction of essence and existence in every creature. If so, it combines participation with a movement from God to creatures.

At this point some texts will be considered from Thomas's later writings where he moves from participation to the essence-existence distinction. Although Fabro has cited a host of such texts, only a few will be examined here. One such text appears in SCG II, ch. 52 (ca. 1262). As we have already seen, in this particular chapter Thomas is arguing for distinction and composition of essence (*quod est*) and existence (*esse*) in created intellectual substances, even though he has denied matter-form composition of them. As his last (philosophical) argument in this discussion, Thomas observes that *esse* belongs to God by his very nature.[55] In proof he recalls that he has already shown (see Bk. I, ch. 22) that God's essence (*substantia*) is his existence. But, continues Thomas, what belongs to something by its very nature cannot be found in others except by participation. Therefore existence (*esse*) pertains to other things only because they participate in it. But what belongs to something by participation is not its substance. Therefore it is impossible for the substance of any other being apart from the first agent to be its *esse*.[56]

In this argument Thomas moves from identity of essence and existence in God to the fact that existence belongs to God essentially. Then, by contrast, he concludes that existence can belong to other things only by participation. From this he draws the conclusion that in other things essence and existence are not identical or are distinct. In this text, therefore, God's existence is presupposed, as is identity of essence and existence in him. The argument moves from his unparticipated character to participation in existence by all other beings. From this it concludes to real distinction of essence and existence in all else.

Another interesting version of this approach appears in Quodlibet 3, q. 8, a. 1 (dating from 1270). Here Thomas is discussing alleged matter-form composition of the human soul, and wishes to show that every created substance is composed of potency and act. He begins by recalling that God

---

55. The chapter concludes with a reference to the well-known text from Exodus 3:14: "Hinc est quod *Exodi* III, 14, proprium nomen Dei ponitur esse QUI EST . . . " (*ed. cit.*, p. 146).

56. Note in particular: "Quod autem competit alicui secundum propriam naturam suam, non convenit aliis nisi per modum participationis . . . . Ipsum igitur esse competit omnibus aliis a primo agente per participationem quandam. Quod autem competit alicui per participationem non est substantia eius. Impossibile est igitur quod substantia alterius entis praeter agens primum sit ipsum esse" (*ibid.*).

alone is his very existence (*esse*), and exists, as it were, essentially: for his existence is identical with his essence (*substantia*). This can be said of no other being, argues Thomas, since just as there could be only one subsisting whiteness, if such were possible, there can be only one subsisting *esse*. Therefore, he continues, every other thing is a being (*ens*) by participation. Given this he concludes that in every such being the substance which participates in existence differs from the participated existence itself. But every participant is related to that in which it participates as potency to act. Therefore, every created substance is composed of potency and act, or to use Boethian language, of *quod est* and *esse*.[57]

In this argument Thomas begins by taking as granted God's existence as well as identity of essence and existence in God. By contrast he reasons that this—identity of essence and existence—can be said of no other being. Here he appeals to a familiar theme, the impossibility of there being more than one subsisting existence. As I have suggested in other contexts, this part of the argument, based as it is on the impossibility of there being more than one subsisting *esse*, should hold even without one's assuming that God actually exists. Thomas moves from the uniqueness of that being which is its existence to the conclusion that everything else is being only by participation. And he reasons from the participated character of such entities to distinction in them of essence and existence. It should be noted, if only in passing, that the reasoning used in this argument is quite similar to that found in the text taken from Thomas's Commentary on *Physics* VIII and examined in the previous section of this chapter.[58]

Another brief but interesting version of this kind of argumentation occurs in Thomas's Commentary on the *Posterior Analytics,* Bk. II, lect. 6. As regards the immediate context, Thomas is attempting to show that it is not possible for someone by a single demonstration to establish both *quid est* and *quia est* concerning something. He begins by observing that the quiddity (the "what it is") of man differs from a man's existence. In proof he notes that *esse* and quiddity are one and the same only in the first principle of being, which is being essentially. In all other things, which are beings by participation, *esse* and quiddity must differ.[59]

---

57. *Ed. cit.*, pp. 60–61. Note in particular: "Manifestum est enim quod solus Deus est suum esse, quasi essentialiter existens, in quantum scilicet suum esse est eius substantia. Quod de nullo alio dici potest: esse enim subsistens non potest esse nisi unum, sicut nec albedo subsistens non potest esse nisi unum. Oportet ergo quod quaelibet alia res sit ens participative, ita quod aliud sit in eo substantia participans esse, et aliud ipsum esse participatum."

58. For this see n. 37 above and the corresponding text.

59. *In Aristotelis libros Peri Hermeneias et Posteriorum Analyticorum Expositio*, R. Spiazzi, ed. (Turin-Rome, 1964), p. 344, n. 462: "Sed aliud est *quod quid est homo*, et *esse*

This argument moves from identity of essence and existence in God, who is being essentially, to distinction of essence and existence in all others, which are beings by participation. But the contrast seems to be especially between essential being (in which essence and existence are identical) and participated being. From this the argument quickly concludes to distinction of quiddity and existence in every participated being. If so, this is another example of argumentation which moves from God to the participated character of all else, and from that in turn to essence-existence distinction in the latter.

Enough representative arguments based on participation have now been examined to show that this is an important approach to the essence-existence distinction, especially for the later Aquinas. Many of the texts just examined do begin with the assumption that God exists. At the same time, at least one does not (see the second argument offered in the Commentary on the *De Hebdomadibus*). And if my interpretation is correct, others would not have to do so in terms of their inner logic (see, for instance, that found in Quodlibet 3, q. 8, a. 1, or that taken from the Commentary on *Physics* VIII).

4: Argumentation Based on the Limited Character of Individual Beings

With this we come to the final kind of argumentation for the essence-existence distinction in created beings which I have singled out above. This particular argument incorporates principles which recur frequently throughout Thomas's writings; but it appears most rarely as a formal argument for the real distinction in his texts. In fact, to the best of my knowledge, the only instance where it is explicitly used for this purpose occurs in his Commentary on I *Sent.*, d. 8, q. 5, a. 1. And even there it is found in the *sed contra* rather than in the *corpus*. Nonetheless, since it draws on principles which Aquinas clearly accepts and since it supports the conclusion he is there attempting to establish, one seems justified in presuming that he accepts it.

In this particular article, as will be recalled, Thomas is attempting to determine whether any creature is simple. In rejecting the claim that some creature is completely simple, the second argument to the contrary runs this way. Every creature has limited *esse*. But any *esse* which is not received in something is not finite but unrestricted (*absolutum*). Therefore, every creature has an *esse* which is received in something else; hence it must consist of at least two (principles), existence (*esse*), and that which receives existence.[60]

---

hominem: in solo enim primo essendi Principio, quod est essentialiter ens, ipsum *esse* et *quidditas* eius est unum et idem; in omnibus aliis, quae sunt entia per participationem, oportet quod sit aliud *esse* et *quidditas* entis."

60. *Ed. cit.*, Vol. 1, p. 226. "Praeterea, omnis creatura habet esse finitum. Sed esse non receptum in aliquo, non est finitum, immo absolutum. Ergo omnis creatura

This argument starts from the fact that creatures have only limited *esse*. For Thomas it would be evident that beings are limited; and if they are limited, their existence (*esse*) must also be limited. This would also follow from Thomas's conviction that there cannot be two infinite beings. As we have seen, he explicitly argues against this possibility in SCG II, ch. 52.[61] Also presupposed by this argument is the claim that if *esse* were not received in something else it would not be finite, but infinite. If one concedes this point — that unreceived *esse* is unlimited or infinite — one has a powerful philosophical argument for the essence-existence distinction in all finite beings. One will have to admit the presence of an existence principle (*esse*) in such beings to account for their actual existence, and another principle which receives and limits their existence (an essence principle) to account for their limitation. This will follow because existence as such is not self-limiting.

The view that act as such or that existence (*esse*) as such is not self-limiting frequently recurs in Thomas's writings.[62] At the same time, I must admit that I have never succeeded in finding a demonstration or even an attempted demonstration of this point in his texts. One might suggest that he bases it on the infinity of God. This will not do, however, since on many occasions

---

habet esse receptum in aliquo; et ita oportet quod habeat duo ad minus, scilicet esse, et id quod esse recipit."

61. For this argument see above, n. 31 and the corresponding text. Not quite the same as the argument for the essence-existence distinction based on limitation is another which appears in this same context (SCG II, ch. 52), that is, one based on the claim that *esse* insofar as it is *esse* is not self-diversifying. Hence it can only be diversified (or divided) by something that is other than *esse*, that is to say, by essence. "Esse autem, inquantum est esse, non potest esse diversum: potest autem diversificari per aliquid quod est praeter esse; sicut esse lapidis est aliud ab esse hominis" (*ed. cit.*, p. 145). But rather than let this argument stand alone, Thomas then moves into one of his God-to-creatures arguments, based on the uniqueness of *esse subsistens*. (For continuation of the text see n. 27 above in the present chapter.)

62. For some representative texts see *In I Sent.*, d. 43, q. 1, a. 1 (*ed. cit.*, Vol. 1, p. 1003) where Thomas first applies this to any form considered in itself and abstractly, and then moves from this to the case of *esse*, and from this to divine infinity ("Et ideo illud quod habet esse absolutum et nullo modo receptum in aliquo, immo ipsemet est suum esse, illud est infinitum simpliciter . . . "); *In I Sent.*, d. 8, q. 2, a. 1 (used to show that only the divine *esse* is not limited ["terminatum"] in any way [p. 202]); SCG I, ch. 43 (p. 41) where it is used to prove divine infinity ("Actus igitur in nullo existens nullo terminatur . . . "); ST I, q. 7, a. 1 (to prove divine infinity); and *Compendium theologiae*, ch. 18 (to prove divine infinity): "Nullus enim actus invenitur finiri nisi per potentiam, quae est vis receptiva . . . ." *ed. cit.*, p. 18/Leonine ed. Vol. 42, p. 88:7–8. On the other hand, in *De spiritualibus creaturis*, q. 1, a. 1, he uses the same kind of reasoning to move in the opposite direction; that is, given the infinity of God, his *esse* cannot be received by any distinct nature; for then it would be limited to that nature (*ed. cit.*, p. 370).

he turns to this principle in order to prove that God is infinite.[63] Hence my strong suspicion is that for Aquinas it is a self-evident axiom. I stress "for Aquinas," because it seems to hold only if one has a certain understanding of being, and above all, of existence, viewed as the actuality of all acts and the perfection of all perfections.[64] If this is one's understanding of existence, and it certainly is Thomas's, it will not be unreasonable to conclude that existence (*esse*) — the act of all acts and the perfection of all perfections — is not self-limiting. To say anything else would be to account for the limitation and imperfection (taken as the negation of further perfection) of a being by appealing to that which is its ultimate principle of actuality and perfection.

Finally, one may ask whether this argument presupposes prior knowledge of God's existence. Its starting point, the fact that limited beings exist, clearly does not. Nor does its appeal to the axiom that unreceived *esse* is unlimited seem to require such knowledge. Against this, however, one may object that by my own admission this axiom rests on Thomas's particular way of understanding being and especially existence (*esse* viewed as the actuality of all acts and the perfection of all perfections). Did not Thomas depend on prior knowledge of God's existence, perhaps even on his reading of Scripture (Exodus 3:14), in order to reach this understanding of existence?

In reply to any such suggestion I would recall one of Thomas's finest discussions of his particular views concerning *esse*—*De potentia*, q. 7, a. 2, ad 9. In this text there is no indication that Thomas must presuppose God's existence

---

63. See most of the texts cited in the preceding note. Also see L. Sweeney, "Presidential Address: Surprises in the History of Infinity from Anaximander to George Cantor," *Proceedings of the American Catholic Philosophical Association* 45 (1981), pp. 11–12; and in the same D. L. Balas, "A Thomist View on Divine Infinity," pp. 91–98. On the importance of this axiom for Thomas's metaphysics (that unreceived act is unlimited) see W. N. Clarke, "The Limitation of Act by Potency: Aristotelianism or Neoplatonism," *The New Scholasticism* 26 (1952), pp. 167–94; de Finance, *Etre et agir*, pp. 51–56; Fabro, *Participation et causalité*, pp. 64ff., and his references to J.-H. Nicolas.

64. See, for instance, Quodlibet 9, q. 4, a. 1 (quoted above, n. 25); *In De Hebdomadibus*, lect. 2 (cited above in n. 45 and discussed in my corresponding text); Quodlibet 12, q. 5, a. 1: "Primus autem actus est esse subsistens per se; unde completionem unumquodque recipit per hoc quod participat esse; unde esse est complementum omnis formae, quia per hoc completur quod habet esse, et habet esse cum est actu: et sic nulla forma est nisi per esse. Et sic dico quod esse substantiale rei non est accidens, sed actualitas cuiuslibet formae existentis . . . " (p. 227); ST I, q. 3, a. 4: " . . . esse est actualitas omnis formae vel naturae: non enim bonitas vel humanitas significatur in actu, nisi prout significamus eam esse . . . " (*ed. cit.*, p. 17); ST I, q. 4, a. 1, ad 3: " . . . ipsum esse est perfectissimum omnium: comparatur enim ad omnia ut actus. Nihil enim habet actualitatem, nisi in quantum est: unde ipsum esse est actualitas omnium rerum et etiam ipsarum formarum. Unde non comparatur ad alia sicut recipiens ad receptum, sed magis sicut receptum ad recipiens" (p. 21). For discussion and other texts see de Finance, *op. cit.*, pp. 111–19.

in order to account for his view of existence. There he comments that what he calls *esse* is the most perfect of all for this reason, that act is always more perfect than potency. But any given form is not understood as enjoying actuality except insofar as it is held to be. Thus humanity or the nature of fire can be considered as existing (1) in the potency of matter; or (2) within the power of an agent which could bring it into being; or (3) in the intellect. But it is only (4) by reason of what Thomas calls *esse* that any such thing is rendered actually existing. Because of this, continues Thomas, *esse* is the actuality of all acts and the perfection of all perfections.[65] This text does not

---

65. Here Thomas is replying to the 9th objection against the position he here defends—that in God substance or essence and *esse* are identical. The objection runs: That which is most imperfect cannot be attributed to God, who is most perfect. But, like prime matter, *esse* is most imperfect; just as prime matter is determined by all forms, *esse*, since it is most imperfect, must be determined by all of the predicaments. From his reply, note: " . . . quod hoc quod dico *esse* est inter omnia perfectissimum: quod ex hoc patet quia actus est semper perfectio[r] potentia. Quaelibet autem forma signata non intelligitur in actu nisi per hoc quod esse ponitur. Nam humanitas vel igneitas potest considerari ut in potentia materiae existens, vel ut in virtute agentis, aut etiam ut in intellectu: sed hoc quod habet *esse*, efficitur actu existens. Unde patet quod hoc quod dico *esse* est actualitas omnium actuum, et propter hoc est perfectio omnium perfectionum. Nec intelligendum est, quod ei quod dico *esse*, aliquid addatur quod sit eo formalius, ipsum determinans, sicut actus potentiam: *esse* enim quod huiusmodi est, est aliud secundum essentiam ab eo cui additur determinandum" (*ed. cit.*, p. 192). Real distinction between existence (*esse*) and that to which it is "added" (nature or essence) seems to be implied by the final part of this text. Though our approaches differ in a number of respects, the reader will find it interesting to consult J.-D. Robert, "Le principe: 'Actus non limitatur nisi per potentiam subjectivam realiter distinctam,'" *Revue philosophique de Louvain* 47 (1949), pp. 44–70. While never finding Thomas reasoning explicitly from the principle that limited act must be received by a distinct potency to the essence-existence distinction, he does conclude that this kind of argument is in accord with Thomas's metaphysical thought (see pp. 51, 53ff.). As regards Thomas's reasons for holding that act as such and especially that *esse* as such is not self-limiting, a number of years ago I had considered the possibility of connecting this with Thomas's views concerning *separatio*. If through *separatio* one judges that that by reason of which something is recognized as being need not be identified with that by reason of which it is recognized as enjoying a given kind of being, perhaps through *separatio* Thomas would also have us infer that that by reason of which something enjoys *esse* need not be identified with that by reason of which its *esse* is limited. Therefore *esse* as such need not be limited and hence is not self-limiting. It now seems to me that this approach will not do. First of all, the axiom makes a stronger claim. Not only does it assert that *esse* in order to be realized as such *need* not be limited but that it *is* not self-limiting. Secondly, it also seems to me that *separatio* is applied by Aquinas to one's discovery of being (*ens*) as being, the subject of metaphysics, and not merely to *esse* (taken as existence). Thomas's reasons for holding that *esse* is not self-limiting surely deserve further investigation, but this will have to be deferred for another occasion.

convey the impression that, according to Aquinas, one must depend on prior knowledge of God's existence in order to arrive at this understanding of *esse*. Hence, an argument for the distinction between essence and existence based on the limited character of existence as we discover it in individual entities need not do so either.

CHAPTER VII

THOMAS AQUINAS, HENRY OF GHENT, AND GODFREY OF FONTAINES ON THE REALITY OF NONEXISTING POSSIBLES

In this chapter I shall concentrate on three leading philosophical and theological thinkers of the thirteenth century: Thomas Aquinas, Henry of Ghent, and Godfrey of Fontaines. Of these, Thomas is surely the best known. But I have selected these three because their discussions of nonexisting possibles are sufficiently different from one another to illustrate some of the major solutions proposed to this issue at that time.

Before turning to these three thinkers in particular, I should like to sharpen the focus of this chapter by reducing its major concern to three questions. A first has to do with what one might term the ontological or metaphysical status of not-yet-existent possibles, or, for that matter, even of those that will never in fact enjoy actual existence, even though they could do so. By this I have in mind the following. Do such "possibles" enjoy any reality, any real being (*ens reale*) in themselves, and if so, to what extent? For instance, before any individual man actually existed, did the essence of man or of any particular man enjoy some kind of reality, some kind of real being, in itself? Secondly, if nonexisting possibles do enjoy any kind of reality, what is the ultimate ontological foundation for this? Thirdly, since most medieval thinkers who do assign any kind of reality to possibles in some way ground this in God, one may also ask: Can God do or make certain things only because they are possible in themselves? Or is it only because God can produce them that they are possible? In discussing the answer to this third question in two of these thinkers, Thomas and Henry, I shall introduce another and closely related issue: Are possibles freely or necessarily such from eternity?

With these three major questions in mind, I now propose to return to the University of Paris and the second half of the thirteenth century. I shall first consider Aquinas, who served as Master in Theology there from 1256 until 1259 and again from 1269 until 1272; then Henry of Ghent, who functioned there as Master from 1276 until ca. 1292; and finally, Godfrey of Fontaines, whose career as a Parisian Master runs from 1285 until ca. 1303 or 1304. It is worth mentioning in passing that both Godfrey and Henry were already present in Paris during Thomas's second teaching period there, that is, from 1269 to 1272.[1]

I

On various occasions Aquinas distinguishes between two fundamentally different usages of the term "possible." On the one hand, something may be described as possible insofar as it is in potency. This kind of possible may be subdivided, in that something may be possible by reason of an active potency, or else by reason of some kind of passive potency. In the first case, something is said to be possible because an agent exists with the capacity or power to bring it into being. Thus that which is within human capability is said to be possible for man. In the second case, something is possible because of some already existing passive potentiality. Thus it is possible for wood to be burnt because of its capacity, its passive potentiality, to be ignited.

On the other hand, Thomas points out, something may be said to be possible, but not by reason of any active or passive potency or power. It will be possible in this absolute or unqualified sense when the terms in which it is expressed are not self-contradictory or incompatible. Because a given predicate is not repugnant to a given subject, one might say that something is possible in this way, for instance, that it is possible for man to be a rational animal. Conversely, something is described as impossible in this absolute sense if the terms in which it is expressed are repugnant to one another, or, in other words, if it entails self-contradiction (for instance, a square circle).[2]

---

1. For Henry's life and works see R. Macken, ed., *Henrici de Gandavo Quodlibet I* (Louvain-Leiden, 1979), pp. vii–xxiv. For Godfrey's life and works see my *The Metaphysical Thought of Godfrey of Fontaines*, pp. xv–xxxiv.

2. See, for instance, SCG II, ch. 37, where Thomas comments that it was possible for created being to exist before it actually did because of the preexisting power of an agent which could bring it into being and because of the lack of repugnance between the terms involved in saying that a given creature exists. He notes that this latter way of describing the possible is that whereby something is possible by reason of no potency or potentiality. He spells out his understanding of the divisions of the possible more fully in his *De potentia Dei* (1265–1266). There, in q. 3, a. 14, with acknowledged dependency upon Aristotle's *Metaphysics* V (see ch. 12), he comments that something may be said to be possible either by reason of some potency, or else not by reason of any potency. In the first case, it may be described as possible either

Thomas frequently connects his discussions of the possible with God. Before creation, he reasons, the world could exist, or was possible, not in the sense that there was any preexisting passive potency or matter from which it might be formed, but in the other two senses distinguished above. From all eternity God had the active power or ability to create the world from nothingness even though, according to Christian religious belief, he did not choose to actualize this capacity from eternity. And before it actually existed, the world was also possible in the absolute sense, in that no intrinsic contradiction would have been entailed by the statement "The world exists" had God then chosen to actualize its possibility.[3] (In fact, against many of his contemporaries, Aquinas maintained that one cannot demonstrate that the world began to be and, or so I would contend, in his final discussion of this in his *De aeternitate mundi,* defended the possibility of an eternally created world.)[4]

Given this understanding of the term "possible," we are now in position to direct the first of our three questions to Thomas: Do such nonexistent or not-yet-existent possibles enjoy any reality, any real being, in themselves, prior to their realization as actually existing entities? Thomas touches on this issue in some of his discussions of the notion of eternal truths. For instance, in the *Summa theologiae* I, q. 16, a. 7, he comments that there is only one eternal truth — God himself. If there were no eternally existing intellect, there could be no eternal truth. And since in his opinion only the divine intellect is in fact eternal, in it alone does truth enjoy eternity.[5] It seems to follow from this that for Thomas, apart from God, there is not and cannot be any eternal truth.

---

by reason of an active power or agent, or by reason of a passive potentiality. In the latter case, where something is said to be possible but not by reason of any potency or power, the term possible can be applied metaphorically (see the geometrical description of a line as a rational power or as potentially commensurable [see q. 1, a. 3]), or in the absolute sense, as when the terms of a proposition are not repugnant to one another. On the other hand, something is to be described as absolutely impossible when it does entail self-contradiction. Also see *De potentia Dei,* q. 1, a. 3. Cf. *In V Met.,* lect. 14, M.-R. Cathala and R. M. Spiazzi, eds. (Turin-Rome, 1950), nn. 954–76; ST I, q. 25, a. 3.

3. See *De potentia Dei,* q. 3, a. 1, ad 2; q. 3, a. 17, ad 10; SCG II, ch. 37; ST I, q. 46, a. 1, ad 1.

4. See Ch. VIII below.

5. Note Thomas's warning at the end of the corpus of his reply: "Nec propter hoc sequitur quod aliquid aliud sit aeternum quam Deus: quia veritas intellectus divini est ipse Deus . . . " See his reply to objection 4 where he comments that propositions formed by us do not enjoy eternal truth, since our intellects are not eternal. See A. Maurer, "St. Thomas and Eternal Truths," *Mediaeval Studies* 32 (1970), pp. 91–107; *St. Thomas and Historicity* (Milwaukee, 1979), pp. 26–31.

One might ask, as did some of Thomas's contemporaries, whether statements concerning nonexistent possibles can be true. If no man existed, for instance, would this statement be true — that man is a rational animal? It is clear enough that in discussing this issue Thomas assigns no distinctive ontological reality to the referents of such statements apart from their existence in some intellect. Prior to the creation of men, or at least of angels, such truths did not exist, maintains Thomas, except in the divine intellect. To say that they exist there is not to assign to them any reality in distinction from that of God. Prior to the creation of some created intellect, then, would it still be true that two and three equal five? "Yes," replies Thomas, "but only in the divine intellect."[6]

Another way of approaching Thomas's answer to our first question is to recall that for him a divine idea is nothing but a given way in which God views his essence as capable of being imitated by a creature. Prior to the actual creation of a given entity there is a divine idea to which that creature will correspond if it is ever brought into actual being. Simply viewed as a principle whereby God knows creatures, a divine idea is also known as a divine *ratio*. But if a given creature is to be brought into actual existence at any point in time, then the divine idea to which it corresponds will also serve as a principle of divine production, and may be called an *exemplar*.[7] In other words, divine ideas or divine *rationes* obtain even for possibles in the purest sense, that is, for those that will never be realized in fact. But divine ideas in the sense of *exemplars* obtain only for those that will indeed enjoy actual existence.[8] Before the actual creation of a given entity, however, and

---

6. For Thomas see ST I, q. 16, a. 7, ad 1. See, for instance, the important work by Siger of Brabant, "Quaestio utrum haec sit vera: homo est animal, nullo homine existente," in *Siger de Brabant, Ecrits de logique, de morale et de physique*, B. Bazán, ed. (Louvain-Paris, 1974), pp. 53–59. Also see Bazán's discussion of this in his "La signification des termes communs et la doctrine de la supposition chez Maître Siger de Brabant," *Revue philosophique de Louvain* 77 (1979), pp. 366–70. Also cf. an interesting anonymous text published by A. Zimmermann, "Eine anonyme Quaestio: Utrum haec sit vera: Homo est animal, homine non existente," *Archiv für Geschichte der Philosophie* 49 (1967), pp. 183–200; and a series of texts edited by Sten Ebbesen and Jan Pinborg, "Studies in the Logical Writings Attributed to Boethius of Dacia," *Cahiers de l'Institut du moyen âge grec et latin* (Copenhagen) 3 (1970).

7. See ST I, q. 15, a. 1; q. 15, a. 3 and ad 2 (on the distinction between a divine idea as *ratio* and as exemplar).

8. ST I, q. 15, a. 3, ad 2: "Ad secundum dicendum quod eorum quae neque sunt neque erunt neque fuerunt, Deus non habet practicam cognitionem, nisi virtute tantum. Unde respectu eorum non est idea in Deo, secundum quod idea significat exemplar, sed solum secundum quod significat rationem." For detailed discussion of God's knowledge see *De veritate*, q. 2. There see a. 7 on the universal scope of that knowledge: "Et ideo Deus cognoscit de unoquoque singulari quod nunc est vel non

before the actual creation of the universe, its divine idea is the maximum degree of reality enjoyed by any possible entity, whether or not it will eventually come into actual existence. From the ontological standpoint, any such divine idea is really identical with the divine essence.[9] This point is important for Aquinas, I might add, because of his view that there is real composition of essence and existence (*esse*) in actually existing creatures. He insists, for instance in *De potentia*, q. 3, a. 5, that when a creature is actually created, being created applies both to its essence principle and its existence principle. Neither in fact actually preexists as such.[10]

Given this, there is no place within Thomas's metaphysics for any eternally preexisting possible that would enjoy some kind of being in distinction from that of the divine essence itself. According to Thomas, prior to its realization as an existing individual, a possible enjoys no distinctive reality from eternity apart from its presence in the divine intellect as a divine idea. And since a divine idea is really identical with the divine essence, a possible enjoys no reality in itself apart from that of God.

---

est; et cognoscit omnia alia enuntiabilia quae formari possunt vel de universalibus, vel de individuis." See *ed. cit.*, p. 43/Leonine ed., Vol. 22.1, p. 68. See a. 8 on God's knowledge of possibles that will never come into actual existence. Given this, God's knowledge extends to an infinity of things since he not only knows things past, present and future, but also all things which can imitate his unlimited goodness, or, in other words, an infinity of possibles (a. 9, pp. 46–47/Leonine ed., Vol. 22.1, pp. 72–73). For more on this also see ST I, q. 14, a. 9 (God's knowledge of things that actually have been, are, or will be, is called his *scientia visionis*. His knowledge of possibles that neither are, were, nor will be is called his *scientia simplicis intelligentiae*); ST I, q. 14, a. 12 (God's knowledge extends to an infinity of things, since he knows all that is within his power); q. 15, a. 2 (God perfectly knows his essence; hence he knows it in every way in which it can be participated in by creatures). For more on Thomas's theory of divine ideas see L. Geiger, "Les idées divines dans l'oeuvre de s. Thomas," in *St. Thomas Aquinas 1274–1974: Commemorative Studies*, ed. A. Maurer (Toronto, 1974), Vol. 1, pp. 175–209.

9. See *In I Sent.*, d. 19, q. 5, a. 3, ad 2, *ed. cit.*, Vol. 1, p. 496: "Ad secundum dicendum quod rationes ideales rerum, quae sunt in Deo ab aeterno, non sunt aliud secundum rem ab ipso intellectu et essentia divina." Also see *De veritate*, q. 2, a. 3, ad 3 (p. 33/Leonine ed., Vol. 22.1, p. 52): "Similiter nec in deo cum agat per suam essentiam, effectus eius in eo non est distinctus ab essentia sua, sed omnino unum; et ideo hoc quo cognoscit creaturam, non est aliud quam essentia sua." Also, ST I, q. 15, a. 1, ad 3: "Ad tertium dicendum quod Deus secundum essentiam suam est similitudo omnium rerum. Unde idea in Deo nihil est aliud quam Dei essentia."

10. "Ad secundum dicendum, quod ex hoc ipso quod quidditati esse attribuitur, non solum esse, sed ipsa quidditas creari dicitur: quia antequam esse habeat, nihil est, nisi forte in intellectu creantis, ubi non est creatura, sed creatrix essentia" (*ed. cit.*, p. 49).

With this we have really also come to Thomas's answer to our second question. The ultimate ontological foundation for a possible is the divine essence itself, insofar as it is viewed as capable of being imitated in a given way. From the ontological standpoint, one may say that a possible is identical with its appropriate divine idea. And since the divine idea is a particular way in which God views his essence as capable of imitation by a creature, from the ontological standpoint a divine idea and a possible are really one and the same. One might suggest that there is a distinction between them, though only a logical one, from the psychological side. For a divine idea also implies that God understands that he understands his essence as being imitable in a given way.[11]

It is true that Thomas would admit that, after the creation of the universe, a not-yet-existent material entity may be described as possible or as potential in more derivative senses as well, such as those mentioned above. It might now be said to be possible by reason of a preexisting passive potency, or matter, as well as by reason of preexisting active potencies, that is, created agents. And from eternity it would have been possible by reason of God's active potency. But these usages of the term "possible" are not the most fundamental. They all presuppose the fact that something is not self-contradictory, not impossible in the absolute sense. And the ultimate ontological foundation for this — that which accounts for the fact that a possible is not self-contradictory and is therefore possible in the absolute sense — is the divine essence itself insofar as it is viewed by God as capable of being imitated in a given way. Hence, even though at times Thomas expresses this most basic kind of possibility by appealing to the absence of incompatibility between the terms which describe such a thing, the possibility in question is not merely linguistic, nor merely logical, but ontological. Like the principle of noncontradiction itself, for Thomas possibility in its most fundamental sense is grounded in being, in this case in the divine being.[12]

11. See ST I, q. 15, a. 2, ad 2. "Deus autem non solum intelligit multas res per essentiam suam, sed etiam intelligit se intelligere multa per essentiam suam. Sed hoc est intelligere plures rationes rerum; vel, plures ideas esse in intellectu eius ut intellectas." On this see L. Dewan, "St. Thomas and the Possibles," *The New Scholasticism* 53 (1979), p. 83. Given this, Dewan comments that "one should not altogether identify the doctrines of the ideas and the possibles. The doctrine of the ideas is more complex, as including the notion of God understanding himself to understand many things." But this distinction can only be logical, not real, according to Aquinas. From the ontological side any reality enjoyed by the possibles is reducible to that of the divine ideas, which reality itself is in turn ultimately identical with the divine essence.

12. ST I, q. 25, a. 3c. Note in particular: "Esse autem divinum super quod ratio divinae potentiae fundatur, est esse infinitum, non limitatum ad aliquod genus entis,

With this we come to Thomas's answer to our third question: Is it because things are possible in themselves that God can do or make them, or is it rather because he can produce them that they are possible in themselves? Closely related to this in certain recent discussions of Thomas's position is an effort to determine his answer to another question: Are possibles dependent for their constitution as possibles on an act of the divine will as well as of the divine intellect, or are they *necessarily* possible from eternity? In considering the last-mentioned question first, we shall be led to Thomas's answer to our third major question as well. In a widely cited article written in 1943 Gerard Smith stressed the role of both the divine intellect and the divine will when it comes to God's knowledge of himself as imitable in given ways by creatures, and, therefore, in constituting possibles. In fact, he used this as a major point of differentiation between Thomas's understanding of the possibles and that proposed by Avicenna.[13]

More recently, another advocate of this same interpretation finds Avicenna defending in some way an independent order of possibles. In contrast with this, " . . . for St. Thomas what makes possibles to be possibles is that they proceed from a will which freely constitutes them in accord with wisdom."[14] Or as Smith himself had phrased it: "Which is true: God can create something, or something can be created by God? According to Thomas, it is the first: God gives to St. Thomas's creatures both their to-be and their to-be-able-to-be."[15] While I would agree that Thomas's God gives

---

sed praehabens in se totius esse perfectionem. Unde quidquid potest habere rationem entis, continetur sub possibilibus absolutis, respectu quorum Deus dicitur omnipotens. Nihil autem opponitur rationi entis, nisi non ens. Hoc igitur repugnat rationi possibilis absoluti, quod subditur divinae omnipotentiae, quod implicat in se esse et non esse simul. Hoc enim omnipotentiae non subditur, non propter defectum divinae potentiae, sed quia non potest habere rationem factibilis neque possibilis." Also see *De potentia Dei,* q. 1, a. 3. There, while explaining how something can be possible or impossible but not by reason of any potency, he comments: "Hoc autem quod est affirmationem et negationem esse simul, rationem entis habere non potest, nec etiam non entis, quia esse tollit non esse, et non esse tollit esse: unde nec principaliter nec ex consequenti potest esse terminus alicuius actionis potentiae activae" (*ed. cit.,* p. 14). Cf. *In I Sent.,* d. 42, q. 2, a. 2.

13. See G. Smith, "Avicenna and the Possibles," *The New Scholasticism* 17 (1943), pp. 340–57; also in *Essays in Modern Scholasticism,* A. Pegis, ed. (Westminster, Md., 1944), pp. 116–33; also, in shortened form, in *Readings in Ancient and Medieval Philosophy,* J. Collins, ed. (Westminster, Md., 1960), pp. 200–205.

14. B. Zedler, "Another Look at Avicenna," *The New Scholasticism* 50 (1976), pp. 504–21. See p. 519.

15. Smith, p. 350. Also: "It is rather to say that the state of affairs whereby two and two, of themselves, make four and cannot make five, is   1) such as it is, in

to actually existing creatures both their intrinsic potential principle, or essence, and their actual existence, I question the claim that his God freely gives to creatures their very possibility.[16] And I also question the claim that according to Thomas it is only because God can create something that it is possible in itself.

To concentrate on the first point for a moment, our discussion so far has indicated that for Thomas a possible is nothing but a given way in which God views his essence as capable of imitation by a creature. The divine essence itself necessarily exists as such from eternity. There can be no question of its being freely constituted by anyone, not even by God. If Thomas's God is not a *causa sui*, and he surely is not, then there is even less likelihood that he could freely cause himself. Given Thomas's view that God knows all that is actual and all that is possible, it is difficult to see how his God could fail to view himself as imitable in any given way,[17] or in other words, how any possible could be freely rather than necessarily such from eternity.

---

itself, because   2) God knows and wills it to be such as it is, in itself. God, in short, is the source of *posse esse*." See p. 357: " . . . they [creatures] depend for their possibility upon God's knowing and willing them to be possible." While agreeing that God is the source of *posse esse* insofar as the latter is simply a given way in which God knows himself as imitable, it does not seem to me that Thomas would admit that possibles depend for their *posse esse* upon God's *willing* them to be possible. Smith himself seems to qualify the above statements somewhat by the following remark: " . . . their [St. Thomas's creatures'] to-be-able-to-be God gives necessarily" (p. 357). But Zedler clearly interprets Smith as I have done, though she also defends that position. See the article cited in n. 14. In his stress on a role for the divine will in constituting possibles, Smith himself seems to have been influenced by A. Forest. See his *La structure métaphysique du concret selon saint Thomas d'Aquin* (Paris, 1956), pp. 151–53; also, end of note, pp. 152–53; p. 161. Note the following: "Pour saint Thomas, ce qui fait que les notions sont possibles, c'est qu'elles ne sont pas contradictoires, autrement dit, qu'elles sont de l'être et par là une imitation du premier être. Mais ce qui fait que les possibles sont tels, c'est qu'ils procédent d'une volonté qui les constitue librement en accord avec la sagesse" (p. 153). Cf. Smith, p. 340, n. 1; p. 347, n. 12. Zedler, too, seems to find support in Forest (see pp. 518–19).

16. This claim has already been sharply challenged by L. Dewan. See his "St. Thomas and the Possibles," pp. 78–81, 83. For some more recent clarifications regarding her position see Zedler, "Why Are the Possibles Possible?" *The New Scholasticism* 55 (1981), pp. 113–30.

17. See ST I, q. 15, a. 2c, and other texts as cited above in n. 8. Also see ST I, q. 14, a. 15, ad 2. Also see *De veritate*, q. 3, a. 2: " . . . unde essentia sua est idea rerum; non quidem ut essentia, sed ut est intellecta." Also see ad 6: " . . . dicendum, quod una prima forma, ad quam omnia reducuntur, est ipsa essentia divina secundum se considerata; ex cuius consideratione divinus intellectus adinvenit, ut ita dicam, diversos modos imitationis ipsius, in quibus pluralitas idearum consistit." (*Ed. cit.*, pp. 66, 67/Leonine ed., Vol. 22.1, pp. 104–5.)

Precisely because the divine essence viewed as imitable in a given way is the ultimate ontological foundation for any possible, possibles are necessarily such from all eternity. So much, then, for the claim that the divine will intervenes in their constitution.

As to the second claim — that possibles depend upon divine power for their very possibility — this too seems to be undermined by all that we have seen so far. If Thomas's God necessarily knows himself from eternity, then he necessarily knows all the ways in which he can be imitated by creatures. The ultimate foundation for this is not the divine power or divine omnipotence, but the divine being itself. As Thomas himself writes: "It is not the case that he [God] can [make them] because he wills, but [he can] because he is such in his own nature."[18] Here, then, we have Thomas's answer to our third question. God can effect certain things only because they are possible in themselves. They are possible in themselves only because the divine essence is as it is in itself.

Before concluding this discussion of Thomas's views on nonexisting possibles, I should refer to two other disputed issues. First of all, Thomas's interpreters disagree as to whether he would place possibles under purely intentional or mind-dependent being, on the one hand, or under real being, on the other. Thus, W. Norris Clarke has suggested that it would be better to classify them under purely intentional or mind-dependent being rather than under real being. But he acknowledges that a more traditional interpretation would place them under real being.[19]

Appeal to Thomas's distinction between that which is possible in the absolute sense (free from self-contradiction) and that which is possible by

---

18. See ST I, q. 25, a. 5, ad 1: "Ideo enim Deus aliquid facit, quia vult: non tamen ideo potest, quia vult, sed quia talis est in sua natura." See q. 25, a. 3, especially: "Unde quicquid potest habere rationem entis, continetur sub possibilibus absolutis, respectu quorum Deus dicitur omnipotens . . . . Quaecumque igitur contradictionem non implicant, sub illis possibilibus continentur, respectu quorum dicitur Deus omnipotens. Ea vero quae contradictionem implicant, sub divina omnipotentia non continentur: quia non possunt habere possibilium rationem. Unde convenientius dicitur quod non possunt fieri, quam quod Deus non potest ea facere." Also see ad 4: " . . . dicendum quod possibile absolutum non dicitur neque secundum causas superiores, neque secundum causas inferiores, sed secundum seipsum." See q. 25, a. 4, ad 2: " . . . sed quaedam non subiacent eius potentiae, quia deficiunt a ratione possibilium." In all of these passages the implication is that it is because things are possible in themselves that they fall under God's omnipotence, not vice versa. And it is because others are impossible in themselves and hence cannot be made that they do not fall under God's power. See Dewan's remarks, pp. 80–81, and n. 9.

19. See Clarke, "What Is Really Real?" in *Progress in Philosophy: Philosophical Studies in Honor of Rev. Doctor Charles A. Hart,* J. A. McWilliams, ed. (Milwaukee, 1955),

reason of an active and/or a passive potency may be helpful here. If one concentrates on possibles taken in the absolute sense, then, according to Thomas, they enjoy no actual reality in themselves apart from that of their respective divine ideas and, therefore, apart from that of the divine essence. If one restricts one's usage of the term "possible" to this, one should not assign any real being to a possible apart from that of the divine essence. So understood, therefore, a possible, when it is simply viewed in itself, will fall under purely intentional being. But if one understands by a possible that which is such by reason of some active and/or passive potency, then one should place it under *real potential* being, I would think, although not under *real actual* being. As has been indicated above, within his division of the possible Thomas has included both of these, that which is possible in the absolute sense, and that which is possible by reason of some potency.[20] The fact that he has included both may account for the divergent interpretations to which reference has just been made. But one should also note that Thomas has singled out for special consideration that which is possible in the absolute sense. Nevertheless, it also seems to follow from his position that if something is possible by reason of an active or a passive potency, it must be possible in the absolute sense as well. In fact, the former kind of possibility presupposes the latter.

Secondly, some fifty years ago J. Benes maintained that Thomas identifies the possible with a nature or essence when it is considered absolutely and in itself, rather than as realized in the intellect or in an individual existent. He argued from Thomas's Quodlibet 8, q. 1 and his usage there of

---

pp. 62–63 (for his statement of the question); pp. 64–66 (for defenders of the "traditional" interpretation); pp. 68–74 (for Clarke's defense of his interpretation); pp. 74–78 (for more on the "traditional" interpretation); and pp. 85–90 (for philosophical argumentation for his interpretation). Recent conversation with Fr. Clarke indicates that we are in some disagreement about another point which he stresses in this article (p. 85, n. 45; p. 88). Commenting on texts taken from *De potentia*, q. 1, a. 5, ad 11 ("rationes quasi excogitatas") and from *De veritate*, q. 3, a. 2, ad 6, he emphasizes the "inventive" role of the divine intellect as it "excogitates" the divine ideas. I prefer to stress the fact that God, in knowing his own essence, also knows (or "discovers") the many ways in which it is imitable and, therefore, the divine ideas and the possibles. But Fr. Clarke also comments: " . . . but [the divine mind] literally 'invents', 'excogitates' them, using the infinitely simple plenitude of *Esse* that is his essence as supreme *analogical* mode or norm, so that all His 'inventions' will be only so many diversely limited modes . . . of the one great central perfection of His own act of existence" (p. 85, n. 45). Our difference seems, therefore, to be largely a matter of emphasis.

20. See the diagram of his division of the possible presented in the Appendix concluding this chapter.

Avicenna's distinction between the three ways in which an essence or nature can be considered.[21] As will be seen in the next section, Henry of Ghent does identify possibles with natures or essences considered in themselves or absolutely. But, in my opinion, Thomas does not do so. Rather, in this same Quodlibet 8, q. 1, he sets up the following sequence. The first consideration of any caused nature occurs insofar as it is present in the divine intellect. Secondly, and following upon this first consideration and presupposing it, such a nature can be considered absolutely or in itself. Following upon this, such a nature admits of a third consideration insofar as it enjoys being in existing things (or in an angelic intellect, adds Thomas). Finally and fourthly, it may also be considered insofar as it exists in a human intellect.[22]

Far from identifying a nature considered absolutely with a possible, Thomas rather makes God's view of such a nature insofar as it exists in his intellect the foundation for any absolute consideration of the same. And this, its divine idea, is really identical with the divine essence itself, even though they are logically distinct. But, as we have already seen, for such a thing to exist as a divine idea is for it to be a possible. Consequently, rather than identify a possible with a nature or essence considered absolutely in the Avicennian sense, Thomas holds that the latter presupposes the former.

II

With Henry of Ghent we enter a very different metaphysical world, one that is considerably more influenced than was that of Aquinas by Augustine

---

21. "Valor 'Possibilium' Apud S. Thomam, Henricum Gandavensem, B. Iacobum de Viterbio," *Divus Thomas* (Piac.) 29 (1926), pp. 622–24. For more on this Avicennian distinction see below, in our discussion of Henry of Ghent's theory. On this in Thomas also see J. Owens, "Common Nature: A Point of Comparison between Thomistic and Scotistic Metaphysics," in J. F. Ross, ed., *Inquiries into Medieval Philosophy: A Collection in Honor of Francis P. Clarke* (Westport, Conn., 1971), pp. 191–95. This article is reprinted from *Mediaeval Studies* 19 (1957), pp. 1–14.

22. See *Quaestiones quodlibetales*, R. Spiazzi, ed. (Marietti ed., 1956), Quodlibet 8, q. 1, pp. 158–59. See in particular: "Unde uniuscuiusque naturae causatae prima consideratio est secundum quod est in intellectu divino; secunda vero consideratio est ipsius naturae absolute; tertia secundum quod habet esse in rebus ipsis, vel in mente angelica; quarta secundum esse quod habet in intellectu nostro . . . . Similiter etiam intellectus divinus est ratio naturae absolute consideratae, et in singularibus; et ipsa natura absolute considerata et in singularibus est ratio intellectus humani, et quodammodo mensura ipsius. . . . Sic autem senarius non erit creatura, sed ratio creaturae in creatore, quae est idea senarii, et est idem secundum rem quod divina essentia, ratione tantum differens."

and by certain themes taken from Avicenna's version of Neoplatonism. Nonetheless, Henry was also quite familiar with the thought of Aristotle. Reflecting an interest already manifested by certain members of the Arts Faculty at Paris in the 1260s, Henry is much concerned with accounting for the possibility of there being some kind of knowledge, even scientific knowledge, of nonexistent possible entities. Going hand in hand with this concern is his effort to show that a creaturely essence is in some way indifferent to its actual existence and nonexistence. At the same time he denies that the actual existence of any created existing entity is really distinct from its essence. On this final point he is directly opposing another contemporary in the Paris Theology Faculty, Giles of Rome, who had defended a somewhat exaggerated version of real distinction between essence and existence. And, if perhaps only indirectly, he is also differing from Aquinas's theory of real composition of essence and *esse* in creatures.[23]

In his effort to account for there being true knowledge of nonexistent possibles, on the one hand, but not of mere beings of reason or chimeras, on the other, Henry draws upon a distinction originally proposed in Avicenna's *Logic* and again in his *Metaphysics*. (Both of these were available to thirteenth-century scholastics in Latin translation.) According to the Latin Avicenna, essences or natures exist in only two ways, either in an intellect, or in individual things. But they may be considered in three ways: (1) absolutely, or simply in themselves, without one's adverting to their existence either in singulars or in the intellect; (2) insofar as they exist in singular things; (3) insofar as they are present in an intellect and hence are in some way universal.[24]

23. See, for instance, his Quodlibet 3, q. 9, where he asks: "Utrum sit ponere aliquam essentiam per indifferentiam se habentem ad esse et ad non esse." *Quodlibeta* (Paris, 1518; repr. Louvain, 1961; in 2 vols. with continuous pagination), fol. 60v. See the *sed contra*, where he presents the argument that for science of a thing to take place neither its *esse* nor its *non esse* is required (fol. 60v). For his ultimate agreement with this claim see fol. 62r, at bottom. For explicit connection of Henry's development of his metaphysics of *esse essentiae* with his concern to account for there being knowledge of nonexistent possibles, see J. Paulus, *Henri de Gand: Essai sur les tendances de sa métaphysique* (Paris, 1938), pp. 124–25 and p. 124, n. 2. On Henry's rejection of real distinction between essence and existence see Paulus, pp. 279–84; "Les disputes d'Henri de Gand et de Gilles de Rome sur la distinction de l'essence et de l'existence," *Archives d'Histoire Doctrinale et Littéraire du Moyen Age* 13 (1940–1942), pp. 323–58; W. Hoeres, "Wesen und Dasein bei Heinrich von Gent und Duns Scotus," *Franziskanische Studien* 47 (1965), pp. 121–86; J. Wippel, "The Relationship between Essence and Existence in Late-Thirteenth-Century Thought: Giles of Rome, Henry of Ghent, Godfrey of Fontaines, and James of Viterbo," in *Philosophies of Existence: Ancient and Medieval*, P. Morewedge, ed. (New York, 1982), pp. 131–64, and other references as cited there.

24. For the medieval Latin translation of both of these sources see *Avicennae perhypatetici philosophi . . . Logica, Philosophia prima* (Venice, 1508; repr. Frankfurt am

As Henry interprets Avicenna, this first way of considering natures or essences, absolutely and in themselves, is prior to the other two. Thus I can think of man simply as man without noting whether the nature of man exists only in the intellect and as universal, or in a particular and therefore as individual. Because of this, Henry also takes Avicenna to assign not only a distinctive intelligible content to an essence or nature when it is considered absolutely and in itself, but also a distinctive kind of *esse*, a distinctive kind of being, which he constantly refers to as the thing's *esse essentiae*. Although this expression is difficult to translate into English, I will refer to it as the thing's essential being.[25] Even though Henry does not admit that a thing's

---

Main, 1961). See, in particular, *Logica* (fol. 2rb): "Essentiae vero rerum aut sunt in ipsis rebus aut sunt in intellectu. Unde habent tres respectus. Unus respectus essentiae est secundum quod ipsa est non relata ad aliquod tertium esse, nec ad id quod sequitur eam secundum quod ipsa est sic. Alius respectus est secundum quod est in his singularibus. Et alius secundum quod est in intellectu." Also see the immediately following context. For Henry's citations of Avicenna's *Metaphysics*, see the following note.

25. See Henry, Quodlibet 1, q. 9 (ed. R. Macken [Louvain-Leiden, 1979], p. 53), where he cites Avicenna's *Metaphysics* V to this effect, that there is a certain *esse* which a thing has essentially and of itself (which Henry names its *esse essentiae*) and another which it receives from something else (called *esse existentiae* by Henry). For Avicenna see *Metaphysica* V, chs. 1-2 (ff. 86va-87va). In Quodlibet 3, q. 9 (fol. 60v), Henry cites Avicenna's *Metaphysica* I, ch. 5 (*ed. cit.*, fol. 72va; also in *Avicenna Latinus, Liber de Philosophia Prima sive Scientia Divina: I-IV*, S. Van Riet, ed. [Louvain-Leiden, 1977], pp. 34-35) to this effect, that each and every thing in its nature has a proper *certitudo* which is its quiddity and that whereby it is what it is. Because of this it is a *res*. This is different from that *intentio* whereby *esse* is ascribed to it. Henry does not hesitate to assign primacy to this proper *certitudo*. As he puts it: "Quoniam intentio de re, est intentio prima simpliciter, ad quam concomitatur intentio de esse, ex hoc scilicet quod certitudo rei qua est id quod est, secundum se habet esse in anima, sive in conceptu intellectus creati vel increati, aut in singularibus extra." Here, too (in Quodlibet 3, q. 1) Henry argues that a thing has this absolute concept, whereby one simply knows what it is without one's adverting to it either as existing in the mind or in singulars. Henry does not here say that it will ever enjoy this *esse absolutum* (as he also describes it) without its also being in some intellect or in singulars. But it is not determined by its absolute quiddity to be either one or the other, either universal or individual. See fol. 60v. Note that Avicenna, while not referring to this as *esse essentiae* (Henry's favored term), does state: "Et hoc est quod fortasse appellamus *esse proprium*, nec intendimus per illud nisi intentionem esse affirmativi . . . ." In the same context Henry develops his view by noting that one's absolute understanding of animal, for instance, or of man, taken as such, is prior to one's consideration of animal or man as realized in individuals or as existing in an intellect. To consider man (or animal) together with universality is to view it with that which pertains to it only as it exists in the intellect. To consider such a nature together with its properties and accidents is to view it as existing in the individual.

actual existence (*esse existentiae*) is really distinct from its essential being (*esse essentiae*), he does contend that the distinction between them is not merely mind-imposed or merely logical. It is not a mere distinction of reason (*distinctio rationis*). In addition to real distinction and purely logical or mind-dependent distinctions, he introduces a third kind, an "intentional" distinction. This, he maintains, is the kind that obtains between an actually existing entity's essential being and its existence.[26]

In order to appreciate more fully Henry's understanding of the ontological status of nonexistent possibles, one must connect the above with his view of divine causality. In brief, he contends that God may be viewed as a formal exemplar cause of all creatures, on the one hand, and as their efficient cause, on the other. Divine formal causality is directed to their

---

For support Henry refers to Avicenna's *Metaphysica* V, chs. 2 and 10. Henry then goes on to assign three modes of *esse* to correspond to these three modes of consideration, namely: an *esse naturae*, which such a nature enjoys in individual things; an *esse rationis*, presumably that which it enjoys in an intellect; and finally, its *esse essentiae*. This last-mentioned *esse*, he comments, is prior to the other two just as the simple is prior to the composite. Then he writes: "Et ut dicit Avicenna, capitulo octavo, hoc esse proprie dicitur definitivum esse, et est dei intentione. Quod intelligo: quia tale esse non convenit alicui nisi cuius ratio exemplaris est in intellectu divino, per quam natum est fieri in rebus extra" (fol. 61r, bottom). For this last in Avicenna see V, 1 (fol. 87rb): "Animal ergo acceptum cum accidentibus suis est res naturalis; acceptum vero per se est natura, de qua dicitur quod esse eius prius est quam esse naturale, sicut simplex prius est composito, et hoc est cuius esse proprie dicitur divinum esse, quoniam causa sui esse ex hoc quod est animal est dei intentione." Also see fol. 87ra. For the recent critical edition now see *Avicenna Latinus, Liber de Philosophia Prima sive Scientia Divina: V–X*, S. Van Riet, ed. (Louvain–Leiden, 1980), p. 237.

26. See, for instance, Quodlibet 1, q. 9 (Macken ed., p. 55); Quodlibet 10, q. 7 (especially ff. 417v–418r/also ed. by R. Macken, *Henrici de Gandavo Quodlibet X* [Leuven-Leiden, 1981], pp. 163–66); Quodlibet 11, q. 3 (especially ff. 441r–441v). For another good presentation of Henry's general theory see his *Summae quaestionum ordinariarum*, a. 28, q. 4 (Paris, 1520; repr. St. Bonaventure, N.Y., 1953), Vol. 1, ff. 167v–168v. For more on this see, in addition to the references given above in n. 23, Paulus, *Henri de Gand* . . . , pp. 220–36, 284–91; J. Gómez Caffarena, *Ser participado y ser subsistente en la metafísica de Enrique de Gante* (Rome, 1958), pp. 65–92. One might also wonder whether Henry defends a purely logical distinction or an intentional distinction between the *esse* and the *essentia* of essential being. In fact, at different points in his career he seems to have defended each position. But since each is consistent with his view that possibles depend for their constitution as possibles on their respective divine ideas as that which is exemplated depends upon its exemplar, it will not be necessary for us to pursue this rather subtle point here. For further discussion of Henry's views on this see Paulus, *Henri de Gand* . . . , pp. 311–14; Hoeres, p. 146, n. 77, p. 156, n. 14; F. A. Cunningham, "Some Presuppositions in Henry of Ghent," *Pensamiento* 25 (1969), p. 129; Gómez Caffarena, *Ser participado y ser subsistente* . . . , pp. 104–17, 263–69.

essential being, their *esse essentiae*, while divine efficient causality results in their actual existence. Henry goes on to argue that the essences of creatures are eternally present to the divine intellect as objects of its knowledge. Insofar as they are objects of God's knowledge, they depend upon their respective divine ideas as upon their formal cause. Given this, some kind of being, essential being, must be ascribed to them, and this from eternity. If they are eventually brought into actual existence, this will be because of the intervention of the divine will and because God communicates existential being to them by serving as their efficient cause. But it is by means of his exemplar ideas that God communicates an eternal essential being to possibles and thereby constitutes them as possibles. And it is because they enjoy this essential being that they can be objects of knowledge prior to their realization as actually existing entities.[27]

Henry is not content simply to identify the essential being of a possible with the merely intentional reality (*esse cognitum*) it enjoys within the divine intellect. In knowing his essence as capable of being imitated by a creature in a given way in terms of its appropriate divine idea, God also knows the creaturely possible essence as distinct in some way both from God himself and from his knowledge of it as possible. As Henry puts it in Quodlibet 9, q. 2, insofar as such essences exist as objects of God's knowledge, their being is not so minimal that they are not also something in themselves.[28] And in some texts he goes so far as to say that such creaturely essences, possibles, if you will, prior to their reception of actual existence, are already and from all eternity *really* related to God as their formal exemplar cause.[29] Because of

<hr />

27. See Quodlibet 1, q. 9 (Macken ed., pp. 53–55); Quodlibet 3, q. 9 (ff. 61r–61v); Quodlibet 9, qq. 1, 2 (ff. 341v, 343v, 345v); Quodlibet 10, q. 7 (fol. 416r/Macken ed., pp. 151–52); *Summae quaestionum ordinariarum*, a. 28, q. 4 (Vol. 1, fol. 167v).

28. "Ista autem non sunt sic diminuta respectu entis quod deus est et existentia in esse cognito quin in illo esse sint aliquid ad se per essentiam . . . . Est enim praedicamentum contentivum talium rerum non secundum quod sunt in esse cognito, neque secundum quod sunt in esse vero, sed secundum quod sunt aliquid simpliciter; per indifferentiam se habens quantum ad illud quod est per essentiam ad utrumque illorum esse . . . ." (fol. 345r).

29. See Quodlibet 9, q. 1 (fol. 341v): "Ex consideratione enim divini intellectus circa divinam essentiam ut est intellecta ab ipso sunt in ipso rationes ideales . . . quae sunt relationes ex hoc in deo secundum rationem ad ipsas essentias creaturarum, quae ex hoc sunt aliquid secundum essentiam quae respondent rationibus idealibus in deo existentibus. Et ratione ipsius essentiae earum habent *relationem realem* ad deum" (italics mine). See Paulus, *Henri de Gand* . . . , pp. 293–94; J. Benes, "Valor 'Possibilium' Apud S. Thomam, Henricum Gandavensem, B. Iacobum de Viterbio," *Divus Thomas* (Piac.) 30 (1927), pp. 107–9. Note in particular Quodlibet 5, q. 4 (fol. 158v): " . . . oportet scire quod ea quae alia sunt ab ipso, dupliciter possunt considerari: Uno modo quoad esse essentiae eorum quod est esse eorum quidditativum;

this, from all eternity they can be described as "things" or *res* (taken strictly as derived from *ratitudo* rather than merely from *reor, reris*). And they can be said to belong to their proper predicament or class. Such is not true, he insists, of mere chimeras.[30] But when they are actually realized in concrete existents, these possible entities are then also really related in time to God as to their efficient cause.[31]

It follows from this that, according to Henry, nonexistent possibles are not simply to be identified with the divine ideas or the divine essence. Divine ideas are distinctive ways in which God views his essence as capable of being

---

alio modo quoad esse existentiae. Primo modo, ea quae sunt extra ipsum essentialem habent dependentiam ad ipsum et ad eius bonitatem. Quod enim est aliquid per essentiam et naturam, licet non sit in existentia aliqua extra intellectum, non potest non esse tale, nec potest non habere rationem perfectionis idealis in deo. Nec e converso Deus potest non habere rationem perfectionis suae idealis ad illud. Habet enim de necessitate perfectionis suae rationem perfectionis idealis et imitabilitatis ad omne illud quod est aliquid in esse quidditativo et essentiae, et quod potest esse aliquid in esse existentiae; quamvis ratio talis non sit in Deo nisi ex respectu et comparatione ad creaturam, sicut dictum est supra in prima quaestione; ut relatio secundum huiusmodi respectum dei ad creaturas sit secundum rationem tantum; e converso, creaturae ad ipsum sit secundum rem."

30. According to Henry the term *res* can be taken as deriving from *reor, reris,* and then is used so broadly and loosely that it could be applied to mere chimeras. In other words, when so derived, it does not imply that something is really possible or capable of enjoying actual existence, or even of being an object of genuine knowledge. But *res* can also be derived from *ratitudo* (*res a ratitudine*), and then signifies that the thing in question is at least capable of actually existing since it has an exemplar idea in the divine mind. For this see Quodlibet 5, q. 2 (fol. 154r): " . . . sciendum quod primus conceptus communissimus et communis ad conceptum vanum quo concipitur saltem modo privatorio id cui nihil natum est respondere in re, ut est conceptus fictitius chimaerae vel hircocervi, et ad conceptum verum quo concipitur modo positivo id quod est aliquid per essentiam, et natum existere extra intellectum in rerum existentia, ut est conceptus divinae essentiae et creaturae. Primus inquam conceptus communissimus et communis ad illum conceptum et ad istum, est conceptus quo concipitur res a reor reris dicta, quae continet sub se rem imaginariam quae est purum non ens, quia neque ens per essentiam neque natum esse per existentiam . . . et continet sub se rem veram quae est natura et essentia alicuius vel rei increatae vel creatae habentis ideam in mente divina et natae existere extra, in quo non consideratur ratio eius quod est esse aliquid per essentiam nisi ex respectu quodam ad rationem exemplaris in Deo. Res enim quaecumque sive existens sive non existens, si habet esse in deo secundum exemplarem rationem, non solum dicitur quod est res dicta a reor reris, sed etiam quod sit natura et essentia aliqua, et ideo dicitur res a ratitudine. Et haec res est super quam fundatur prima ratio praedicamenti." Also see Benes, pp. 104–5; Paulus, pp. 22–27.

31. For more details on Henry's discussion of the ways in which possible and actual entities are related to God, see Quodlibet 9, q. 1, ff. 341r–344r.

imitated by creatures. But the essential being of a genuine possible depends upon its divine idea as that which is modelled depends upon its model, or as that which is exemplated depends upon its exemplar.[32] In Quodlibet 9, q. 2 Henry distinguishes different "objects" of God's cognitive activity. The primary object of divine cognition is the divine essence itself. Secondary objects — the possibles — may simply be viewed as virtually present in God. So considered, they are to be regarded as identical with the divine essence itself. But they may also be viewed as enjoying some reality in themselves from eternity and hence in some way as distinct from the divine ideas and the divine essence, though as always dependent upon them.[33]

With this background in mind we are now in position to direct our three questions to Henry. First of all, what is the ontological status of a nonexisting possible? It does not enjoy any actual existence, maintains Henry, apart from that of the divine essence itself. But it does have essential being (*esse essentiae*) from eternity, and this is in some way to be distinguished from the being of its appropriate divine idea and hence from that of the divine essence. To repeat, a possible depends upon its respective idea just as that which is exemplated depends upon its exemplar. In other words, Henry seems to be assigning a strange and intermediate kind of reality to nonexistent possibles. In some way they are distinct from the being of the divine essence, but they do not enjoy actual existence in themselves. They

32. See Quodlibet 9, q. 2 (ff. 344r–347r). Note in particular: "Illa autem ratio in divina essentia secundum quam sua essentia est ratio qua cognoscit alia a se nihil aliud est quam imitabilitas quae ab aliis imitetur, quam vocamus ideam . . . . Et est talis haec dei cognitio in cognoscendo se secundum rationem formae exemplaris; a quo secundum rationem causae formalis habent esse aliquid per essentiam ipsa exemplata in esse suo cognito" (fol. 344v). Also see fol. 345v: " . . . quemadmodum divina essentia secundum rationes ideales est forma exemplaris qua essentiae tiae creaturarum sunt id quod sunt ut quaedam exemplata . . . " See Benes, pp. 107–10; Gómez Caffarena, *Ser participado* . . . , pp. 30–32; Paulus, *Henri de Gand* . . . , pp. 87–88; Hoeres, "Wesen und Dasein . . . ," pp. 154–55.

33. Ff. 344r–344v. See in particular: "Obiectum primarium . . . non est nisi ipsa divina essentia, quae per se intelligitur a Deo, et nihil aliud ab ipso . . . . Obiectum autem secundarium est aliud a se . . . . Sed aliud a se ut obiectum secundarium suae cognitionis potest cognoscere dupliciter. Uno modo cognoscendo de creatura id quod ipsa est in Deo. Alio modo cognoscendo de ipsa id quod ipsa habet esse in seipsa aliud a Deo, quamvis non habeat esse extra eius notitiam . . . . Hoc [primo] modo Deus cognoscit alia a se ut sunt in sua essentia idem quod ipsa, et sic non ut alia . . . . Secundo autem modo cognoscit alia a se vere. . . . Sic autem sua essentia qua cognoscit se cognoscit alia a se . . . . ut ipsa essentia est ratio et habet rationem respectus quo respicit alia a se, non ut quae sunt per existentiam aliquid extra in seipsis, sed ut quae sunt per essentiam aliquid in divina cognitione, videlicet in eo quod divina essentia est ratio et forma exemplaris illorum . . . ." (344v). See Paulus, pp. 87–92, for discussion of this.

rather seem to fall into a kind of metaphysical "no man's land" between purely intentional being, on the one hand, and actually existing being, on the other. So true is this that one may fairly represent Henry's division of being taken most broadly by three different levels: (1) purely intentional or mental being, the kind enjoyed even by *entia rationis* or chimeras; (2) the essential being (*esse essentiae*) that is enjoyed by nonexistent possibles, and which suffices for one to refer to a possible as a thing (*res a ratitudine*) and as an object of true knowledge; (3) actual existence, which is enjoyed only by actually existing entities. But one can also place class two, essential being, and class three, actually existing being, under the general heading of *ens reale* or real being, as I have done in the diagram in this chapter's Appendix. Given all of this, it is clear that Henry has assigned to possibles a greater degree of reality or of ontological density than did Aquinas.

Secondly, what is the ultimate ontological foundation for Henry's possibles, or for their essential being? As already indicated, it is the divine intellect insofar as it views the divine essence as capable of being imitated in given ways. In other words, it is the divine ideas, which are really identical with the divine essence. If these ideas are distinctive ways in which God views himself as capable of being imitated by creatures, pure possibles are in some way to be distinguished from them and depend upon them as that which is exemplated depends upon its exemplar.

Thirdly, is it because things are possible that God can bring them to pass, or is it rather because God can do or make them that they are possible? Here we meet with some difficulty in Henry's texts. In discussing the ultimate explanation for the fact that certain things are possible and others impossible, his thought seems to have changed. In Quodlibet 6, q. 3 (of 1281 or 1282), he first attempts to identify the ultimate ground for possibility. Here, after a rather involved discussion, he concludes that a creature's intrinsic possibility depends on God's power. Things are possible in themselves because and only because God has the power to make them. He is not saying that God can do or make them because they are possible in themselves. But in this same context, in accounting for impossibility, Henry reverses his field. If things are absolutely impossible, this is first of all because they are impossible in themselves. It is because of this that God cannot bring them to pass. In other words, it is because something is impossible in itself that it cannot be done by God.[34]

---

34. See Quodlibet 6, q. 3 (ff. 220r–221r). Note in particular: " . . . sicut possibile simpliciter primo attribuitur Deo active secundum se, et ex hoc attribuitur creaturae posse passive secundum se primo, et deinde in respectu ad Deum, ex quo demum attribuitur Deo in respectu ad creaturam . . . , sic impossibile simpliciter primo attribuitur creaturae secundum se, et ex hoc in respectu ad Deum, ex quo deinde

Some two years later, however, Henry returns to this topic again. He continues to assign intrinsic possibility to creatures only because of God's

---

attribuitur Deo in respectu ad creaturas. Nullo autem modo attribuitur ipsi secundum se et ex seipso" (ff. 220v–221r). For discussion of Henry's reasoning here see A. B. Wolter, "Ockham and the Textbooks: On the Origin of Possibility," *Franziskanische Studien* 32 (1950), pp. 70–96; reprinted in J. F. Ross, ed., *Inquiries into Medieval Philosophy*, pp. 243–73. See especially in the last-mentioned source pp. 244–47. In brief, Henry reasons here as follows. Whatever is not a pure and simple perfection (*aliquid dignitatis simpliciter*) — that is, the kind of perfection that entails no imperfection — cannot be attributed to God primarily but only in some secondary way. Included among those which are not pure and simple perfections are what we might call relative perfections or attributes, reasons Henry. By these he means those perfections which God enjoys only because of some reference or relationship to creatures. Thus he can hardly be regarded as Master (*dominus*) without some reference to creatures as his servants. So too, active power can be attributed to God with reference to some creature only insofar as the creature is capable of receiving some action from God. In addition, Henry notes that possibility can be assigned to God viewed actively either in terms of that in which this active power resides (subjectively) or in terms of that towards which it is directed (objectively). So too, a creature's passive possibility can be viewed either subjectively (as that in which this resides) or objectively (in terms of that upon which the creature depends for this, namely God). Given this, Henry arrives at the fourfold relationship that applies to power or possibility insofar as these are affirmed of God and creatures and which is implied by the text cited above. One may apply active power to God (1) simply insofar as he is viewed in himself; or (2) insofar as he is viewed in relationship to creatures. And as regards passive possibility, this can be applied to a creature (3) simply insofar as it is viewed in itself; or (4) insofar as it is viewed as related to God. Henry then assigns these four different usages of potentiality and possibility to God and to creatures according to the following order. First of all, active power should be assigned to God insofar as he is viewed in himself. Secondly, and resulting from this, is the creature's passive potentiality or ontological possibility, when that creature is simply viewed in itself. This second moment, the creature's intrinsic possibility, if you will, presupposes the first. Thirdly, passive possibility can now be applied to the creature insofar as it is referred back to God, or viewed as possible with reference to divine power. Fourthly, one may assign active power to God in a relative sense, that is, with respect to creatures. By this procedure Henry has, he believes, allowed for one to apply power to God in the primary sense in the first moment, when he is simply viewed in himself, and as an absolute perfection. Power is applied to him in secondary fashion, or taken relatively, only in the fourth moment as distinguished above. But in this discussion impossibility is to be attributed first of all to that which is impossible in itself. Note how he connects this view (which he later reverses) with his theory of the divine ideas: "Licet enim res a ratitudine dicta ex hoc est res et natura vel essentia aliqua quod habet ideam in Deo; illud tamen quod non est res a ratitudine dicta, et maxime nec a reor reris dicta, non ex hoc non est res quia non habet ideam in Deo, sed potius non habet ideam in Deo quia secundum se non est res" (fol. 221r).

ability or power. But now he changes his position regarding the impossible. No longer will he say that certain things cannot be done by God because they are impossible in themselves. Rather, if certain things are impossible in themselves, this is because God cannot bring them about. Or as he phrases it, this is because there is no power in God to do such things, just as there is in him no capacity to sin.[35]

Two additional difficulties might be raised concerning Henry's views on nonexisting possibles. First of all, since in Quodlibet 6, q. 3 and in Quodlibet 8, q. 3, he has argued that things are possible in themselves only because God has the power to make them, one might wonder whether they are freely or necessarily possible from eternity. Secondly, one might also wonder whether Henry's grounding of possibles in God's power can be reconciled with his usual practice of basing them on the divine ideas.

As to the first difficulty, discussion above of Henry's position concerning the ultimate ontological foundation for possibles has strongly suggested that, according to him, they are not freely but necessarily such from eternity. This follows from his assertion that a divine idea is a given way in which the divine intellect views the divine essence as capable of being imitated by a creature, and his claim that possibles result from their respective divine ideas and are related to them as that which is exemplated is related to its exemplar. If God necessarily knows himself from eternity, he necessarily knows from eternity all the ways in which his essence can be imitated. In other words, his divine ideas are necessarily such from eternity. Given the relationship Henry has established between divine ideas and the possibles that correspond to them, there seems to be no place for the divine will to intervene in constituting possibles. On the contrary, Henry's theory clearly implies that possibles are necessarily such from eternity.

This same impression is confirmed by a text taken from Henry's Quodlibet 5, q. 4. There he comments that that which is something (*aliquid*) in terms of its essence and nature, even though it does not enjoy actual existence, cannot fail to be such, nor can it fail to have its appropriate divine idea. Nor, he adds, can God fail to serve as an "ideal" (that is, as an exemplar) with respect to it.[36] In other words, it follows from God's perfection that he must serve as the exemplar for every possible and, therefore, that possibles are necessarily

---

35. See Quodlibet 8, q. 3 (fol. 304v). Note in particular: "Ita quod non est verum dicere de impossibili simpliciter quod Deus non potest illud facere quia non potest fieri, sed potius, non potest fieri quia Deus non potest facere, sicut et in affirmativa non dicitur Deum possibile aliquid facere quia illud possibile est fieri, sed e converso, quia Deus potest illud facere, ideo, possibile est fieri, aut obiective aut subiective."

36. See ff. 158v–159r, as cited above in n. 29. Also see Paulus, *Henri de Gand* . . . , pp. 295–98.

constituted as such from eternity. This point is worth emphasizing, because it indicates that according to Henry something can depend on God's power in some way for its constitution and still not be *freely* constituted. If actual existence is ever to be given to it, of course, God's will must also intervene. But God's will does not enter into the eternal constitution of possibles as such.

It is more difficult to determine Henry's answer to the second problem. On the one hand, he has clearly grounded possibles on the divine ideas. Possibles are related to them as that which is exemplated is related to its exemplar. As I have just argued, there is no need within Henry's perspective to introduce the divine will to account for their possibility. But, on the other hand, in Quodlibet 6, q. 3 and in Quodlibet 8, q. 3 he has introduced divine power. If things are possible in themselves, this is only because God has the power to produce them. Can these two positions be reconciled?

Although he does not apply it directly to our difficulty, the distinction introduced by Henry in Quodlibet 9, q. 2 may be helpful here. There, as will be recalled, he distinguishes between the primary object of God's knowledge — the divine essence itself, and secondary objects — including possibles. As regards the latter, he notes that they may be viewed as virtually present in God. When they are so viewed they are simply identical with the divine essence. But they may also be viewed as enjoying some reality in themselves from eternity and hence in some way as distinct from the divine ideas and the divine essence. It is only when they are viewed in this second way that they are formally constituted as possibles.[37] But, though he does not say this in so many words, it may be that when Henry refers to them as being viewed in the first way — as virtually present in God and as really identical with his essence — he is also implying that in some way they presuppose some reference to divine power. And it may be this first view of them as virtually present in God that Henry also has in mind in the texts from Quodlibet 6, q. 3 and Quodlibet 8, q. 3 where he has explicitly introduced divine power as being in some way prior to and required for things to be possible in themselves. If so, in this first moment or view Henry would have us assign power to God only as an absolute perfection (*subiective*), not as a relative perfection (*obiective*).[38] And some reference to divine power taken as an absolute perfection would be presupposed for possibles to be viewed in this first way and, therefore, a fortiori, for them to be viewed in the second way and to be constituted formally as possibles in themselves. But reference to God's power taken as a relative perfection would not be required either for possibles to be considered in the first way

---

37. See ff. 344r–345r, and the citation above in n. 33.
38. See my discussion of Quodlibet 6, q. 3 in n. 34 above.

(as virtually present in God and as really identical with him) or in the second (as formally constituted in themselves).

III

Godfrey of Fontaines had been a student in the Theology Faculty at Paris during Henry's earlier days as a Master (ca. 1276–1285), and they were colleagues in that same Faculty until Henry's retirement ca. 1292. Godfrey was also quite familiar with the thought of Thomas Aquinas. And while he would differ from Thomas on many points, he was much more sympathetic to his stronger Aristotelian thrust than to the Avicennian and Neo-Augustinian thinking of his colleague from Ghent.[39]

In reacting to Henry's theory of possibles and of *esse essentiae*, Godfrey quickly identifies two important features in Henry's solution. First of all, Henry is much concerned with accounting for our ability to have knowledge of nonexistent possibles. Secondly, Henry has relied heavily on Avicenna's discussion of the three different ways in which an essence or nature can be considered, and has assigned a distinctive *esse* to Avicenna's essence or nature when it is considered simply in itself or absolutely. As to the second point, Henry's interpretation of Avicenna, Godfrey dismisses it as a misinterpretation.[40]

Before turning to Godfrey's discussion of the first point, I should note that he rejects Henry's intentional distinction between essence and existence in actually existing creatures. But he agrees with him in opposing any kind of real distinction between them. As far as Godfrey is concerned, essence and existence are really identical, so much so that any kind of distinction we may introduce between them because of grammatical usage can only be mind-imposed or purely logical.[41]

---

39. On Godfrey's life and career see my *The Metaphysical Thought of Godfrey of Fontaines: A Study in Late Thirteenth-Century Philosophy*, pp. xv–xxi. On his writings see pp. xxi–xxxiv.

40. Godfrey's major contribution to philosophical and theological writing is to be found in a series of fifteen quodlibetal questions, ranging from 1285 until 1303/1304. These have been edited in the series *Les Philosophes Belges* in Vols. 2, 3, 4, 5, and 14, and will be cited hereafter as follows: *PB* (for *Les Philosophes Belges*), followed by numbers indicating the volume and the page. For Godfrey's recognition of Henry's effort to account for knowledge of nonexisting entities see Quodlibet 2, q. 2 (*PB* 2.54–56) and Quodlibet 8, q. 3 (*PB* 4.36). For Godfrey's discussion of Henry's usage of Avicenna see Quodlibet 2, q. 2 (*PB* 2.56–59, 61–63). On this see Wippel, pp. 68–79.

41. On this see Wippel, ch. 2, *passim;* also, "Godfrey of Fontaines and the Real Distinction between Essence and Existence," *Traditio* 20 (1964), pp. 385–410; "Godfrey of Fontaines and Henry of Ghent's Theory of Intentional Distinction between Essence and Existence," in *Sapientiae procerum amore: Mélanges Médiévistes offerts à Dom Jean-Pierre Müller, O.S.B., Studia Anselmiana* 63 (Rome, 1974), pp. 289–321.

Godfrey first addresses himself to this problem at length in Quodlibet 2, q. 2 of 1286. There he is attempting to determine whether any created essence can be said to be indifferent to its actual existence and nonexistence.[42] A created essence can never enjoy real being, argues Godfrey, apart from its given existence. Whatever is true of one is true of the other. But if one were to defend real distinction between essence and existence in creatures, then one might regard essence as indifferent to actual existence and nonexistence in a weaker sense, that is, in the order of consideration. This would simply mean that one could think of a given essence without at the same time thinking of its actual existence.[43]

But since Godfrey denies that essence and existence are either really distinct or intentionally distinct, his answer is clear. Essence is not indifferent to existence or nonexistence, not even in the order of consideration. Whatever is true of essence is also true of existence. And whatever is known of a thing's essence is also known of its existence, since they are one and the same. Given this, Godfrey denies that one can understand what a thing is in itself or in terms of its essential being without at the same time knowing its existence.[44]

How, then, is Godfrey to account for knowledge of nonexistent possibles, when such cannot be had of mere chimeras? This, of course, was of major concern to Henry. Godfrey replies by appealing to his own way of dividing being, a division that was to become fairly influential after his time and which would be referred to by others as "Godfrey's way" of dividing being.[45] As he presents this in Quodlibet 8, q. 3 of the early 1290s, being may be divided into purely cognitive or mental being, on the one hand, and real being, on the other. The first kind of being is assigned to something only to the extent that it exists in an intellect, and does not imply any corresponding reality in that which is known. This kind is enjoyed even by mere beings of reason such as chimeras. The second kind of being, real being, is itself divided into being in act and being in potency. Some things exist formally and in actuality, as is true of concrete existents. Others exist only virtually

42. "Utrum essentia creaturae sit aliquid indifferens ad esse et non esse" (*PB* 2.53).
43. See *PB* 2.60.
44. *PB* 2.60–61. Also see Quodlibet 4, q. 2 (*PB* 2.235).
45. See, for instance, the anonymous catalogue of Godfrey's quodlibets edited by J. Hoffmans, "La Table des divergences et innovations doctrinales de Godefroid de Fontaines," *Revue Néoscolastique de Philosophie* 36 (1934), p. 430: "Ibi dividit suo modo ens in potentiam et actum, et respondet rationibus Henrici omnibus multum bene." (Here the author is commenting on Godfrey's Quodlibet 8, q. 3.) Also see Walter Burley's presentation and adoption of Godfrey's division in his *Quaestiones in librum Perihermeneias* of 1301. See S. Brown, ed., "Walter Burley's *Quaestiones in Librum Perihermeneias*," *Franciscan Studies* 34 (1974), pp. 271–72.

or potentially by reason of the preexisting potency of their cause or causes. Real potential being can be subdivided into the kind that exists by reason of a preexisting passive potency — an intrinsic cause — and that which exists by reason of a preexisting active power or potency — an extrinsic cause.[46]

To illustrate, something will enjoy real potential being by reason of its intrinsic cause if some kind of matter preexists that may enter into its formal constitution. It will enjoy real but potential or possible being by reason of a preexisting active or extrinsic cause when an agent preexists with the power to bring it into actual existence. Prior to the creation of the universe, real potential being and, therefore, possible being, could be assigned to it and its parts by reason of God's creative power. And God would then have true knowledge of our possibles by reason of his divine ideas. After creation, it may be that created efficient causes also exist which can bring a given possible into actual existence. If so, then real potential and possible being can be assigned to it by reason of such causes, as well as by reason of the preexistence of matter. And because of its potential being by reason of such preexisting causes, Godfrey is confident that one can account for the fact that we can have genuine knowledge of it even when it does not actually exist.[47]

Given this, Godfrey emphatically rejects Henry's defense of a distinctive real essential being which would be enjoyed by possibles simply insofar as they depend upon God's formal exemplar causality. For Godfrey, appeal to a nonexisting thing's real potential being by reason of its preexisting causes is sufficient for him to account both for its status as a possible and for the fact that there can be knowledge of it prior to its actual existence. As may be seen from the diagram in the Appendix, what is missing from Godfrey's division of being is Henry's realm of purely essential being. At the same time, since chimeras do not enjoy real being in any way, whether actual or potential, they are not possibles and cannot become objects of scientific knowledge.[48]

Godfrey offers a host of arguments against Henry's theory of essential being, some of which I will merely mention in passing. For instance, Henry's view really leads to a denial that creatures are created from nothing. If a creature enjoys real essential being from eternity, how can Henry maintain that it is created from nothing when it receives actual existence due to the intervention of the divine will at some point in time?[49] Again, Henry's

---

46. *PB* 4.38-40. Also see Quodlibet 2, q. 2 (*PB* 2.63-65); Quodlibet 4, q. 2 (*PB* 2.237-38); and Wippel, *The Metaphysical Thought* . . . , pp. 15-19, 78-79.

47. See the references cited in n. 46.

48. See the Appendix at the end of this chapter.

49. See Quodlibet 8, q. 3 (*PB* 4.45); Quodlibet 9, q. 2 (*PB* 4.190-92).

theory assigns eternal reality to possibles and, therefore, entails defending an eternal world.[50]

We are now in position to address our three questions to Godfrey. First, what degree of reality is to be assigned to a nonexisting possible? Prior to its reception of actual being, any such entity simply enjoys potential being. In itself it enjoys no real and actual being apart from that of the divine essence, and after creation of the universe, apart from the reality of other causes, intrinsic and extrinsic, that might contribute to its actual existence. From eternity it is potentially distinguishable from the divine essence and its corresponding divine idea, but not actually so. Prior to the creation of the universe, then, the potential being of a possible, the divine essence, and its corresponding divine idea are one and the same in the ontological order.[51] One can readily see how greatly Godfrey differs from Henry on this point. In fact, in spite of his rejection of real distinction between essence and existence in creatures, here Godfrey is much closer to Aquinas. However, he does not see fit to distinguish the possible in the absolute sense from that which is possible by reason of some potency or power. This may be because he realizes that there will never be a case where something is possible in the absolute sense (free from self-contradiction) without its also being possible or potential at least by reason of God, its extrinsic cause.

Secondly, for Godfrey as for Aquinas the ultimate ontological foundation for a possible is the divine essence itself. Godfrey, too, regards a divine idea as a given way in which the divine intellect views the divine essence as capable of being imitated by a creature. In other words, a possible is ultimately grounded in God's knowledge of himself as imitable in a given way. But against Henry he denies that this results in any real essential being

---

50. See Quodlibet 9, q. 2 (*PB* 4.196–97). On these and other arguments against Henry, see Wippel, *The Metaphysical Thought* . . . , pp. 137–43. These and other arguments already directed by Godfrey against Henry's position would be repeated a few years later by Duns Scotus. See *Ordinatio* 1, d. 36, q. un., nn. 13–18, 23 (Vatican City, 1958), Vol. 6, pp. 276–81.

51. See Quodlibet 9, q. 2 (*PB* 4.201–2). Also see Quodlibet 8, q. 3 (*PB* 4.46–48). In the latter context Godfrey makes an interesting comment with respect both to our knowledge and God's knowledge of nonexisting possibles: "Et sic ad hoc quod aliquid sit obiectum cognitum non requiritur ipsius existentia actualis, sed sufficit quod sit quid possibile; sic enim potest cognosci per illud per quod et in quo est possibile" (*PB* 4.48). If one wonders how Godfrey would account for this in terms of his theory of knowledge, the immediately preceding sentence gives an important clue: "Immo etiam intellectus noster potest habere intellectum de re non existente per aliquam eius similitudinem in memoria remanentem et intellectus divinus per suam essentiam omnia perfecte intelligit antequam sint."

that might be assigned to the possible in distinction from its divine idea and as eternally caused by it. In other words, he would not admit that possibles are eternally *caused* by God's exemplar ideas. In fact, in another criticism of Henry, he had denied that an intelligent being can serve as exemplar cause of anything without simultaneously functioning as its efficient cause.[52]

His answer to our third question is more difficult to discern since he devoted less attention to it. But in Quodlibet 6, q. 1, he implies that if something is impossible in itself, not even God can do it.[53] And according to Quodlibet 6, q. 2, that which does not entail self-contradiction is possible in itself and can, therefore, be done by God. There again he repeats the point that if something does entail contradiction, not even God can do it.[54] Hence his position seems to be this. It is not because God can do certain things that they are possible. It is rather because they are possible in themselves that he can do or make them. And it is because others are impossible in themselves that God cannot produce them. Here, too, then, he differs with Henry's final position on both counts, and appears to be much closer to Aquinas.

So much, then, for our three thinkers and their answers to our three questions concerning nonexisting possibles.

---

52. See Quodlibet 8, q. 3 (*PB* 4.43–44). Also see Quodlibet 9, q. 2 (*PB* 4.195); Quodlibet 2, q. 2 (*PB* 2.67–68). For more on this see Wippel, *The Metaphysical Thought* . . . , pp. 138–40. For discussion of Godfrey's theory of divine ideas see the same, pp. 124–30. Most distinctive of his theory is the claim that divine ideas are not multiplied to correspond to individuals within species. See Quodlibet 4, q. 1 (*PB* 2.229–33). On this point, at least, he is in agreement with a position defended by Henry of Ghent in the latter's Quodlibet 7, qq. 1–2 (ff. 255r–257r) of 1282.

53. See *PB* 3.107: "Sed quia concedere Deum posse aliquid quod tamen non possit, non sic derogat eius potentiae quia hoc non contingit nisi ex impossibilitate ex parte rei, sicut negare eum posse aliquid quod potest quia hoc contingeret ex defectu suae potentiae; quando sermo est de his quae Deus facere potest, debemus esse largissimi in concedendo eum posse omne illud quod non multum manifestam contradictionem includit."

54. *PB* 3.110–12. Here Godfrey is attempting to determine "Utrum Deus possit eumdem motum numero qui fuit reparare." He denies that God can do this because, he maintains, it cannot be done. See in particular, "Respondeo dicendum, quod Deus cuius potentia est infinita potest quicquid est possibile fieri. Possibile est autem fieri id quod enti universaliter non opponitur; hoc autem est quicquid contradictionem non importat. Ea ergo quorum reparatio secundum identitatem numeralem contradictionem implicat Deus non potest eadem numero reparare" (*PB* 3.110). Also see Quodlibet 5, q. 3, where Godfrey remarks: "confiteor tamen Deum posse omne illud quod contradictionem non includit, licet non intelligam omnia quae facere potest" (*PB* 3.8).

APPENDIX

Thomas Aquinas's Division of the Possible

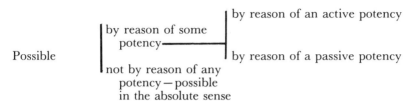

Henry of Ghent's Division of Being

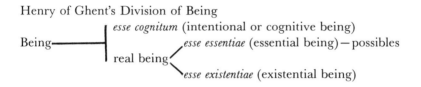

Godfrey of Fontaines' Division of Being

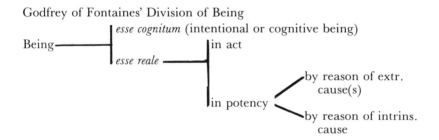

CHAPTER VIII

THOMAS AQUINAS ON THE POSSIBILITY OF ETERNAL CREATION

As is well known, Thomas Aquinas repeatedly found wanting all argumentation offered in support of eternity of the world. So great was his respect for Aristotle, however, that at times he seized upon a passage from the latter's *Topics* in order to suggest that the Stagirite himself may not have really intended to demonstrate the eternity of the world, but only to show that argumentation presented by others against its eternity was not demonstrative.[1] But later in his career, while commenting on the *Physics*, Thomas appears to reject this more benign reading of Aristotle.[2] As is equally well known, Thomas also dismissed as inconclusive argumentation offered by

---

1. See *Scriptum super libros Sententiarum*, Bk. II, d. 1, q. 1, a. 5 (*ed. cit.*, Vol. 2, pp. 33–34): "Dico ergo quod ad neutram partem quaestionis sunt demonstrationes, sed probabiles vel sophisticae rationes ad utrumque. Et hoc significant verba Philosophi dicentis, I *Top.*, cap. vii, quod sunt quaedam problemata de quibus rationem non habemus, ut utrum mundus sit aeternus; unde hoc ipse demonstrare nunquam intendit . . . ." For Aristotle see *Topics* I, ch. 11 (104b12–17). Thomas's apparent source for this reading of Aristotle was Moses Maimonides. See his *The Guide of the Perplexed*, trans. S. Pines (Chicago, 1963), II, ch. 15, p. 292. On this text in Aristotle and Maimonides' interpretation of it see E. Behler, *Die Ewigkeit der Welt* (Munich, 1965), pp. 54–55, 260–61.

2. See *In VIII Physic.*, lect. 2, in *In octo libros Physicorum Aristotelis Expositio* (Turin and Rome, 1954), n. 986, pp. 509–10. "Quidam vero frustra conantes Aristotelem ostendere non contra fidem locutum esse, dixerunt quod Aristoteles non intendit hic probare quasi verum, quod motus sit perpetuus; sed inducere rationem ad utramque partem, quasi ad rem dubiam: quod ex ipso modo procedendi frivolum apparet. Et praeterea, perpetuitate temporis et motus quasi principio utitur ad probandum primum principium esse, et hic in octavo et in XII Metaphys.; unde manifestum est, quod supponit hoc tanquam probatum." Cf. *In XII Met.*, lect. 5, in *In duodecim libros Metaphysicorum Aristotelis expositio* (Turin and Rome, 1950), nn. 2496–97, p. 584. Weisheipl dates the Commentary on the *Physics* 1269–70 and that on the *Metaphysics* 1269–72. See his *Friar Thomas d'Aquino,* pp. 375, 379.

his Christian contemporaries in support of creation in time. In sum, then, it appears that in Thomas's eyes one cannot demonstrate either eternity or noneternity of the world.[3] The Christian can only accept the noneternal character of the same as a matter of religious belief.

Eternity of the world was obviously a much discussed point during Thomas's time at the University of Paris and for some years thereafter. Condemnations of propositions relating to the same in 1270 and 1277 attest to this,[4]

3. For the Latin text and discussion of many of Thomas's treatments of eternity of the world see A. Antweiler, *Die Anfangslosigkeit der Welt nach Thomas von Aquin und Kant* (Trier, 1961), 2 vols. For English translations of many of these texts as well as important selections from Bonaventure and Siger of Brabant on this same topic and for a discussion of the same see C. Vollert, L. Kendzierski, and P. Byrne, *St. Thomas Aquinas, Siger of Brabant, St. Bonaventure, On the Eternity of the World* (Milwaukee, 1964). For some other discussions of this in Thomas and for further references see F. Van Steenberghen, *La philosophie au XIIIe siècle* (Louvain, 1966), pp. 458-64; "La controverse sur l'éternité du monde au XIIIe siècle," in his *Introduction à l'étude de la philosophie médiévale* (Louvain, 1974), esp. pp. 520-25; "Le mythe d'un monde éternel," *Revue philosophique de Louvain* 76 (1978), pp. 157-79 (with discussion of a number of other recent treatments of this); O. Argerami, "La cuestión 'De aeternitate mundi': posiciones doctrinales," *Sapientia* 27 (1972), pp. 313-34; 28 (1973), pp. 99-124, 179-208 (which considers the views of the more conservative group, especially Bonaventure, then of Thomas [pp. 325-34], and then of Boethius of Dacia and Siger of Brabant, to whom he attributes some doubtful and even some inauthentic writings [see Van Steenberghen, "Le mythe . . . ," p. 175]); E. Bertola, "Tommaso d'Aquino e il problema dell'eternità del mondo," *Rivista di filosofia neoscolastica* 66 (1974), pp. 312-55; J. I. Saranyana, "La creación 'ab aeterno': Controversia de Santo Tomás y Raimundo Marti con San Buenaventura," *Scripta theologica* 5 (1973), pp. 27-74; F. Kovach, "The Question of the Eternity of the World in St. Bonaventure and St. Thomas — A Critical Analysis," in *Bonaventure and Aquinas: Enduring Philosophers*, ed. R. W. Shahan and F. J. Kovach (Norman, Oklahoma, 1976), pp. 155-86; A. Zimmermann, "'Mundus est aeternus' — Zur Auslegung dieser These bei Bonaventura und Thomas von Aquin," in *Die Auseinandersetzungen an der Pariser Universität im XIII. Jahrhundert, Miscellanea Mediaevalia* 10 (Berlin, 1976), pp. 317-30.

4. For the Condemnation of 1270 see *Chartularium Universitatis Parisiensis* I (Paris, 1889), pp. 486-87. See propositions 5 ("Quod mundus est eternus") and 6 ("Quod nunquam fuit primus homo"). On the Condemnation of 1270 see my "The Condemnations of 1270 and 1277 at Paris," *The Journal of Medieval and Renaissance Studies* 7 (1977), pp. 179-83; Van Steenberghen, *La philosophie au XIIIe siècle*, pp. 472-74; *Maître Siger de Brabant* (Louvain, 1977), pp. 74-79. For the text of the 1277 Condemnation see *Chartularium . . .* I, pp. 543-60; P. Mandonnet, *Siger de Brabant et L'Averroïsme latin au XIIIe siècle*, 2d ed., 2 vols. (Louvain, 1911, 1908), Vol. 2, pp. 175-91. For some propositions touching on eternity of the world see 4-87, 87-85, 89-89, 91-80, 98-84, 99-83, 101-91, 107-112, 202-111, 205-88 (with the Chartularium number listed first). On the Condemnation of 1277 see Wippel, pp. 185-201; Van Steenberghen, *Maître Siger . . .*, pp. 146-58; R. Hissette, *Enquête sur les 219 articles condamnés à Paris le 7 mars 1277* (Louvain, 1977), *passim* (on articles touching on eternity of the world see pp. 147-60).

as do discussions of this topic by Henry of Ghent in 1276,[5] by Giles of Rome in apparent connection with his rehabilitation in the Theology Faculty in 1285,[6] and by Godfrey of Fontaines in his Quodlibet 2 of 1286.[7] Some years ago Edgar Hocedez drew attention to some important passages in Giles of Rome as well as some manuscript marginal notations to suggest that Giles himself may have originally defended the possibility of an eternally created world, and that this may have been one of the positions leading to his "exile" from the Theology Faculty from about 1278 until 1285.[8]

In fact, in later reference to this problem, Giles distinguishes three conceivable positions: (1) one might assert that eternity of the world is possible; (2) one might maintain that it is not possible to demonstrate the impossibility of the eternity of the world; (3) one might claim only that the impossibility of the eternity of the world has not yet been demonstrated. Giles himself here protests that he has never defended the first assertion, even though his earlier remarks might have given that impression. In fact, he does not even defend the second formulation, according to which it is not possible to demonstrate the impossibility of the eternity of the world. He has only maintained that no one has yet succeeded in so doing.[9]

And in his treatment of this in 1286, wherein he is obviously heavily influenced by Thomas's *De aeternitate mundi*, Godfrey of Fontaines carefully refrains from defending the first formulation. He contends not that eternity

---

5. See Henry's *Quodlibet* 1, qq. 7–8, where he considers together these two questions: "Utrum creatura potuit esse ab aeterno . . . . Utrum repugnat creaturae fuisse ab aeterno." (Paris, 1518, reprod. Louvain, 1961), Vol. 1, ff. 4r–6r. For a critical edition of these two questions see R. Macken, "La temporalité radicale de la créature selon Henri de Gand," *Recherches de Théologie ancienne et médiévale* 38 (1971), pp. 257–72 (and pp. 221–56 for a detailed study of the same); and now, his *Henrici de Gandavo, Quodlibet I* (Leuven-Leiden, 1979), pp. 27–46.

6. For Giles see his *In Secundum Librum Sententiarum*, d. 1, p. 1, q. 4, a. 2 (Venice, 1581; repr. Frankfurt, 1968), pp. 54–70.

7. For Godfrey see Quodlibet 2, q. 3 ("Utrum mundus sive aliqua creatura potuit esse vel existere ab aeterno"), in *Les Philosophes Belges*, Vol. 2 (Louvain, 1904), pp. 68–80.

8. See "La condamnation de Gilles de Rome," *Recherches de Théologie ancienne et médiévale* 4 (1932), pp. 42–46; also, Macken, "La temporalité radicale . . . ," pp. 243–47.

9. *In Secundum Librum* . . . , d. 1, p. 1, q. 4, a. 2, pp. 57 and 70. Note in the latter context: " . . . tamen ut supra tangebamus, quia multa sunt vera, quae demonstrari non possunt, et multa sunt demonstrabilia ad quae nondum inventae sunt demonstrationes, ideo non tenemus quod mundus potuerit esse ab aeterno, nec quod non possit demonstrari, sed quod rationes ad hoc factae non videntur nobis esse demonstrationes. Si ergo in hac quaestione aliquando visi sumus dicere quod mundus potuit esse ab aeterno, non tanquam hoc asserentes diximus sed gratia disputationis hoc assumebamus, ut possemus ostendere rationes contra hoc factas non concludere."

of the world is possible but only that its impossibility is not demonstrable.[10] In sum, then, he seems to accept both propositions 2 and 3 as distinguished by Giles, and thus does defend a bolder position than does Giles. But he had not, of course, been exiled from the Theology Faculty for a number of years.

One might wonder how Thomas Aquinas would have reacted to these three propositions. He certainly denied that anyone had demonstrated the impossibility of eternal creation, and he thus set himself at odds with Bonaventure and the Neo-Augustinian tradition represented by John Peckham and to be continued somewhat later by Henry of Ghent.[11] But what of the first and second formulations: Did he claim that eternity of the world is possible? Or if not, did he at least maintain that one cannot demonstrate its impossibility? Raymond Macken has recently suggested that he did not defend the first formulation at all and that if some of his words might indicate that he accepted the second, his real position is best captured by the third. For his reservations about actual infinite multitudes and series point to some doubt on his part about his contention that noneternity of the world cannot be demonstrated. The first formulation, then — the claim that eternity of the world is indeed a possibility — is really an exaggeration of the true Thomistic position.[12] (Macken's point was partially anticipated some

10. See Quodlibet 2, q. 3, p. 80. Throughout much of this discussion Godfrey obviously has the text of Thomas's *De aeternitate mundi* before him. For reference to the presence of this work in Godfrey's Student Notebook, see below. For fuller analysis of Godfrey's discussion of this and his usage of Thomas therein see my *The Metaphysical Thought of Godfrey of Fontaines*, pp. 160–64.

11. For Bonaventure on the impossibility of an eternally created world see especially *In II Sent.*, d. 1, p. 1, a. 1, q. 2, in *Opera Omnia*, 10 vols. (Quaracchi, 1882–1902), Vol. 2, pp. 20–22. For some more recent discussions of Bonaventure's position see Van Steenberghen, *La philosophie au XIIIe siècle*, pp. 225–26; "Saint Bonaventure contre l'éternité du monde," in his *Introduction à l'étude de la philosophie médiévale*, pp. 404–20; A. Coccia, "De aeternitate mundi apud s. Bonaventuram et recentiores," in *S. Bonaventura 1274–1974*, 5 vols. (Grottaferrata [Rome]: Collegio S. Bonaventura, 1973), Vol. 3, pp. 279–306; B. Bonansea, "The Impossibility of Creation from Eternity According to St. Bonaventure," *Proceedings of the American Catholic Philosophical Association* 48 (Washington, D.C., 1974), pp. 121–35; "The Question of an Eternal World in the Teaching of St. Bonaventure," *Franciscan Studies* 34 (1974), pp. 7–33; J. F. Quinn, *The Historical Constitution of St. Bonaventure's Philosophy* (Toronto, 1973), pp. 594–603; and the references already cited above in n. 3 which compare Thomas and Bonaventure. For Henry's adamant refusal to admit that an eternally created world is possible, see the references cited above in n. 5, including Macken's study. For Peckham see his *Quaestiones de aeternitate mundi* as edited and introduced by Ignatius Brady, "John Pecham and the Background of Aquinas's *De aeternitate mundi*," in *St. Thomas Aquinas 1274–1974: Commemorative Studies* (Toronto, 1974), Vol. 2, pp. 141–78.

12. See Macken, "La temporalité radicale de la créature selon Henri de Gand," p. 256.

centuries ago by Cardinal Cajetan in his Commentary on the *Summa theologiae* I, q. 46, a. 2, where he urges caution on the part of Thomists who would say that the world could have existed from eternity. While apparently agreeing that Thomas would concede this on the subhuman level, Cajetan will not say the same for man himself.)[13] Others evidently disagree with Macken's interpretation in that they attribute to Aquinas the view that an eternal and created world is a possibility. Among more recent studies of this question in Thomas mention should be made of those by Van Steenberghen, Kovach, Zimmermann, Argerami, Bertola, and Bonansea.[14] In light of

13. See Thomas's *Opera omnia*, Vol. 4 (Rome: Leonine ed., 1888), p. 483b, IX. Given Thomas's doctrine on the immortality of the human soul, and without some theory of circulation of souls, it is not intelligible, remarks Cajetan, to say that man has been generated from eternity. Therefore, he continues: "Et propterea cauti sint Thomistae in concedendo mundum *potuisse ab aeterno*. Concedant mundum quoad substantiam, constantem ex quinque corporibus simplicibus; concedant mundum etiam quoad motum caeli, et generationes omnes praeter humanam."

14. In *La philosophie au XIIIe siècle* (p. 462, n. 98) Van Steenberghen comments that while Thomas rejects the Aristotelian arguments for eternity of the world, he does not take a position on the *possibility* of an eternal world. His thesis is purely negative. Here he seems to have especially in mind ST I, q. 46, aa. 1-2. In his "La controverse sur l'éternité du monde au XIIIe siècle," in the course of commenting on Thomas's *De aeternitate mundi*, Van Steenberghen observes that certain manuscripts entitle this treatise *De possibilitate aeternitatis mundi*, which corresponds better to its content. Perhaps he would admit that here Thomas does defend the possibility of an eternally created world (p. 523). And in the *Résumé* following his "Le mythe d'un monde éternel," reference is made to the fact that "S. Thomas ait defendu la possibilité d'un monde éternel . . . " (p. 179), though it is not clear whether Van Steenberghen himself is responsible for this résumé. For Kovach's repeated assertion that Thomas did defend the possibility of an eternally created world see "The Question of the Eternity . . . ," pp. 165, 167, 170, 182, 185. Zimmermann seems to be of the same mind (see his "'Mundus est aeternus'—Zur Auslegung . . . ," esp. p. 330). So, too, is Argerami (see "La cuestión 'De aeternitate mundi' . . . ," pp. 326ff. [on the *De aeternitate mundi*], p. 331 [also on *In II Sent.*, d. 1, q. 1, a. 5], p. 333). Without saying so in so many words, Bertola seems to recognize that in the *De aeternitate mundi* Thomas does defend the possibility of an eternally created world rather than merely criticize argumentation offered in support of creation in time (see "Tommaso d'Aquino e il problema . . . ," pp. 349, 352). But like most of the authors just mentioned, Bertola is not primarily concerned with the distinction between Thomas's defense (whether real or imagined) of the possibility of an eternally created world, on the one hand, and his critique of all argumentation offered for its temporal beginning, on the other. See p. 355 where he seems to equate the two and states that Thomas always defended "la possibilità teorica e razionale che il mondo avrebbe potuto non avere avuto inizio." In his "The Question of an Eternal World in the Teaching of St. Bonaventure" Bonansea notes in passing that "the school of thought headed by Aquinas" admitted "the theoretical possibility of an eternally created world" (p. 7).

this disagreement, therefore, it may be rewarding for us to examine Thomas's texts on this point once more. My purpose here will be not to determine whether or not he was correct in rejecting argumentation to prove that the world began to be, but to ascertain whether he did, in fact, defend the possibility of eternal creation.

Among Thomas's major discussions of eternity of the world, we shall begin with that found in his Commentary on Bk. II of the *Sentences*, d. 1, q. 1, a. 5 (dating ca. 1253).[15] There the question proposed for discussion is straightforward: whether the world is eternal.[16] Thomas offers a series of arguments in support of the contention that the world is eternal, and then a series of arguments against this claim. In his solution he lists three general positions: that of the philosophers, who hold that certain things apart from God are also eternal (which Thomas here rejects both as false and heretical); that of those who say that the world began after not having existed, and that God could not have created an eternal world, not because he lacks the power, but because an eternal and created world is an impossibility; finally, the view of those who maintain that everything apart from God began to be, but that human reason cannot demonstrate this. This can be known only by revelation.[17]

Thomas accepts the third position and comments that in his opinion noneternity of the world, like the Trinity, cannot be demonstrated.[18] Therefore, nothing more than probable or sophistic argumentation can be offered for either side, that is, for eternity or for noneternity of the world. He cites with approval the passage from Aristotle's *Topics* to which reference has been made above in order to show that the Stagirite did not really intend to demonstrate the world's eternity. He then attempts to show that the arguments offered both for eternity and for noneternity of the world are not conclusive.[19] In sum, in this discussion Thomas does *not* explicitly defend the possibility of an eternally created world (see position 1 as formulated by Giles of Rome), but contents himself with refuting argumentation both for and against its eternity.[20] Neither eternity nor noneternity can be demonstrated.

15. Weisheipl dates Thomas's Commentary on the Four Books of the *Sentences* from 1252 until 1256 (pp. 358–59).

16. See *Scriptum super libros Sententiarum*, Vol. 2, p. 27: "Utrum mundus sit aeternus."

17. *Ibid.*, pp. 32–33.

18. " . . . sed tamen mundum incepisse non potuit demonstrari, sed per revelationem divinam esse habitum et creditum . . . . Et huic positioni consentio: quia non credo, quod a nobis possit sumi ratio demonstrativa ad hoc; sicut nec ad Trinitatem . . . " (p. 33).

19. See pp. 34–41.

20. Here I differ from Argerami, who does find Thomas defending the possibility of an eternally created world in this context (see his "La cuestión . . . ," p. 331).

Not only does he defend the weakest of the three positions singled out by Giles—position 3—but he also defends the second position by asserting that noneternity of the world cannot be demonstrated.

Thomas next addresses himself to this problem in considerable detail in his *Summa contra gentiles* II, chs. 31–38 (dating from 1261 or thereafter). In ch. 31 he defends the position that creatures need not have always existed. In chs. 32–37 he presents a series of arguments in support of the world's eternity and then refutes these in turn. He does not, of course, appeal to the impossibility of creation from eternity in refuting these arguments since, as is conceded by all of his interpreters, he did not accept as conclusive any alleged demonstration that eternal creation is impossible. In ch. 38 he presents and rejects a series of arguments offered by "some" to prove that the world is not eternal. Here he comments that while these arguments are not demonstrative, they do not lack some probability. And he suggests that a more effective (though still not demonstrative) procedure might be based on the divine goodness and the purposiveness of the divine will. It was most fitting for God to assign to creatures a beginning in duration. Thomas's intent throughout this general discussion is once more to show that neither argumentation for nor argumentation against eternity of the world is demonstrative. But nowhere in this context does he assert in positive terms that an eternally created world is possible.[21]

One might wonder, perhaps, if he has not at least implied that such is possible in ch. 37, in the course of refuting the third argument for eternal creation, which he had presented in ch. 34. According to that argument, what begins to exist must have enjoyed possible being before it actually exists. But a possible being is a subject, a being in potency. Therefore, before anything can begin to be, a subject or a being in potency must preexist. And rather than regress to infinity, one must postulate some first subject which never began to be. As one would expect, Thomas replies that there

---

Apparently Kovach also does ("The Question . . . ," p. 170). For fuller discussion of this article from the Commentary on the *Sentences* see Bertola, "Tommaso d'Aquino . . . ," pp. 314–25.

21. It is interesting to observe that in this context (ch. 38) Thomas limits himself to a series of arguments that have been offered against the world's eternity and then meets these by noting how they might be refuted by those who defend an eternal world. Here his claim does not appear to be quite so strong as in *In II Sent.* Thus he contents himself with refuting argumentation offered in favor of an eternal world, but he does not state in explicit terms either that its noneternity *cannot* be demonstrated or that its eternity is *possible*. Hence here he explicitly defends only the weakest of the three positions distinguished by Giles. For some other differences between the discussions in SCG II and in *In II Sent.* see Bertola, "Tommaso d'Aquino e il problema . . . ," pp. 325–30.

need be no preexisting passive potency or subject prior to the existence of all created being. Such is required only for things that come into being by way of motion. He comments that prior to its actual existence a created entity may be described as possible in two ways: first, by reason of the preexisting power of an agent that can bring it into being; and second, by reason of lack of repugnance between the terms that describe it or, in other words, because its existence does not entail intrinsic contradiction. Evidently the possible in this last-mentioned sense requires no preexisting passive potential principle. Therefore, since the predicate "to exist" is not repugnant to a subject such as "the world" or "man," the existence of such a subject is not intrinsically impossible. Rather than defend the possibility of an eternally created world in this discussion, however, all that Thomas has done is to indicate two ways in which any being, including the entire universe, may be described as possible prior to its actual existence.

In his *De potentia*, q. 3, a. 17 (1265–66) Thomas again addresses himself to the question whether the world has always existed.[22] Once more he first presents a long series of arguments in support of this contention and then a few against it. In the corpus of this article he recalls that according to Catholic faith one must hold that the world did not always exist. And he remarks that this Catholic position cannot be effectively countered by any physical demonstration. Just as the present dimensions of the universe depend upon the divine will, so does its duration. He spends most of his time here arguing against alleged demonstrations that the world is eternal, but concludes by also rejecting alleged demonstrations that it began to be. In replying to the tenth argument for an eternal world he returns to the different ways in which the world might be said to be possible before it actually existed: first, by reason of the power of a cause (God) that could bring it into being; secondly, not by reason of any potency, but simply because of the absence of contradiction in the statement "the world exists." Once more, then, this is to state only that the world was possible before it actually existed, not that it could have always existed.[23]

Somewhat earlier in this same q. 3 of the *De potentia* Thomas had considered an issue that is more directly related to our immediate concern. In q. 3, a. 14 he asks whether that which is distinct from God in essence could have always existed.[24] The immediately preceding article (q. 3, a. 13) may well have suggested this question to him since he had there contended on

---

22. "*Decimoseptimo* quaeritur utrum mundus semper fuerit" (in *Quaestiones disputatae*, Vol. 2 [Turin and Rome, 1953], p. 90).

23. See pp. 93–94 and for his reply to the tenth argument, p. 95.

24. "*Decimoquarto* quaeritur utrum id quod est a Deo diversum in essentia, possit semper fuisse" (p. 79).

theological grounds that some being which proceeds from another (*ens ab alio*) can indeed be eternal, namely, the Son insofar as he proceeds from the Father in the Trinity.[25] In any event, Thomas begins article 14 by presenting a number of arguments in support of the view that something that differs in essence from God could have always existed. These are then followed by another series of arguments against any such possibility.[26]

In the corpus of article 14 Thomas develops somewhat more fully the different ways in which the term "possible" may be used. Taking his cue from Aristotle's *Metaphysics* V, he observes that something may be said to be possible either by reason of some potency or else by reason of no potency. In the former case it may be possible by reason of an active potency or power (it is possible for a builder to build something because he has the active power) or by reason of a passive potency (it is possible for wood to be burnt). In the latter case (when something is said to be possible by reason of no potency or power) the name "possible" can be applied metaphorically (as when in geometry a line is referred to as a rational power) or in the absolute sense (as when two terms of a proposition are not incompatible with one another). On the other hand, something is to be described as impossible only when it involves self-contradiction, and not merely because it is not possible for a given agent or a given recipient.[27]

Thomas now applies these distinctions to the case at hand. The statement that something which differs in substance from God has always existed is not self-contradictory and is not, therefore, impossible in itself. This follows because "to be from another" is not repugnant to "always existing" except in cases where one thing proceeds from another by way of motion, something which is not true of creative production. The additional note "differing in substance" likewise introduces nothing that is intrinsically repugnant to or incompatible with "to have always existed."[28]

What Thomas has here defended is the absence of any intrinsic contradiction in the claim that some creature could have always existed. But one might wonder whether other conditions do not militate against such a

---

25. "*Decimotertio* quaeritur utrum aliquod ens ab alio possit esse aeternum." For this see pp. 78–79.

26. For these see pp. 79–80.

27. *Ibid.*, p. 80. Though admittedly inspired by Aristotle's discussion in *Metaphysics* V, ch. 12, Thomas's division of the possible is not exactly reducible to it, especially as regards the possible in the absolute sense and the impossible. For an interesting commentary on Aristotle's text see Thomas's *In V Metaphysicorum*, lect. 14, nn. 954–76.

28. *Ibid.*, p. 80. Note in particular: "Per hoc autem quod additur, *diversum in substantia*, similiter nulla repugnantia absolute loquendo datur intelligi ad id quod est semper fuisse."

possibility. Thomas then goes on to apply the various members of his division of the possible. If one takes the possible as referring to active potency or power, it is clear that there can be no lack or deficiency in God's ability to produce something that differs from himself from all eternity. But, in a curious turn in his argumentation, Thomas comments that if one takes the possible in the sense of passive potency, then, given the truth of Catholic belief, one cannot say that anything could be produced by God from eternity and still differ from him in essence. For according to the teaching of faith there was no eternally existing passive potency from which the world might have been produced. Thomas's point here seems to be this. Under the supposition that nothing which differs in essence from God has always existed, it is not possible for it to have always existed by reason of any pre-existing passive potency. But this is only hypothetical impossibility, the kind that obtains only under the supposition of the opposite — that the entire created universe in fact began to be.[29]

One might still wonder whether as of this writing Thomas would not go farther and admit the possibility of an eternally created universe under a different supposition, namely, that God has willed it to exist from eternity. But instead of committing himself on this point, Thomas now turns to the series of arguments he had offered in defense of the view that something distinct from God could have been produced by him from eternity. Interestingly enough, rather than accept this position without qualification, Thomas criticizes each of these arguments. It seems, then, that he does not here regard as definitively established the claim that an eternally created effect is possible. For instance, several of these arguments merely show, he contends, something which he has already conceded — that there is no deficiency from the side of God (see his replies to arguments 1, 4, 5, and 9). The eighth argument had maintained that God can produce in a creature anything that is not contrary to its essence, and that it is not contrary to such an essence to have always existed and to be produced. Thomas replies that this shows only that it is not intrinsically contradictory for something to be made and to have always existed.[30]

In sum, then, in De potentia, q. 3, a. 14, Thomas has argued that there is no intrinsic repugnance between being produced as distinct in essence from

29. Ibid. Note Thomas's concluding remark in the corpus: "Unde et dicitur a quibusdam quod hoc quidem est possibile ex parte Dei creantis, non autem ex parte essentiae a Deo procedentis, per suppositionem contrarii, quam fides facit." For much the same see Quodlibet 5, q. 1, a. 1, which dates from December, 1271.

30. Ibid., pp. 80–81. See in particular: "Ad octavum dicendum, quod ratio illa non probat nisi quod esse factum, et esse semper, non habeant ad invicem repugnantiam secundum se considerata; unde procedit de possibili absolute."

God and having always existed. In other words, such is possible in this sense, that it does not entail intrinsic contradiction. Moreover, he has also noted that such is possible from the standpoint of God's power, granted that it is not possible by reason of any eternally preexisting passive potency. He would now seem to have all the necessary ammunition at hand in order to take the final step and to assert positively that an eternally created effect is indeed possible. Yet he hesitates to do so, and he sees fit to criticize all the arguments offered to establish this possibility. One wonders why. Perhaps he is still not quite certain that he has considered and eliminated every conceivable obstacle that might preclude the possibility of an eternally created entity.

In two well-known articles in the *Summa theologiae* (I, q. 46, aa. 1–2) Thomas again takes up this discussion (ca. 1266–68). In article 1 he considers and rejects the claim that the world has always existed. Here he is content to show that arguments designed to prove that the world has always existed are not conclusive and that eternity of the world cannot be demonstrated. He again comments that the arguments offered by Aristotle in support of the world's eternity are not intended to be demonstrations as such, but only to refute other arguments offered by some of the ancients. Once more, along with other indications, he cites the text from the *Topics* to buttress his assessment of Aristotle's intentions. In his reply to the first objection he repeats his earlier contention that the world, before it actually existed, was possible, not in terms of any preexisting passive potency or matter, to be sure, but by reason of God's active power, and also insofar as its existence was not self-contradictory. This, however, is not for him to claim that an eternally created world is possible.

In article 2 Thomas contends that our conviction that the world did not always exist rests on faith alone and cannot be demonstrated.[31] Here, then, he defends both positions 3 and 2 as they were to be formulated by Giles of Rome, and as he had already done in his Commentary on Bk. II of the *Sentences*.[32] Not only has the noneternity of the world not been demonstrated, it cannot be demonstrated. But now he attempts to indicate why this is so. First of all, this cannot be demonstrated by reasoning from the side of the world itself. For it is the quiddity (*quod quid est*) of a thing that serves as its principle of demonstration. But when something is considered simply in terms of its specific definition, it abstracts from the here and now. Wherefore, it cannot be demonstrated that man, or the heavens, or stones, have

31. "Respondeo dicendum quod mundum non semper fuisse, sola fide tenetur, et demonstrative probari non potest: sicut et supra de mysterio Trinitatis dictum est" (Turin and Rome: Marietti, 1950), p. 237.
32. See above, pp. 196–97.

not always existed. Nor can this be demonstrated by reasoning from the side of God, since this decision depends upon the divine will.[33]

In his reply to the seventh argument presented to show that the world could not be eternal, Thomas counters that an infinite series of efficient causes wherein each depends upon that which is prior to it is not repugnant when such causes are related to one another only *per accidens*. Viewed from this perspective, therefore, it is not impossible for one man to have been generated by another to infinity, extending backward into a beginningless past. But for Thomas to say this is not yet for him to assert unequivocally that an eternal world is possible. And in his reply to the eighth argument against creation from eternity he grapples with the problem of the actual infinite multitude of human souls that might result from such a situation. Even if one accepts this as an argument against the existence of man from eternity, he responds, one might hold that the world itself, or at least some creature, such as an angel, has existed from eternity.[34] Once more he is directly concerned with refuting argumentation in favor of the noneternity of the world rather than with positively asserting that an eternal world is possible.

Reference has been made above to the fact that two propositions asserting eternity of the world or of man were condemned by Stephen Tempier in December, 1270. This would lead one to assume that this topic continued to be discussed during Thomas's second teaching period at Paris, that is to say, from 1269 until 1272. Not surprisingly, therefore, in works dating from that period this issue reappears. Thus in Quodlibet 3, q. 14, a. 2 (Easter, 1270), the following question was put to Thomas by one of those attending this particular quodlibetal session: "Whether it can be demonstrated that the world is not eternal."[35] Thomas replies that matters which simply depend upon the divine will cannot be demonstratively proved.

---

33. *Ibid.* Thomas then reemphasizes his point that it cannot be demonstrated that the world began to be: "Unde mundum incoepisse est credibile, non autem demonstrabile vel scibile."

34. In this same context he notes that some, such as Algazel, do not reject the possibility of an infinity of souls, though, as he also observes, he himself has rejected such a possibility earlier in this same work (see ST I, q. 7, a. 4). Some hold that the soul is corrupted with the body; some maintain that only one soul survives; and some appeal to circulation of a finite number of souls in different bodies. Thomas himself does not comment on each of these suggestions here, but it is clear that he can accept none of the three last-mentioned theories, and that he will later have some doubts about the impossibility of an actual infinite multitude of spiritual entities (see his *De aeternitate mundi*).

35. "Utrum possit demonstrative probari quod mundus non sit aeternus" in *Quaestiones quodlibetales* (Turin, 1956), p. 68.

Such is true of our conviction that the world began to be.[36] Here again, then, he is not content to say that no one has yet demonstrated that the world began to be, but asserts that such cannot be demonstrated. Such a position surely did little to appease more conservative theologians who had espoused Bonaventure's position.

In Quodlibet 12, q. 6, a. 1 (perhaps of Christmas, 1270), this question is proposed for Thomas's consideration: — "Whether the heaven or the world is eternal."[37] Although only a brief résumé of Thomas's reply has been preserved, presumably as a *reportatio*, he quickly moves from the safe contention that neither the heaven nor the world is eternal to the more controversial statement that our knowledge that the world began to be is a matter of faith only, not of demonstration.[38] In his *Compendium theologiae,* which may have been written circa 1269–73 at either Paris or Naples, Thomas considers eternity of the world in chs. 98 and 99. In both of these chapters he presents and then rejects argumentation for either the eternity of the world or the eternity of matter. In replying to the last of these he again explains in what ways the world may be said to have been possible before it actually existed.[39] In none of these texts, as in no other examined until this point, does he maintain positively and without qualification that an eternal world is indeed possible.

But when one turns to Thomas's more polemical discussion of this topic in his *De aeternitate mundi* (ca. 1270), one has the impression from the outset that he will explicitly address himself to our particular concern.[40] Here he

---

36. *Ibid.* Note in particular: " . . . unde ea quae ad principium mundi pertinent, demonstrative probari non possunt, sed sola fide tenentur . . . ." For more on this see Bertola, pp. 345–47.

37. "Utrum caelum vel mundus sit aeternus." *Ibid.,* p. 227.

38. "Sed mundum incepisse est de numero eorum quae cadunt sub fide, non sub demonstratione" (*ibid.*).

39. See *Compendium theologiae,* ch. 99.2 and reply to the *secunda obiectio,* in *Opuscula theologica,* Vol. 1 (Turin and Rome: Marietti, 1954), pp. 48–49/Leonine ed., Vol. 42, pp. 117–18.

40. Granted that the date for this work continues to be disputed, there are strong reasons, in my opinion, for placing it during Thomas's second Parisian teaching period, and ca. 1270 or possibly 1271. For references to Mandonnet, Glorieux, Van Steenberghen, Walz, and Brady in support of this later dating see the introduction to the *De aeternitate mundi* in the Leonine critical edition: *Sancti Thomae de Aquino opera omnia,* Vol. 43 (Rome, 1976), pp. 54–56. The Leonine editors themselves favor this later dating and side against Pelster, Bukowski, and Hendrickx, who argue for an earlier date. And if Brady is correct in his effort to show that Thomas directed this treatise against John Peckham's two *Quaestiones de aeternitate mundi,* which he has recently edited, and especially against the second of these ("Utrum mundus potuit fieri ab

begins by observing that if one supposes, in accord with Catholic belief, that the world did not always exist but began to be, doubt has been raised as to whether it *could have always existed.* [41] After eliminating the possibility of there being any eternally existing thing apart from God that would not have been created by him, Thomas concentrates on this issue: Is it possible for something to be caused by God in terms of its entire being (to be created), and yet to have always existed?[42] He then proceeds by process of elimination. This might be said to be impossible either because God lacked the power to bring it about or else because it simply could not be done in itself. All parties concede, he quickly comments, that God does not lack such power, because his power is infinite. But if it be said that this is something that simply cannot be done, this can only be either because of the absence of any (eternally existing) passive potency or because it is intrinsically contradictory in itself.[43] One now has the impression that Thomas intends to consider and to eliminate every conceivable obstacle that might be raised against the possibility of eternal creation and, therefore, to defend that possibility.

Thomas quickly dismisses the first suggested reason for holding that it is impossible in itself for something to have always existed and to have been created by God, namely, the absence of any passive potency from which an eternally existing creature might be formed. Granted that in accord with the teaching of faith one cannot defend the eternal existence of any creature or of any such passive potency, this admission does not prove that God *could*

---

aeterno"), the case for the later dating becomes even stronger. See Ignatius Brady, "John Pecham and the Background of Aquinas's *De aeternitate mundi*," pp. 141–78. If, as I shall now maintain, Thomas does defend the possibility of an eternally created world in the *De aeternitate*, his position is diametrically opposed to Peckham. According to the latter, the world could not be without a beginning (*ibid.*, p. 176). Another Franciscan Master of Theology, William of Baglione, had contended some years before that it can be demonstrated both that the world *is not* and *cannot be eternal.* See Brady, "The Questions of Master William of Baglione O.F.M., *De aeternitate mundi* (Paris, 1266–1267)," *Antonianum* 47 (1972), pp. 368, 370.

41. " . . . dubitatio mota est utrum potuerit semper fuisse." Unless otherwise indicated I shall cite this work according to the edition by J. Perrier, *S. Thomae Aquinatis Opuscula omnia necnon opera minora*, Vol. 1 (Paris, 1949), pp. 52–61. For the above see par. n. 1.

42. See in particular: "Si autem intelligatur aliquid semper fuisse, et tamen causatum fuisse a Deo secundum totum id quod in eo est, videndum est utrum hoc possit stare" (n. 1).

43. See nn. 1–2. Note in particular: "Restat ergo videre utrum sit possibile aliquid fieri quod semper fuerit. Si autem dicatur quod hoc non potest fieri, hoc non potest intelligi nisi duobus modis vel duas causas veritatis habere: vel propter remotionem potentiae passivae, vel propter repugnantiam intellectuum."

not bring such to pass.[44] Implied in Thomas's answer is his conviction that creative production needs no preexisting passive potency. He devotes considerably more attention to the second suggested obstacle, the claim that it is intrinsically repugnant or contradictory for that which has been created by God to have always existed. One might argue that this is as impossible as it is for affirmation and negation to be true simultaneously (with respect to the same subject). Though some would say that God could bring this about, or even make the past not to have been, Thomas regards such claims as false, although not as heretical. As far as he is concerned, not even God can do such things, since they cannot be done.[45]

As regards the present issue, then, this is the crucial question: Is it intrinsically contradictory for something to be created by God and to have always existed?[46] In line with his preceding observation, Thomas first comments that whatever answer to this question may be correct, it is not heretical for someone to maintain that it could be brought to pass by God that something created by him should have always existed. Nevertheless, if these two notions are incompatible, such a claim would, in Thomas's opinion, be false.[47] But if these two notions are not incompatible, then not only is it *not false* to maintain this, but such is also possible. And to say anything else would be *erroneous*, he immediately adds.[48]

This passage is extremely important for a proper understanding of Thomas's *De aeternitate mundi*. First of all, as is well known, he quickly proceeds in the remainder of this opusculum to show that these two notions — to be created by God and to have always existed — are not intrinsically incompatible: neither because a creative efficient cause must precede its effect in duration nor because the nonexistence of a creature must precede its existence

---

44. See n. 2, and in particular: "Tamen ex hoc non sequitur quod Deus non possit facere ut fiat aliquid semper ens."

45. See n. 2: "Tamen manifestum est quod non potest facere ut hoc fiat, quia potentia qua ponitur esse destruit se ipsam. Si tamen ponatur quod Deus hujusmodi potest facere ut fiant, positio non est haeretica, quamvis, ut credo, sit falsa; sicut quod praeteritum non fuerit, includit in se contradictionem . . . . Et tamen quidam magni pie dixerunt Deum posse facere de praeterito quod non fuerit praeteritum; nec fuit reputatum haereticum."

46. "Videndum est ergo utrum in his duobus repugnantia sit intellectuum, quod aliquid sit creatum a Deo et tamen semper fuerit" (n. 3).

47. "Et quidquid de hoc verum sit, non est haereticum dicere quod hoc possit fieri a Deo ut aliquid creatum a Deo semper fuerit. Tamen credo quod, si esset repugnantia intellectuum, falsum esset" (n. 3).

48. "Si autem non est repugnantia intellectuum, non solum non est falsum sed etiam possibile; aliter esset erroneum, si aliter dicatur" (n. 3).

in duration.[49] Given the opening statement of his treatise ("doubt has been raised as to whether it [the world] could have always existed"), and given his careful listing of and elimination of all conceivable obstacles to this possibility, it seems in light of the passage just analyzed that in this work Thomas does indeed defend the possibility of an eternally created world.[50]

Secondly, Thomas has carefully prepared the ground for his position by noting that if the notions of being created by God and having always existed are incompatible, to say that an eternally created effect is possible would be false but not heretical.[51] In other words, he seems to be disarming his opponents in the theological faculty by suggesting in advance that the stronger position for which he is about to argue, the possibility of an eternally created world, is not heretical, whether it be true or false.

Finally, Thomas contends that if there is no intrinsic repugnance or incompatibility between the two notes in question, not only is it *not false* to defend this possibility; eternal creation is also possible. So true is this, he continues, that to hold otherwise would be erroneous. Presumably he means theologically erroneous, for he justifies this claim by pointing out that to deny that such is possible would be to detract from God's omnipotence![52] Here Thomas neatly turns the tables against his opponents by suggesting that their apparently more conservative position is, in fact, theologically erroneous. If he has rejected as *false* but *not* as *heretical* the claim that God can do that which is contradictory or make the past not to have been, now he is saying that it is not only *not false* to defend the possibility of eternal creation, but that such is indeed possible and, moreover, that to deny this possibility is *erroneous*. (This is not for him to say that this denial is heretical, for that would also require that one be pertinacious in rejecting an article of

---

49. "Si enim repugnant, hoc non est nisi propter alterum duorum vel propter utrumque: aut quia oportet quod causa agens praecedat suum effectum duratione, aut quia oportet quod non esse praecedat esse duratione; propter hoc dicitur causatum a Deo ex nihilo fieri" (n. 3). For his effort to show that it is not necessary for a creative efficient cause (God) to precede his effect in duration see nn. 4–5. For his proof that the nonexistence of something created need not precede its existence in duration see nn. 6–7.

50. See n. 8: "Sic ergo patet quod in hoc quod dicitur aliquid esse factum a Deo et nunquam non fuisse, non est intellectus aliqua repugnantia." For some appeals to and discussion of authorities such as Augustine, John Damascene, Hugh of St. Victor, and Boethius, see nn. 8–10.

51. See the text cited above in n. 47.

52. "Cum enim ad omnipotentiam Dei pertineat ut omnem intellectum et virtutem excedat, expresse omnipotentiae Dei derogat qui dicit aliquid posse intelligi in creaturis quod a Deo fieri non possit" (n. 3, in continuation of the text cited in n. 48 above).

faith.)[53] But his usage of the term "erroneous" would surely have given little comfort to his opponents.

To return to the main theme of our investigation, it seems that in the *De aeternitate mundi* Thomas would have defended all three propositions as formulated by Giles of Rome. Not only has no one yet demonstrated that the world began to be. Not only can this not be demonstrated. An eternal world is possible. Unfortunately, there is one difficulty with this reading of the *De aeternitate*, a difficulty that arises from textual variants in the central passage analyzed above.[54] We have followed the Perrier edition, but that printed by Marietti differs from this in important respects.[55] Moreover, the oldest surviving manuscript of this work, that preserved in a student notebook compiled by Godfrey of Fontaines in the 1270s, differs from both Perrier and the Marietti text.[56] Finally, as the editors of the recently published Leonine critical edition both acknowledge and illustrate, the manuscript tradition for this particular passage is especially troubled. In their edition they have assigned a privileged position to the group of manuscripts they refer to as Phi (φ), and within that family especially to Godfrey's manuscript (P[23]).[57]

53. See for instance ST II-IIae, q. 5, a. 3c: "Et sic manifestum est quod haereticus qui pertinaciter discredit unum articulum non est paratus sequi in omnibus doctrinam Ecclesiae (si enim non pertinaciter, iam non est haereticus, sed solum errans)" (Turin and Rome, 1948), p. 50.

54. See the text cited above in n. 48.

55. See *Opuscula Philosophica*, ed. R. M. Spiazzi (Turin and Rome: Marietti, 1954), p. 106, n. 297.

56. On Godfrey's Student Notebook see P. Glorieux, "Un recueil scolaire de Godefroid de Fontaines (Paris, Nat. Lat. 16297)," *Recherches de Théologie ancienne et médiévale* 3 (1931), pp. 37–53; J. J. Duin, *La doctrine de la providence dans les écrits de Siger de Brabant* (Louvain, 1954), pp. 130–35. For Thomas's *De aeternitate mundi* see ff. 68ra–69rb. Glorieux dates this manuscript ca. 1270–72 (see pp. 47–48). For further discussion of this dating see Duin, pp. 271–75, 292. It may be that Godfrey's compilation of his notebook was not completed until as late as ca. 1277. (See R. Wielockx, "Le ms. Paris Nat. lat. 16096 et la condamnation du 7 mars 1277," *Recherches de Théologie ancienne et médiévale* 48 [1981], p. 236; "Gottfried von Fontaines als Zeuge der Echtheit der Theologischen Summe des Albertus Magnus," *Miscellanea Mediaevalia* 15 [1982], pp. 214–16.) But the position of Thomas's *De aeternitate* in the manuscript suggests that his treatise was incorporated into the collection before that date, but after Thomas's Quodlibet 5, which seems to have been conducted in December, 1271.

57. *Sancti Thomae* . . . , pp. 79–80. Among the various readings they have found and reproduced there note: "non solum non est falsum sed etiam impossibile, aliter esset erroneum si aliter dicatur" (φ); "non solum non est falsum sed etiam possibile aliter enim esset erroneum si aliter dicatur" (N[1]); "non solum non est falsum sed etiam impossibile aliter esse et erroneum si aliter dicatur"; and a complete reversal in

As regards the present passage of the various manuscripts, only group Phi (identical in this case with Godfrey's text), and Naples, *Biblioteca Nazionale* VII. B. 16 (N[1]), have correctly understood it. And in N[1] the term *possibile* has been substituted for the *impossibile* found in Godfrey's notebook (P[23]).[58] This substitution also appears in the Perrier edition. And if they follow Godfrey's reading in their edition, they offer a rather unusual way of interpreting it.

Given this confusing textual situation, therefore, I have judged it advisable to present in turn the Perrier edition, the Marietti edition, Godfrey's text, and finally the interpretation of P[23] (Godfrey's text) proposed by the Leonine editors.

Perrier, n. 3

Si autem non est repugnantia intellectuum, non solum *non* est *falsum* sed etiam *possibile;* aliter esset *erroneum,* si aliter dicatur.

But if these two notions are not incompatible, then not only is it *not false* (to maintain this), but it is also *possible.* Otherwise it would be *erroneous* to say anything else.

Marietti, n. 297

Si autem non est repugnantia intellectuum, non solum *non* est *falsum,* sed etiam est *impossibile* aliter esse, et *erroneum,* si aliter dicatur.

But if these two notions are not incompatible, then not only is it *not false* (to maintain this), but it is also *impossible* for it to be otherwise. And it is *erroneous* to say anything else.

Godfrey, *Paris, Nat. Lat.* 16.297, fol. 68rb

Si autem non est repugnantia intellectuum, non solum *non* est *falsum* sed etiam *impossibile,* aliter esset *erroneum* si aliter dicatur.

But if these two notions are not incompatible, then not only is it *not false* (to maintain this), but also *impossible.* Otherwise it would be *erroneous* to say anything else.

According to Godfrey's manuscript there is a punctuation point between *impossibile* and *aliter*. Given this, in order to make sense out of the first sentence, it seems that one will have to interpret it as the Leonine editors propose by carrying forward the *non est* so as to apply it to the *impossibile* as well.[59]

---

the following one: "non solum est falsum sed etiam impossibile aliter esse . . . ." On group φ and the privileged place of P[23] (Godfrey's manuscript) therein see pp. 71, 73, 79.

58. *Ibid.,* pp. 79–80.

59. Here we are relying on a microfilm of Godfrey's manuscript, but the punctuation mark seems to be clear enough. And this is confirmed by the Leonine editors' transcription of the same (p. 73). For their way of interpreting the text see pp. 79–80.

Leonine, p. 86:68–71

si autem non est repugnantia intellec-tuum, non solum *non* est *falsum* sed etiam <*non est*> impossibile: aliter esset *erroneum,* si aliter dicatur.	But if these two notions are not incom-patible, then not only is it *not false* (to maintain this), but also <*it is not*> im-*possible:* otherwise, it would be *erroneous* to say anything else.

Some comments are called for with respect to these proposed readings and translations. First of all, in each of these versions I have referred the term "false" directly to the position or statement that "this could be brought about by God that something created by him has always existed." I have done so because of the two preceding sentences wherein Thomas clearly refers the expressions "not heretical" and "false" to this rather than imme-diately to possibility in the ontological order, and because it would seem strange for him to describe ontological possibility as not false.[60]

Secondly, in each of these versions one might wonder whether the term "possible" (Perrier) or "impossible" (other versions) should be referred directly to this same statement or directly to ontological possibility or im-possibility. This is more difficult to determine, although there might seem to be some predisposition in favor of directly referring this expression to the ontological order. The opening lines of the treatise indicate that Thomas is here concerned with the real or ontological possibility of an eternally created universe. This concern with the ontological order is confirmed by subse-quent remarks.[61] Still, the final sentence (according to our English transla-tion) obviously refers the term "erroneous" to the earlier statement or position by indicating that it would be "erroneous" to *say* or maintain anything else. It may be helpful, then, for us to attempt to resolve this by turning to each of the versions in turn, and at the same time to seek to determine what each of them has to tell us about the possibility of an eternally created universe.

As we have already seen above, the Perrier text implies that eternal cre-ation is possible if one grants the absence of contradiction between the notes of being created and having always existed. And this will follow whether one refers the term "possible" directly to the ontological order or directly to the controlling statement ("that this could be brought to pass by God that something created by him has always existed"). Even in the latter case it in-dicates that it is possible for one to defend this statement. Still, to state this is hardly more emphatic than to say that this statement is not false, as one would expect from the construction: "*not only* is it not false (to maintain this), *but also* possible." Hence I would prefer to refer the term "possible" as it appears here directly to the ontological order. Thomas's point would then

60. See the text cited above in n. 47. Cf. that quoted in n. 45.
61. See the texts cited above in nn. 41, 42, 43, 44, 46.

be this. Not only is it not false to state that something created by God could have always existed, but this (an eternally created effect) is also possible in itself.

The Marietti text is more perplexing. While the term "false" should, it would seem, again be referred to the controlling statement as cited above, the "impossible for it to be otherwise" can be directly referred to the ontological order only with some difficulty. Thomas surely does not want to state that the world must be eternal! Perhaps one could take the statement to mean that it is impossible for an eternally created effect not to be possible. But this seems to be a rather contrived reading. If one refers this to the statement ("that this could be brought to pass by God that something created by him has always existed"), the passage will mean: not only is this statement not false, but it is impossible for it to be anything but true. Hence it is correct to state that something created by God could have always existed, or that an eternally created world is a possibility. But in light of the Leonine editors' examination of the manuscript tradition, there seems to be little justification for accepting the Marietti reading at all.[62]

If Godfrey's manuscript does indeed accurately record Thomas's original text, then one can understand why subsequent scribes (as well as certain thirteenth-century thinkers) might have been puzzled as to his opinion in this treatise, and especially in this passage.[63] There would be little difficulty with the opening remark according to which, if there is no incompatibility between the two notes in question, it is not false to state that something created by God could have always existed. But how can Thomas go on to say in that eventuality either that this statement is "impossible" or that an eternally created effect is "impossible"? In brief, one has difficulty whether

62. See their comments on the reading in manuscript Sg⁴ (Stuttgart, Württembergische Landesbibliothek, H.B. I 2) and group Lambda (λ) which corresponds here (in a slightly different word order) with the Marietti text: "non solum non est falsum sed etiam impossibile aliter *esse et* erroneum si aliter dicatur" (as reproduced on p. 79). As the editors indicate, the crucial misreading is *esse et* (as italicized above) for *esset* (see pp. 79–80).

63. Thus the substitution of *possibile* for *impossibile* in N¹ (and in Perrier) seems to reflect an effort on the part of a scribe to clarify the passage by removing all ambiguity therefrom. See the Leonine ed., p. 79. For some remarks about some earlier printed editions of the *De aeternitate* see p. 80. For the Franciscan William of Falegar's refusal to attribute to Thomas the claim that at least some effect could be produced from eternity by God which would differ essentially from him see p. 56, n. 10, and A.-J. Gondras's edition of William's text in *Archives d'Histoire Doctrinale et Littéraire du Moyen Age* 39 (1972), p. 212. Reference has been made above to Godfrey's refusal to defend the possibility of eternal creation, and this notwithstanding his close dependence upon Thomas's *De aeternitate mundi* in his own discussion of this in his Quodlibet 2, q. 3 of 1286. See note 10 above.

one refers the term "impossible" to the controlling statement or directly to ontological possibility. If one were to join the *aliter* and the *impossibile*, then the text might be taken to mean either that it is impossible for one to state otherwise (which would hardly convey the greater emphasis demanded by the "but also") or that it is impossible for it to be otherwise. In either event the text would by implication or else directly state that an eternally created effect is possible. But this punctuation is precluded by that present in Godfrey's manuscript, as we have already indicated above. Given this, one seems to be forced to interpret the passage as the Leonine editors have proposed.

According to the Leonine interpretation, therefore, the term "false" will presumably refer to the key statement that an eternally existing effect can be produced by God. But in order properly to understand the term *impossibile* one must carry forward and repeat the *non est*. Not only is it not false to say this (that an eternally existing effect can be produced by God), but it is not impossible. Once more, one might attempt to refer the "not impossible" to the same controlling statement. Not only is this statement not false, but it is also not impossible. In other words, it is possible for one to state that something can be eternal and be created by God. However, then the *sed etiam* ("but also") in the passage would seem to lose its force. For to say that this statement is not impossible (or that it is possible) is hardly more emphatic (as the *sed etiam* would lead one to expect) than to state that it is not false. It would seem, therefore, that the "not impossible" should be directly referred to the ontological order. Not only is it not false to say that something can be eternal and be created by God, but it is *not impossible* for this to be the case. By the double negation, the statement explicitly defends the possibility of an eternally created effect and, consequently, of an eternally created world. If the "impossible" were referred back to the controlling statement, it would still defend this possibility, but less directly.

It is true that in the passage examined above and in the immediately preceding context, Thomas discusses the nonrepugnance of holding that "something" could be created by God and nonetheless have always existed. One might wonder, does his subsequent effort to show that such is not repugnant indicate that the world might possibly be eternal, or only that some creature, perhaps something purely spiritual, might be eternal? It will be recalled that Thomas has opened this treatise by asking whether or not the world could have always existed.[64] After eliminating either way in which

---

64. "Supposito, secundum fidem catholicam, mundum ab aeterno non fuisse, sed quod mundus durationis initium habuit, dubitatio mota est utrum potuerit semper fuisse" (Perrier, n. 1).

it might be thought that it is impossible in itself for an effect to be created and to have always existed, he has, it would seem, also eliminated any such reason for denying that an eternally existing and created world is possible. At the end of the treatise he returns to the frequently raised objection based on the infinity of human souls that would seem to result from a world that has always existed. He refers to this objection as "more difficult," but replies that it is not to the point. For God could have made a world without men and souls. Or he could have produced men when he did, even if he had created the world from eternity. (Thomas is evidently again discussing the possibility of an eternally created world.) And finally he remarks: "Moreover, it has not yet been demonstrated that God could not produce an infinity (of things) in act."[65]

If, then, Thomas has defended the possibility of an eternally created effect in this treatise, he has also defended the possibility of an eternally created world, whether or not that world was always populated by human beings. And if our interpretation of the various proposed readings of the key passage has been correct, this follows from each of the more authoritative versions, that is to say, from the Leonine edition and also from the Perrier edition. This is especially so if one interprets the expression *possibile* (in N^1 and Perrier) or *impossibile* (in the Leonine edition) as referring immediately to the ontological order. But it also follows even if one refers the expression in question back to the controlling statement that "this could be brought about by God that something created by him has always existed."

---

65. See n. 12. Note in particular: "Et praeterea non est adhuc demonstratum quod Deus non possit facere ut sint infinita in actu." Thomas's thinking on the possibility of an actual infinity of created entities, at least of spiritual entities, evidently shifted during his career. Although limitations of space will not permit fuller examination of this here, simply compare his flat rejection of any such possibility in ST I, q. 7, a. 4 or in the earlier Quodlibet 9, q. 1, a. 1 (1258) with the uncertainty expressed in the passage from the *De aeternitate*, or with SCG II, chs. 38 and 81. And for a crucial distinction between number and multitude as applied to an Aristotelian argument against the possibility of an actual infinite see *In III Phys.*, lect. 8, nn. 351–52, p. 175. Note in particular: "Attendendum est autem quod istae rationes sunt probabiles, et procedentes ex iis quae communiter dicuntur. Non enim ex necessitate concludunt: . . . Similiter qui diceret aliquam multitudinem esse infinitam, non diceret eam esse numerum, vel numerum habere. Addit enim numerus super multitudinem rationem mensurationis: est enim numerus multitudo mensurata per unum, ut dicitur in X Metaphys. Et propter hoc numerus ponitur species quantitatis discretae, non autem multitudo; sed est de trancendentibus." Also see *In XI Met.*, lect. 10, n. 2329, for this same reasoning. The Commentaries on the *Physics* and *Metaphysics* seem to date respectively from 1269–70 and 1269–72 (see Weisheipl, pp. 375–76 and 379).

As regards the major concern of this study, therefore, in my opinion Thomas Aquinas did not clearly defend the possibility of eternal creation or of an eternally created world prior to his *De aeternitate mundi*. From the beginning of his career he had insisted that no one had successfully demonstrated that the world began to be, and at times, even that this could not be demonstrated. In *De potentia,* q. 3, a. 14, he seems to come very close to asserting that an eternally created effect (and therefore an eternally created world) is possible, but he hesitates to take the final step. In the *De aeternitate mundi* he again applies the divisions of possibility which he had developed in the *De potentia.* Here he seems to be satisfied that since an eternally created effect is possible from the standpoint of God, on the one hand, and from the standpoint of the effect viewed in itself, on the other, such is possible without further qualification. Since these two notes — to be created and always to exist — are not mutually exclusive, he now concludes that it is possible for an effect (and for the world) to be produced from eternity by God.

If the above interpretation of Thomas's thinking concerning the possibility of an eternally created world is correct, two additional questions might be raised: (1) Why did Thomas hesitate to defend this stronger position — that an eternally created world is possible — prior to his *De aeternitate mundi?* (2) Why did he go farther in the *De aeternitate mundi* itself and maintain not only that one cannot demonstrate that the world began to be, but that an eternally created world is possible?

As regards the first question, we can only conjecture. But I strongly suspect that Thomas's primary concern in his earlier writings was to show that the noneternity of the world (as well as its eternity) had not been demonstrated and could not be demonstrated and, therefore, that one could be certain that the world began to be only because of religious belief. *De potentia,* q. 3, a. 14 indicates interest on Thomas's part in the question with which we have been concerned, the *possibility* of an eternally created effect. It may be that he was then not yet completely satisfied that his proposed division of the different kinds of possibility was sufficiently all-inclusive for him to be certain that no other obstacle to the possibility of eternal creation could be raised, once he had eliminated any that might follow from his application of that division.

As regards the second question, if I. Brady is correct, the *De aeternitate mundi* was occasioned by a particular attack on the part of John Peckham against Thomas's earlier denials that noneternity of the world could be demonstrated. It is evident in this treatise that Thomas's feelings have been aroused by some conservative theologian (or theologians), as his biting sarcasm in the following remark attests: "Therefore they who so subtly perceive (this contradiction) alone are men, and with them did wisdom come into being!"[66] Whether his immediate target is merely Peckham or others as well, it may be that the heat of controversy provoked Thomas to take a stronger stand. Not only has the noneternity of the world not been demonstrated. Not only can it not be demonstrated, as he had long maintained. An eternally created world is possible! At the same time, his procedure in this treatise indicates that he is now convinced of the success of his application of the division of the different ways in which something might be termed possible, and of his corresponding elimination of any way in which eternal creation might be thought to be impossible.[67]

66. "Ergo illi qui tam subtiliter eam percipiunt soli sunt homines et cum eis oritur sapientia" (Perrier, n. 9). For Brady see n. 40 above.

67. Though I have referred above to the "Leonine editors," special credit for the final version of Vol. 43 (and hence of the *De aeternitate mundi*) should be given to H. F. Dondaine (see p. 400). It seems that Perrier's materials, assembled while he himself had been a member of the Leonine Commission, were made available to Dondaine. This information has been communicated to me by William A. Wallace, who is currently serving as Director both of the American Section and of the International Leonine Commission.

CHAPTER IX

QUIDDITATIVE KNOWLEDGE OF GOD

In a well-known statement in his *Summa contra gentiles* Thomas Aquinas observes: "Concerning God, we cannot grasp what he is, but what he is not, and how other things are related to him."[1] This statement, reechoed as it is in many other passages in his writings, comes from a Thomas Aquinas who is equally well known, if not more so, for having developed a theory of analogical predication of divine names. This is the same Thomas who had also criticized others, especially Moses Maimonides, for having unduly restricted our knowledge of God.[2] Without intending here to discuss Thomas's theory of analogy of being (that would be subject-matter for another study), I would like to stress the following point.[3] Not only does Aquinas maintain that we can reason from knowledge of the existence of effects to knowledge of God as their cause; he also holds that we can predicate certain names of God in more than metaphorical fashion. Of course, one may reply, but only negatively, by removing from any such name all that implies limitation or imperfection or any creaturely mode of being. To say, for instance, that God is eternal is really to make the point that he is not temporal. To say that God is simple is to deny any kind of composition to him. To say that he is immutable is to deny all change of God. In short, in each of these cases the perfections signified by such names are negative, not positive, and cannot, therefore, tell us what God is in himself.[4]

---

1. "Non enim de Deo capere possumus quid est, sed quid non est, et qualiter alia se habeant ad ipsum, ut ex supra dictis patet." *Summa contra gentiles* I, ch. 30 (Rome, 1934), p. 32.

2. Reference will be made below to Thomas's critique of Maimonides in *De potentia*, q. 7, a. 5, and ST I, q. 13, a. 2.

3. For what is perhaps the finest single treatment of Thomas's doctrine of analogy see B. Montagnes, *La doctrine de l'analogie de l'être d'après saint Thomas d'Aquin* (Louvain-Paris, 1963).

4. For forceful statements of the negative side of our knowledge of God according to Thomas see A. D. Sertillanges, *Les grandes thèses de la philosophie thomiste* (Paris, 1928), pp. 67–80; E. Gilson, *The Christian Philosophy of St. Thomas Aquinas* (New York, 1956), pp. 108–10; A. Pegis, "Penitus Manet Ignotum," *Mediaeval Studies* 27 (1965), pp. 212–26.

Granted all of this, however, there are other names. When we say that God is good, we do not simply mean that he causes goodness in creatures. According to Aquinas, it is rather because God is good that he can produce goodness in creatures.[5] Here, then, one may ask, are we not dealing with a positive name and thereby saying something positive about God? And if so, are we not also thereby implying that we have some knowledge concerning what God is? Or to take the name frequently singled out by Aquinas as most appropriate for God, what do we mean when we describe God as "He who is" (*Qui est*)? Does not this name, which expresses a most sublime truth, as Thomas himself has phrased it, tell us something about the divine nature?[6] Does it not signify something more than what God is not and the mere fact that he is? Against any such conclusion, however, there still stands the Thomistic stricture: when it comes to our knowledge of God we can know that he is; we cannot know what he is.

My purpose in this chapter will be to examine somewhat more fully Thomas's reasons for defending this seemingly restrictive view concerning our knowledge of God, as well as what he understands by it. The first section of this study will concentrate on some representative texts taken from Thomas's earlier discussions of this issue, that is, from his *Expositio super librum Boethii De Trinitate* and his somewhat later *Summa contra gentiles*. The second part will be devoted to discussions taken from later works, especially from the Disputed Questions *De potentia Dei* and from the First Part of the *Summa theologiae*.

I

Thomas's reasons for defending this position are complex. At the risk of some oversimplification, one may suggest that they follow both from his theory of knowledge and from his great appreciation for the transcendence of God, for the sublime otherness of the divine reality. While both of these considerations enter into Thomas's various discussions of this issue, I shall begin by focusing on his theory of knowledge insofar as this controls his thinking about man's knowledge, especially man's philosophical knowledge, of God. Perhaps nowhere else has Thomas so carefully spelled out his thoughts on this point as in one of his early writings, his Commentary on the *De Trinitate* of Boethius (ca. 1258–1259).[7] There, in q. 1, a. 2, Thomas

---

5. See, for instance, *De potentia*, q. 7, a. 2; ST I, q. 13, a. 6.

6. "Hanc autem sublimem veritatem Moyses a Domino est edoctus . . . . osten-dens suum proprium nomen esse Qui Est." SCG I, ch. 22, p. 24. Cf. ST I, q. 13, a. 11. Also see Gilson, *The Christian Philosophy* . . . , pp. 92–95.

7. For this date and for those of other works by Aquinas cited here see Weisheipl, *Friar Thomas d'Aquino: His Life, Thought, and Work*. For this work see p. 381.

asks whether the human mind can arrive at knowledge of God.[8] In beginning his reply Thomas notes that a given thing may be known in one of two
different ways. On the one hand, it may be that it is known by its proper
form, as when the eye sees a stone by means of the form (*species*) of that
stone. On the other hand, something may be known by means of a form
which belongs to something else, but which bears some likeness to the thing
that is known. For instance, a cause may be known through its likeness insofar as this likeness is found in its effect; or a man may be known by means
of the form that is present in an image of that same man, such as a statue or
a picture. Even when something is known in the first way — by means of its
proper form — this can happen in one of two ways: either (1) by means of a
form which is identical with that thing itself (as God knows himself through
his essence); or (2) by means of a form which is in some way derived from
the object that is known (as when a form is abstracted from the thing that is
known; or when a form is impressed on the intellect of the knower by the
object known, as in knowledge by means of infused species).[9]

Thomas immediately examines each of these possibilities with respect to
his immediate concern — man's knowledge of God. According to Aquinas's
theory of knowledge, in this life the human intellect is necessarily directed
to forms which are abstracted from sense experience. Given this, in this life
we cannot know God by means of that form which is identical with the
divine essence. (Thomas does comment in passing that it is in this way that
God will be known by the *beati* in the life to come.)[10] Appeal to a form or
species which might be impressed by God on our intellect — some kind of
infused species — will not resolve our problem, continues Thomas. No such
likeness will enable us to know the divine essence because God infinitely
surpasses every created form. Moreover, God cannot be known by us in
this life by means of purely intelligible (and infused) forms, since our intellect is naturally ordered to forms derived from phantasms and hence from
sense experience.[11]

Having eliminated the possibility that in this life we might know God in
any of these ways, Thomas is forced to fall back on the one that remains —
God may be known by means of a form that is proper to something else but
which bears some likeness to him. As Thomas puts it, in this life God can be
known by us only by means of forms found in his effects. But, continues

8. *Expositio super librum Boethii De Trinitate*, Decker ed. (Leiden, 1959), p. 63.
"Utrum mens humana possit ad dei notitiam pervenire."

9. *Ibid.*, pp. 64:21–65:9.

10. *Ibid.*, p. 65:9–13. For more on this see H.-F. Dondaine, "Cognoscere de Deo
'quid est'," *Recherches de Théologie ancienne et médiévale* 22 (1955), pp. 72–78.

11. *Expositio super librum Boethii*, p. 65:14–20.

Thomas, effects are of two kinds. One kind is equal to the power of its cause. Knowledge of such an effect can lead fully to knowledge of the power of its cause and, therefore, to knowledge of that cause's quiddity. Here Thomas has in mind what in other contexts he describes as univocal causes.[12] There is another kind of effect which falls short of the power of its cause. Knowledge of this kind of effect will enable us to know that its cause exists. In other contexts Thomas describes such causes as equivocal.[13] It is in this second way that every creature stands with respect to God. Because of this, in the present life we are unable to arrive at any knowledge of God beyond our awareness that he is (*quia est*). Nonetheless, Thomas does allow for some gradation in our knowledge that God is. One knower may reach more perfect knowledge that God is than another; for a cause is known more perfectly from its effect insofar as through that effect the relationship between the two is more fully grasped.[14]

With this last point in mind, Thomas now introduces some further precisions into his analysis of the kind of knowledge "that God is" which is available to man in this life. Always bearing in mind that no creature can ever be equal to the power of its divine cause, Thomas singles out three elements which enter into our examination of the relationship which obtains between creatures, viewed as effects, and God, their cause. First of all, any such effect comes forth from God. Secondly, in some way any such effect is like its cause. Thirdly, any such effect falls short of its cause.[15]

Corresponding to these, Thomas distinguishes three ways in which the human intellect can advance in its knowledge that God is, even though, he hastens to add, it will not reach knowledge what God is. Such knowledge that God is will be more perfect, first of all, insofar as God's power in producing is more perfectly known through his effects; secondly, insofar as God is known as the cause of nobler effects, which bear a greater likeness to him; and thirdly, insofar as we come to realize more and more clearly how far removed God is from everything that is found in his effects. This corresponds to the threefold approach to knowledge of divine things which Thomas here, as on so many other occasions, traces back to Dionysius: the

---

12. *Ibid.*, p. 65:20–23. For more on Thomas's distinction between univocal and equivocal causes see Montagnes, *La doctrine de l'analogie*, pp. 47–49 and especially n. 62.

13. *Expositio super librum Boethii*, p. 65:23–26. For other passages in Thomas see the references cited by Montagnes, as indicated in the preceding note.

14. *Ibid.*, pp. 65:26–66:5. Note in particular: "Et tamen unus cognoscentium quia est alio perfectius cognoscit, quia causa tanto ex effectu perfectius cognoscitur, quanto per effectum magis apprehenditur habitudo causae ad effectum."

15. *Ibid.*, p. 66:6–10.

way of causality, the way of eminence, and the way of negation.[16] What must be stressed here, of course, is Thomas's unyielding warning that none of these ways will ever deliver *quid est* or quidditative knowledge of God to man in this life. In fact, in replying to the first objection, Thomas comments that in this life we reach the peak of our knowledge of God when we come to realize that we know him as unknown (*tamquam ignotum*), in other words, when we come to recognize that his essence surpasses anything we can apprehend in this life and, therefore, that what God is remains unknown to us.[17]

Interestingly, in concluding the corpus of his reply in this same article, Thomas notes that the human intellect can be aided in its effort to arrive at greater knowledge of God by a new illumination, given through the light of faith and the gifts of wisdom and understanding. Nonetheless, even when elevated by such supernatural gifts, the human intellect remains incapable of achieving knowledge of the divine essence.[18] In other words, neither faith nor the infused gifts of the Holy Spirit will give us knowledge of the divine essence or quiddity in this life. Hence we cannot overcome this difficulty

---

16. *Ibid.*, p. 66:10–16. For discussion of these texts also see S. Neumann, *Gegenstand und Methode der theoretischen Wissenschaften nach Thomas von Aquin aufgrund der Expositio super librum Boethii de Trinitate*, Beiträge zur Geschichte der Philosophie und Theologie des Mittelalters 41/2 (Münster, 1965), pp. 152–53; L. Elders, *Faith and Science: An Introduction to St. Thomas's Expositio in Boethii De Trinitate* (Rome, 1974), pp. 31–33; R. Imbach, *Deus est intelligere: Das Verhältnis von Sein und Denken in seiner Bedeutung für das Gottesverständnis bei Thomas von Aquin und in den Pariser Quaestionen Meister Eckharts*, Studia Friburgensia 53 (Freiburg, 1976), pp. 121–24. For Dionysius see *De divinis nominibus* 7.3 (PG 3.872).

17. *Expositio super librum Boethii*, p. 67:2–6: "Ad primum ergo dicendum quod secundum hoc dicimur in fine nostrae cognitionis deum tamquam ignotum cognoscere, quia tunc maxime mens in cognitione profecisse invenitur, quando cognoscit eius essentiam esse supra omne quod apprehendere potest in statu viae, et sic quamvis maneat ignotum quid est, scitur tamen quia est." Also see his reply to objection 2 (ll. 7–9). For another text dating from roughly the same period (1256–1259), see *De veritate*, q. 2, a. 1, ad 9: "Ad nonum dicendum, quod tunc intellectus dicitur scire de aliquo quid est, quando definit ipsum, id est quando concipit aliquam formam de ipsa re quae per omnia ipsi rei respondet. Iam autem ex dictis patet quod quidquid intellectus noster de Deo concipit, est deficiens a repraesentatione eius; et ideo quid est ipsius Dei semper nobis occultum remanet; et haec est summa cognitio quam de ipso in statu viae habere possumus [Leonine ed: possimus], ut cognoscamus Deum esse supra omne id quod cogitamus de eo; ut patet per Dionysium in I cap. *de Mystica Theologia*." See *S. Thomae Aquinatis Quaestiones disputatae*, Vol. 1, *De veritate*, R. Spiazzi, ed. (Turin-Rome, 1953), p. 26. For the same in the Leonine edition see *Sancti Thomae de Aquino opera omnia*, T. 22, vol. 1 (Rome, 1975), p. 42.

18. *Expositio super librum Boethii*, pp. 66:18–67:1.

simply by falling back on religious faith, or by taking refuge in a theology which presupposes faith.

In other discussions within this same Commentary on the *De Trinitate* Thomas continues to develop this thinking. For instance, in q. 6, a. 3 he asks whether our intellect can view the divine form itself.[19] In his reply he again distinguishes between knowing that something is and knowing what it is. For us to arrive at *quid est* knowledge of a thing we must have access to the essence or quiddity of that thing either immediately or else by means of other things which do manifest its quiddity. Once more Thomas appeals to his theory of knowledge in order to remind the reader that in this life the human intellect cannot immediately grasp the essence of God or, for that matter, of other separate substances. Man's intellect is immediately directed only to concepts that are drawn from phantasms and hence ultimately based on sense experience. At best, therefore, we can *immediately* grasp the quiddities of sensible things, but not of things that are purely intelligible.[20]

Thomas does concede that we can arrive at *mediate* quidditative knowledge of some intelligibles, that is, of those whose quiddity or nature is perfectly expressed by the quiddities of sensible things. Here he has in mind our capacity to know the quiddity of a genus or species by beginning with *quid est* knowledge of man and animal and then by noting the relationship between them. But sensible natures cannot express or reflect the divine essence or, for that matter, the essence of created separate substances, in sufficient fashion for us to attain to quidditative knowledge of either. Neither God nor created separate substances belong to the same genus as corporeal entities, at least when genus is taken in the natural or physical sense. Moreover, as Thomas explicitly states farther on in this discussion, God himself falls under no genus. Wherefore, concludes Thomas, names which are extended to separate substances apply to them and to sensible creatures almost equivocally. He cites with approval Dionysius's description of such names as "unlike likenesses."[21] And if the way of similitude is not sufficient of itself to make known to us the essences or quiddities of separate substances, neither is the way of causality. The effects produced by separate substances in our world are not equal to the power of their causes, and hence cannot enable us to reach quidditative knowledge of those causes.[22]

In developing a point to which he had already referred in q. 1, a. 2, Thomas reiterates his contention that in this life we cannot reach quidditative knowledge of separate substances even by means of revelation.

---

19. "Utrum intellectus noster possit ipsam formam divinam inspicere" (*ibid.*), p. 218.
20. *Ibid.*, p. 220:5–14.
21. *Ibid.*, pp. 220:16–221:3. For Dionysius see *Cael. hier.* 2.4 (PG 3.141).
22. *Ibid.*, p. 221:2–6.

Revelation itself is expressed in human language. Language presupposes concepts. Concepts are derived from sense experience. But, as we have already seen, according to Aquinas no path that begins from sense experience can deliver *quid est* knowledge of immaterial entities.[23]

Having stated this point so forcefully, Thomas must now come to terms with the Aristotelian view that we cannot know that something is unless in some way we also know what it is — either by perfect knowledge, or at least by some kind of confused knowledge.[24] For instance, if someone knows that man exists and wishes to determine what man is by defining him, he must already understand the meaning of the term "man." Presumably, in this case he will already have some prior knowledge of man in terms of his proximate or remote genus and by means of certain accidents. In other words, just as in demonstration so too in definition some kind of foreknowledge is presupposed.[25]

How, then, can one know that God and other separate entities exist unless one also knows what they are in some way? Direct knowledge of them by reason of any proximate or remote genus has been ruled out. Nor can one appeal to knowledge of them by reason of their accidents. God has no accidents. If created separate substances do have accidents, their accidents remain unknown to us.[26]

At this point Thomas seems to have reached an impasse. All is not lost, however, since it is here that he introduces knowledge by way of negation. Instead of knowing separate substances in terms of any genus, we may substitute negative knowledge. For instance, when we know that such entities are incorporeal, we are really negating configuration and other corporeal qualities of them. The more negations we know of them, the less confused is our resulting knowledge. Thus by successive negations prior negations are contracted and determined just as is a remote genus by its appropriate differences. Hence, as regards separate substances and especially as regards God, Thomas concludes that we can know that they are by reasoning from effect to cause. Instead of knowing what they are we must substitute knowledge of

<hr />

23. *Ibid.*, p. 221:7-20. Note in particular: "Et sic restat quod formae immateriales non sunt nobis notae cognitione quid est, sed solummodo cognitione an est, sive naturali ratione ex effectibus creaturarum sive etiam revelatione quae est per similitudines a sensibilibus sumptas."

24. *Ibid.*, p. 221:21-24. Here Thomas refers to the beginning of Aristotle's *Physics*, for which see *Phys.* I, ch. 1 (184a23–b12).

25. *Expositio super librum Boethii*, pp. 221:24–222:2.

26. *Ibid.*, p. 222:5-21. See l. 4: " . . . eo quod deus in nullo genere est, cum non habeat quod quid est aliud a suo esse . . . ."

them by negation, by causality, and by transcendence (*per excessum*).[27] Thomas reaffirms this same conclusion in q. 6, a. 4.[28]

It is interesting to turn from the Commentary on the *De Trinitate* to the somewhat later *Summa contra gentiles* (1259–1264). We began this chapter by citing a text from Bk. I, ch. 30 of that work to this effect: we cannot understand what God is, but only what he is not, and how other things are related to him.[29] Already in ch. 14 of Bk. I Thomas had set the stage for this dictum. There, after his lengthy presentation of argumentation for God's existence in ch. 13, Thomas comments that when it comes to our knowledge of God's properties, we must make special use of the way of negation (*via remotionis*). Perfectly consistent with the reasoning we have seen in his Commentary on the *De Trinitate*, he again writes that the divine substance completely surpasses any form our intellect can reach. Hence we are unable to grasp the divine substance by knowing what it is. Still, he adds, we can have some knowledge of it by knowing what it is not. Insofar as we negate more and more things of God, we come closer to knowledge of him. One negative difference will be contracted by another, and that by still others, thereby leading us to more precise knowledge of God. By continuing this procedure in ordered fashion, we will be able to distinguish God from all that he is not. Still, even though we may thereby reach a proper consideration (*propria consideratio*) of God's substance by knowing that he is distinct from everything else, our knowledge will not be perfect. We will still not know what God is in himself.[30]

---

27. *Ibid.*, pp. 222:22–223:17. For an even earlier statement on our knowledge of God by way of negation see *In I Sent.*, d. 8, q. 1, a. 1, ad 4 (Mandonnet ed., Vol. 1, pp. 196–97). For helpful commentary see J. Owens, "Aquinas—'Darkness of Ignorance' in the Most Refined Notion of God," in *Bonaventure and Aquinas: Enduring Philosophers*, ed. R. W. Shahan and F. J. Kovach (Norman, Oklahoma, 1976), pp. 69–86.

28. Article 4 is directed to this question: "Utrum hoc possit fieri per viam alicuius scientiae speculativae" (*ibid.*, p. 223), that is, whether we can behold the divine form through any speculative science. From his reply note in particular: "Et ideo per nullam scientiam speculativam potest sciri de aliqua substantia separata quid est, quamvis per scientias speculativas possimus scire ipsas esse et aliquas earum condiciones, utpote quod sunt intellectuales, incorruptibiles et huiusmodi" (p. 227:25–28). Also see his reply to objection 2: " . . . quamvis quiditas causae sit semper ignota, et ita accidit in substantiis separatis" (p. 228:18–19).

29. See above, n. 1.

30. *Summa contra gentiles* I, ch. 14, p. 15. Note in particular: " . . . et sic ipsam apprehendere non possumus cognoscendo quid est. Sed aliqualem eius habemus notitiam cognoscendo quid non est . . . . et sic per ordinem ab omni eo quod est praeter ipsum, per negationes huiusmodi distinguetur; et tunc de substantia eius erit propria consideratio cum cognoscetur ut ab omnibus distinctus. Non tamen erit perfecta: quia non cognoscetur quid in se sit."

In the succeeding chapters of Bk. I Thomas proceeds to do just this.[31] He applies the *via negationis* in ordered fashion in order to show, for instance, that God is eternal (ch. 15); that there is no passive potency in him (ch. 16); that there is no matter in him (ch. 17); that there is no composition in God (ch. 18); that he is not subject to violence (ch. 19); that he is not a body (ch. 20); that he is his essence (ch. 21); that in him *esse* and essence are identical, i.e., not distinct (ch. 22); that he is without accidents (ch. 23); that no substantial difference can be added to God (ch. 24); that he is not in any genus (ch. 25); that he himself is not the formal *esse* of other things (ch. 26);[32] and that he is not the form of any body (ch. 27). Even in ch. 28, in attempting to establish the divine perfection, Thomas continues to use the way of negation — by showing that any absence or limitation of perfection is to be denied of God.[33]

In ch. 29 Thomas offers some precisions concerning the likeness that does and does not obtain between God and creatures. Granted that no created effect can be equal to its divine cause either in name or in definition, still there must be some likeness between them. This follows because it is of the very nature of action for an agent to produce something that is like itself. And this in turn follows from the fact that something can act or function as an agent only insofar as it is in act. Since God is an equivocal cause and therefore surpasses in perfection any and all of his effects, any form present in an effect will be realized in God only in higher and more eminent fashion. In other words, there will be likeness and unlikeness between God and creatures at one and the same time — likeness because as a cause he produces things that are in some way like himself; unlikeness because whatever is found in God can be present in other things only in deficient fashion and by participation.[34] (If only in passing, it should be noted that defense of

---

31. Note that he uses as a point of departure and as a working principle in this procedure the conclusion from his argumentation for God's existence in ch. 13 — that God is completely free from being moved in any way ("Ad procedendum igitur circa Dei cognitionem per viam remotionis, accipiamus principium id quod ex superioribus iam manifestum est, scilicet quod Deus sit omnino immobilis"). *Ibid.*, ch. 14, p. 15.

32. Thomas also uses this discussion to make the point explicitly that God is not in any way to be identified with *esse commune* (*ibid.*, p. 27).

33. One of Thomas's arguments rests upon the identity of essence and *esse* in God. Because that being which is its own *esse* must possess *esse* according to the total capacity (*virtus*) of being itself, it can lack nothing of the perfection which may pertain to being. As we have mentioned in passing, in ch. 22 Thomas establishes identity of essence and *esse* in God by following the negative way, that is, by showing that in God essence and *esse* are not distinct. For the argument in ch. 28 see pp. 29–30.

34. *Ibid.*, p. 31. Note in particular: "Ita etiam et Deus omnes perfectiones rebus tribuit, ac per hoc cum omnibus similitudinem habet et dissimilitudinem simul . . . ."

some kind of likeness between creatures and God will be absolutely crucial for Thomas's rejection of purely equivocal predication of names of God in ch. 33, and for his defense of analogical predication of divine names in ch. 34.)

In ch. 30 Thomas distinguishes between two kinds of names that one might wish to apply to God. Some names signify perfection without including any limitation or imperfection in their formal meaning. Names such as these, here illustrated by goodness, wisdom, and *esse* and often referred to as pure perfections in the scholastic tradition — can be said of God in some nonmetaphorical way. This is not true of another kind of name which necessarily implies some creaturely and imperfect mode of being in its very definition. No such name can be applied to God except metaphorically.[35]

At this point one might wonder whether Thomas is not now preparing to go beyond the way of negation and to allow for some kind of affirmative naming of God, perhaps even for some kind of quidditative knowledge of the divine. Almost as if in anticipation of our query, Thomas immediately introduces a crucial distinction. Granted that certain names such as those he has just mentioned do not include any imperfection in that which they signify (*quantum ad illud ad quod significandum nomen fuit impositum*), they do involve some deficiency in the way in which they signify, in their *modus significandi*. This follows because we express perfections by names in accord with the ways in which we conceive these perfections. Since our intellect derives its knowledge from sense experience, in conceiving such perfections it does not surpass the mode in which it finds them realized in sensible things. Because of the matter-form composition of sensible things, in conceiving them we distinguish between a form and that which has the form. Hence, when we signify any perfection concretely, we also signify it as involving distinction between itself and the subject in which it is realized. If we signify the perfection in abstract fashion, we cannot then signify it as something which subsists but only as that by means of which something else subsists. According to either mode of signification imperfection is implied.[36]

Quia igitur id quod in Deo perfecte est, in rebus aliis per quandam deficientem participationem invenitur . . . ."

35. Thomas adds that names which express (pure) perfections together with the mode of supereminence whereby they pertain to God can be said of God alone. What he has in mind are complex names such as "supreme good," "first being," etc. (" . . . sicut summum bonum, primum ens, et alia huiusmodi"), p. 31.

36. See in particular: "Dico autem aliqua praedictorum nominum perfectionem absque defectu importare, quantum ad illud ad quod significandum nomen fuit impositum: quantum enim ad modum significandi, omne nomen cum defectu est . . . . Forma vero in his rebus invenitur quidem simplex, sed imperfecta, utpote non subsistens: habens autem formam invenitur quidem subsistens, sed non simplex, immo

For instance, we might apply the name "good" to God in concrete fashion by saying that God is good. In this case the way in which "good" signifies — concretely — implies some kind of composition and distinction between the perfection, on the one hand, and the subsisting subject on the other. Or we might apply this same name to God in abstract fashion, by describing God as goodness. The abstract way of signifying will imply that divine goodness is not itself subsistent. In either event, even when we are dealing with pure perfections, some kind of deficiency is implied by the *modus significandi* of any such name. Thomas now cites Dionysius to this effect, that such names (those signifying pure perfections) are both affirmed and denied of God — affirmed because of the meaning of the name; denied because of their *modus significandi*, the way in which they signify. Shortly thereafter, Thomas makes the remark with which our chapter began: "Concerning God we cannot grasp what he is, but what he is not, and how other things are related to him."[37]

Two important points should be kept in mind from Thomas's discussion in ch. 30. First of all, his application of the distinction between the *res significata* and the *modus significandi* appears to be all-embracing. No matter what name we may apply to God, its creaturely *modus significandi* must be denied of him. Secondly, in the final part of this chapter Thomas seems to distinguish between names which are negative in their formal meaning (*res significata*), such as eternal or infinite, and others which are not, such as

---

concretionem habens. Unde intellectus noster, quidquid significat ut subsistens, significat in concretione: quod vero ut simplex, significat non ut *quod est*, sed ut *quo est*. Et sic in omni nomine a nobis dicto, quantum ad modum significandi, imperfectio invenitur, quae Deo non competit, quamvis res significata aliquo eminenti modo Deo conveniat . . ." (*ibid.*, pp. 31–32). For earlier appeal to this distinction when discussing the divine names see Thomas, *In I Sent.*, d. 22, q. 1, a. 2 (Mandonnet ed., Vol. 1, p. 535). Note in particular: " . . . omnia illa nomina quae imponuntur ad significandum perfectionem aliquam absolute, proprie dicuntur de Deo, et per prius sunt in ipso quantum ad rem significatam, licet non quantum ad modum significandi, ut sapientia, bonitas, essentia, et omnia hujusmodi . . . " For further discussion of this distinction see H. Lyttkens, *The Analogy between God and the World* (Uppsala, 1952), pp. 375–82; "Die Bedeutung der Gottesprädikate bei Thomas von Aquin," in *Philosophical Essays Dedicated to Gunnar Aspelin on the Occasion of his Sixty-fifth Birthday*, ed. H. Bratt et. al. (Lund, 1963), pp. 80–84. For more on Thomas's usage of this distinction in his Commentary on the *Sentences* see B. Mondin, *St. Thomas Aquinas' Philosophy in the Commentary to the Sentences* (The Hague, 1975), pp. 92–93, 100–101 (note the additional references given in n. 29). Also see L. Clavell, *El nombre propio de Dios segun santo Tomás de Aquino* (Pamplona, 1980), pp. 143–46.

37. SCG I, ch. 30, p. 32. For the reference to Dionysius the editors cite *Cael. hier.*, ch. 2, §3, and also refer to *De div. nom.*, ch. 1, 5.

goodness, wisdom, etc.[38] But even when names of the second type are applied to God, one must deny of them the creaturely *modus significandi*. In other words, the *via negativa* seems to apply in three different ways. First of all, the perfections assigned to God until the discussion in ch. 30 all seem to have been discovered by the process of successive negations. Secondly, they also seem to include the negation of something in their formal meaning, as, for instance, infinity is the negation of finiteness. Thirdly, while names such as goodness and wisdom do not include anything negative in their formal meaning, even they carry with them a creaturely *modus significandi* when they are applied to God. This too must in turn be denied of him.

In ch. 37 Thomas explicitly attempts to show that God is good. If one would expect him to admit of some kind of knowledge of God that is positive rather than negative, and perhaps even quidditative, it would be here. In arguing for God's goodness Thomas recalls that he has already shown that God is perfect. God's goodness follows from this. In establishing God's perfection in ch. 28 Thomas had in fact used the *via negativa* (taken in the first of the three senses I have just distinguished, as the process of successive negations). He continues to do so here, at least by implication. For instance, he recalls that in ch. 13 he had shown that God is the first unmoved mover. But God moves insofar as he is an object of desire, as the *primum desideratum*. This implies that he is truly good. Thomas assumes that we will recall that he has shown that God is the first unmoved mover by proving that he is not a moved mover. Another argument reasons that because God is pure actuality, and because all things desire to be in actuality according to their proper mode — which is for them to be good — God himself is good. But, one may ask, why does Thomas describe God as pure actuality? His answer is that he has already shown (see ch. 16) that God is not in potency.[39]

---

38. "Modus autem supereminentiae quo in Deo dictae perfectiones inveniuntur, per nomina a nobis imposita significari non potest nisi vel per negationem, sicut cum dicimus Deum aeternum vel infinitum; vel etiam per relationem ipsius ad alia, ut cum dicitur prima causa, vel summum bonum" (SCG I, ch. 30, p. 32).

39. Even the final argument in this chapter, based upon the axiom that the good tends to diffuse itself, presupposes the way of negation. Thomas interprets this Neoplatonic axiom in the sense of final rather than efficient causality. He notes that the good of any given thing is its act and its perfection. But everything acts insofar as it is in act. By acting it passes on being and goodness to other things. Hence a sign of a thing's perfection is that it can produce its like. But the essence of the good consists in the fact that it is desirable. This is to identify the good with the end, the final cause. It is this that moves an agent to act, and justifies the Neoplatonic axiom just mentioned — *bonum est diffusivum sui et esse*. But such diffusion of goodness and being pertains to God. For it has been shown above (see ch. 13) that God is the cause of

In succeeding chapters Thomas shows that God is goodness itself, that there is no evil in God, and that God is the good for every other good.[40] Since many of the particular arguments introduced in these chapters also follow the negative way, since all of them presuppose that God is good, and since Thomas has used the way of negation to show that God is good, one may conclude that even in establishing God's goodness Thomas has continued to use the process of successive negations. This is not to say, of course, that the name "goodness" itself is negative in its formal meaning (negative in the second sense distinguished above).[41]

For confirmation one may turn to Thomas's own assessment of his procedure in SCG I, chs. 14–42 as he refers back to this in Bk. III of the same work. In Bk. III, ch. 39 he is attempting to show that no demonstrative knowledge of God can ever suffice to give perfect happiness to man. Thomas comments that by the path of demonstration one does come closer to a proper knowledge of God. By this procedure one removes from God many things and thereby understands more clearly how different he is from all else. Thomas recalls that he had used this approach in Bk. I in demonstrating that God is immobile, eternal, perfectly simple, one, and other things of this kind. In reviewing the path he had followed there, Thomas remarks that one can arrive at proper knowledge of something not only by affirmations but by negations. Thomas stresses this important difference between these two kinds of proper knowledge. Proper knowledge gained by succeeding affirmations may yield *quid est* knowledge of a thing as well as knowledge concerning its difference from all else. If one reaches proper knowledge of a thing by succeeding negations, granted that one will know how that thing differs from others, the quiddity of that same thing will

---

being for all other things. Therefore he is truly good. Presupposed, therefore, for application of goodness to God is one's previous demonstration that he is the first cause, that is, that he is not a caused cause.

40. See chs. 38 ("Quod Deus est ipsa bonitas"), 39 ("Quod in Deo non potest esse malum"), 40 ("Quod Deus est omnis boni bonum"). As regards ch. 38, Thomas argues, for instance, that actual *esse* for a given thing is its good. But God is not only being in act, but *ipsum suum esse*. Therefore he is not only good but goodness itself. In ch. 22 Thomas had used the way of negation to show that God is *ipsum suum esse*, by showing that there is no distinction in him between essence and *esse*. In two other arguments in ch. 38 Thomas shows that God is not good by participation. Therefore he is goodness itself.

41. For Thomas's procedure in arriving at knowledge that God is good see the remarks in the preceding note. As I interpret him, however, even though he continues to use the way of succeeding negations to establish the conclusion that God is good or goodness, he acknowledges that the name "goodness" is not negative but positive in content.

remain unknown to him. Only this second kind of proper knowledge of God is available to man in this life.[42]

In ch. 49 Thomas argues that neither created separate substances nor men can arrive at *quid est* knowledge of God by reasoning from effect to cause. By following this path at best we can know that God is, that he is the cause of all else, and that he supereminently surpasses all else. At this highest point in our knowledge of God, we are conjoined to a God who remains, as it were, unknown. This happens when we know of God what he is not. What he is remains completely unknown to us (*penitus ignotum*).[43]

II

In order to determine whether Thomas ever softened his views concerning this final point, we shall now turn to two somewhat later sets of texts: (1) a series of articles in q. 7 of the *De potentia* (disputed at Rome, 1265-1266); and (2) the slightly later discussion of the divine names in the First Part of the *Summa theologiae* (ca. 1266-1268).[44]

To begin with the *De potentia*, in q. 7 Thomas examines in considerable detail the issue of divine simplicity.[45] In a. 1 he follows the path of negation to establish the fact that God is simple.[46] In a. 2 Thomas denies to God any kind of distinction between substance (or essence) and existence (*esse*). While this is evidently phrased in negative fashion, one might wonder

---

42. SCG III, ch. 39, p. 263. Note in particular: " . . . per negationes autem habita propria cognitione de re, scitur quod est ab aliis discreta, tamen quid sit remanet ignotum. Talis autem est propria cognitio quae de Deo habetur per demonstrationes." Compare this with Thomas's remark in SCG I, ch. 14 about the *propria consideratio* concerning God's substance which is available to us by following the path of successive negations.

43. SCG III, ch. 49, pp. 279-81. Note in particular: "Et hoc est ultimum et perfectissimum nostrae cognitionis in hac vita, ut Dionysius dicit, in Libro *De Mystica Theologia* [capp. I, II], *cum Deo quasi ignoto coniungimur*: quod quidem contingit dum de eo *quid non sit* cognoscimus, quid vero sit penitus manet ignotum. Unde et ad huius sublimissimae cognitionis ignorantiam demonstrandam, de Moyse dicitur, *Exodi xx*, quod *accessit ad caliginem in qua est Deus*" (p. 280). For Dionysius see especially 1.3 (PG 3.1000). For more on this see Pegis, "Penitus Manet Ignotum," pp. 217-18. Opinions vary concerning the precise dating of Bk. III of the *Summa contra gentiles*. For discussion see Weisheipl, *Friar Thomas d'Aquino*, pp. 359-60. But whether one places this as early as 1259 or as late as 1264 (the latest likely date for Bk. IV), it clearly antedates both q. 7 of the *De potentia* and the First Part of the *Summa theologiae*, which are to be examined below.

44. For these datings see Weisheipl, pp. 363, 361.

45. See *S. Thomae Aquinatis Quaestiones disputatae*, Vol. 2, *De potentia*, ed. P. Pession (Turin-Rome, 1953), pp. 188-90.

46. *Ibid.*, pp. 188-89.

whether Thomas has not in some way here gone beyond the way of negation. Such a suspicion is envisioned by the first objection. According to
John Damascene: "That God is is manifest to us, but what he is in his substance is completely incomprehensible and unknown [to us]." But what is
known to us cannot be unknown at the same time. Therefore, God's *esse* is
not identical with his substance or essence.[47]

In replying Thomas distinguishes two ways in which *ens* or *esse* may be
understood. They may signify the essence of a thing or its act of existing, on
the one hand; but on other occasions they simply signify the truth of a
proposition. Given this distinction, continues Thomas, when Damascene
says that God's *esse* is manifest to us he is taking *esse* only in the second
way — as signifying the truth of the proposition "God is." But it is only when
esse is taken according to the first usage that we can say God's *esse* is identical
with his essence or substance. When *esse* is taken in this first way, God's *esse*
remains unknown to us, just as does his essence.[48]

In a. 4 Thomas uses the way of negation to show that divine names such
as "good" or "wise" or "just" do not predicate anything accidental of God. At
the same time, at least some such names do not appear to be negative in the
second of the three ways we have distinguished above — in their definition.
Hence, introduction of names such as "good" and "wise" naturally gives rise
to the important discussion in a. 5.[49] There Thomas asks whether such
names signify the divine substance. First of all, he presents what he regards
as extreme versions of the negative view. Some, most particularly Moses

47. For objection 1 see p. 190: "Dicit enim Damascenus, in I lib. *Orth. Fidei* [cap.
I et III]: *Quoniam quidem Deus est, manifestum est nobis; quid vero sit secundum substantiam
et naturam, incomprehensibile est omnino et ignotum.* Non autem potest esse idem notum et
ignotum. Ergo non est idem esse Dei et substantia vel essentia eius." For the text
from John Damascene see *Saint John Damascene, De fide orthodoxa* (Burgundio translation), ed. E. M. Buytaert (St. Bonaventure, N.Y., 1955), Bk. I, ch. 4, p. 19:3-5.

48. *De potentia*, q. 7, a. 2, ad 1 (pp. 191-92): "Ad primum ergo dicendum, quod
ens et esse dicitur dupliciter, ut patet V *Metaph*. . . . . Quandoque enim significat
essentiam rei, sive actum essendi; quandoque vero significat veritatem propositionis, etiam in his quae esse non habent: sicut dicimus quod caecitas est, quia
verum est hominem esse caecum. Cum ergo dicat Damascenus, quod esse Dei est
nobis manifestum, accipitur esse Dei secundo modo, et non primo. Primo enim
modo est idem esse Dei quod est substantia: et sicut eius substantia est ignota, ita et
esse. Secundo autem modo scimus quoniam Deus est, quoniam hanc propositionem
in intellectu nostro concipimus ex effectibus ipsius." Cf. ST I, q. 3, a. 4, ad 2. For
Gilson's usage of these passages to support his interpretation of Thomas's views concerning quidditative knowledge of God see *Elements of Christian Philosophy* (Garden
City, New York, 1960), pp. 143-45.

49. "Quinto quaeritur utrum praedicta nomina significent divinam substantiam"
(*De potentia*, q. 7, a. 5, p. 196).

Maimonides, hold that such names do not signify the divine substance. As applied to God, they may be understood in two different ways. On the one hand, they may be taken to point to some similarity between God's effects and the effects of other things which are known to us. For instance, to say that God is wise is not to imply that wisdom is really anything in God, but rather that he acts after the manner of one who is wise in ordering his effects to their proper ends. To say that he is living is only to indicate that he acts in the fashion of one who is living, that is, that he acts of himself. On the other hand, such names may be applied to God negatively. In this sense, to say that God is living is not to imply that life is anything really present in God. It is rather to negate of him any inanimate mode of being. To say that God is intelligent is not to signify that intellect is present in the divine being, but rather to deny of God the mode of being enjoyed by brutes.[50]

Thomas criticizes each of these ways of applying divine names as insufficient and even as unfitting (inconveniens). Against the first he objects that there would then be no difference between saying that God is wise and that God is angry or that he is fire. God would be called angry simply because he acts like someone who is angry when he punishes. He would be called fire because in purging he acts as does fire. So too, according to the theory, he would be named wise only because he acts in the manner of one who is wise in ordering his effects. This, counters Thomas, stands in opposition to the practice of saints and prophets. They permit us to apply some names to God, but not others. According to the present position, all such names could with equal justification be affirmed or denied of God. As a second argument against Maimonides, Thomas recalls that Christians hold that creation has not always existed—a point, he adds, that is conceded by Maimonides. Before creation God did not in fact operate in any of his effects. According to this way of understanding divine names it would therefore follow that before creation God could not have been described as good or as wise, something Thomas rejects as contrary to faith. He does soften this criticism by allowing that Maimonides might counter that before creation God could have been called wise, not because he then acted as one who is wise, but because he could so act. But, counters Thomas, this would be to concede that the term "wise" does signify something which is really present

50. *Ibid.*, p. 198. For this in Maimonides see *The Guide of the Perplexed*, tr. S. Pines (Chicago, 1963), I, chs. 52–59 (pp. 114–43). Note in particular ch. 58 (pp. 134–37). For the medieval Latin version see *Liber Rabi Moysi Aegyptii Qui dicitur Dux Neutrorum seu dubiorum* (Paris, 1520; repr. Frankfurt am Main, 1964), I, chs. 51–58 (ff. 18v–23v). For the all-important ch. 57 (according to the numbering in the Latin version) see ff. 22r–22v. For an earlier reference to Maimonides (and to Avicenna) see Thomas, *In I Sent.*, d. 2, q. 1, a. 3 (Mandonnet ed., Vol. 1, pp. 67–68).

in God, and hence that this name does signify the divine substance; for whatever is in God is identical with his substance.[51]

Thomas next turns to the second way in which such names might be understood, that is, as pure negations. Against this he comments that there is no name of any species by which something could not be denied of God as unfitting for him. The name of any species includes a difference by which other species are excluded. For instance, the name "lion" includes this difference — that it is fourfooted. By means of this lion differs from bird, since it excludes a bird's mode of being. If names were applied to God only in order to deny things of him, not only might we say that God is living in order to deny of him the mode of inanimate things; we might also say that he is a lion in order to deny of him a bird's mode of being. Thomas's point again seems to be that according to this approach, any name could be applied to God. Thomas follows this up with an interesting reflection. Our understanding of any negation is based on some prior affirmation, just as any negative proposition is proved by means of one that is affirmative. Therefore, unless the human intellect could affirm something of God, it would be unable to deny anything of him. But it will know nothing of God in affirmative fashion unless something that it knows is positively realized in him.[52]

Thomas now cites Dionysius for support in developing his own position. Names of this kind, he counters, do signify the divine substance, but in deficient and imperfect fashion. Immediately the reader wonders, is this not to say something more about God than what he is not? Thomas justifies his claim that such names do in some albeit imperfect way signify the divine substance by recalling that every agent acts insofar as it is in act and, therefore, produces something that is like itself. Hence the form found in an effect must in some way also be present in its cause although, as we have seen, this may happen in different ways. When an effect is equal to the power of its agent, the form of that effect will be of the same kind as that of its cause (*secundum eamdem rationem*). When the effect is not equal to the power of its cause, the form of the effect will be present in the cause in more eminent fashion; for the agent must have the power to produce that effect. Such is true of equivocal agents, as when the sun generates fire. Since no

51. *De potentia*, q. 7, a. 5, p. 198. Note in particular the concluding part of Thomas's second counterargument: "Et sic sequeretur quod aliquid existens in Deo per hoc significetur, et sit per consequens substantia, cum quidquid est in Deo sit sua substantia."

52. *Ibid*. Note in particular: " . . . unde nisi intellectus humanus aliquid de Deo affirmative cognosceret, nihil de Deo posset negare. Non autem cognosceret, si nihil quod de Deo dicit, de eo verificaretur affirmative."

effect is equal to the power of God, the form of no effect will be present in God in the same way it is present in that effect, but in more eminent fashion. Hence forms which are realized in divided and distinct fashion in different effects are united in God as in one single though common power.[53]

In developing this point Thomas notes that the various perfections realized in creatures are likened to God by reason of his unique and simple essence. Since the human intellect derives its knowledge from created things, it is informed by the likenesses of perfections it discovers in creatures, such as wisdom, power, goodness, etc. If creatures are in some though deficient way like God because of the presence of such perfections in them, our intellect can be informed by intelligible species of these same perfections. When the human intellect is assimilated to a given thing through an appropriate intelligible form or species, that which it conceives and formulates by means of such a species must be verified in that thing itself. This follows from Thomas's conviction that knowledge involves an assimilation of the intellect to that which is known. If this is so, those things which the intellect thinks or says about God insofar as it is informed by such intelligible species must in fact be truly present in him.[54]

Thomas immediately cautions, however, that such intelligible species which are present in the human intellect cannot be adequate likenesses of the divine essence. Otherwise, our intellects would comprehend the divine essence and our conception of God would perfectly capture his essence (*esset perfecta Dei ratio*).[55] Given all of this, Thomas concludes that while names of this kind do signify "that which is the divine substance," they do not perfectly signify it (the divine substance) as it is in itself but only as it is known by us.[56]

---

53. *Ibid.* Note Thomas's opening remark in this discussion: "Et ideo, secundum sententiam Dionysii (capit. XII *de divinis Nominibus*), dicendum est, quod huiusmodi nomina significant divinam substantiam, quamvis deficienter et imperfecte." This seems to be an interpretation rather than an exact quotation on Thomas's part. I have been unable to find any precise statement in ch. 12 of *The Divine Names* indicating that such names signify the divine substance. J. Durantel rather sees in Thomas's text a general reference to ch. 13, §3. See his *Saint Thomas et le Pseudo-Denis* (Paris, 1919), p. 197.

54. *De potentia*, q. 7, a. 5, pp. 198–99.

55. "Si autem huiusmodi intelligibilis species nostri intellectus divinam essentiam adaequaret in assimilando, ipsam comprehenderet, et ipsa conceptio intellectus esset perfecta Dei ratio, sicut animal gressibile bipes est perfecta ratio hominis" (*ibid.*).

56. " . . . et ideo licet huiusmodi nomina, quae intellectus ex talibus conceptionibus Deo attribuit, significent id quod est divina substantia, non tamen perfecte ipsam significant secundum quod est, sed secundum quod a nobis intelligitur" (*ibid.*). Note how differently this crucial passage is interpreted by Maritain and by Gilson. For Maritain see his *Distinguish to Unite or The Degrees of Knowledge*, tr. G. B. Phelan (New York, 1959), p. 425: "Names signifying, although only ananoetically, *'id quod*

Presumably by "names of this kind" Thomas still has in mind those which signify pure perfections — names such as "good," "wise," "just," etc. In concluding the corpus of this article, he comments that while such names do signify the divine substance, they do so only in imperfect fashion, and not so as to comprehend it. Because of this the name "He who is" (*Qui est*) is most fittingly applied to God; for it does not determine any form for God, but signifies *esse* without determination.[57]

Additional clarifications appear in some of Thomas's replies to objections in this same article 5. Objection 1 counters that according to Damascene names such as those here under discussion do not tell us what God is in his substance. Hence they are not predicated substantially of God.[58] In replying Thomas comments that Damascene's point is to show that such names do not signify what God is, if this be taken to mean that they define and comprehend his essence. This is why Damascene has added that the name *Qui est* is most properly attributed to God, since it signifies God's substance without determining it (*indefinite*).[59] Here, then, we seem to find Thomas distinguishing between some kind of imperfect knowledge of God's substance, on the one hand, and comprehensive and defining knowledge, on the other. Apparently it is only the latter that is denied when Thomas

---

est divina substantia' do indeed tell us in some manner what God is," although only in a "more-or-less imperfect, but always true fashion." Here Maritain is rejecting Sertillanges' general interpretation of this issue. For Gilson see his *The Christian Philosophy of St. Thomas Aquinas*, p. 109 and especially p. 458, n. 47. There, in criticizing Maritain's reading, Gilson comments: "In using this text . . . we must keep in mind the exact thesis which St. Thomas is developing, namely, that the divine names signify the substance of God, that is, they designate it as actually being what the names signify. It does not follow from this that these designations give us a positive conception of what the divine substance is."

57. *De potentia*, q. 7, a. 5, p. 199. "Sic ergo dicendum est, quod quodlibet istorum nominum significat divinam substantiam, non tamen quasi comprehendens ipsam, sed imperfecte: et propter hoc, nomen *Qui est*, maxime Deo competit, quia non determinat aliquam formam Deo, sed significat esse indeterminate." In support of the last point in his text Thomas cites John Damascene, *De fide orthodoxa* I, ch. 9, pp. 48–49:13–17. He finds his general solution confirmed by Dionysius's remark in ch. 1 of the *Divine Names:* "quia Divinitas omnia simpliciter et incircumfinite in seipsa existentia praeaccipit, ex diversis convenienter laudatur et nominatur." For this see ch. 1, §7, trans. John the Saracen (*Dionysiaca*, 1 [1937], p. 50).

58. *Ibid.*, pp. 196–97. For the citation from Damascene see his *De fide orthodoxa* I, ch. 9 (p. 48:8–12).

59. "Ad primum ergo dicendum, quod Damascenus intelligit, quod huiusmodi nomina non significant quid est Deus, quasi eius substantiam definiendo et comprehendendo; unde et subiungit quod hoc nomen *Qui est*, quod indefinite significat Dei substantiam, propriissime Deo attribuitur" (*De potentia*, q. 7, a. 5, ad 1, p. 199).

says that we cannot know what God is. The former, which does not seem to be purely negative in content, is here defended by Aquinas.

In replying to the second objection, Thomas reminds us that he has not forgotten the restriction which follows from the way in which we signify divine names. According to this objection, no name which signifies the substance of a thing can truly be denied of it. But according to Dionysius, in the case of God negations are true while affirmations are inexact (*incompactae*). Hence such names do not signify the divine substance.[60] Thomas counters that as regards the *res significata*—the perfection signified by such names—these names are truly applied to God because that which they signify is really present in him in some way. But as regards their *modus significandi*, such names can be denied of him. Every such name signifies a definite form, and cannot be realized in God in that fashion. Hence these names can also be denied of him insofar as they do not belong to him in the way in which they are signified. Dionysius has this restriction in mind—their *modus significandi*—when he describes such names as *incompactae*. Thomas concludes by again appealing to the threefold way according to which Dionysius states that such names are predicated of God. First, there is the way of affirmation, as when we say that God is wise. This we must affirm of God because there must be in him a likeness of that wisdom we discover in his effects. Secondly, because wisdom is not realized in God in the way we understand and name it, we introduce the way of negation and say that God is not wise. In other words, we deny of God the creaturely *modus significandi* which is always conjoined with our speech about God. Thirdly, since wisdom is not denied of God because he falls short of it but rather because it is present in him in supereminent fashion, we can say that God is superwise (*supersapiens*)—the way of eminence.[61] Presumably, what we do in this third case is negate all imperfection and limitation of wisdom as we apply this to God.

As Thomas points out in replying to objection 4, he does not intend to say that God is wise only in this sense that he causes wisdom in us. On the contrary, it is because God is wise that he can cause wisdom (cf. q. 7, a. 6).[62]

---

60. *Ibid.*, p. 197. For the citation from Dionysius's *De caelesti hierarchia*, ch. 2 ("in divinis negationes sunt verae, affirmationes vero incompactae") Thomas seems to have combined the translations by John Scotus Eriugena and by John the Saracen. See Durantel, *Saint Thomas et le Pseudo-Denis*, p. 73. For confirmation see ST I, q. 13, a. 12, ad 1.

61. *De potentia*, q. 7, a. 5, ad 2, p. 199.

62. *Ibid.* For q. 7, a. 6 see pp. 201–2: "quia cum effectus a causa secundum similitudinem procedat, prius oportet intelligere causam aliqualem quam effectus tales. Non ergo sapiens dicitur Deus quoniam sapientiam causet, sed quia est sapiens, ideo sapientiam causat."

On the other hand, in replying to objection 6, Thomas again reminds us that his claim that such names signify the divine substance does not imply that we can therefore either define or comprehend God's quiddity. It is this defining or comprehensive knowledge that Damascene has in mind when he denies that we can know what God is.[63]

As we turn to the slightly later First Part of the *Summa theologiae*, we find Thomas again defending essentially the same position as in the *De potentia*. In q. 2, a. 3 he presents his famed "five ways" to establish God's existence. In introducing q. 3 he remarks that once we have recognized that something is, it remains for us to investigate how it is in order to arrive at *quid est* knowledge of it. In the case of God, however, we cannot know what he is, but what he is not. Thomas then lays down a program for his subsequent discussion. He will proceed by examining (1) how God is not; (2) how God is known by us; and (3) how God is named by us.[64]

In qq. 3-11 Thomas concentrates on the first phase—determining how God is not. It is only in q. 12 that he asks how God is known by us, and in q. 13 that he takes up the issue how God is named by us. Accordingly, we have it on Thomas's own word that in examining God's simplicity, perfection, infinity, immutability, and unity, he is determining how God is not. We should also note that after discussing God's perfection in q. 4, Thomas devotes q. 5 to a study of goodness taken generally, and q. 6 to God's goodness. In other words, even Thomas's defense of divine goodness continues to fall under the *via negativa*, or his effort to determine how God is not. As we shall find confirmed below, this is not to say that goodness itself is negative in meaning, but that we apply it to God by following the path of negation (see the first sense of the way of negation). Even in q. 12 ("How God is known by us") Thomas continues to stress the *via negativa* and to deny that human reason can arrive at *quid est* knowledge of God.[65]

In q. 13, a. 2, Thomas again asks whether any name can be said of God substantially. He comments that neither those names which are said of God

---

63. *Ibid.*, pp. 199-200. "Ad sextum dicendum, quod ratio illa probat quod Deus non potest nominari nomine substantiam ipsius definiente, vel comprehendente vel adaequante: sic enim de Deo ignoramus quid est." Cf. also his reply to objection 14: " . . . illud est ultimum cognitionis humanae de Deo quod sciat se Deum nescire, in quantum cognoscit illud quod Deus est, omne ipsum quod de eo intelligimus, excedere" (p. 200).

64. *Summa theologiae*, Leonine manual edition (Marietti: Turin-Rome, 1950), p. 13. "Sed quia de Deo scire non possumus quid sit, sed quid non sit, non possumus considerare de Deo quomodo sit, sed potius quomodo non sit. Primo ergo considerandum est quomodo non sit; secundo, quomodo a nobis cognoscatur; tertio, quomodo nominetur."

65. See in particular q. 12, a. 12. Note his reply to objection 1: "Ad primum ergo dicendum quod ratio ad formam simplicem pertingere non potest, ut sciat de ea *quid est*: potest tamen de ea cognoscere, ut sciat *an est*" (p. 62).

negatively (that is, which are negative in content) nor those which signify God's relationship to creatures can signify his substance in any way. But concerning names which are said absolutely and affirmatively of God — names such as "good," "wise," etc., Thomas once more presents the two extreme versions of the negative position we have already seen from the *De potentia*. According to some, even though such names are said affirmatively of God, they really deny something of him. To say that God is living is really to make the point that God is not in the way inanimate things are. Thomas continues to assign this position to Maimonides. He notes that according to another view (which he does not here attribute to Maimonides) such names signify nothing but God's relationship to creatures. To say that God is good is merely to make the point that he causes goodness in creatures.[66]

Thomas rejects both of these positions, and for three reasons. First of all, neither position can explain why certain names can be said of God with greater justification than others. Secondly, it would follow that all names are said of God *per posterius* rather than *per prius* (as medicine is said to be healthy only because it causes health in an animal). Thirdly, such theories run counter to the intention and practice of those who speak of God. When they say that God is living, they intend to signify something more than that he causes life in us, or that he differs from the inanimate.

After rejecting these positions as too restrictive, Thomas concludes that names of this type do signify the divine substance. They are predicated of God substantially, but fall short of any adequate representation of him.[67] As Thomas recalls, such names can signify God only insofar as our intellect can know him. But the human intellect derives its knowledge of God by reasoning from creatures. Hence it can know God only insofar as creatures represent him. God contains in himself in simple and undivided fashion all perfections found in creatures. Wherefore, any creature can represent God and be like him only insofar as it possesses some perfection. Since God belongs to no genus or species, no creature can represent him by belonging to the same genus or species. Hence, creatures can represent God only as the supreme principle from whose likeness all effects fall short, but each of which achieves some degree of likeness to him. This is enough for Thomas to continue to insist here, as he had in the *De potentia*, that such names (affirmative ones) do signify the divine substance, but imperfectly, just as creatures imperfectly represent God.[68] Thomas reinforces his point by noting

66. *Ibid.*, p. 64.

67. "Et ideo aliter dicendum est, quod huiusmodi quidem nomina significant substantiam divinam, et praedicantur de Deo substantialiter, sed deficiunt a repraesentatione ipsius" (p. 65).

68. *Ibid.* Note in particular: "Sic igitur praedicta nomina divinam substantiam significant: imperfecte tamen, sicut et creaturae imperfecte eam repraesentant."

that when we say God is good we do not merely mean that he is the cause of goodness (Theory II), or that he is not evil (Theory I). Rather, what we call goodness in creatures preexists in God according to a higher mode. Wherefore, it does not follow that God is good because he causes goodness; rather, because he is good, he produces goodness in creatures.[69]

In replying to objection 1, Thomas once more must contend with John Damascene's statement that those things which we say of God do not signify what he is in his substance, but what he is not. Thomas again interprets this to mean that no such name perfectly expresses what God is; but every such name does imperfectly signify him, just as creatures imperfectly represent him.[70] As in the *De potentia,* therefore, we find Thomas distinguishing between a perfectly comprehensive and quidditative knowledge of God, which he continues to deny to man, and an imperfect knowledge of the divine substance or essence, which he now defends.

In q. 13, a. 3, Thomas asks whether any names can be said of God properly (*proprie*). In replying Thomas once more reminds us that we know God from perfections which we find in creatures, and that such perfections are realized in God in more eminent fashion. Since our intellect understands these perfections as they are present in creatures, it can only signify them as it understands them. This leads Thomas to recall the distinction between that which such names signify when they are applied to God and the way in which they signify. Some names — names that signify pure perfections — are properly said of God as regards that which they signify. This is not true, however, of their *modus significandi*, since the way in which these names signify is still that which is appropriate to creatures.[71] In replying to objection 2, Thomas appeals to this same distinction to account for Dionysius's statement that such names are more truly denied of God. What Dionysius really has in mind is that the creaturely *modus significandi* of such names is to be denied of God.[72]

---

69. *Ibid.* "Cum igitur dicitur *Deus est bonus,* non est sensus, *Deus est causa bonitatis,* vel *Deus non est malus:* sed est sensus, *id quod bonitatem dicimus in creaturis, praeexistit in Deo,* et hoc quidem secundum modum altiorem. Unde ex hoc non sequitur quod Deo competat esse bonum inquantum causat bonitatem: sed potius e converso, quia est bonus, bonitatem rebus diffundit . . . "

70. *Ibid.*, pp. 64, 65. For the citation from Damascene see n. 58 above. Note Thomas's reply: "Ad primum ergo dicendum quod Damascenus ideo dicit quod haec nomina non significant quid est Deus, quia a nullo istorum nominum exprimitur quid est Deus perfecte: sed unumquodque imperfecte eum significat, sicut et creaturae imperfecte eum repraesentant."

71. *Ibid.*, pp. 65–66. Also see his reply to objection 1.

72. *Ibid.*, p. 66.

In subsequent articles of this same q. 13 Thomas draws out the implications from these conclusions.[73] Because different divine names signify different concepts which are themselves drawn from different perfections as realized in creatures, these divine names are not mere synonyms (a. 4). In a. 5 Thomas offers his well-known critique of univocal and equivocal predication of such names of God, and again falls back on predication of such divine names only by analogy or proportion. Here, as in the *Summa contra gentiles* and in the *De potentia*, he rejects the analogy of many to one and accepts only the analogy of one to another.[74] Although Thomas's doctrine of analogy has not been my primary concern in this chapter, perhaps I should here stress the point that if Thomas has admitted that as regards their *res significata* some names can be predicated of God substantially and properly, such can happen only by analogy. Not only must one deny of God the creaturely *modus significandi* which such names carry with them when we apply them to God; even as regards that which they signify (their *res significata*), such names cannot be applied to God univocally. For one to say anything else would be to reduce Thomas's doctrine of analogy to veiled univocity.

In q. 13, a. 6 Thomas writes that certain names such as "good" are said of God not merely metaphorically and not merely because God causes goodness in creatures, but essentially (*essentialiter*). Hence, as regards that which such names signify, they are said of God *per prius*. But as regards the order of discovery, such names are first applied by us to creatures. Because of this they retain their creaturely *modus significandi*.[75] According to a. 11 the name

---

73. For some interesting reflections on Thomas's procedure in q. 13 see K. Riesenhuber, "Partizipation als Strukturprinzip der Namen Gottes bei Thomas von Aquin," in *Sprache und Erkenntnis im Mittelalter, Miscellanea Mediaevalia* 13/2 (Berlin-New York, 1981), pp. 969–82. For another interesting but more widely ranging study see Ludwig Hödl, "Die philosophische Gotteslehre des Thomas von Aquin O.P. in der Diskussion der Schulen um die Wende des 13. zum 14. Jahrhundert," *Rivista di filosofia neo-scolastica* 70 (1978), pp. 113–34, especially 114–20.

74. ST I, q. 13, a. 5 (pp. 67–68). Cf. *De potentia*, q. 7, a. 7 (p. 204); SCG I, ch. 34 (p. 34). It is interesting to observe that as in the *Summa theologiae*, so too in the *De potentia* Thomas explicitly takes up the question of analogical predication of divine names only after he has already defended the possibility of substantial predication of some names of God (see *De pot.*, q. 7, a. 5). This would suggest that when discussing Thomas's doctrine of analogical predication of divine names in these two works (ST, *De pot.*), one would be well advised to do so only after having addressed oneself to the issue of substantial (or essential) predication of divine names.

75. "Utrum nomina per prius dicantur de creaturis quam de Deo" (pp. 68–69). Note in particular from Thomas's reply: "Sed supra ostensum est quod huiusmodi nomina non solum dicuntur de Deo causaliter, sed etiam essentialiter. Cum enim dicitur *Deus est bonus*, vel *sapiens*, non solum significatur quod ipse sit causa sapientiae vel bonitatis, sed quod haec in eo eminentius praeexistunt."

"He who is" is supremely proper or appropriate to God. As Thomas clarifies in replying to objection 1, this is true if one concentrates on that by reason of which this name is assigned, that is, *esse*, and if one has in mind its *modus significandi*. But if one rather thinks of that which the divine name is intended to signify — the *res significata* — the name "God" is more appropriate. And even more appropriate than this is the name "Tetragrammaton," which is intended to signify the singular and incommunicable substance of God.[76] Finally, according to a. 12, affirmative statements can be made about God.[77]

III

In concluding this chapter I would like to recall that from the beginning of his career until its end Thomas consistently denies to man in this life quidditative knowledge of God. He has frequently made this point by stating that we can know that God is and what God is not, but not what God is. On the other hand, even in earlier discussions such as those in the *Summa contra gentiles* or, for that matter, in his Commentary on the *Sentences* he has defended the validity of some kind of nonmetaphorical predication of divine names.[78] What I have not found in these earlier discussions, however, is explicit defense of man's ability to apply some names to God substantially or, according to the language of ST I, q. 13, a. 6, essentially. Nonetheless, joined with this admission in these later works is Thomas's continuing refusal to admit that we can arrive at quidditative knowledge of God in this life. How, then, is one to fit all of this together?

First, I would suggest, one should define quidditative knowledge or knowledge of what God is very strictly, even as Thomas himself has done. He has made it clear, for instance, in the *De potentia* and in the First Part of the *Summa theologiae*, that when he agrees with John Damascene that we cannot know what God is, what he is thereby excluding is comprehensive and defining knowledge of God. This kind of knowledge of God Thomas had always

---

76. *Ibid.*, p. 74. For fuller discussion of this see A. Maurer, "St. Thomas on the Sacred Name 'Tetragrammaton'," *Mediaeval Studies* 34 (1972), pp. 275–86. Maurer finds this view that the name "Tetragrammaton" is in one sense more proper to God than the name "He Who is" unique to Thomas's *Summa theologiae* in contrast with his earlier works (p. 278), and also identifies Maimonides as Thomas's source for this later precision (pp. 282–85). This is another indication that Thomas was taking Maimonides very seriously at this point in his career. For more on Thomas's discussion of these names see Clavell, *El nombre propio de Dios*, pp. 146–56.

77. ST I, q. 13, a. 12 (pp. 74–75).

78. For an interesting examination of key texts taken from *In I Sent.*, *De ver.*, SCG, *Comp. theol.*, *De potentia*, and ST I, see Montagnes, *La doctrine de l'analogie de l'être*, pp. 65–93.

denied to man in this life. In fact, as he had explained in another early work, the *De veritate*, our intellect is said to know of something what it is when it defines it, that is, when it conceives some form concerning that thing which corresponds to it in every respect.[79]

Secondly, as we have seen, in the *De potentia* and in the *Summa theologiae*, Thomas has explicitly stated that we can apply some names to God substantially or essentially. This type of divine naming is restricted, of course, to names which are positive in content and which imply no limitation or imperfection in their formal meaning—in other words, to names signifying pure perfections. On this point there seems to have been some development in Thomas's thinking between the time of the *Summa contra gentiles* and the *De potentia.*

Thirdly, if one wonders why such development has occurred, I would suggest that it is because Thomas came to take Moses Maimonides' restrictive position concerning the divine names very seriously. It is within the context of his refutation of Maimonides both in the *De potentia* and then in the *Summa theologiae* that Thomas counters by defending the possibility of substantial predication of certain divine names.

Fourthly, even in these later discussions Thomas continues to insist that one should distinguish between the perfection (*res*) that is signified by such names, and the way in which the perfection is signified. If these names can be affirmed of God as regards that which they signify, one must always deny of them their creaturely *modus significandi*. This is why Thomas can continue to say that such names are both to be affirmed and denied of God.

Finally, if one wonders why in the *Summa theologiae* and even thereafter, for instance, in his Commentary on the *Liber de causis,* Thomas continues to say that we cannot know what God is, or even that what God is remains completely unknown to us, this is for the reasons already indicated.[80] In

---

79. See *De veritate*, q. 2, a. 1, ad 9, as cited above in n. 17. For much the same point that I am making here see J. H. Nicolas, "Affirmation de Dieu et connaissance," *Revue thomiste* 44 (1964), p. 221, n. 2. Texts such as these, argues Nicolas, exclude "seulement une connaissance des attributs divins *à partir de son essence*, autrement dit ils excluent une connaissance quidditative de Dieu, non la connaissance de son essence." On the other hand, allowance for some chronological development on Thomas's part between the SCG and the *De potentia* such as I am here proposing might have made Nicolas's task of reconciling Thomas with himself less difficult. See, for instance, the remarks on p. 200 and n. 2 of his article.

80. See *Sancti Thomae de Aquino super Librum de causis expositio*, H. D. Saffrey, ed. (Fribourg-Louvain, 1954), p. 43. There, in commenting on proposition 6, Thomas writes: " . . . ille enim perfectissime Deum cognoscit qui hoc de ipso tenet quod, quidquid cogitari vel dici de eo potest, minus est eo quod Deus est." After citing Dionysius's *Mystical Theology* (ch. 1) to this effect that man "*secundum melius* suae

such contexts he is taking the expression *quid est* knowledge strictly, as equivalent to comprehensive and defining knowledge. This he will never grant to man in this life. Moreover, he is also reminding us that no matter what name we may apply to God, its creaturely *modus significandi* must be denied of him.

---

cognitionis *unitur* Deo sicut *omnino ignoto*," Thomas comments on this remark from prop. 6 of the *Liber de causis:* "Causa prima superior est narratione." Thomas explains that the term *narratio* is to be taken as meaning "affirmation" because: "quidquid de Deo affirmamus non convenit ei secundum quod a nobis significatur; nomina enim a nobis imposita significant per modum quo nos intelligimus, quem quidem modum esse divinum transcendit." In other words, the creaturely *modus significandi* is to be denied of any positive statement we may make about God. See Thomas's concluding remark from his commentary on this same proposition: "Sic ergo patet quod *causa prima superior est narratione*, quia neque per causam, neque per seipsam, neque per effectum sufficienter cognosci aut dici potest" (p. 48). Thomas's Commentary seems to date from 1271–1272 (Weisheipl, *Friar Thomas d'Aquino*, p. 383). For Dionysius see *De mystica theologia* 1.3 (PG 3.1001), and *Dionysiaca* 1, p. 578. For fuller discussion see Pegis, "Penitus Manet Ignotum," pp. 212–16.

CHAPTER X

DIVINE KNOWLEDGE, DIVINE POWER, AND HUMAN FREEDOM IN THOMAS AQUINAS AND HENRY OF GHENT

In this chapter I shall limit myself to two thinkers from the thirteenth century, Thomas Aquinas and Henry of Ghent. Since Thomas devoted considerably more attention to this topic than did Henry, and since Aquinas's position was to become the focal point for centuries of subsequent controversy, the greater part of my remarks will be devoted to him. As will be recalled, Henry lectured as Master in Theology at the University of Paris from 1276 until ca. 1292. Concerning the present topic he may serve as an interesting link between Aquinas and Duns Scotus (though Scotus's position will not be examined here).[1] Henry had developed a radically different kind of metaphysics from that of Aquinas.[2] Of greatest interest to us will be Henry's explanation of God's knowledge of future contingents.

1: Thomas Aquinas

In discussing Thomas's position I shall try to cover the points suggested in my title by reducing them to two major concerns: (1) Thomas's explanation of God's knowledge of future contingents; (2) his views concerning the causal character of God's knowledge and God's will. In each case I shall attempt to show how Thomas reconciles his explanation with man's freedom.

---

1. On Henry's life and career see R. Macken, ed., *Henrici de Gandavo Quodlibet I* (Louvain-Leiden, 1979), pp. vii–xxiv. For a comparison of Thomas, Henry, and Duns Scotus on the question of divine foreknowledge of future contingents see Hermann Schwamm, *Das göttliche Vorherwissen bei Duns Scotus und seinen ersten Anhängern*, Philosophie und Grenzwissenschaften V (Innsbruck, 1934), especially pp. 91–108.
2. For what continues to be the best overall account of Henry's metaphysical thought see J. Paulus, *Henri de Gand: Essai sur les tendances de sa métaphysique* (Paris, 1938).

1.1: God's Knowledge of Future Contingents

As is well known, Thomas Aquinas always maintained that God knows individuals and individual events, including future contingents. For instance, to take a representative text from the mid-1250s, in q. 2, a. 12 of his *De veritate* he explicitly addresses himself to this issue.[3] He begins his reply by criticizing two unsatisfactory solutions. According to one position, which errs by likening God's knowledge to that of man, God does not know future contingents. Aquinas immediately rejects this view because it would imply that God's providence does not extend to human affairs. According to another extreme position, God does know future contingents, but only because they happen out of necessity, in other words, because they are not really contingent. Thomas rejects this view because it would result in a denial of man's freedom. He concludes by defending the more difficult middle position. God does know future events, but this does not prevent some of them from being contingent.[4]

In developing his defense of this position in the same context, Thomas begins by noting that even in man some of his cognitive powers and habits do not admit of falsity. He cites sensation, science, and our intuition of first principles. Then Thomas contrasts the necessary with the contingent. As he understands the necessary here, it refers to that which cannot be prevented from occurring even before it exists. This is so because its causes are unchangeably ordered to its production. Given this, such necessary things or events, even when they are future, can be known by habits and powers such as those he has just mentioned.[5] By the contingent Thomas here means that which can be impeded before it is actually brought into being. Once such a contingent thing has actually been produced, however, it cannot be prevented from having actually existed. Hence, even the contingent can be grasped by one or other of those powers or habits which do not admit of falsity. For instance, when Socrates is actually sitting, my sense perception of him as sitting is correct.[6]

---

3. "Duodecimo quaeritur utrum Deus sciat singularia futura contingentia," in *S. Thomae Aquinatis Quaestiones disputatae*, Vol. 1, *De veritate*, R. Spiazzi, ed. (Turin-Rome, 1953), p. 52. For the same in the Leonine edition see *Sancti Thomae de Aquino opera omnia*, T. 22, Vol. 1 (Rome, 1975), p. 81. Here I shall normally cite from the first-mentioned edition (Marietti), although all citations have been compared with the Leonine edition.

4. *Ed. cit.*, p. 53.

5. *Ibid.* Thomas illustrates this with our knowledge that the sun will rise, or that an eclipse will occur.

6. *Ibid.* Cf. *In I Sent.*, d. 38, q. 1, a. 5 (*Scriptum super libros Sententiarum*, P. Mandonnet, ed., Vol. 1 [Paris, 1929], p. 910). There Thomas distinguishes three situations. Before a thing exists it enjoys being only in its causes. But these may be causes

Thomas is attempting to make the point that even something contingent can be truly or correctly grasped once it has been realized in actuality. At the same time, he also acknowledges that insofar as something contingent is future, certain knowledge cannot be had of it. Since falsity cannot be admitted of God's knowledge, Thomas remarks that not even God can know future contingents, if this be taken to imply that he would know them *as* future.[7] For something to be known as future there must be some passing of time between one's knowing it and the actual realization of that thing in itself. Such, however, cannot be admitted of God's knowledge of the contingent or, for that matter, of anything else. God's knowledge is always ordered to that which he knows as that which is present (his knowledge) to that which is present (the object known). In order to illustrate this point Thomas offers the example of someone who observes many people passing along a road in succession. Within a given period of time our observer will have seen every individual passing by that road during a particular part of that time. During the total period of time, therefore, he will have seen each one who passed by as present to him; but he will not have seen them all as simultaneously present to him. Now if his vision of all these passersby could be simultaneous, then he would view them all as simultaneously present to him, though they would not be simultaneous with one another.[8]

Ultimately inspired here by Boethius, Thomas goes on to apply this to the case at hand. Since God's "vision" is measured only by eternity, which itself is *tota simul* and includes the whole of time, whatever takes place in the course of time is not viewed by God as future to himself but as present.

---

(1) from which an effect necessarily follows in the sense that they (the causes) cannot be impeded; or (2) causes from which an effect usually follows; or (3) causes which are open to both possibilities. We can have science (certain knowledge) concerning future effects which follow from the first kind of cause, conjectural knowledge concerning the second, and no knowledge in the proper sense concerning the third. But as regards effects which follow from the third type of cause, once they have actually been realized in their own determined being, they can be known with certainty.

7. " . . . unde cum divinae scientiae non subsit falsitas nec subesse possit, impossibile esset quod de contingentibus futuris scientiam haberet Deus, si cognosceret ea ut futura sunt" (*ed. cit.*, p. 53). Also see at 6 (p. 54). Cf. *In I Sent.* (p. 910): "et ideo contingentia ad utrumlibet in causis suis nullo modo cognosci possunt."

8. *Ed. cit.*, pp. 53–54. In *In I Sent.*, d. 38, q. 1, a. 5, Thomas offers a slightly different illustration. Suppose that five different human observers saw five different events successively over a period of five hours. One can say that the five saw these contingent events successively as present to each of them. Now suppose that these five cognitive acts on the part of our observers could become one act of cognition. It could then be said that there was one cognition of these five successive events as present to that single knowing act (*ed. cit.*, p. 911).

Nonetheless, Thomas also insists that what is seen by God as present to him may still be future with respect to other things which come before it in time. Because God's vision is not in time but outside time, any such event is not future to God but present. Because we are measured by time, any such event is future for us.[9]

From this Thomas concludes that just as our power of sight is not deceived when it sees an actual contingent object as present to it, so too God infallibly knows all contingents as present to him. And if our knowledge of an actually present contingent does not rob that event of its contingency, neither does God's knowledge of anything that is contingent.[10]

Thomas comments that it is difficult for us to understand this. This is because we cannot signify divine knowledge except by thinking of knowledge as we find it in ourselves, and then by also cosignifying certain differences.[11] It should be recalled that in the immediately preceding article of the *De veritate* Thomas had argued that *scientia* cannot be predicated of God and creatures either univocally or purely equivocally, but only analogically. It is true that his defense there of analogy of proportionality as the only kind to be used in such cases is something of an anomaly, and is at odds both with his earlier discussions of this in his Commentary on the *Sentences* and especially with all his major treatments after the *De veritate*. Nonetheless, throughout his career he consistently rejects both univocity and equivocation when it comes to naming God and creatures, and defends some kind of analogy.[12]

Granted the difficulty of our adequately understanding knowledge as this is realized in God, Thomas comments that it would be better for us to say that God knows that a given contingent *is* than to say God knows that it *will be*. Or to use the language of Boethius in Bk. V of his *Consolation of Philosophy,* Thomas

9. *De veritate*, p. 54. For much the same see *In I Sent.*, d. 38, q. 1, a. 5 (pp. 910-11). There Thomas explicitly makes the point that the divine intellect knows from eternity every contingent not only as it exists in its causes (and hence as potential or as capable of being brought into being), but also as it is in its determined being. Otherwise one would have to say that God's knowledge of such a thing changes when that thing passes from potential being to actual being.

10. *De veritate*, p. 54.

11. "Difficultas autem in hoc accidit eo quod divinam cognitionem significare non possumus nisi per modum nostrae cognitionis consignificando differentias" (*De veritate*, p. 54). According to the Leonine edition's preferred reading, it is differences in time that are cosignified ("temporum differentias" [p. 84]).

12. See *De veritate*, q. 2, a. 11. The literature on Thomas's doctrine of analogy is vast. For an excellent discussion of this in Thomas and for much of the earlier bibliography see B. Montagnes, *La doctrine de l'analogie de l'être d'après saint Thomas d'Aquin* (Louvain, 1963). For the unusual character of his defense of analogy of proportionality in the *De veritate* see especially pp. 65-93.

suggests that God's knowledge of the future is more properly called *providentia* than *praevidentia* (providence rather than foreknowledge). Still, adds Thomas, in another sense divine knowledge can be styled *praevidentia* on account of the order which something known by God may have to other things to which it is future. Presupposed by all of this, of course, is the distinction between divine eternity, on the one hand, and human existence in time, on the other.[13]

As one might expect, a number of objections having to do with free future contingents were raised at this disputation. For instance, according to objection 1, only that which is true can be known. But according to Aristotle's *De interpretatione*, individual future contingents enjoy no determined truth. Therefore, God cannot have certain knowledge of them. In replying to this objection Thomas concedes that any such contingent is not determined so long as it is future. Once it is actually realized, however, it does have determined truth. And it is in this way that it is known by God. In other words, he is again applying the Boethian view that such events are not future for God but eternally present to him. Hence, in the divine and eternal present they are not unrealized but realized, not undetermined but determined.[14]

In replying to the fourth objection, Thomas appeals to the distinction between that which is necessary *de dicto* and that which is necessary *de re*. Here he is considering the statement that whatever is known by God is necessary. Taken *de dicto* the statement is composite and therefore true, since it simply means this: whatever is known by God is necessary in the sense that it is not possible for God to know that something is and for that thing not to be. But if this statement is understood *de re*, it is taken in divided fashion and is false. It would then mean this: that which is known by God is a necessary being. Thomas reminds us once more that the mere fact that things are known by God does not of itself impose necessity upon them.[15] In replying to the fifth objection Thomas makes basically the same point. If such a proposition were understood *de re*, the necessity would apply to the very thing that is known by God. In other words, the thing itself would exist

---

13. *De veritate*, p. 54. Cf. *In I Sent.*, d. 38, q. 1, a. 5 (pp. 911–12) for much the same. In both contexts Thomas explicitly acknowledges his debt to Boethius. For this in Boethius see *The Consolation of Philosophy*, in H. F. Stewart and E. K. Rand, *Boethius, The Theological Tractates and the Consolation of Philosophy* (Cambridge, Mass., 1968), Bk. V, pr. 6 (pp. 398–410). On this in Boethius see E. Stump and N. Kretzmann, "Eternity," *The Journal of Philosophy* 78 (1981), pp. 429–58; J. Groblicki, *De scientia Dei futurorum contingentium secundum S. Thomam eiusque primos sequaces* (Krakow, 1938), pp. 40–44.

14. *De ver.*, pp. 52, 54. For the same objection and essentially the same reply see *In I Sent.*, *loc. cit.*, p. 907 (obj. 2), and p. 912 (ad 2).

15. *De veritate*, p. 52 (obj. 4); p. 54 (ad 4).

necessarily. But when any such statement is taken *de dicto*, the necessity in question does not apply to the thing itself but only to the relationship between God's science, on the one hand, and the thing known, on the other.[16]

Thomas devotes considerable attention to the seventh objection and, I should add, discusses it in detail on a number of other occasions as well. The objection runs this way. In every true conditional, if the antecedent is absolutely necessary, the consequent is also absolutely necessary. But this conditional proposition is true: If something was known by God, it will be. Since the antecedent ("This was known by God") is absolutely necessary, the consequent ("It will be") is also absolutely necessary. Hence, it follows that whatever was known by God will necessarily be, and with absolute necessity. To strengthen the argument the objector reasons that the antecedent ("This was known by God") is a statement concerning the past. Statements concerning the past, if true, are necessary, since what was cannot not have been.[17]

In replying to this objection Thomas first proposes and rejects three inadequate responses.[18] Rather than delay here over these, I shall turn immediately to his personal solution. In such a proposition, he concedes, the antecedent is necessary without qualification (*simpliciter*). But the consequent is absolutely necessary only insofar as it follows from the antecedent. Thomas distinguishes between characteristics which are attributed to something insofar as it exists in itself, and others which apply to it only insofar as it is known. Those which are attributed to the thing as it is in itself apply to it according to its proper mode of being; but those which are attributed to it or follow from it insofar as it is known apply to it only according to the mode of the power that knows it, not according to the mode of being of the object that is known.[19]

In other words, Thomas here employs the scholastic axiom that whatever is known is known according to the modality of the knower. To illustrate he proposes this statement: "If I understand something, it is immaterial." From this one need not conclude that the thing in question is in fact an immaterial being in itself, but only that it is immaterial insofar as it is present in my

16. *De veritate*, p. 52 (obj. 5); p. 54 (ad 5). For the same reply see *In I Sent.*, p. 908 (obj. 5); pp. 914–15 (ad 5).

17. *De veritate*, p. 52 (obj. 7). Cf. *In I Sent.*, pp. 907–8 (obj. 4).

18. For these see *De veritate*, p. 55 (ad 7). Compare with the inadequate solutions discussed in *In I Sent.*, d. 38, q. 1, a. 5, ad 4 (pp. 912–14).

19. *De veritate*, p. 55. Note that this particular point is brought out much more fully here than in the parallel discussion in *In I Sent.*, where it appears only implicitly at best (p. 914). However, it is clearly implied by Boethius in an earlier part of Bk. V of his *Consolation*. See pr. 4 (*op. cit.*, p. 388:75–77): "Omne enim quod cognoscitur non secundum sui vim sed secundum cognoscentium potius comprehenditur facultatem."

knowing power. So too, when I state, "If God knows something, it will be," the consequent is not to be interpreted as applying to the thing according to its own mode of being, but according to the mode of its knower—in this case God himself. Granted that such a thing is future in terms of its own and temporal mode of being, according to the mode of its eternal divine knower it is present, and eternally present, to God. Given this, Thomas again comments that it would be more exact for us to say: "If God knows something, it is," than to say "If God knows something, it will be."

Thomas also notes that the necessity in such statements is like that which applies to the following: "If I see that Socrates is running, he is running."[20] In each case we can say that the thing in question necessarily is when it is. In neither case need we conclude that the thing in question enjoys a necessary mode of being in itself, or that it is a necessary being. Or to put this another way, granted that in such propositions the consequent follows necessarily from the antecedent, this does not imply that the consequent enjoys a necessary mode of being. To state this in still another way, Thomas is here distinguishing between logical necessity, on the one hand, or that which applies to propositions, and ontological necessity, on the other. To say that such a proposition is logically necessary is to say that if its antecedent is given, its consequent necessarily follows. But this is to tell us nothing about the ontological structure or mode of being of the referent of that consequent in itself.[21]

Since Thomas evidently regards this as a serious objection, two features should be recalled from his reply. First of all, he has distinguished between that which applies to a thing in terms of its own mode of being, on the one hand, and that which applies to it only insofar as it is present to a knowing power, on the other. Secondly, equally crucial to his reply is the distinction between divine duration or eternity, on the one hand, and creaturely duration or time, on the other. Given these two points, he can insist that while

---

20. *De veritate*, p. 55. Also note Thomas's concluding remark in his reply to objection 9 (objection 8 in the Leonine ed.): " . . . sic enim non loquimur nunc de cognitione futuri, prout scilicet a Deo in suis causis videtur, sed in quantum cognoscitur in seipso; sic enim cognoscitur ut praesens."

21. In other contexts, such as *De veritate*, q. 24, a. 1, ad 13, Thomas identifies absolute necessity with *necessitas consequentis*, and contrasts this with conditioned necessity (*necessitas consequentiae*). See *ed. cit.*, p. 436: "Ad decimumtertium dicendum, quod ex praescientia Dei non potest concludi quod actus nostri sint necessarii necessitate absoluta, quae dicitur necessitas consequentis; sed necessitate conditionata, quae dicitur necessitas consequentiae, ut patet per Boëtium in fine *de Consol. philosophiae*." Also see SCG I, ch. 67. For fuller discussion of the difference between "logical" necessity or contingency, on the one hand, and "ontological" necessity or contingency, on the other, see H. J. McSorley, *Luther: Right or Wrong?* (New York, N.Y., and Minneapolis, 1969), pp. 150–53. McSorley concedes that this precise terminology is not that of Aquinas.

all things are eternally present to God insofar as they are known by him in accord with his eternal mode of being, they also unfold in time in accord with their own modes of being. Failure to take both of these points seriously may account, at least in part, for some recent criticisms of Thomas's reply to this seventh objection.[22]

Before moving on to the next major part of this chapter, I should mention that the general thinking found in this article from the *De veritate* is closely paralleled by an even earlier discussion in Thomas's Commentary on I *Sentences* (d. 38, q. 1, a. 5). The similarity applies in large measure even to the major objections and replies we have just examined in the *De veritate*.[23] Moreover, one finds essentially the same general solution with many of the

22. See A. Kenny, "Divine Foreknowledge and Human Freedom," in *Aquinas: A Collection of Critical Essays*, A. Kenny, ed. (Garden City, N.Y., 1969), pp. 262–64. Kenny finds the notion of "timeless eternity" rather hopeless. As regards the first point, he does not clearly connect Thomas's distinction between *necessitas consequentis* and *necessitas consequentiae* with the distinction between that which applies to a thing in terms of its own mode of being and that which applies to it only insofar as it is present to a knowing power. For another writer who has difficulty with Thomas's and Boethius's views concerning the eternal character of divine knowledge see P. Streveler, "The Problem of Future Contingents: A Medieval Discussion," *The New Scholasticism* 47 (1973), pp. 238–40, 246. He seems to regard as more fruitful Kenny's suggestion that doubt should be cast "upon our belief that the past is somehow necessary in a way that the future is not" (p. 241). Without pausing here to discuss this point at length, it seems to me that Aquinas would assign to a past event the same kind of necessity that he assigns to a present event, that is, conditioned necessity (*necessitas consequentiae*) or necessity *ex suppositione*. See *De veritate*, q. 2, a. 12, ad 7: "Quamvis autem res in seipsa, sit futura, tamen secundum modum cognoscentis est praesens; et ideo magis esset dicendum: Si Deus scit aliquid, illud est; quam: Hoc erit; unde idem est iudicium de ista: Si Deus scit aliquid, hoc erit; et de hac: Si ego video Socratem currere, Socrates currit: quorum utrumque est necessarium dum est" (p. 55). Granted that here Thomas explicitly refers to God's knowing something rather than to his having known it, Thomas has already explained that for God there is no past. Since any event that is temporally past in itself is eternally present to God, it enjoys the same kind of necessity as any present event that is perceived by us. Under the supposition that it is happening (or has happened), it is happening (or has happened). This does not imply that it is absolutely or ontologically necessary in itself. For a critical reaction to Kenny's critique see W. Mulligan, "Divine Foreknowledge and Freedom: A Note on a Problem of Language," *The Thomist* 36 (1972), pp. 293–99.

23. A number of these parallels have already been pointed out in preceding notes. Unlike the discussion in the *De veritate*, however, Thomas begins his response in *In I Sent.* by distinguishing two major kinds of reasons which might be offered against the possibility of reconciling God's knowledge with future contingents. A first approach would reject this possibility because of the relationship that obtains between a cause and its effect. Because God's science is the cause of things, and because a necessary effect seems to result from a necessary and unchangeable cause, the possibility of any kind of contingent effect would seem to be eliminated. A second approach would be based on the relationship between science and its object. Because science is certain knowledge, it

same objections and replies in major later treatments, such as SCG I, chs. 66–67 (ca. 1259–1261, for Bk. I);[24] *Summa theologiae* I, q. 14, a. 13 (ca. 1266–1268);[25] *De malo*, q. 16, a. 7 (after November, 1267, and inserted into this set of Disputed Questions at a later date);[26] and *Compendium theologiae* I, ch. 133 (ca. 1269–1273).[27]

seems to require certitude and determination in that which is known. We shall defer consideration of Thomas's discussion and refutation of the first approach for the next section of this chapter. It is in addressing himself to the second kind of objection, which he here regards as the more difficult, that Thomas proposes the solution we have already examined from the *De veritate*. See *In I Sent.*, pp. 909ff. Also see M. Benz, "Das göttliche Vorherwissen des freien Willensakte des Geschöpfe bei Thomas von Aquin: *In I Sent.*, d. 38. q. 1 a. 5," *Divus Thomas* (Freib.) 14 (1936), pp. 255–73; 15 (1937), pp. 415–32.

24. In ch. 66 Thomas is attempting to account for the fact that God can know nonexistent entities. Here again he stresses the point that because of his eternity God's knowledge is not subject to any kind of successive duration. Divine eternity is present to all parts or instants of time, even as the center of a circle, being outside its circumference, bears an equal relationship to all points on that circumference. Consequently: "Quicquid igitur in quacumque parte temporis est, coexistit aeterno quasi praesens eidem: etsi respectu alterius partis temporis sit praeteritum vel futurum" (Leonine manual edition [Rome, 1934], p. 61). As regards things which are not yet but will be, God knows them by his *scientia visionis* not only in knowing his own power and in knowing their proper causes, but also in knowing them in themselves. In ch. 67 Thomas explicitly appeals again to the distinction between divine eternity and the temporal duration of creatures to account for God's knowledge of free future contingents. Once more he applies the distinction between *necessitas consequentiae* and *necessitas consequentis* (or between conditional and absolute necessity).

25. In this well-known discussion Thomas notes that something contingent can be considered in itself as it now exists in actuality, or only as it exists in its cause and hence as future. Considered in the first way it can be an object of certain knowledge, even on the level of sense perception. Considered in the second way, it is not yet determined *ad unum*, and hence cannot be known with certainty by any knower. But God knows all contingents not only in the second way, but also in the first, once again, argues Thomas, because God's knowledge is measured by eternity, just as is his *esse*. See in particular obj. 2 and the reply which is essentially the same as his reply to objection 7 in the *De veritate*, q. 2, a. 12. See his reply to obj. 3 for more on the difference between God's eternity and the temporal duration of creatures and for appeal to the difference between the necessary *de dicto* and *de re*. Also cf. ST I, q. 86, a. 4.

26. On the date of this question in the *De malo* see J. Weisheipl, *Friar Thomas d'Aquino*, pp. 363, 366. I have also followed Weisheipl for the datings of Thomas's other works. Art. 7 is directed to the question whether demons can know the future. In replying Thomas again distinguishes between knowing future things in themselves, and in their causes. Only God can know future things in themselves, something that is impossible for knowledge that is subject to the order of time. God knows all things as present to him, since his knowledge is above the temporal order. Also see the reply to obj. 15.

27. See ch. 132 for a series of objections against God's providence concerning particulars, two of which apply to our immediate concern: ("adhuc") there can be no certain knowledge of individual contingents; ("praeterea") not all particulars are simultaneous.

In addition to these, Thomas's Commentary on ch. 9 of the *De interpretatione* merits special attention. This Commentary seems to date from ca. 1270–1271. It has been shown that while writing it Thomas made considerable use of earlier commentaries by Boethius and by Ammonius.[28] In commenting on ch. 9 Thomas devotes three *lectiones* to the question of future contingents. In brief, in *Lectio* 13 he asks, following Aristotle, whether individual propositions concerning the future are either determinately true or determinately false. He agrees with Aristotle that individual propositions concerning the past or present are either determinately true or determinately false (see n. 167).[29] He notes that individual propositions concerning that which is necessary are either determinately true or determinately false when they deal with the future, just as they are when they have to do with the past or present (see n. 168). But what of individual propositions concerning future contingents? Here he also agrees with Aristotle that such are neither true nor

---

For this see *S. Thomae Aquinatis Opuscula theologica*, Vol. 1, R. Verardo, ed. (Turin-Rome, 1954), p. 63; and T. 42 (Opuscula III) of the Leonine edition, p. 131. See ch. 133 for Thomas's replies to these objections, replies to which the distinction between divine eternity and temporal duration as realized in creatures is again crucial. In ch. 134 Thomas makes the point that only God can know individual future contingents in themselves ("prout sunt actu in suo esse"), although in some cases creatures can know things that are future insofar as they necessarily follow from their causes, or insofar as it is likely that they will do so. For fuller discussion of most of the texts cited in the last few notes see J. Groblicki, *De scientia Dei futurorum* . . . , pp. 15–39. Groblicki also considers Thomas's *In De interpretatione*, ch. 9, for which see below.

28. See Weisheipl, *Friar Thomas d'Aquino*, pp. 374–75. As Weisheipl points out, Thomas commented on the Greek-Latin version of Aristotle accompanied by Ammonius's commentary on the same, the translation of which was completed by William of Moerbeke in September, 1268. For a critical edition of the commentary by Ammonius see G. Verbeke, ed., *Ammonius, Commentaire sur le Peri Hermeneias d'Aristote, Traduction de Guillaume de Moerbeke* (Louvain-Paris, 1961). On Thomas's usage of Ammonius in preparing his own commentary see pp. XI–XXXV. Verbeke suggests that Thomas's commentary may have remained unfinished because during the time he was preparing it he did not yet have in his hands the complete translation of Ammonius's commentary (see pp. XXXIII, XXXV). On Thomas's usage of this commentary as well as of that by Boethius see J. Isaac, *Le Peri Hermeneias en Occident de Boèce à saint Thomas* (Paris, 1953), pp. 100–105. As far as Boethius's commentaries are concerned, it seems that Thomas used only the second of these in preparing his own commentary.

29. See the Leonine edition, R. Spiazzi, ed., *In Aristotelis libros Peri Hermeneias et Posteriorum Analyticorum Expositio* (Turin, 1964), pp. 64ff. Often in citing it I shall simply list the paragraph numbers in my text or in the notes. For the present point see n. 167: "Unde Philosophus dicit, ex praemissis concludens, quod *in his quae sunt*, idest in propositionibus de praesenti, et *in his quae facta sunt*, idest in enunciationibus de praeterito, necesse est quod affirmatio vel negatio determinate sit vera vel falsa."

false in determined fashion.[30] He will not conclude from this, however, that they are entirely devoid of truth value.

As Thomas interprets Aristotle, the Stagirite reaches this conclusion by showing that to defend the opposite, that is, to hold that individual propositions concerning future contingents are determinately true or determinately false, will lead to unacceptable consequences — to some kind of fatalism or determinism. If it is necessary to hold that every affirmation or negation concerning individual future events is determinately true or false, it is also necessary to maintain that he who affirms or denies them determinately speaks truly or falsely. From this it will follow that every such event will be controlled by necessity (*ex necessitate*).[31] Such a conclusion would exclude three kinds of contingents: (1) those that happen by chance or fortune; (2) those that are equally open to opposites and which result from choice; (3) those which happen in the majority of cases.[32] Because Aristotle finds such exclusion of contingency completely unacceptable, comments Thomas, he must reject the position which leads to such absurdity.[33] On the other hand, Thomas also warns that one should not conclude from this that in individual contingent propositions concerning the future neither opposite is true. If such were the case, we could then only say of such a contingent that it neither will be nor will it not be.[34]

If we may bypass *Lectio* 14 for a moment, in *Lectio* 15 Thomas continues his commentary on Aristotle's text and finds him eventually reversing his earlier procedure in this same ch. 9. Instead of reasoning from propositions about future contingents to things themselves and arriving at an impasse, Aristotle now reasons from the way in which truth and necessity apply to things and then only back to the status of propositions concerning them. In brief, Thomas finds Aristotle distinguishing between absolute necessity and necessity *ex suppositione*. It is one thing to say that a thing necessarily is (and thus to assign absolute necessity to it). It is another to say that a thing

---

30. *Ibid.*, n. 169. "Sed in singularibus et futuris est quaedam dissimilitudo. Nam in praeteritis et praesentibus necesse est quod altera oppositarum determinate sit vera et altera falsa in quacumque materia; sed in singularibus quae sunt de futuro hoc non est necesse, quod una determinate sit vera et altera falsa. Et hoc quidem dicitur quantum ad materiam contingentem: nam quantum ad materiam necessariam et impossibilem similis ratio est in futuris singularibus, sicut in praesentibus et praeteritis."

31. N. 171.

32. Nn. 171–72.

33. See n. 173, near end.

34. N. 175.

necessarily is when it is. This is to assign necessity *ex suppositione* to it.[35] So too, that which is not absolutely necessary in itself becomes necessary under the supposition that its opposite is negated (*per disiunctionem oppositi*). This follows because it is necessary of each and every thing either that it is or that it is not; and again, that it will be or that it will not be. These statements are true when they are taken disjunctively.[36] As regards statements concerning future contingents, therefore, one cannot say determinately that there will be a sea battle tomorrow, or determinately that there will not be. But one can say that the following statement is true when taken disjunctively: It is necessarily the case either that there will be a sea battle tomorrow or that there will not be.[37]

Of greater interest for my immediate purpose, however, is the section from *Lectio* 14 where Thomas goes far beyond Aristotle's text in order to meet objections against human freedom. Thomas directs considerable attention to two such objections. One is based on God's knowledge and the other on God's volition. According to the first, since God's knowledge is infallible, whatever he knows must take place. According to the second, since the divine will cannot be without effect, all that God wills must happen necessarily.[38] Before replying to each of these in turn, Thomas remarks that each objection mistakenly assumes that God's knowledge or God's willing is like our own. In other words, each objection is guilty of anthropomorphism. Against this Thomas counters that divine knowledge and divine willing are very different from our own (*cum tamen multo dissimiliter se habeant*).[39]

Thomas's reply to the objection against freedom based on divine knowledge is very similar to that which we have already examined from other sources. Again he contrasts the temporal character of human knowledge with the eternity of divine knowledge. Because our knowledge is subject to temporal succession, we cannot know future things as they are in themselves but only through their causes. If they are totally determined so as to

---

35. Nn. 200–201. See in particular: "Et ideo manifeste verum est quod omne quod est necesse est esse quando est; et omne quod non est necesse est non esse pro illo tempore quando non est: et haec est necessitas non absoluta sed ex suppositione. Unde non potest simpliciter et absolute dici quod omne quod est, necesse est esse, et omne quod non est, necesse est non esse: quia non idem significant quod omne ens, quando est, sit ex necessitate, et quod omne ens simpliciter sit ex necessitate; nam primum significat necessitatem ex suppositione, secundum autem necessitatem absolutam" (n. 201).

36. See n. 201, near end; and n. 202.

37. See n. 202. Note in particular: " . . . sed necesse est quod vel sit futurum cras vel non sit futurum: hoc enim pertinet ad necessitatem quae est sub disiunctione."

38. N. 192.

39. N. 193.

follow necessarily from their causes, we can have certain knowledge of them. If they are not so determined to follow from their causes, we cannot know them; for something is not knowable insofar as it is in potency but only insofar as it is in act (n. 194).[40] In contrast, God's knowledge is eternal and therefore *tota simul*. All that unfolds in time is eternally grasped by God through one single act of intuition. By this single intuition he sees all that takes place over the course of time, and he sees each particular thing as it exists in itself. He does not, therefore, merely see or understand things as they exist in their causes.[41]

In replying to the objection against human freedom based on the divine will, Thomas continues to stress the difference between God's way of willing and ours. The divine will exists outside the order of created beings as a cause that produces every other being and every difference within created being. But the possible and the necessary are differences within the realm of being. Therefore, both necessity and contingency arise from the divine will. The divine will disposes necessary causes to produce those effects which it wills to be necessary. And it orders causes which act contingently to produce effects which it wills to be contingent. Even though all effects depend upon the divine will as upon their first cause, effects are said to be necessary or contingent by reason of the nature of their proximate causes. The first cause itself transcends the order of necessity and contingency. Such cannot be said, however, of the human will or of any creaturely cause. Every such cause falls under the order of necessity or contingency. Hence every such cause either can fail to produce its effect (which effect is therefore contingent), or else it cannot fail to produce its effect. Such an effect will therefore be necessary. The divine will, on the other hand, cannot fail. Nonetheless, not all of its effects are necessary; some are contingent.[42]

Thomas's reply to this objection may serve as a point of transition to the next section of this chapter.

1.2: The Causal Character of God's Knowledge and God's Will

In the first part of this chapter I have concentrated on Thomas's attempt to reconcile divine knowledge with the freedom of future contingents. Central

40. In this same context (n. 194) Thomas notes that we can have conjectural knowledge of the kind of thing that is not so determined to follow from its causes that it cannot be impeded from doing so.

41. See n. 195. Note in particular: "et ideo uno intuitu videt omnia quae aguntur secundum temporis decursum, et unumquodque secundum quod est in seipso existens, non quasi sibi futurum quantum ad eius intuitum prout est in solo ordine suarum causarum (quamvis et ipsum ordinem causarum videat), sed omnino aeternaliter sic videt unumquodque eorum quae sunt in quocumque tempore . . . ."

42. See n. 197. Also see C. Boyer, "Providence et liberté dans un texte de saint Thomas (In Perihermeneias, lib. 1, 2. lect. 13, 14)," *Gregorianum* 19 (1938), pp. 194–209. For much the same, but much more briefly stated, see *De malo*, q. 16, a. 7, ad 15.

to Thomas's proposed solution is his view that in the strict sense nothing is future for God. Because of God's eternal mode of being, every creature and every creaturely activity is eternally present to him. This holds whether that creature or its activity is past or present or future from our perspective. In a word, Thomas seems to have reduced the problem of divine knowledge of free future contingents to the problem of God's knowledge of free present contingents.

Still, even if accepted, this procedure seems to leave a major metaphysical problem unexamined. According to Aquinas, God's knowledge and God's providence are in some way causal in character. To the extent that divine knowledge causes creatures and, more important for our purposes, the actions of creatures, the problem of safeguarding a place for free creaturely activity becomes more complex. It is this aspect of the problem that one does not find examined in Boethius's *Consolation of Philosophy*. And it is to this that we must now turn.

In his earliest works and continuing throughout his career, Thomas steadfastly maintains the causal character of God's knowledge.[43] For instance, in his Commentary on I *Sentences* (d. 38, q. 1, a. 1), Thomas observes that science taken simply as science does not necessarily cause objects. Otherwise, all science would be causal. But insofar as the science is that of an artist who is making something, science may be said to be causal with respect to that which is produced by means of the art of that artist. Thomas develops this analogy in order to clarify the causal character of divine science. In the case of a human artist, the artist's knowledge presents an end that is to be attained. The artist's will intends the end, and finally commands that the appropriate act or acts be performed to produce the artefact. In sum, while science enters into the production of the artefact by manifesting the end,

---

43. In his Commentary on I *Sentences* Thomas begins to discuss divine science in distinction 35, and continues this through distinction 36. Only after all of this, in d. 38, q. 1, a. 1, does he explicitly ask whether God's science is the cause of things (p. 897). After having given an affirmative answer to this, it is in article 5 of that same question that Thomas addresses himself to God's knowledge of future contingents (p. 907). Thomas follows roughly the same procedure in the much later First Part of the *Summa theologiae*. In q. 14, a. 1, he discusses the fact that there is divine knowledge. In a. 8 he asks whether God's knowledge causes things and only thereafter, in a. 13, does he consider God's knowledge of future contingents. On the other hand, in q. 2, a. 1 of the *De veritate* Thomas discusses the fact that science is to be said of God. In a series of subsequent articles he develops his account of divine science. In q. 2, a. 12, as we have already seen, Thomas discusses God's knowledge of future contingents. But only after all of this, in a. 14, does he finally address himself to the fact that God's knowledge causes things. Unlike the *De veritate*, therefore, in *In I Sent.* and in ST I he had discussed the causal character of God's knowledge before taking up divine knowledge of future contingents.

the will does so by directing the artist's productive activity.[44] In developing his position in a parallel passage from the *De veritate* (q. 2, a. 14), Thomas comments that one should either maintain that science causes that which is known, or else that the thing known causes science, or else that both are caused by something else. He notes that one cannot hold that the things known by God are the causes of his knowledge; they are temporal and God's knowledge is eternal. Nor can one say that both God's knowledge and the objects known by him are caused by any other single cause; for nothing in God can be caused. Therefore, God's science is the cause of things.[45]

In this same context Thomas again remarks that science *qua* science is not in itself an efficient cause, just as form *qua* form is not. Form rather exercises its causality by perfecting that in which it resides. But action, and therefore efficient causal activity, involves the production of something that flows forth from an agent. Given this, a form can serve as a principle of such productive activity only by means of some power. Hence nothing will be efficiently caused by the science of a knower except by means of that knower's will. Will of its very nature implies some kind of influx with respect to the thing willed. To this Thomas adds a second point. While God is the first cause of everything else, effects also proceed from God by means of second causes. Therefore, between God's science which is the first cause of things and those things themselves there may be two intermediaries: one from the side of God—the divine will; and another from the side of creatures—those second causes which enter into the production of so many effects.[46] As Thomas succinctly sums up the first point in ST I, q. 14, a. 8, God's science causes things insofar as his science is conjoined with his will to produce them. Thomas must make this precision, of course, in order to distinguish between God's knowledge of pure possibles, on the one hand, and God's knowledge of actual existents (whether past, present, or future), on the other.[47] One may still wonder, however, whether the causal character

44. *Ed. cit.*, p. 899.
45. *Ed. cit.*, p. 59.
46. *Ed. cit.*, p. 59.
47. "Unde necesse est quod sua scientia sit causa rerum, secundum quod habet voluntatem coniunctam" (Leonine edition, prepared by P. Caramello and published by Marietti [Turin-Rome, 1950], p. 82). On God's knowledge of pure possibles see, for instance, *De ver.*, q. 2, a. 8 (where Thomas refers to God's knowledge of pure possibles as speculative, and to his knowledge of possibles that were, are, or will be realized in actuality as "quasi-practical"); ST I, q. 14, a. 9 (where Thomas refers to God's knowledge of things that were, are, or will be, as his *scientia visionis*, and to his knowledge of pure possibles as his *scientia intelligentiae*). Also see ST I, q. 15, a. 3, and ad 2 (where Thomas discusses divine ideas insofar as they may be called divine *rationes*—principles whereby God knows creatures; and divine exemplars—principles

of God's science when it is conjoined with the divine will leaves any place for free creaturely activity.

In discussing God's knowledge of future contingents in his Commentary on I *Sentences* (d. 38, q. 1, a. 5), Thomas had noted that one might think that contingents do not fall under divine knowledge for either of two reasons — either because God's knowledge is an unchanging cause of things, or because God's knowledge must be certain. Thomas's answer to the second difficulty — that based on the certitude of God's knowledge and which Thomas himself here seems to regard as the more serious — is essentially the same as that we have already examined in the first part of this chapter.[48] His answer to the first difficulty — that based on the causal character of divine knowledge — is much like his later reply in his Commentary on the *De interpretatione*, ch. 9.[49] In brief, he reasons that when various causes are ordered (*ordinatae*) to one another so as to produce a given effect, that effect is not to be regarded as contingent or as necessary by reason of its first cause but by reason of its proximate cause. This is so because the power of a first cause is received in a second cause in accord with the mode of the latter. Thus God's science is the unchanging cause of all other things. But effects are often produced by God through the activities of second causes. Therefore, by means of necessarily acting second causes God produces necessary effects. And by means of contingently acting second causes God produces contingent effects. Presumably, Thomas would have us conclude that by means of freely acting second causes God produces free effects.[50]

In order to appreciate more fully Thomas's thinking on this, it may be helpful for us to recall the broader context of his views concerning the relationship that obtains between God as first cause and the activities performed by any created or second cause. Thomas has worked this out in considerable detail in q. 3, a. 7 of the *De potentia* (1265–1267), and his discussion there is more or less paralleled by that found in his slightly later *Summa theologiae* I, qq. 104–105 (1266–1268). While much of Thomas's discussion in the text from the *De potentia* is especially concerned with the ways in which God intervenes in the operations of nature, his remarks also apply to God's role in free activities performed by created wills.[51] Thomas begins by

for God's production of creatures). For more on Thomas's theory of the divine ideas see L. Geiger, "Les idées divines dans l'oeuvre de s. Thomas," in *St. Thomas Aquinas 1274–1974: Commemorative Studies*, A. Maurer, ed. (Toronto, 1974), Vol. 1, pp. 175–209.

48. See the text cited above in our note 23.

49. See above in our text p. 255.

50. *Ed. cit.*, pp. 909–10. Cf. ad 1 (p. 912).

51. "Respondeo. Dicendum, quod simpliciter concedendum est Deum operari in natura et voluntate operantibus." See *Quaestiones disputatae*, Vol. 2 (Turin-Rome,

reporting and then refuting two different forms of occasionalism, one of which he attributes to the *loquentes in lege Maurorum* on the authority of Moses Maimonides, and the other to Avicebron.[52]

Thomas next distinguishes four different ways in which God may be said to cause the actions performed by creatures: (1) by giving to the created agent the power by means of which it acts or, in other words, by creating the creature's active power; (2) by continuously sustaining or conserving in being this created power; (3) by moving or applying the creaturely operative power to its activity; (4) by serving as principal cause with respect to that of which the created agent is an instrumental cause. Near the end of the corpus of this same article Thomas expresses the fourth way in slightly different terms, explaining that it is by God's power that every other power acts.[53] Thomas comments that if we join to all of this the fact that God is identical with his power (*virtus*) and that he is present to every creature by keeping it in being, we may conclude that God himself operates immediately in the activities performed by creatures, including their acts of volition.[54]

In the parallel discussion in the *Summa theologiae* Thomas follows a somewhat different procedure. In q. 104, aa. 1–2 he discusses God's conservation of creatures. In q. 105, a. 5, while defending the fact that God intervenes in the activities performed by created agents, Thomas notes that three of the four causes can in some way be regarded as principles of action. Accordingly, God works in the causal activities exercised by other agents (1) by serving as their final cause (insofar as every other operation is for the sake of some real or apparent good, and nothing can serve as such a good except insofar as it participates in some likeness of the Supreme Good, God himself); (2) by serving as an efficient cause insofar as second causes act by reason of the first cause, which moves them to act; (3) insofar as God gives to creatures the forms which serve as their principles of operation and keeps these forms in being. (An interesting difference between this treatment and that in the *De potentia* is the fact that here Thomas correlates created agents and God as second causes and first cause respectively rather than as instrumental causes and principal cause. To correlate them as second causes and

---

1953), p. 56. For discussion of this text and its parallels see C. Fabro, *Participation et causalité selon s. Thomas d'Aquin* (Louvain-Paris, 1961), pp. 397–409.

52. *Ed. cit.*, pp. 56–57.

53. *Ed. cit.*, pp. 57–58. Note near the end of the corpus: "Sic ergo Deus est causa actionis cuiuslibet in quantum dat virtutem agendi, et in quantum conservat eam, et in quantum applicat actioni, et in quantum eius virtute omnis alia virtus agit" (p. 58).

54. "Et cum coniunxerimus his, quod Deus sit sua virtus, et quod sit intra rem quamlibet non sicut pars essentiae, sed sicut tenens rem in esse, sequetur quod ipse in quolibet operante immediate operetur, non exclusa operatione voluntatis et naturae" (p. 58).

first cause seems less likely to run the risk of robbing creaturely causes of their proper causal activity, something Thomas would never permit one to do.)[55]

For our immediate purposes we may combine the third and fourth ways in which, according to the *De potentia*, God works in the actions performed by creatures. God moves the creaturely power to act (or applies it to action), and he serves as first cause with respect to those effects of which creatures are, properly speaking, second causes, according to the terminology from the *Summa*. [56] In other words, in moving any created power to act, God does so in such fashion that he is the first cause of that creature's action, while the created cause is itself a proper but second cause of that same action. Thomas would not have us take this to mean that God causes one part of the action or the effect, and the creature another part, as for instance, an elephant and a horse might combine to pull the same wagon. At times Thomas makes this point by insisting that any such action is to be attributed entirely to God as its first cause, and entirely to the created agent as its second cause.[57]

If this is Thomas's general view concerning God's role in causal activities exercised by creaturely or second causes, does he apply the same to freely acting creatures and hence to human volition? Indeed he does. Not only does God cause the free volitions of the human will insofar as he creates and sustains in being both man and his will; God causes man's acts of volition.

---

55. For parallels see SCG III, ch. 67. For texts from the *De potentia*, SCG, and ST see J. de Finance, *Etre et agir dans la philosophie de Saint Thomas* (Rome, 1960), pp. 232–33. It is not my intention here to enter into discussion of the appropriateness of the expression "physical premotion" to describe God's moving influence upon created causes in their activity. For some references and for brief discussion see de Finance, pp. 230–31, n. 51. Also see F. X. Meehan, *Efficient Causality in Aristotle and St. Thomas* (Washington, D.C., 1940), pp. 299ff.; R. Moore, "Motion divine chez Saint Thomas d'Aquin," *Studia Montis Regis* 1 (1958), pp. 93–137; H. Degl'Innocenti, "De actione Dei in causas secundas liberas iuxta S. Thomam," *Aquinas* 4 (1961), pp. 28–56. On the text from ST I, q. 105, a. 5, see Fabro, *op. cit.*, pp. 499–501. See n. 163 on the change in terminology from the *De potentia* and SCG, on the one hand, to ST, on the other. But, as Fabro notes, the language of "instrumental" cause to signify second causes reappears in the *Compendium theologiae*, chs. 3, 135. For both usages and for an important distinction between two ways in which creatures may be described as "instrumental" causes see *De veritate*, q. 24, a. 1, ad 3; ad 4; ad 5 (*ed. cit.*, p. 435).

56. At the same time Thomas may have in mind by the fourth way (according to the *De potentia*) in which God causes the causal activities performed by creatures an additional point—his view that God alone is the proper and principal cause of *esse*, and that creatures can cause *esse* only insofar as they act as "instruments" of God. For this see Fabro, pp. 401–2, 468–88; Meehan, pp. 298–302. This could lead to the interesting question whether Aquinas admits that creatures can cause *esse*, a point which cannot be pursued here.

57. See SCG III, ch. 70. Note in particular: "Sicut igitur non est inconveniens quod una actio producatur ex aliquo agente et eius virtute, ita non est inconveniens

In fact, in a. 4 of q. 105 of the *Summa theologiae*, Thomas argues that God can move the human will by serving as its object (and hence as its final cause) in that God alone is the universal good capable of moving man's will both sufficiently and efficaciously. But in addition to this, Thomas also holds that God moves the will efficiently, by inclining it from within. Thomas assigns special priority to this interior divine causing of the will's action in that same passage,[58] and strongly defends God's efficient causation of human volition in other contexts. For instance, in the key passage from *De potentia,* q. 3, a. 7, Thomas has stated that God immediately works in every created agent, including the activity of the will.[59]

In the *Summa contra gentiles*, Bk. I, ch. 68, Thomas maintains that God knows the inner motions of the will. By knowing his essence God knows all that to which his causality extends. But his causality extends to the operations of both the intellect and the will. In other words, God causes, as first cause to be sure, the acts of the human will. Near the end of this same chapter, Thomas argues that God's causation of our acts of willing does not destroy the fact that the will has dominion over its own acts. If the will were by its nature determined only to one thing, or if it were subject to violence from an external agent, its capacity to will or not will would be destroyed. But such is not destroyed by the influence of a higher cause which gives it both its being and its operation. Hence God is the first cause of the motions of the will.[60]

In SCG III, ch. 88, Thomas comments that the only kind of agent that can cause the motion of the will without doing violence to it is that which causes the intrinsic principle of this same motion, that is to say, the very power of the will itself. This is God, since he alone creates the soul. Because of this, he alone can move the will as an agent. Or as Thomas puts it in

---

quod producatur idem effectus ab inferiori agente et Deo: ab utroque immediate, licet alio et alio modo . . . . Patet etiam quod non sic idem effectus causae naturali et divinae virtuti attribuitur quasi partim a Deo, et partim a naturali agente fiat, sed totus ab utroque secundum alium modum: sicut idem effectus totus attribuitur instrumento, et principali agenti etiam totus" (*ed. cit.*, p. 306).

58. ST I, q. 105, a. 4. Note in particular: "Potest autem voluntas moveri sicut ab obiecto, a quocumque bono; non tamen sufficienter et efficaciter nisi a Deo . . . . Similiter autem et virtus volendi a solo Deo causatur. Velle enim nihil aliud est quam inclinatio quaedam in obiectum voluntatis, quod est bonum universale. Inclinare autem in bonum universale est primi moventis, cui proportionatur ultimus finis . . . . Unde utroque modo proprium est Dei movere voluntatem: sed maxime secundo modo, interius eam inclinando" (*ed. cit.*, p. 498).

59. See n. 54 above.

60. *Ed. cit.*, p. 64.

ch. 89, not only is the power of the will caused by God; so is its very act of willing. Here Thomas appeals to his broader metaphysical claim that no agent can act by its own power unless it also acts by the power of God (see SCG III, chs. 67, 70). But that by whose power an agent acts not only causes that agent's power, but the acts performed by that power as well. Hence God causes the created will's acts of volition.[61]

Thomas is aware of objections which might be raised against human freedom because of this position. For instance, in replying to some of these in *De potentia*, q. 3, a. 7, he counters that the fact that the human will has dominion over its action does not exclude the causal influence of the first cause. It rather means that the first cause does not so act on the will as to determine it of necessity to one thing rather than another (ad 13).[62] Again he reasons, not every cause excludes freedom in that which it causes but only one that is compelling (*cogens*). It is not in this way that God is the cause of our volitions (ad 14).[63] Or as he puts it in ST I, q. 19, a. 8, not only do those things happen which God wills to happen; they happen in the way he wills them to happen. He wills some things to happen necessarily, and others to happen contingently. Here Thomas adds an interesting precision. It is not because proximate causes are contingent that certain effects which are willed by God happen contingently. It is rather that because God wills them to happen contingently, he has prepared contingent causes for them.[64] Even so, it does not follow from this that all that is willed by God is absolutely necessary. Such things have the kind of necessity God wills them to have, which may be either absolute or only conditional (ad 3).

In ST I, q. 83, a. 1, Thomas replies to the following objection. Whatever is moved by something else is not free. But God moves the will. Therefore, man

---

61. See in ch. 88: "Solus igitur Deus potest movere voluntatem, per modum agentis, absque violentia" (p. 331). Ch. 89 is entitled: "Quod motus voluntatis causatur a Deo, et non solum potentia voluntatis." Note in particular: "Deus non solum dat rebus virtutes, sed etiam nulla res potest propria virtute agere nisi agat in virtute ipsius, ut supra ostensum est. Ergo homo non potest virtute voluntatis sibi data uti nisi inquantum agit in virtute Deo. Illud autem in cuius virtute agens agit, est causa non solum virtutis, sed etiam actus . . . . Deus igitur est causa nobis non solum voluntatis, sed etiam volendi" (pp. 331–32). Cf. SCG III, ch. 67, p. 300.

62. "Ad decimumtertium dicendum, quod voluntas dicitur habere dominium sui actus non per exclusionem causae primae, sed quia causa prima non ita agit in voluntate ut eam de necessitate ad unum determinet sicut determinat naturam; et ideo determinatio actus relinquitur in potestate rationis et voluntatis" (*ed. cit.*, p. 59).

63. "Ad decimumquartum dicendum, quod non quaelibet causa excludit libertatem, sed solum causa cogens: sic autem Deus non est causa operationis nostrae" (*ibid.*).

64. Note in particular: "Non igitur propterea effectus voliti a Deo, eveniunt contingenter, quia causae proximae sunt contingentes; sed propterea quia Deus voluit eos contingenter evenire, contingentes causas ad eos praeparavit" (*ed. cit.*, p. 114).

is not free. In replying Thomas notes that the will is a cause of its own motion, since by means of free will man moves himself to act. Still, adds Thomas, the presence of freedom does not require that a free agent be the first cause of its own motion. Thus, for something to be regarded as the cause of something else, it need not be a first cause; it can be a second cause. So too, God, as first cause, moves both natural agents and voluntary agents. Just as his moving natural causes does not destroy the fact that they are causes, neither does his moving voluntary agents militate against the fact that they are still voluntary causes. Rather, he moves each in accord with its nature.[65]

This seems to be Thomas's final philosophical thought on this point. God moves every created agent to act in accord with its nature. He moves freely acting agents to act in accord with their nature, which is to say, freely. Neither the certitude of divine science nor the causal character of the divine will detracts from man's freedom. In fact, remarks Aquinas, it would be more repugnant to the divine motion if the created will were thereby moved to act necessarily rather than to act freely. Only the latter kind of divine motion is in accord with the nature of the created will.[66]

2: Henry of Ghent

In the final part of this chapter I shall concentrate on Henry's account of God's knowledge of future events, including future contingents. Since medieval times and continuing onward into the twentieth century there has been disagreement about a particular feature of Aquinas's position. Mention of this will serve to set the stage for our consideration of Henry. In brief the problem reduces to this. In order to account for the fact that God knows future contingents, does Aquinas appeal to God's eternal mode of

---

This statement should not be taken as contradicting Thomas's view that effects are said to be necessary or contingent by reason of the nature of their proximate cause (see citations given in notes 42 and 50 above). In those passages Thomas was indicating that if we wonder whether an effect is necessary or contingent, we should look to the nature of the proximate cause. Here he is rather making the point that, viewed from the standpoint of divine final causality, God has prepared contingent causes for given effects because he wills these effects to be contingent.

65. Compare this with ST I-IIae, q. 10, a. 4: "Quia igitur voluntas est activum principium non determinatum ad unum, sed indifferenter se habens ad multa, sic Deus ipsam movet, quod non ex necessitate ad unum determinat, sed remanet motus eius contingens et non necessarius, nisi in his ad quae naturaliter movetur" (*ed. cit.*, p. 60). For discussion of this passage see Degl'Innocenti, pp. 39–43. Also see ST I-IIae, q. 9, a. 6, and ad 3. For discussion see Degl'Innocenti, pp. 44–52.

66. See ST I-IIae, q. 10, a. 4, ad 1: "Et ideo magis repugnaret divinae motioni, si voluntas ex necessitate moveretur, quod suae naturae non competit; quam si moveretur libere, prout competit suae naturae" (*ed. cit.*, p. 60).

being and hence to the eternal presence of future contingents to God's knowledge? Or does Thomas rather appeal to the eternal and determining decrees of the divine will?[67] Without delaying here over this controversy among interpreters of Aquinas, we should recall that both points have appeared in texts examined above.[68] Nonetheless, if we ask Thomas how it is and why it is that God can know things that are future for us, it seems to me that Thomas appeals to their eternal presence in their divine knower. Because they are eternally present to God they can be known with certainty by him, and as they are in themselves.[69]

67. For a brief sketch of differences among contemporary interpreters of Aquinas on this see Groblicki, *op. cit.*, pp. 7–10. Much of his study is devoted to an examination of the interpretations proposed by Thomas's earliest critics and followers concerning this point. For an effort to trace this theme through the great classical commentators on Aquinas see F. Schmitt, *Die Lehre des hl. Thomas von Aquin vom göttlichen Wissen des zukünftig Kontingenten bei seinen grossen Kommentatoren* (Nijmegen, 1950). See in particular his concluding remarks, pp. 196–202.

68. Thomas's dependency upon his understanding of divine eternity in order to account for God's knowledge of future contingents is evident from the first part of this chapter (see Section 1.1 – "God's Knowledge of Future Contingents"). That God's science (when conjoined with his will) also serves as the first cause of all creaturely activities, including those that are free, has been developed in the second section of this chapter. As I have observed near the end of that discussion (p. 261), in SCG I, ch. 68, Thomas notes that God by knowing his essence knows all of that to which his causality extends. This includes operations of the intellect and will. Is this not for Thomas to appeal to God's knowledge of himself as cause of the will's activity in order to account for divine knowledge of free human activity? Not necessarily, it seems to me, since Thomas's purpose in this chapter is not to indicate how God knows free human activity, but only to marshal evidence to show that God does know the motions of the will since he knows himself as cause of the same. When Thomas wants to explain how this can be so he introduces the theme of divine eternity and the eternal presence of all such things to God. It is because of this that Thomas can also hold that God does not merely know them by knowing himself as their cause, but as they are in themselves. Cf. SCG I, ch. 66.

69. In addition to the many passages cited in the first section of this chapter, see the strong endorsement of this view by H. Schwamm, in his *Das göttliche Vorherwissen bei Duns Scotus und seinen ersten Anhängern* (Innsbruck, 1934), pp. 91–99. See p. 99: "Den einzigen Grund für die unfehlbare Sicherheit des Vorherwissens sieht der hl. Thomas darin, dass das kontingent Zukünftige in seiner eindeutig bestimmten aktuellen Wirklichkeit von Ewigkeit her dem göttlichen Erkennen gegenwärtig vorliegt." For a more cautious reply see Groblicki, *op. cit.*, pp. 37–39. He comments that Thomas replies to the question how God knows future contingents in two different ways, that is, by appealing to God's knowledge of them as eternally present to him, and by appealing to God's causation of them. Groblicki proposes the following as a probable solution. When Thomas wants to show that God knows future contingents in terms of their real being, he does not merely appeal to their intentional

As we turn to Henry of Ghent's Quodlibet 8, q. 2 of Christmas, 1284, a subtle shift seems to have occurred. In both qq. 1 and 2 of this particular Quodlibet Henry is much concerned with divine science. In q. 1 he asks whether there are practical ideas in God.[70] Strictly speaking, he replies, practical ideas are not to be admitted in God. One can allow for practical ideas in God when they are taken in a broader sense, as an "extension" of his speculative knowledge and ideas.[71] As far as Henry is concerned, if by practical knowledge one means that an agent must do that which he judges to be advantageous for himself, no such knowledge can be admitted of God. Henry will permit one to speak of practical knowledge in God when, as we have noted, this is taken in a broader sense and as an extension of divine speculative knowledge. By such knowledge God knows that certain things might or might not be done insofar as they are fitting or appropriate for the

---

presence in his ideas or in their causal principles but to their eternal presence to him. But when Thomas wants to account for the fact that such things are indeed real, he then appeals to the fact that they are caused by the divine will (see pp. 38–39).

70. *Quodlibeta* (Paris, 1518; repr. Louvain, 1961; in 2 vols. with continuous pagination), fol. 299v. "Utrum in Deo sint ideae practicae." Henry accepts the classical notion that a divine idea is nothing but the divine essence insofar as it is viewed as imitable in a given way by creatures (fol. 300r). At the same time, he has an unusual view concerning the status of nonexistent possibles, or objects of divine ideas before they are realized in actuality. To them he assigns a special kind of being, *esse essentiae*, and this from all eternity. Actual existence is given to them only in time, due to the added intervention of the divine will. This does not result in real distinction between essence (*esse essentiae*) and existence (*esse existentiae*) in actually existing creatures, however, but only in something called by Henry an "intentional distinction." This distinction is greater than a purely logical distinction (distinction of reason), but less than a real distinction. For more discussion and for references to this see my Ch. VII above.

71. Henry notes that God knows other things according to his ideas (*rationes ideales*) in two different ways: (1) insofar as they are certain essences or existences in themselves, and this by purely speculative knowledge; (2) insofar as they are *quaedam operabilia a deo*. According to some, God would know things in this second way by practical ideas and by practical knowledge. Henry comments that practical and speculative knowledge are to be distinguished not by reason of diversity in the objects that are known, but by reason of diversity in end. The mere fact that knowledge has to do with *operabilia* is not enough to make it practical. The end must be action or operation. Thus the intellect may have speculative knowledge of some *operabile*, e.g., by asking what virtue is or what vice is. But when dealing with such matter the speculative intellect can become practical by a certain extension to an end that is practical. In other words, if one who is speculating about an *operabile* extends his goal so as to know in order for his will to act accordingly, his knowledge thereby will become practical. But when it deals with purely speculative matter the speculative intellect never becomes practical in this way — by extension (ff. 300r-v).

rest of creation. But even here, insists Henry, God remains perfectly free to choose or not to choose to act accordingly.[72]

In q. 2 Henry wonders whether change or variation (*difformitas*) in things known by God will result in any change in God's knowledge.[73] Here Henry distinguishes between God's knowledge of creatures solely in terms of their essences or natures, and his knowledge of things insofar as they are to be made or done by him, that is to say, his practical knowledge of them in the qualified sense just mentioned. The first kind of divine knowledge is purely speculative.[74] Through the second kind of knowledge God knows that certain things are to be made or done by him by knowing the determination of his own will. In this case the divine will itself is the foundation and cause of God's knowledge of such things, rather than vice versa.[75] Henry comments that this is why the philosophers, who hold that God produces things only by his intellect and of necessity, can much more readily postulate practical knowledge in God. Such is not so easy for the theologians, who must defend God's freedom in creating.[76]

Though Henry goes on to develop in considerable detail his explanation of both kinds of divine knowledge, here I shall concentrate on his understanding of the second — God's knowledge of things that are to be made or done by him. Several times Henry repeats the point that God knows such things by knowing the determination of his will, which will itself is unchanging. Henry stresses the point that God does not depend for his knowledge of such things on the reality of those things themselves but, to repeat, on the determination or decrees of his will. It is this that establishes or serves as the foundation for his knowledge of the things he is to bring to pass. By knowing the eternal and unchanging decree of his will, God knows in uniform fashion all creatures taken as individuals. He knows that they are when they in fact are, and that they are not when they are not. By one

72. Here Henry distinguishes two ways of understanding practical knowledge: (1) when the intellect considers what should or should not be done for the sake of that which is fitting for things; (2) when the intellect considers what should or should not be done in order for the agent to gain some advantage. This second type, which Henry regards as practical knowledge in the proper sense, is found only in creatures. Such is not present in God. Henry will admit of divine practical knowledge in the first sense, subject to the qualifications already mentioned. See fol. 300v.

73. "Utrum difformitas scibilium circa creaturas arguat aliquam difformitatem in scientia dei" (fol. 299v).

74. Fol. 301r.

75. "Secundo autem modo scit res sciendo determinationem voluntatis. Quia enim et quae determinat voluntas dei facienda, et hoc modo quo ea determinat, scit intellectus eius ea esse facienda et sic facienda et non e converso, ut in hoc voluntas potius sit ratio et causa scientiae et intellectus dei quam e converso" (*ibid.*).

76. *Ibid.*

single intuition God also knows what individual he will produce at any given moment of time, again because he knows the eternal decree of his will.[77]

If one were to stop here, there could be little doubt that Henry grounds God's knowledge of future things on the determination of the divine will. But then Henry attempts to develop the point that God knows in uniform fashion things that are when they are, and things that are not when they are not. Here Henry introduces the theme of divine eternity. Granted that in its actual existence time flows with motion, still by reason of its essence time (and motion as well) stand as fixed before the science of God. God simultaneously sees all things, both in themselves and in their relations with one another, when they actually exist.[78] But he does this in his eternal now. Hence, things which flow with the course of time stand fixed simultaneously before the divine vision. Therefore, all things which pass through time are present to God's knowledge from eternity. This holds, continues Henry, not only because their divine ideas exist in the divine intellect and because of God's eternal knowledge of the determination of his will concerning such things. It also holds because God's vision bears upon all such things from eternity insofar as they are eternally present to him (*in sua praesentialitate*).[79]

---

77. For Henry's discussion of divine speculative knowledge, see ff. 301r–v. On God's knowledge of things insofar as they are *operabilia ab ipso* see fol. 301v: " . . . sciendum est . . . quod quia intellectus divinus scit operanda inquantum operanda sciendo determinationem suae voluntatis quae omnino est invariabilis, non autem per ipsas res quae variantur extra influendo in esse diversimode, secundum determinationem simplicem et invariabilem divinae voluntatis, qua simul ab aeterno omnia determinavit . . . ." See ff. 301v–302v for an exposition and critique of Avicenna's account of divine knowing. Henry is especially critical both of Avicenna's view that the universe is necessarily produced by God, and of his apparent denial that God knows singulars as singulars. "Sentiendum est quod ideo uniformiter scit ea esse cum sunt et non esse cum non sunt, quia scit determinationem suae voluntatis . . . in cognoscendo se esse causam illius [i.e., of the Antichrist] per suam substantiam secundum actum, sive in producendo, sive in conservando, cognoscit illam rem esse . . . sic et ex parte scientiae, quia scit omnia talia sciendo invariabilem essentiam et invariabilem voluntatis determinationem" (fol. 302v). On all of this see Schwamm, *op. cit.*, pp. 101–4. As Schwamm points out, Henry is not restricting himself to or especially concentrating on God's knowledge of future contingents in this discussion. He is rather accounting for God's knowledge of any existent, whether past or present or future, by appealing to the determination of the divine will (pp. 103–4). However, what Henry says certainly applies in his eyes to future contingents.

78. See fol. 303r.

79. *Ibid.* Note in particular: " . . . et sic simul cum quolibet instanti temporis respicit singula secundum modum quo sunt se habitura, sive secundum esse, sive secundum non esse, in suo nunc aeternitatis. Et quae fluunt extra in tempore stant simul fixa in eius cognitione . . . . Et sic omnia quae fluunt in tempore sibi sunt ab aeterno praesentia; et hoc non solum ea ratione quia habet rationes rerum ideales ex parte intellectus, et determinationes earum ad esse ex parte voluntatis ut principia

At this juncture one might wonder whether Henry has now shifted his position and introduced the eternal presence of things to their divine knower as the means whereby God knows future things. But here Henry interjects a note of caution. One should not take this as implying, he warns, that such creatures actually exist in themselves from eternity. Their eternal presence to their divine knower does not of itself entail anything more than that they exist in the divine knowledge. In other words, it is one thing to say that God knows things as eternally present to him; it is another to say that such things exist from eternity. The second does not follow from the first. As Henry puts it, this eternal presentness of things to God does not imply their actual extramental existence, but only that they are present in their cause from eternity, a cause which is not only productive of them but which also knows them.[80]

Henry's reservations concerning this point may well have been occasioned by William de la Mare's *Correctorium* and his criticism therein of Thomas Aquinas's discussion in ST I, q. 14, a. 13.[81] This seems most likely since some of Henry's language reflects not only Thomas's text but William's critique of the same. In the *Summa* Thomas had written: "Wherefore, all things which are in time are present to God from eternity not only because he has the *rationes* of these things present to himself, as some say, but because his vision is directed to all things from eternity [*ab aeterno*] as they are in their presentness."[82]

---

productiva earum . . . sed quia eius intuitus fertur super omnia ab aeterno prout sunt in sua praesentialitate; ut non solum dicamus deum scire omnia tam contingentia ad utrumlibet quam alia quia cognoscit ea in seipso ut in sua causa productiva, etiam secundum rationem esse particularis et individualis . . . sed dicamus deum scire omnia tam contingentia ad utrumlibet quam alia quia praesentialitate essentiae ipsius creaturae secundum praedictum modum subduntur suo conspectui." For close parallels between this and Thomas's ST I, q. 14, a. 13, see Schwamm, *op. cit.*, pp. 105–6.

80. See fol. 303v. Note in particular: "Et sic est illa praesentialitas rerum in Deo non in rerum existentia, sed in earum causa, non solum productiva sed formali cognitiva, ut dictum est."

81. I would like to express my thanks to Stephen Brown for having first suggested to me that William's critique might account, at least in part, for Henry's reservations. My subsequent comparison of the texts of the two has convinced me that Henry's knowledge of William's critique can hardly be denied.

82. "Unde omnia quae sunt in tempore, sunt Deo ab aeterno praesentia, non solum ea ratione qua habet rationes rerum apud se praesentes, ut quidam dicunt: sed quia eius intuitus fertur ab aeterno super omnia, prout sunt in sua praesentialitate" (*ed. cit.*, pp. 86–87). My rendering of *ab aeterno* as "from eternity" could perhaps be misleading, as could the Latin expression itself. As is clear from our discussion in the first part of this chapter, Thomas does not wish to suggest thereby that there is any kind of successive duration in God's eternity, or in the eternal presence of things in God's knowledge.

Because of this, Thomas had argued, contingents are infallibly known by God even though they may still be future for us.[83]

William counters that this passage implies that all contingents and, for that matter, all created necessary things, are produced by God from eternity and in eternity (*ab aeterno in aeternitate*), even though they are also said to be created in time. In support William argues that things may be said to be present to God in only two ways: either as in their causal principle, or in terms of their actual existence. Since Thomas has stated that temporal beings are present to God and not merely in the first way, William concludes that Thomas must hold that all such things actually exist from eternity and in eternity.[84]

Without explicitly naming him, Henry repeats the key passage from Aquinas and seems to accept it as his own.[85] As we have already seen, Henry argues that this does not imply that temporal beings actually exist in themselves from eternity. He counters that their presentness to God applies to their eternal causal *rationes* in God, which *rationes* themselves account for the fact that such creatures are eternally known by God.[86]

Although Henry's explanation of this could be clearer, he seems to have introduced the theme of divine eternity and of the eternal presence of future things in God's knowledge in order to show that changes in this world or in

83. "Unde manifestum est quod contingentia et infallibiliter a Deo cognoscuntur, inquantum subduntur divino conspectui secundum suam praesentialitatem: et tamen sunt futura contingentia, suis causis comparata" (*ibid.*).

84. For William's text see *Les premières polémiques thomistes: I. — Le Correctorium Corruptorii 'Quare'*, P. Glorieux, ed. (Le Saulchoir, Kain, Belgium, 1927), p. 18. Note in particular: "Hoc enim est simpliciter falsum et erroneum; quia hoc est ponere omnia contingentia, et multo fortius necessaria ab aeterno in aeternitate, licet in tempore sint producta de non esse in esse."

85. "Non enim sequitur omnia quae sunt in tempore sunt deo ab aeterno praesentia non solum ea ratione quia habet rationes rerum apud se praesentes secundum modum iam expositum, sed quia eius intuitus fertur super omnia ab aeterno prout sunt in sua, scilicet ipsius dei praesentialitate; ergo sunt in aeternitate; sicut non sequitur, ergo sunt in tempore, vel ergo sunt in seipsis extra intellectum" (fol. 303v). Compare with Thomas's text as cited in n. 82. Note also that Henry here assigns the "presentness" directly to God rather than to creatures.

86. See fol. 303v, and the passage cited above in n. 80. For practically verbatim citation of William see Henry, lines 12–14; William, as cited above in n. 84. Also note: "Et sic quae non sunt in sua natura propria, sunt praesentia aeternitati, non solum pro tanto quia rationes ideales ut sunt causales ad producendum ea in effectu, tempus, et omnia temporalia, sint praesentes aeternitati et Deo ab aeterno, et per hoc ipsa aeternitas praesens istis rationibus, sed etiam pro tanto quia istae rationes ut sunt cognitivae ad causandum cognitionem rerum in divina sapientia sunt praesentes aeternitati et Deo ab aeterno; et similiter ipsae rerum essentiae praesentes sunt aeternitati et Deo ab aeterno, sicut obiecta cognita per illas rationes in divina essentia fundatas . . . ." (fol. 303v).

creatures do not entail any kind of change in God's knowledge.[87] His development of the notion of God's eternal knowledge of creatures is evidently deeply indebted to Aquinas. At the same time, Henry seems to be sensitive to William's critique. Even though he refuses to admit that a proper understanding of the eternal presence of things to God's knowledge will result in defending their actual eternal existence, he is hard pressed to justify his refusal. What he seems to have done is to compromise Thomas's view that because of their eternal presence to God as their knower, God views all creatures, including those that are still future for us, as they are in themselves, not merely as they exist in God as their productive cause. This may be because Henry, like William, does not really grasp the significance of Thomas's claim that whatever is known is known according to the mode of being of its knower. In any event, Henry does not seem to have abandoned his earlier statements in this same question to this effect, that the ultimate foundation which accounts for God's knowledge of future things is his knowledge of the eternal decrees of his will.[88]

While both the notions of eternity and the causal character of the divine will have entered into Thomas's account of God's knowledge of contingents and into Henry's, there are considerable differences between the two. According to Thomas, it is because things are eternally present to the divine mind that God can know future contingents with certainty and as they are in themselves. It is also true, of course, that for such events to be realized in actuality in the course of time, the divine will must intervene; but this is required to account for their actual existence, not for God's knowledge of them. According to Henry, it is because God knows the eternal decrees of his will that he knows with certainty the things he will produce and, therefore, things that are future for us. Even so, in order to avoid introducing any change into God's knowledge, Henry has also drawn upon the concept of eternity. Whether his account will allow for divine knowledge of such things as they are in themselves, or only as they are in God, their productive cause, might well be questioned.

---

87. See ff. 303v (near bottom)–304r (top).

88. Thus he returns to the theme of the divine will in the closing part of his discussion. See fol. 304r: "Similiter quantum est ex parte sua quoad eius scientiam quasi practicam qua novit operanda determinata per eius voluntatem. Idem enim est iudicium quoad hoc de scire particularia et universalia, plura vel pauciora, quia scientia Dei secundum praedicta etsi non determinat facienda vel non facienda, perfecte tamen perscrutatur determinationem suae voluntatis quoad facienda et non facienda." Though Henry clearly defends divine knowledge of particulars, he does not multiply divine ideas in accord with individuals within species. See his Quodlibet 7, qq. 1–2, ff. 255r–257r. For discussion see my The Metaphysical Thought of Godfrey of Fontaines, pp. 125 (and n. 71 for references), 129–30.

Bibliography

Algazel. *"Logica Algazelis*, Introduction and Critical Text," ed. C. Lohr. *Traditio* 21 (1965), pp. 223–90.

Ammonius. *Ammonius, Commentaire sur le Peri Hermeneias d'Aristote, Traduction de Guillaume de Moerbeke*, ed. G. Verbeke. Louvain-Paris, 1961.

Anawati, G. C. *Essai de bibliographie avicennienne.* Cairo, 1950.

————. "La tradition manuscrite orientale de l'oeuvre d'Avicenne." *Revue thomiste* 51 (1951), pp. 407–40.

————. "Chronique avicennienne 1951–1960." *Revue thomiste* 60 (1960), pp. 614–34.

————. "Bibliographie de la philosophie médiévale en terre d'Islam pour les années 1959–1969." *Bulletin de philosophie médiévale* 10–12 (1968–70), pp. 316–69.

————. "St. Thomas d'Aquin et la *Métaphysique* d'Avicenne," in *St. Thomas Aquinas 1274–1974: Commemorative Studies*, ed. A. Maurer. Toronto, 1974. Vol. 1, pp. 449–66.

————. *La Métaphysique du Shifā' Livres I à V. Introduction, traduction et notes.* Paris, 1978.

Ando, T. *Metaphysics: A Critical Survey of Its Meaning.* The Hague, 1963.

Anonymous. "La Table des divergences et innovations doctrinales de Godefroid de Fontaines," ed. J. Hoffmans. *Revue Néoscolastique de Philosophie* 36 (1934), pp. 412–36.

Antweiler, A. *Die Anfangslosigkeit der Welt nach Thomas von Aquin und Kant.* 2 Vols., Trier, 1961.

Argerami, O. "La cuestión 'De aeternitate mundi': posiciones doctrinales." *Sapientia* 27 (1972), pp. 313–34.

Aubenque, P. *Le problème de l'être chez Aristote: Essai sur la problématique aristotélicienne.* Paris, 1962.

Avicenna. *Metaphysica Avicennae sive eius Prima Philosophia.* Venice, 1495; repr. Louvain, 1961.

————. *Avicennae perhypatetici philosophi ac medicorum facile primi Opera in lucem redacta ac nuper quantum ars niti potuit per canonicos emendata.* Venice, 1508; repr. Frankfurt am Main, 1961.

————. *Avicenna Latinus, Liber de Philosophia Prima sive Scientia Divina: I–IV*, ed. S. Van Riet. Louvain-Leiden, 1977.

————. *Avicenna Latinus, Liber de Philosophia Prima sive Scientia Divina: V–X*, ed. S. Van Riet. Louvain-Leiden, 1980.

Bazán, B. "La signification des termes communs et la doctrine de la supposition chez Maître Siger de Brabant." *Revue philosophique de Louvain* 77 (1979), pp. 345–72.

Beach, J. "A Rejoinder to Armand A. Maurer's Review of *The Thomism of Etienne Gilson: A Critical Study* by John M. Quinn." *The Thomist* 38 (1974), pp. 187–91.

————. "Another Look at the Thomism of Etienne Gilson." *The New Scholasticism* 50 (1976), pp. 522–28.

Behler, E. *Die Ewigkeit der Welt.* Munich, 1965.

Benes, J. "Valor 'Possibilium' Apud S. Thomam, Henricum Gandavensem, B. Iacobum de Viterbio." *Divus Thomas* (Piac.) 29 (1926), pp. 612–34; 30 (1927), pp. 94–117, 333–55.

Benz, M. "Das Göttliche Vorherwissen des freien Willensakte des Geschöpfe bei Thomas von Aquin: *In I Sent.*, d. 38, q. 1. a. 5." *Divus Thomas* (Freib.) 14 (1936), pp. 255–73; 15 (1937), pp. 415–32.

Bertola, E. "Tommaso d'Aquino e il problema dell'eternità del mondo." *Rivista di filosofia neo-scolastica* 66 (1974), pp. 312–55.

Bobik, J. *Aquinas on Being and Essence.* Notre Dame, Ind., 1965.

Boethius. *The Consolation of Philosophy,* in Boethius, *The Theological Tractates and the Consolation of Philosophy,* ed. H. F. Stewart and E. K. Rand. Cambridge, Mass., 1968.

Bonansea, B. "The Impossibility of Creation from Eternity According to St. Bonaventure." *Proceedings of the American Catholic Philosophical Association* 48 (1974), pp. 121–35.

――――. "The Question of an Eternal World in the Teaching of St. Bonaventure." *Franciscan Studies* 34 (1974), pp. 7–33.

Bourke, V. *The Pocket Aquinas.* New York, 1960; 6th printing, 1968.

Boyer, C. "Providence et liberté dans un texte de saint Thomas (In Perihermeneias, Lib. 1, 2. lect. 13, 14)." *Gregorianum* 19 (1938), pp. 194–209.

Brady, I. "The Questions of Master William of Baglione O.F.M., *De aeternitate mundi* (Paris, 1266–1267)." *Antonianum* 47 (1972), pp. 576–616.

――――. "John Pecham and the Background of Aquinas's *De aeternitate mundi,*" in *St. Thomas Aquinas 1274–1974: Commemorative Studies,* ed. A. Maurer. Toronto, 1974. Vol. 2, pp. 141–78.

Clarke, W. N. "The Limitation of Act by Potency: Aristotelianism or Neoplatonism." *The New Scholasticism* 26 (1952), pp. 167–94.

――――. "The Meaning of Participation in St. Thomas Aquinas." *Proceedings of the American Catholic Philosophical Association* 26 (1952), pp. 147–57.

――――. "What Is Really Real?" in *Progress in Philosophy: Philosophical Studies in Honor of Rev. Doctor Charles A. Hart,* ed. J. A. McWilliams (Milwaukee, 1955), pp. 61–90.

Clavell, L. *El nombre propio de Dios segun santo Tomás de Aquino.* Pamplona, 1980.

Coccia, A. "De aeternitate mundi apud s. Bonaventuram et recentiores," in *S. Bonaventura 1274–1974,* 5 vols. Grottaferrata (Rome): Collegio S. Bonaventura, 1973. Vol. 3, pp. 279–306.

Collins, J. *The Thomistic Philosophy of the Angels.* Washington, D.C., 1947.

Cosgrove, M. "Thomas Aquinas on Anselm's Argument." *The Review of Metaphysics* 27 (1974), pp. 513–30.

Counahan, J. "The Quest for Metaphysics." *The Thomist* 33 (1969), pp. 519–72.

Cunningham, F. A. "Some Presuppositions in Henry of Ghent." *Pensamiento* 25 (1969), pp. 103–43.

d'Alverny, M.-T. "Avicenna Latinus I." *Archives d'Histoire Doctrinale et Littéraire du Moyen Age* 28 (1961), pp. 281–316.

de Finance, J. *Etre et agir dans la philosophie de Saint Thomas.* 2d ed., Rome, 1960.

Degl'Innocenti, U. (or H.). "La distinzione reale nel 'De ente et essentia' di S. Tommaso." *Doctor Communis* 10 (1957), pp. 165–73.

――――. "De actione Dei in causas secundas liberas iuxta S. Thomam." *Aquinas* 4 (1961), pp. 28–56.

Denifle, H. and Chatelain, A. *Chartularium Universitatis Parisiensis.* Vol. I, Paris, 1889.

De Raeymaeker, L. "La esencia avicenista y la esencia tomista." *Sapientia* 11 (1956), pp. 154–65.

――――. "L'être selon Avicenne et selon s. Thomas d'Aquin," in *Avicenna Commemoration Volume* (Calcutta, 1956), pp. 119–31.

Dewan, L. "St. Thomas and the Possibles." *The New Scholasticism* 53 (1979), pp. 76–85.

Dionysius (Pseudo). *Dionysiaca,* Vol. 1. Paris-Bruges, 1937.

Doig, J. "Science première et science universelle dans le 'Commentaire de la métaphysique' de saint Thomas d'Aquin." *Revue philosophique de Louvain* 63 (1965), pp. 41-96.

————. *Aquinas on Metaphysics: A Historico-Doctrinal Study of the Commentary on the Metaphysics.* The Hague, 1972.

Dolan, S. Edmund. "Resolution and Composition in Speculative and Practical Discourse." *Laval théologique et philosophique* 6 (1950), pp. 9-62.

Dondaine, H.-F. "Cognoscere de Deo 'quid est'." *Recherches de Théologie ancienne et médiévale* 22 (1955), pp. 72-78.

Duin, J. J. *La doctrine de la providence dans les écrits de Siger de Brabant.* Louvain, 1954.

Durantel, J. *Saint Thomas et le Pseudo-Denis.* Paris, 1919.

Ebbesen, S., and Pinborg, J., eds. "Studies in the Logical Writings Attributed to Boethius of Dacia." *Cahiers de l'Institut du moyen âge grec et latin* (Copenhagen) 3 (1970), pp. 1-54.

Elders, L. *Faith and Science: An Introduction to St. Thomas' Expositio in Boethii De Trinitate.* Rome, 1974.

Fabro, C. "Un itinéraire de saint Thomas: l'établissement de la distinction réelle entre essence et existence." *Revue de philosophie* 39 (1939), pp. 285-310.

————. *La nozione metafisica di partecipazione,* 2d ed. Turin, 1950.

————. *Partecipazione e causalità.* Turin, 1960.

————. *Participation et causalité selon s. Thomas d'Aquin.* Louvain-Paris, 1961.

Forest, A. *La structure métaphysique du concret selon saint Thomas d'Aquin,* 2d ed. Paris, 1956.

Gardet, L. "Saint Thomas et ses prédécesseurs arabes," in *St. Thomas Aquinas 1274-1974: Commemorative Studies,* ed. A. Maurer. Toronto, 1974. Vol. 1, pp. 419-48.

Geiger, L. B. "Abstraction et séparation d'après s. Thomas *In de Trinitate,* q. 5, a. 3." *Revue des sciences philosophiques et théologiques* 31 (1947), pp. 3-40.

————. *La participation dans la philosophie de S. Thomas d'Aquin,* 2d ed. Paris, 1953.

————. "Les idées divines dans l'oeuvre de s. Thomas," in *St. Thomas Aquinas 1274-1974: Commemorative Studies,* ed. A. Maurer. Toronto, 1974. Vol. 1, pp. 175-209.

Giles of Rome. *In Secundum Librum Sententiarum.* Venice, 1581; repr. Frankfurt, 1968.

Gilson, E. "Pourquoi saint Thomas a critiqué saint Augustin." *Archives d'Histoire Doctrinale et Littéraire du Moyen Age* 1 (1926-1927), pp. 5-127.

————. "Avicenne et le point de départ de Duns Scot." *Archives d'Histoire Doctrinale et Littéraire du Moyen Age* 2 (1927), pp. 89-149.

————. "Les sources gréco-arabes de l'augustinisme avicennisant." *Archives d'Histoire Doctrinale et Littéraire du Moyen Age* 4 (1929), pp. 5-149.

————. *L'Esprit de la philosophie médiévale.* 2 vols., Paris, 1932; 2d ed. (in 1 vol.), Paris, 1948.

————. *The Spirit of Mediaeval Philosophy,* tr. A. H. C. Downes. London, 1936; repr. 1950.

————. *The Philosophy of St. Bonaventure,* tr. I. Trethowan and F. J. Sheed. New York, 1938.

————. *Christianity and Philosophy,* tr. R. MacDonald. New York, 1939.

————. "La preuve du 'De ente et essentia.'" *Acta III Congressus Thomistici Internationalis: Doctor Communis* 3 (Turin, 1950), pp. 257-60.

————. *Reason and Revelation in the Middle Ages.* New York-London, 1950.

————. *Being and Some Philosophers,* 2d ed. Toronto, 1952.

————. *Jean Duns Scot: Introduction à ses positions fondamentales.* Paris, 1952.

————. *History of Christian Philosophy in the Middle Ages.* New York, 1955.

————. *The Christian Philosophy of St. Thomas Aquinas,* tr. L. K. Shook. New York, 1956.

_____. "Thomas Aquinas and Our Colleagues," in *A Gilson Reader*, ed. A. Pegis (Garden City, N.Y., 1957), pp. 278-97.

_____. "What is Christian Philosophy?" in *A Gilson Reader*, ed. A. Pegis (Garden City, N.Y., 1957), pp. 177-91.

_____. "La possibilité philosophique de la philosophie chrétienne." *Revue des sciences religieuses* 32 (1958), pp. 168-96.

_____. *God and Philosophy.* New Haven, 1959.

_____. *The Christian Philosophy of Saint Augustine*, tr. L. E. M. Lynch. New York, 1960.

_____. *Elements of Christian Philosophy.* Garden City, New York, 1960.

_____. *Introduction à la philosophie chrétienne.* Paris, 1960.

_____. "Trois leçons sur le problème de l'existence de Dieu." *Divinitas* 5 (1961), pp. 23-87.

_____. *The Philosopher and Theology*, tr. C. Gilson. New York, 1962.

_____. *Le thomisme*, 6th ed. Paris, 1965.

_____. "Avicenne, en Occident au Moyen Age." *Archives d'Histoire Doctrinale et Littéraire du Moyen Age* 36 (1969), pp. 89-121.

Glorieux, P. "Un recueil scolaire de Godefroid de Fontaines (Paris, Nat. Lat. 16297)." *Recherches de Théologie ancienne et médiévale* 3 (1931), pp. 37-53.

Godfrey of Fontaines. *Les quatre premiers Quodlibets de Godefroid de Fontaines*, ed. M. De Wulf and A. Pelzer. Les Philosophes Belges, Vol. 2, Louvain, 1904.

_____. *Les Quodlibets cinq, six et sept*, ed. M. De Wulf and J. Hoffmans. Les Philosophes Belges, Vol. 3, Louvain, 1914.

Gómez Caffarena, J. *Ser participado y ser subsistente en la metafísica de Enrique de Gante.* Rome, 1958.

Grisez, G. "The 'Four Meanings' of Christian Philosophy." *The Journal of Religion* 42 (1962), pp. 103-18.

Groblicki, J. *De scientia Dei futurorum contingentium secundum S. Thomam eiusque primos sequaces.* Krakow, 1938.

Heidegger, M. *Einführung in die Metaphysik.* Tübingen, 1958.

_____. *An Introduction to Metaphysics*, tr. R. Manheim. Garden City, New York, 1961.

Henry of Ghent. *Quodlibeta.* Paris, 1518; repr. Louvain, 1961.

_____. *Summae quaestionum ordinariarum.* Paris, 1520; repr. St. Bonaventure, N.Y., 1953.

_____. *Henrici de Gandavo Quodlibet I*, ed. R. Macken. Leuven-Leiden, 1979.

_____. *Henrici de Gandavo Quodlibet X*, ed. R. Macken. Leuven-Leiden, 1981.

Hissette, R. *Enquête sur les 219 articles condamnés à Paris le 7 mars 1277.* Louvain-Paris, 1977.

Hocedez, E. "La condamnation de Gilles de Rome." *Recherches de Théologie ancienne et médiévale* 4 (1932), pp. 34-58.

Hödl, Ludwig. "Die philosophische Gotteslehre des Thomas von Aquin O.P. in der Diskussion der Schulen um die Wende des 13. zum 14. Jahrhundert." *Rivista di filosofia neo-scolastica* 70 (1978), pp. 113-34.

Hoeres, W. "Wesen und Dasein bei Heinrich von Gent und Duns Scotus." *Franziskanische Studien* 47 (1965), pp. 121-86.

Hoffmans, J. "La Table des divergences et innovations doctrinales de Godefroid de Fontaines." *Revue Néoscolastique de Philosophie* 36 (1934), pp. 412-36.

Imbach, R. *Deus est intelligere: Das Verhältnis von Sein und Denken in seiner Bedeutung für das Gottesverständnis bei Thomas von Aquin und in den Pariser Quaestionen Meister Eckharts.* Studia Friburgensia 53. Freiburg, 1976.

Isaac, J. *Le Peri Hermeneias en Occident de Boèce à saint Thomas.* Paris, 1953.

John Damascene. *Saint John Damascene, De fide orthodoxa* (Burgundio translation), ed. E. M. Buytaert. St. Bonaventure, N.Y., 1955.

John of St. Thomas. *Cursus Philosophicus Thomisticus*, Vol. 1, *Ars logica*, ed. B. Reiser. Turin, 1930.

Judy, A. "Avicenna's *Metaphysics* in the *Summa contra gentiles*." *Angelicum* 52 (1975), pp. 340–84, 541–86.

Kennedy, L. Review of J. M. Quinn's *The Thomism of Etienne Gilson: A Critical Study*, in *The New Scholasticism* 49 (1975), pp. 369–73.

Kenny, A. "Divine Foreknowledge and Human Freedom," in *Aquinas: A Collection of Critical Essays*, ed. A. Kenny (Garden City, N.Y., 1969), pp. 255–70.

Klubertanz, G. "St. Thomas on Learning Metaphysics." *Gregorianum* 35 (1954), pp. 3–17.

_____. "The Teaching of Thomistic Metaphysics." *Gregorianum* 35 (1954), pp. 187–205.

_____. *Introduction to the Philosophy of Being*, 2d ed. New York, 1963.

_____. "Metaphysics and Theistic Convictions," in *Teaching Thomism Today*, ed. G. McLean (Washington, D.C., 1963), pp. 271–306.

Knasas, J. "Making Sense of the *Tertia Via*." *The New Scholasticism* 44 (1980), pp. 476–511.

König, E. "Aristoteles' erste Philosophie als universale Wissenschaft von den ARXAI." *Archiv für Geschichte der Philosophie* 52 (1970), pp. 225–46.

Kovach, F. "The Question of the Eternity of the World in St. Bonaventure and St. Thomas—A Critical Analysis," in *Bonaventure and Aquinas: Enduring Philosophers*, ed. R. W. Shahan and F. J. Kovach (Norman, Oklahoma, 1976), pp. 155–86.

Krapiec, A. M. "Analysis formationis conceptus entis existentialiter considerati." *Divus Thomas* (Piac.) 59 (1956), pp. 320–50.

Lescoe, F. J. "*De substantiis separatis*: Title and Date," in *St. Thomas Aquinas 1274–1974: Commemorative Studies*, ed. A. Maurer. Toronto, 1974. Vol. 1, pp. 51–66.

Litt, T. *Les corps célestes dan l'univers de saint Thomas d'Aquin*. Louvain-Paris, 1963.

Lobato, A. *De influxu Avicennae in theoria cognitionis Sancti Thomae Aquinatis*. Granada, 1956.

Lotz, J. "Ontologie und Metaphysik." *Scholastik* 18 (1943), pp. 1–30.

Lyttkens, H. *The Analogy between God and the World*. Uppsala, 1952.

_____. "Die Bedeutung der Gottesprädikate bei Thomas von Aquin," in *Philosophical Essays Dedicated to Gunnar Aspelin on the Occasion of his Sixty-fifth Birthday*, ed. H. Bratt et al. (Lund, 1963), pp. 76–96.

McGrath, M. *Etienne Gilson: A Bibliography/Une Bibliographie*. Toronto, 1982.

Macken, R. "La temporalité radicale de la créature selon Henri de Gand." *Recherches de Théologie ancienne et médiévale* 38 (1971), pp. 211–72.

McNicholl, A. "On Judging." *The Thomist* 38 (1974), pp. 768–825.

_____. "On Judging Existence." *The Thomist* 43 (1979), pp. 507–80.

McSorley, H. J. *Luther: Right or Wrong?* New York, N.Y., and Minneapolis, 1969.

Mandonnet, P. *Siger de Brabant et l'Averroïsme latin au XIIIᵉ siècle*, 2d ed., 2 vols. Louvain, 1911, 1908.

Mansion, A. "L'objet de la science philosophique suprême d'après Aristote, *Métaphysique* E I," in *Mélanges de philosophie grecque offerts à Mgr A. Diès* (Paris, 1956), pp. 151–68.

_____. "Philosophie première, philosophie seconde et métaphysique chez Aristote." *Revue philosophique de Louvain* 56 (1958), pp. 165–221.

Maritain, J. *Science and Wisdom*, tr. B. Wall. London, 1940/repr. 1954.

_____. *Existence and the Existent*. New York, 1948.

_____. *An Essay on Christian Philosophy*, tr. E. H. Flannery. New York, 1955.

_____. *Distinguish to Unite or the Degrees of Knowledge*, tr. G. B. Phelan. New York, 1959.

Masiello, R. "A Note on Essence and Existence." *The New Scholasticism* 45 (1971), pp. 491–94.

Maurer, A. "St. Thomas on the Sacred Name 'Tetragrammaton'." *Mediaeval Studies* 34 (1972), pp. 275–86.

_____. Review of J. M. Quinn's *The Thomism of Etienne Gilson: A Critical Study*, in *The Thomist* 37 (1973), pp. 389–91.

Meehan, F. X. *Efficient Causality in Aristotle and St. Thomas*. Washington, D.C., 1940.

Merlan, P. *From Platonism to Neoplatonism*, 2d ed. The Hague, 1960.

Mondin, B. *St. Thomas Aquinas' Philosophy in the Commentary to the Sentences*. The Hague, 1975.

Montagnes, B. *La doctrine de l'analogie de l'être d'après saint Thomas d'Aquin*. Louvain-Paris, 1963.

Moore, R. "Motion divine chez Saint Thomas d'Aquin." *Studia Montis Regis* 1 (1958), pp. 93–137.

Moreno, A. "The Nature of Metaphysics." *The Thomist* 30 (1966), pp. 109–35.

Moses Maimonides. *Liber Rabi Moysi Aegyptii Qui dicitur Dux Neutrorum seu dubiorum*. Paris, 1520; repr. Frankfurt am Main, 1964.

_____. *The Guide of the Perplexed*, tr. S. Pines. Chicago, 1963.

Mulligan, W. "Divine Foreknowledge and Freedom: A Note on a Problem of Language." *The Thomist* 36 (1972), pp. 293–99.

Naud, A. *Le problème de la philosophie chrétienne: Eléments d'une solution thomiste*. Montreal, 1960.

Nédoncelle, N. *Is There a Christian Philosophy?*, tr. I. Trethowan. New York, 1960.

Neumann, S. *Gegenstand und Methode der theoretischen Wissenschaften nach Thomas von Aquin aufgrund der Expositio super librum Boethii De Trinitate*. Beiträge zur Geschichte der Philosophie und Theologie des Mittelalters 41:2. Münster Westf., 1965.

Nicolas, J. H. "Affirmation de Dieu et connaissance." *Revue thomiste* 44 (1964), pp. 200–22.

O'Brien, T. *Metaphysics and the Existence of God*. Washington, D.C., 1960.

Oeing-Hanhoff, L. *Ens et Unum Convertuntur: Stellung und Gehalt des Grundsatzes in der Philosophie des. Hl. Thomas von Aquin*. Münster Westf., 1953.

Owens, J. "The Conclusion of the Prima Via." *The Modern Schoolman* 30 (1953), pp. 33–53, 109–21, 203–15.

_____. "Common Nature: A Point of Comparison between Thomistic and Scotistic Metaphysics." *Mediaeval Studies* 19 (1957), pp. 1–14; repr. in *Inquiries into Medieval Philosophy: A Collection in Honor of Francis P. Clarke*, ed. J. F. Ross (Westport, Conn., 1971), pp. 185–209.

_____. *An Elementary Christian Metaphysics*. Milwaukee, 1963.

_____. "Quiddity and Real Distinction in St. Thomas Aquinas." *Mediaeval Studies* 27 (1965), pp. 1–22.

_____. "Aquinas and the Proof from the 'Physics.'" *Mediaeval Studies* 28 (1966), pp. 119–50.

_____. *An Interpretation of Existence*. Milwaukee, 1968.

_____. "Judgement and Truth in Aquinas." *Mediaeval Studies* 32 (1970), pp. 138–58.

_____. "'Ignorare' and Existence." *The New Scholasticism* 46 (1972), pp. 210–19.

_____. "Metaphysical Separation in Aquinas." *Mediaeval Studies* 34 (1972), pp. 287–306.

_____. "Aquinas as Aristotelian Commentator," in *St. Thomas Aquinas 1274–1974: Commemorative Studies*. Toronto, 1974. Vol. 1, pp. 213–38.

_____. "Aquinas — 'Darkness of Ignorance' in the Most Refined Notion of God," in *Bonaventure and Aquinas: Enduring Philosophers*, ed. R. W. Shahan and F. J. Kovach (Norman, Oklahoma, 1976), pp. 69–86.

_____. "Aquinas on Knowing Existence." *The Review of Metaphysics* 29 (1976), pp. 670–90.

_____. *The Doctrine of Being in the Aristotelian Metaphysics*, 3d ed. Toronto, 1978.

_____. *Aquinas on Being and Thing*. Niagara University Press, 1981.

_____. "Stages and Distinction in *De ente:* A Rejoinder." *The Thomist* 45 (1981), pp. 99–123.

Paulus, J. "La théorie du Premier Moteur chez Aristote." *Revue de philosophie*, n.s. 4 (1933), pp. 259–94, 394–424.

_____. *Henri de Gand: Essai sur les tendances de sa métaphysique*. Paris, 1938.

_____. "Les disputes d'Henri de Gand et de Gilles de Rome sur la distinction de l'essence et de l'existence." *Archives d'Histoire Doctrinale et Littéraire du Moyen Age* 13 (1940–1942), pp. 323–58.

Peghaire, J. *Intellectus et Ratio selon S. Thomas d'Aquin*. Paris-Ottawa, 1936.

Pegis, A. "Penitus Manet Ignotum." *Mediaeval Studies* 27 (1965), pp. 212–26.

_____. "St. Thomas and the Coherence of the Aristotelian Theology." *Mediaeval Studies* 35 (1973), pp. 67–117.

Quinn, J. F. *The Historical Constitution of St. Bonaventure's Philosophy*. Toronto, 1973.

Quinn, J. M. *The Thomism of Etienne Gilson: A Critical Study*. Villanova, 1971.

Régis, L.-M. "Un livre: *La philosophie de la nature*. Quelques 'Apories'." *Etudes et Recherches* 1 (1936), pp. 127–56.

_____. "Analyse et synthèse dans l'oeuvre de saint Thomas," in *Studia Mediaevalia in honorem admodum reverendi patris Raymundi Josephi Martin* (Bruges, 1948), pp. 303–30.

Renard, H. "What is St. Thomas' Approach to Metaphysics?" *The New Scholasticism* 30 (1956), pp. 64–83.

Riesenhuber, K. "Partizipation als Strukturprinzip der Namen Gottes bei Thomas von Aquin," in *Sprache und Erkenntnis im Mittelalter, Miscellanea Mediaevalia* 13/2 (Berlin–New York, 1981), pp. 969–82.

Robert, J.-D. "La métaphysique, science distincte de toute autre discipline philosophique, selon saint Thomas d'Aquin." *Divus Thomas* (Piac.) 50 (1947), pp. 206–22.

_____. "Le principe: 'Actus non limitatur nisi per potentiam subjectivam realiter distinctam.'" *Revue philosophique de Louvain* 47 (1949), pp. 44–70.

Saranyana, J. "La creación 'ab aeterno': Controversia de Santo Tomás y Raimundo Marti con San Buenaventura." *Scripta theologica* 5 (1973), pp. 127–55.

Schmidt, R. "L'emploi de la séparation en métaphysique." *Revue philosophique de Louvain* 58 (1960), pp. 373–93.

Schmitt, F. *Die Lehre des hl. Thomas von Aquin vom göttlichen Wissen des zukünftig Kontingenten bei seinen grossen Kommentatoren*. Nijmegen, 1950.

Schrimpf, G. *Die Axiomenschrift des Boethius (De Hebdomadibus) als philosophisches Lehrbuch des Mittelalters*. Leiden, 1966.

Schwamm, H. *Das göttliche Vorherwissen bei Duns Scotus und seinen ersten Anhängern*. Philosophie und Grenzwissenschaften 5. Innsbruck, 1934.

Sertillanges, A. D. *Les grandes thèses de la philosophie thomiste*. Paris, 1928.

Siger de Brabant. "Quaestio utrum haec sit vera: homo est animal, nullo homine existente," in *Siger de Brabant, Ecrits de logique, de morale et de physique*, ed. B. Bazán. Louvain-Paris, 1974.

Sillem, E. A. "Notes on Recent Work: Christian Philosophy." *The Clergy Review* 46 (1961), pp. 149–74.

Smith, G. "Avicenna and the Possibles." *The New Scholasticism* 17 (1943), pp. 340–57. Also in *Essays in Modern Scholasticism*, ed. A. Pegis (Westminster, Md., 1944), pp. 116–33. Also, in shortened form, in *Readings in Ancient and Medieval Philosophy*, ed. J. Collins (Westminster, Md., 1960), pp. 200–05.

Smith, V. "The Prime Mover: Physical and Metaphysical Considerations." *Proceedings of the American Catholic Philosophical Association* 28 (1954), pp. 78–94.

———. *The General Science of Nature.* Milwaukee, 1958.

Streveler, P. "The Problem of Future Contingents: A Medieval Discussion." *The New Scholasticism* 47 (1973), pp. 233–47.

Stump, E., and Kretzmann, N., "Eternity." *The Journal of Philosophy* 78 (1981), pp. 429–58.

Sweeney, L. "Existence/Essence in Thomas Aquinas's Early Writings." *Proceedings of the American Catholic Philosophical Association* 37 (1963), pp. 97–131.

———. *A Metaphysics of Authentic Existentialism.* Englewood Cliffs, N.J., 1965.

———. "Presidential Address: Surprises in the History of Infinity from Anaximander to George Cantor." *Proceedings of the American Catholic Philosophical Association* 45 (1981), pp. 3–23.

Thomas Aquinas. *Sancti Thomae de Aquino opera omnia*, Leonine ed. Rome, 1882–.

———. *Scriptum super libros Sententiarum*, Vols. 1 and 2, ed. P. Mandonnet. Paris, 1929.

———. *Scriptum super Sententiis*, Vol. 3, ed. M. F. Moos. Paris, 1933.

———. *Summa contra gentiles.* Ed. Leonina Manualis. Rome, 1934.

———. *The Trinity and The Unicity of the Intellect by St. Thomas Aquinas*, tr. Sr. Rose Emmanuella Brennan. St. Louis, 1946.

———. *In librum Boethii De Trinitate, Quaestiones Quinta et Sexta*, ed. P. Wyser. Fribourg-Louvain, 1948.

———. *Le "De ente et essentia" de S. Thomas d'Aquin*, ed. M. D. Roland-Gosselin, repr. Paris, 1948.

———. *De aeternitate mundi*, in *S. Thomae Aquinatis Opuscula omnia necnon opera minora*, ed. J. Perrier. Vol. 1, Paris, 1949.

———. *In duodecim libros Metaphysicorum Aristotelis expositio*, ed. M.-R. Cathala and R. Spiazzi. Turin-Rome, 1950.

———. *In Librum Beati Dionysii De divinis nominibus expositio*, ed. C. Pera. Turin-Rome, 1950.

———. *Summa Theologiae, Prima Pars.* Turin-Rome, 1950; *Prima Secundae*, Turin-Rome, 1950; *Secunda Secundae*, Turin-Rome, 1948.

———. *De potentia*, ed. P. Pession, in *S. Thomae Aquinatis Quaestiones disputatae*, Vol. 2. Turin-Rome, 1953.

———. *De spiritualibus creaturis*, ed. M. Calcaterra and T. Centi, in *S. Thomae Aquinatis Quaestiones disputatae*, Vol. 2. Turin-Rome, 1953.

———. *De veritate*, ed. R. Spiazzi, in *S. Thomae Aquinatis Quaestiones disputatae*, Vol. 1. Turin-Rome, 1953.

———. *S. Thomae Aquinatis Quaestiones disputatae*, Vol. 2, ed. P. Bazzi et al. Turin-Rome, 1953.

———. *In octo libros Physicorum Aristotelis Expositio*, ed. P. M. Maggiòlo. Turin-Rome, 1954.

———. *Divi Thomae Aquinatis Opuscula philosophica*, ed. R. M. Spiazzi. Turin-Rome, 1954.

———. *S. Thomae Aquinatis Opuscula theologica*, Vol. 1, ed. R. Verardo. Turin-Rome, 1954.

———. *S. Thomae Aquinatis Opuscula theologica*, Vol. 2, ed. R. M. Spiazzi and M. Calcaterra. Turin-Rome, 1954

————. *Sancti Thomae de Aquino super Librum de causis expositio*, ed. H. D. Saffrey. Fribourg-Louvain, 1954.

————. *Quaestiones quodlibetales*, ed. R. Spiazzi. Turin-Rome, 1956.

————. *In Aristotelis librum De anima commentarium*, ed. A. Pirotta. Turin-Rome, 1959.

————. *Sancti Thomae de Aquino Expositio super librum Boethii De Trinitate*, ed. B. Decker. 2d ed. Leiden, 1959.

————. *St. Thomas Aquinas, The Division and Methods of the Sciences: Questions V and VI of His Commentary on the De Trinitate of Boethius*, Translated with Introduction and Notes, tr. A. Maurer. 3d rev. ed. Toronto, 1963.

————. *Tractatus de substantiis separatis*, ed. F. Lescoe. West Hartford, Conn., 1963.

————. *In Aristotelis libros Peri Hermeneias et Posteriorum Analyticorum Expositio*, ed. R. Spiazzi. Turin-Rome, 1964.

————. *St. Thomas Aquinas, On Being and Essence*, tr. A. Maurer. 2d rev. ed. Toronto, 1968.

Van Steenberghen, F. "Le problème de l'existence de Dieu dans le 'De ente et essentia' de saint Thomas d'Aquin," in *Mélanges Joseph De Ghellinck, S. J.* (Gembloux, 1951), pp. 837–47.

————. *La philosophie au XIIIe siècle*. Louvain-Paris, 1966.

————. "La controverse sur l'éternité du monde au XIIIe siècle," in *Introduction à l'étude de la philosophie médiévale* (Louvain-Paris, 1974), pp. 512–30.

————. *Maître Siger de Brabant*. Louvain-Paris, 1977.

————. "Le mythe d'un monde éternel." *Revue philosophique de Louvain* 76 (1978), pp. 157–79.

————. "Etienne Gilson, historien de la pensée médiévale." *Revue philosophique de Louvain* 77 (1979), pp. 487–508.

————. *Le problème de l'existence de Dieu dans les écrits de S. Thomas d'Aquin*. Louvain-la-Neuve, 1980.

————. *Thomas Aquinas and Radical Aristotelianism*. Washington, D.C., 1980.

Vansteenkiste, C. "Avicenna-Citaten bij S. Thomas." *Tijdschrift voor Philosophie* 15 (1953), pp. 457–507.

Vollert, C., Kendzierski, L., and Byrne, P. *St. Thomas Aquinas, Siger of Brabant, St. Bonaventure, On the Eternity of the World*. Milwaukee, 1964.

Wallace, W. *The Role of Demonstration in Moral Theology*. Washington, D.C., 1962.

Walter Burley. "Walter Burley's *Quaestiones in librum Perihermeneias*," ed. S. Brown. *Franciscan Studies* 34 (1974), pp. 200–295.

Weidemann, H. *Metaphysik und Sprache: Eine sprachphilosophische Untersuchung zu Thomas von Aquin und Aristoteles*. Freiburg-Munich, 1975.

Weisheipl, J. *Friar Thomas d'Aquino: His Life, Thought, and Work*. Garden City, New York, 1974.

————. "The Relationship of Medieval Natural Philosophy to Modern Science: The Contribution of Thomas Aquinas to Its Understanding." *Manuscripta* 20 (1976), pp. 181–96.

Wielockx, R. "Gottfried von Fontaines als Zeuge der Echtheit der Theologischen Summe des Albertus Magnus." *Miscellanea Mediaevalia* 15 (1982), pp. 209–25.

————. "Le ms. Paris Nat. lat 16096 et la condamnation du 7 mars 1277." *Recherches de Théologie ancienne et médiévale* 48 (1981), pp. 227–37.

William de la Mare. *Les premières polémiques thomistes: I-Le Correctorium Corruptorii 'Quare'*, ed. P. Glorieux. Le Saulchoir, Kain, Belgium, 1927.

William of Falegar. "Guillaume de Falegar: Oeuvres inédites," ed. A.-J. Gondras, in *Archives d'Histoire Doctrinale et Littéraire du Moyen Age* 39 (1972), pp. 185–288.

Wippel, J. "Godfrey of Fontaines and the Real Distinction between Essence and Existence." *Traditio* 20 (1964), pp. 385–410.

_____. "Godfrey of Fontaines and Henry of Ghent's Theory of Intentional Distinction between Essence and Existence," in *Sapientiae procerum amore: Mélanges Médiévistes offerts à Dom Jean-Pierre Müller, O.S.B., Studia Anselmiana* 63 (Rome, 1974), pp. 289–321.

_____. "The Condemnations of 1270 and 1277 at Paris." *The Journal of Medieval and Renaissance Studies* 7 (1977), pp. 169–201.

_____. Review of J. Doig's *Aquinas on Metaphysics: A Historico-Doctrinal Study of the Commentary on the Metaphysics,* in *Speculum* 52 (1977), pp. 133–35.

_____. *The Metaphysical Thought of Godfrey of Fontaines: A Study in Late Thirteenth-Century Philosophy.* Washington, D.C., 1981.

_____. "Essence and Existence," in *The Cambridge History of Later Medieval Philosophy* (New York, N.Y., 1982), pp. 385–410.

_____. "The Relationship between Essence and Existence in Late-Thirteenth-Century Thought: Giles of Rome, Henry of Ghent, Godfrey of Fontaines, and James of Viterbo," in *Philosophies of Existence: Ancient and Medieval,* ed. P. Morewedge (New York, 1982), pp. 131–64.

Wolter, A. B. "Ockham and the Textbooks: On the Origin of Possibility." *Franziskanische Studien* 32 (1950), pp. 70–96; reprinted in *Inquiries into Medieval Philosophy,* ed. J. F. Ross (Westport, Conn., 1971), pp. 243–73.

Zedler, B. "Saint Thomas and Avicenna in the 'De Potentia Dei.'" *Traditio* 6 (1948), pp. 105–59.

_____. "St. Thomas, Interpreter of Avicenna." *The Modern Schoolman* 33 (1955–1956), pp. 1–18.

_____. "Another Look at Avicenna." *The New Scholasticism* 50 (1976), pp. 504–21.

_____. "Why are the Possibles Possible?" *The New Scholasticism* (1981), pp. 113–30.

Zimmermann, A. *Ontologie oder Metaphysik? Die Diskussion über den Gegenstand der Metaphysik im 13. und 14. Jahrhundert.* Leiden-Köln, 1965.

_____. "Eine anonyme Quaestio: Utrum haec sit vera: Homo est animal, homine non existente." *Archiv für Geschichte der Philosophie* 49 (1967), pp. 183–200.

_____. "'Mundus est aeternus'—Zur Auslegung dieser These bei Bonaventura und Thomas von Aquin," in *Die Auseinandersetzungen an der Pariser Universität im XIII. Jahrhundert, Miscellanea Mediaevalia* 10 (Berlin, 1976), pp. 317–30.

Index of Names

Index of Topics

Absolutely impossible: cannot be done by God, 205

Abstraction: in Commentary on the *De Trinitate*, 38; meaning of, 75; different from *separatio*, 75–76; of the whole, 76; of form, 76–77, 217; and mathematics, 77; and physics, 77; of universal from particular, 82n; of quantity, 82n

Accidents: presence in genus does not require composition, 135; not in God, 229

Agent: intelligent must be efficient cause if exemplar cause, 188; produces its like, 231; univocal vs. equivocal, 231–32

Analogy: of being, 215; and divine names, 215, 224; kinds of, 238, 246

Analysis: process of, 59, 60–62, 101 (*See Resolutio*); and synthesis, 60–62

Analysis and synthesis: processes of, 63–67. *See* Synthesis

Angels: not multiplied within species, 138; not composed of matter-form, 138, 142, 143, 144; act-potency composition of, 142, 143; composed of *esse* and *quod est*, 142, 143, 144; essence-existence distinction of, 152. *See* Intelligences

Arabic philosophy: as source for Scholasticism, 37

Autonomy of lower theoretical sciences, 48

Avicenna: as source for Aquinas, 37; Latin translation of his *Metaphysics*, 39n; *Metaphysics* as source for Aquinas, 39–44, 49–53

Beati: knowledge of God, 217

Being: Aquinas on and Exodus 3:14, 16n; primitive notion of, 32; most universal, 57, 66; terminus of analysis *secundum rationem*, 62, 63, 64; notion of, 77; negatively immaterial, 78, 92, 93, 103; subject of metaphysics, 89, 160n; positively immaterial, 92, 102; material and metaphysics, 102; division of in Henry of Ghent, 180, 189; division of in Godfrey of Fontaines, 185, 189; *ab alio* can be eternal, 199

Being as being: subject of metaphysics, 30–32, 41n, 64, 72, 73, 97; and created separate substances, 104n

Being as existing: discovery of, 69; and judgment, 69, 74, 75, 77

Being in general (*ens commune*): subject of metaphysics, 58, 98 (*See* Metaphysics: subject of); negatively immaterial, 72–73; and God, 104

Bonaventure: philosophy or theology in, 6

Caused being: essence and *esse* are distinct, 140, 146

Causes: as most intelligible, 57; knowledge of, 91; knowledge of as goal of science, 92, 93, 94; known through effects, 217; univocal and equivocal, 218; likeness with effect, 223; necessary vs. contingent, 255; first and second, 258–59; principal vs. instrumental, 259, 260

Chimeras: not objects of knowledge, 186

Christianity: as a philosophy, 9

Christian Philosophy: possibility of,